TROTSKY
IN NEW YORK

TROTSKY
IN NEW YORK
1917

A RADICAL ON THE
EVE OF REVOLUTION

KENNETH D. ACKERMAN

COUNTERPOINT
BERKELEY

Library of Congress Cataloging-in-Publication Data is Available

Cover design by Faceout Studios
Interior design by Megan Jones Design

ISBN 978-1-61902-607-0

COUNTERPOINT
2560 Ninth Street, Suite 318
Berkeley, CA 94710
www.counterpointpress.com

Printed in the United States of America
Distributed by Publishers Group West

10 9 8 7 6 5 4 3 2 1

To my grandparents Rubin Mendel and Ides Bronfeld—loved, remembered, and appreciated by five generations of descendants—who fled Poland for America as a result of the 1920 Soviet Russian invasion of Poland led by the then Soviet people's commissar for military and naval affairs, Leon Trotsky.

And to my friend and colleague Bob Hahn, part of our OFW Law family, who touched all who knew him and who, typically, dropped all else to share with me his clear-eyed insights on this manuscript, before we lost him without warning and far too soon. I hope his sense of excellence has rubbed off on these pages.

CONTENTS

ACT I: ON THE EVE

1: Montserrat 5

2: Times Square 29

3: Saint Marks Place 41

4: Brooklyn 55

5: Riverside Drive I 65

6: Paterson 73

7: The Bronx 75

8: Cooper Union 79

9: Riverside Drive II 89

10: Wilson 95

ACT II: OF WAR

11: Spy versus Spy 103

12: Carnegie Hall 115

13: Ziv 129

14: Zurich 139

15: East Broadway 145

16: The Committee 157

17: Lenox Casino 169

18: Russia 177

ACT III: AND REVOLUTION

19: The Whirlwind 185

20: Spies Again 197

21: Consulates 213

22: Missing 225

23: Harlem River Casino 231

24: Kristianiafjord 239

25: Nova Scotia 251

26: Petrograd 273

Loose Ends 291

Acknowledgments 331

Selected Sources 335

Endnotes 343

Index 365

ACT I:

ON THE EVE

LEV DAVIDOVICH BRONSTEIN, a thirty-eight-year-old zealot who went by the nom de guerre Leon Trotsky, burst onto the world stage in November 1917 as co-leader of a Marxist revolution seizing power in Russia. As foreign commissar of the new government under Vladimir Lenin, Trotsky quickly made his name by orchestrating Russia's exit from the First World War. Then, as war commissar, he led Russia's Red Army to victory in a gruesome civil war against White Russians and foreign interveners.

Their rule secure, Trotsky and his Marxist cohorts would tear Russian society to its roots and impose a communist regime that would challenge the world for the next seventy years. With his thick glasses; riveting eyes; and shaggy, unkempt hair, Trotsky emerged as one of the most recognized personalities of the twentieth century.

Yet just months before his great moment in Russia, this same Lev Bronstein/Trotsky was a nobody, a refugee expelled from countries across Europe, writing obscure pamphlets and speeches, barely noticed outside a small circle of quarrelsome fellow travelers. Where had he come from to topple Russia and change the world? Where else: New York.

From January through March 1917, Trotsky had found refuge in the United States. America had kept itself out of the European Great War, leaving New York a safe haven, the freest city on earth, enjoying a last gasp of the belle epoque.

1

MONTSERRAT

"Sunday, January 13: We are nearing New York. At three o'clock in the morning, everybody wakes up. We have stopped. It is dark. Cold. Wind. Rain. On land, a wet mountain of buildings. The New World!"[1]

—Leon Trotsky, aboard the steamer *Montserrat*, on reaching America

SATURDAY NIGHT, JANUARY 13, 1917:

Music played in New York City the night Trotsky's ship entered the harbor. It had nothing to do with Trotsky or his ship. It was just New York.

The New Amsterdam Theater on West Forty-Second Street featured Ziegfeld's Follies that night. The show, *The Country Girl,* included sixty beautiful Ziegfeld Girls with big eyes, pink cheeks, and long legs. They dressed like Caribbean birds while dancing, singing, and kicking up their feet to tunes of a marimba band. Also on the bill were Senegalese acrobats, new singing sensation Eddie Cantor, spritely Fannie Brice, and comedian Will Rogers showing off his cowboy rope tricks.

Broadway was enjoying a golden age in 1917. A few blocks away, George Gershwin, the eighteen-year-old musical prodigy, led the pit orchestra for *Miss 1917,* a new revue featuring original songs by Jerome Kern, including "In the Good Old Summertime" and "Dinah." Laughter erupted across the street at the theater run by George M. Cohan, Broadway's "Yankee Doodle Dandy." Cohan's latest production was *Captain Kidd, Jr.,* a comedy farce about three bumbling misfits who embarrass themselves searching for lost pirate treasure on old Cape Cod.

Over on Fifty-First Street, Al Jolson packed the Winter Garden with his schmaltzy revue of ragtime, dance, and comedy skits, ten years before *The Jazz Singer*.

For sheer spectacle, you couldn't beat the Manhattan Opera House's live production of *Ben-Hur*, in which 350 actors shared the stage with fifty horses. At Reisenweber's restaurant on Columbus Circle, the Original Dixieland Jass Band, with its funny-faced, frog-throated piano player Jimmy Durante ("That's not a banana, that's my nose"), filled the house with a new sound they called jazz.

Further downtown, vaudeville drew big crowds with its eclectic mix of acrobats, musicians, jugglers, trained animals, and comedians, rising unknowns with names like George Burns, the Marx Brothers, and Buster Keaton.

All this, plus piano sonatas at Carnegie Hall, operas at the Metropolitan, and the ballet. And this didn't even start on all the immigrant places.

New York in 1917 had dense, bulging neighborhoods that smelled and sounded like foreign countries, and each of these also had its own music. Almost two million New Yorkers in 1917 had come from across the ocean: 480,000 Russians, 340,000 Italians, 145,000 Poles, 200,000 Germans, 200,000 Irish. Jews comprised the bulk of the Eastern Europeans. Including their American-born children and grandchildren, they totaled well over a million. The Lower East Side, Germantown, Little Italy, Little Russia, and Little Poland; each spoke its own language, read its own newspapers, and drank in its own saloons and cafés. The Yiddish-language פֿאָרווערטס (*Jewish Daily Forward* or *Forward*), with its circulation more than two hundred thousand, rivaled even the *New York Times*.

Second Avenue below Tenth Street belonged to the Yiddish theaters: Kessler's at Second Street, Thomashefsky's at Houston Street, and more. A few blocks over, neighborhoods changed and gave way to German beer gardens, polka halls, Irish saloons, and Italian trattorias, each louder, more boisterous than the next.

New York at that moment lived like no other place on earth. Certainly not Europe. Europe in January 1917 remained trapped in a slow-motion agonizing hell. The world war had entered its third year, having already killed more than 10 million soldiers and civilians. France and England, Russia and Germany, Austria and Turkey; each would lose a million young men or more. They killed and died in gruesome new ways: via poison gas, flamethrowers, artillery bombs, submarine torpedoes, and trench warfare, plus starvation and disease. Europe's great cities, Paris, London, and Vienna, all turned dark, increasingly populated by widows, gripped with hunger, or ruled by military edict.

But not America. Not New York. Here, the music played. Just two months earlier, in November 1916, Americans had reelected Woodrow Wilson as their president largely because, as the slogan went, "He Kept Us Out of War." Meanwhile, America grew rich lending money and selling weapons to the warring powers, particularly the Entente Allies: England, France, and Russia.

Yes, the war caused its problems. Some Americans expected that they too would inevitably join the fight against Germany. In New York they held parades and urged preparedness: a bigger army and military training. German submarines sank ships on the high seas, and increasingly Americans found themselves targets.

On May 7, 1915, a German sub had fired two torpedoes at the British-flag RMS *Lusitania,* a Cunard liner carrying almost two thousand passengers and crew. The strike had sunk the vessel and killed 1,198, including 128 Americans. Protests had erupted but never reached the breaking point. The *Lusitania,* after all, had carried ammunition in its cargo, making it fair game under rules of war, at least so argued the Germans. After the sinking, Germany had ordered its submarines not to attack passenger ships without prior warning. Thus far they had mostly complied.

Just as nerve-shattering to Americans were the big explosions, at least forty since 1914. With American factories producing huge stocks of weapons and ammunition, mostly for Britain and France, accidents proliferated. More than sixty men had died, and each explosion fed talk of sabotage.[2] Just that weekend, a massive blast at the Du Pont powder plant at Haskell, New Jersey, had killed an estimated twenty-one men and demolished 150 houses, breaking windows in five states.

Still, most Americans saw no reason to enter Europe's war. How could Germany ever attack the United States from across the ocean? The idea sounded idiotic. Just weeks earlier, on December 18, 1916, President Wilson had challenged the warring European countries yet again to stop the carnage and publish their conditions for peace talks. Americans applauded. But the gesture had produced only finger-pointing among the Europeans.

Peace in America protected not just music and riches but also freedom. In early 1917, America had no secret police or internal spies like Russia. It had no censors like France or England. Plenty of New Yorkers, especially immigrants, openly backed Germany in the war, and nobody doubted their loyalty. The Metropolitan Opera could produce Wagner's *Der Ring des Nibelungen* (The Ring Cycle) in the original German and nobody complained. Any night in New York, one could stop by Cooper Union or Beethoven Hall to hear an anarchist like Emma Goldman, a socialist like Eugene Debs, a birth control activist like Margaret Sanger, or a pacifist like Ilya Tolstoy, the great Russian novelist's son then lecturing in the United States. A socialist sat in the United States Congress. People could mock politicians as much as they liked.

And then there were the newspapers, millions of copies flooding the city each day. Huge steam presses cranked them out in a dozen languages, often thick with cartoons, fashions, sports, and society gossip. The biggest, William Randolph Hearst's *New York American* (originally *Morning Journal*) and Joseph Pulitzer's *New York World*, vied for top circulation, but the newsstands brimmed with competitors, the *Times*, the *Tribune*, the *Sun*, the *Herald*, the *Globe*, the *Call*, each with its loyal following, plus weeklies like *McClure's* and the *Outlook*. New York supported four daily papers in Russian, six in Yiddish, three in German, and more in other languages.

Amid all the noise that Saturday night, January 13, 1917, a few people knew that Leon Trotsky was coming. Trotsky was a celebrity in some circles. One small Russian-language newspaper called *Novy Mir* (New World), published in Greenwich Village, proudly touted its connection to a small international band of Russian leftists calling themselves Bolsheviks or Mensheviks, depending on who controlled the editorial desk that week. It claimed Trotsky as one of its own and had announced his travel plans on its front page. A few other socialist newspapers repeated the news.

But these interested circles existed almost entirely inside the immigrant neighborhoods of New York City. Otherwise, especially across the Hudson, no one in America had ever heard of Trotsky. They didn't know his name, his face, or his place in the world. Other than the port inspectors, no one noticed his ship's entry into the harbor that night. Instead, New York enjoyed its music, its busy streets, its crowded stores, its noisy theaters, its teeming tenements, its busy churches and synagogues, its sweatshops, its subways, its boxing matches, its horse races and skating rinks, life lived intensely in a thousand flavors.

BACK ABOARD THE *Montserrat,* the Trotskys looked like any nice, respectable young family. Papa Trotsky made a fine impression in his suit, tie, pince-nez glasses, and neatly trimmed mustache. "Trotzky is a young man," a typical newspaper description of the period went. "Tall, well-built, and rather handsome."[3] People who met him noticed mostly his eyes, sharp and deep behind ever-present glasses, and his voice, nasal and usually dominating the talk, a "geyser of speech" as one put it.[4]

Natalya Sedova, the attractive woman at his side, stood a few inches shorter, with dark hair, large eyes, stylish coat. Two young sons—Leon (or Lyova) and Sergei, ages eleven and nine—scampered behind them. Seeing them together strolling the decks, who could imagine the truth about these polite, well-dressed people? They didn't look like radicals or troublemakers. They didn't act like revolutionaries expelled or barred from five different countries: Russia, Austria, Germany, France, and Spain. But they were.

On boarding the *Montserrat* in Barcelona, all 340 passengers had been required to give their names and backgrounds for the official manifest. For Trotsky and his family, this occasion had required a well-rehearsed, creative performance designed to avoid questions.

Asked his name, he told them Zratzky, or at least that's how the ship's officer wrote it down, probably confused by the Russian accent.[5] Asked his occupation, he gave "author." This last part was true. Since last leaving Russia ten year earlier, Trotsky had earned his living editing small Russian-language newspapers, cranking out pamphlets, and writing about politics. In fact, his writing, particularly his wartime accounts from the French and Balkan fronts, had earned him European-wide fame. No, he told the ship's officer, he was no anarchist, no polygamist, and never lived in an almshouse. Yes, he could read and write. Yes, he was born in Russia, near a tiny village called Yanofska, where his father owned a farm. Yes, he had good health, was not deformed or crippled, and had no identifying marks. All true.

He didn't start the serious lying until asked if he had even been to prison. Trotsky said no, and so they recorded it in the manifest. That, as they say, was a doozy.

In fact, Leon Trotsky had a long and intimate history with prisons. It formed part of his celebrity, his calling card. Trotsky was just eighteen years old when tsarist police jailed him the first time. From his father's farm, the family had sent Trotsky for schooling in Odessa on the Black Sea. Here, he grew enamored with underground politics. After his studies, he moved to the nearby town Nikolaev, where he helped organize an illegal workers' union. Police ultimately broke the union and arrested some two hundred members and leaders, including young Trotsky, whom they sentenced to four years' exile in Siberia. He escaped after two, hiding in a hay wagon to cross the frontier under a false name. Then he left the country to join the socialist movement abroad.

They arrested him again in late 1905. This time, Trotsky, living in Switzerland and already well-known as a socialist writer, had snuck back into Russia on hearing of the Bloody Sunday massacre in Saint Petersburg, in which tsarist soldiers had shot down nearly a thousand peaceful protesters. The incident sparked protests across Russia, and Trotsky joined the brewing uprising in Saint Petersburg, ultimately leading the Saint Petersburg Workers Soviet (Council) in its stand against the regime. When police again crushed the revolt and arrested the participants, Trotsky used his public trial—a group trial of fifty-two leaders—as a platform to denounce the government. This made him a national figure while earning him his second conviction and Siberian exile. He again escaped, traveling almost a thousand miles across frozen Siberian wilderness hidden in a sleigh pulled by reindeer.

These jailings had occurred long before, in 1901 and 1906, before Trotsky had matured into a leading journalist, but he had more recent ones too. Just within the past two months, he had been arrested in Paris and imprisoned in Spain, and he remained subject to arrest in Russia, France, and Germany. But to the steamship officials on the *Montserrat* that day, he said not a word about any of this. So far, so good.

Natalya came next. Asked her name for the manifest, she gave it as Natalya Sedova, and they entered it that way beneath his. But then she changed her mind. She had the ship's officer cross out the "Sedova" and replace it with ditto marks under his "Zratsky." She gave her occupation as "his spouse." This too was a lie.

For starters, Sedova in fact was her real name. It came from her father, a well-off factory manager near Kharkov, though both her parents had died when she was about eight years old. And yes, Natalya was the mother of Trotsky's two sons and his companion the past fifteen years. But no, they had never married. Trotsky had a wife still living in Russia whom he had never divorced. He also had two daughters with her. Trotsky's first wife had been a friend from his teenage years, a fellow Marxist arrested with him in the 1898 Nikolaev union crackdown. They had married behind bars awaiting sentence, and the two daughters were born during their exile in Siberia. When Trotsky escaped from Siberia in 1902, he left them behind.

Natalya certainly knew about the prior marriage. She had met Trotsky later that same year in Paris, where she had come as a student and joined the local group of young Russian socialists. One day, a dashing young speaker named Lev Davidovich came to visit them, telling exciting stories of his recent adventures in Siberia and his daring agitation in Russia. Just twenty years old, Natalya was smitten. As she explained it, "It just happened that one day the two of us were standing together looking at Baudelaire's tomb in the Montparnasse Cemetery . . . and from that time on, our lives were inseparable."[6] Marriage or not didn't matter. He became her husband in fact if not law.

Natalya lied again when she told the ship's officer she had never been to prison. But this was a small lie. She had been jailed only once. Russian police had arrested her eleven years earlier, in 1905, for attending an illegal May Day workers meeting near Saint Petersburg. The judge sentenced her to six months at the nearby Dom Predvaritelnogo Zakluchenyo, what Natalya later called "un tres bon prison" (a very nice prison), since it had electric lights and separate cells for inmates.[7] Years later she still had warm memories of the prison mistress there announcing, "Your bath is ready, Madame Sedova."[8]

She and Trotsky both lied about their birthdays for the manifest, declaring themselves ten years younger than their actual ages, thirty-seven and thirty-four. And the boys lied too, about their names, calling themselves Leon and Sergei Zratsky. In fact, neither son had taken their father's last name. Both had taken their mother's name, Sedov.

For Leon Trotsky and his family, all this was nothing new. Over the years, he and Natalya had often traveled using false identities or forged papers, sneaking across borders to avoid police. Many Russian radicals adopted aliases. "The very character of their work compelled them to hide their names," one contemporary explained.[9] "I suppose I've had fifteen or twenty names myself," said another. "Sometimes a fellow will come up to me and hail me by some name and I have to think a minute before I remember it was once mine."[10]

Trotsky himself wasn't really named Trotsky or Trotzki or Zratsky either. Nor Lvov, Yanofsky, Vikentiev, nor Arbuvov, other names he'd called himself.[11] His actual family name, Bronstein, was one he hadn't used in fifteen years. He had adopted Trotsky in 1902 during his first escape from Siberia. The name actually belonged to a jail guard.

So now, in a pinch, to satisfy the steamship officers on the *Montserrat* and the American customs officials who used the ship's manifest, the Trotskys made themselves look on paper like any nice, normal family. No questions. No problems.

The *Montserrat* was an old ship. Its coal-powered engines dragged its 4,377-ton carcass across the water as slow as an old freighter, managing top speeds of fourteen knots and usually far less. It took the ship seventeen days to cross the ocean from Barcelona to New York. Storms ravaged the Atlantic that month. Rough seas and freezing gale winds made the ship roll and pitch. Passengers got seasick. Meals sat untouched. For passengers below deck in steerage, nausea and stale air made the stench unbearable. Trotsky complained about what he called this "wretched little Spanish boat" that "did everything to remind us of the frailty of human life" and practiced what he called "transport barbarism."[12]

To make things worse, German submarines patrolled the waters off the Spanish coast. In the three weeks before the *Montserrat* sailed, they had sunk two American-flag merchant ships, the *Coruna* and the *Columbian,* plus the Italian-flag *Palermo.* The *Palermo* had carried fifty-two Americans and a cargo of two thousand horses and mules. Two of the *Palermo* crewmen, Frank Carney and Dan O'Connor, hitched rides back home to New York aboard the *Montserrat* and happily shared their stories. As they described it, the Germans had attacked the *Palermo* while they were sleeping, sunk the ship with torpedoes and artillery guns, and then left them to row their tiny lifeboat across twenty-five miles of open ocean.[13] One American horse trainer died in the incident.

It is easy to picture nervous *Montserrat* passengers hearing this and spending their days searching the horizon for periscopes. Normally the

Montserrat carried twelve hundred passengers and a crew of eighty on its transatlantic crossings, including a thousand poor souls stuck below in steerage. But wartime and winter left most of the cabins empty this time. The entire ship now held barely four hundred people, including crew.

Trotsky's young sons, Leon and Sergei, seemed the only ones in the family actually to enjoy the cruise. Braving the cold, they ventured outside to explore the *Montserrat* stem to stern, counting the ship's decks and cabins and getting to know the sailors and other passengers. Like kids anyplace, they marveled at the ocean, the ship's engines, its huge smokestacks, the birds and fish, the salty smell and roaring waves.

The boys spoke no Spanish. As sons of Leon Trotsky, their unusual language skills reflected the family's unique odyssey. They'd learned Russian from their parents. Leon, the older son, was actually conceived in a Russian prison during his father's imprisonment after the abortive 1905 Saint Petersburg uprising. Tsarist police had held Trotsky in the notorious Peter-Paul Fortress awaiting trial, and it was during one of Natalya's conjugal visits that she became pregnant with Leon. When the Russian court sentenced Trotsky to lifelong exile in Siberia, Natalya stayed behind in Saint Petersburg to give birth alone. Then, after he escaped, Trotsky quickly reunited the family in Finland and moved them to safety in Austria. As a result, Sergei, the younger son, was born in Vienna in 1908. The boys learned smatterings of German and French from attending public schools in Vienna and Paris, following Papa's various places of refuge.

The Spanish sailors on the *Montserrat* enjoyed playing with the young Trotsky sons and befriended them, using slang and sign language to communicate. One day the boys told their parents a strange story. "Do you know, the fireman is very nice," they reported back to Papa. "He's a Repubicker."

"A Republican?" Trotsky asked, curious at the strange term. "How could you understand him?"

"Oh, he explains everything fine." The boys then told Papa the latest piece of sign language the sailors had taught them. "He said 'Alfonso!'"

The fireman had been telling the boys about Spanish king Alfonso XIII, widely hated among the country's poor. Alfonso had sat on the Spanish throne for thirty-two years. The boys went on: "He said 'Alfonso!' and then went 'Poff-Piff.'" Sergei and Leon then drew their fingers across their necks, as if cutting a man's throat with a knife.

That, they said, was what the sailors wanted to do with Alfonso.[14]

"Oh, then he is certainly a Republican," Trotsky laughed, apparently pleased with these new friends of his young sons. Natalya gave the boys Malaga grapes and other delicacies from their first-class cabin to share with the friendly sailors.[15]

Why were they on this ship at all? Three months earlier, Trotsky and his family were living in Paris in a small apartment on rue Oudry near the Place d'Italie, a pretty spot on the Left Bank with trees, grass, and a small fountain. Trotsky had settled in France in 1914 at the start of the world war after Austria, their home up till then, had forced them to leave. As Russians, they would have been considered alien enemies. Germany had gone further and indicted Trotsky in absentia over an anti-war tract he had written, convicted him of treason, and threatened to arrest him if he entered the country. That left Switzerland as a refuge, where many émigré Russian radicals fled, or France.

Trotsky tried Switzerland but picked France. He enjoyed the French cinema, French novels (which he read in the original language), and the cafés. A favorite became the Rotonde in Montmartre, rich with artists and writers surviving on handouts and cheap coffee. In Paris he had Russian friends and could mingle with leading French socialist politicians, including legislators and cabinet ministers. In Paris Trotsky coedited a small Russian-language newspaper called *Nashe Slovo* (Our Word), a platform for his socialist, antiwar, anti-tsarist views.

French military censors sometimes harassed him, often prompted by complaints from the Russian embassy. Russia, after all, was France's ally in the war, and the Russians resented Trotsky's anti-tsarist articles, particularly the ones he arranged to have smuggled back home. Trotsky haggled with the censors, and sometimes they forced him to publish a blank page or two, but his tabloid survived long enough to produce 213 editions between January 1915 and October 1916.

In addition to the censors, French military intelligence also kept an eye on Trotsky, suspecting him of being pro-German. They noticed, for instance, how *Nashe Slovo* barely mentioned Germany's sinking of the *Lusitania*. In 1915 French military police spotted Trotsky at the French war front near Belgium, snooping around the trenches, an area off-limits to foreign journalists. They followed him back to his room at the Hotel Parisien in Le Havre, confronted him there, and, as they put it, "immediately invited [him] to leave" and return to Paris.[16] After that, they began monitoring his mail and his friends, noting the many registered letters from Switzerland and Russia and his notoriety as a self-proclaimed socialist revolutionary. In a July 1915 report, they claimed that Trotsky's newspaper had received money from a Romanian revolutionary named Rakovsky, a suspected Austrian spy.

All this, to French authorities, made Trotsky an "etranger comme suspect au point de vue national"[17] (suspicious alien from a national viewpoint), a designation likely to cause trouble.

With her common-law husband gallivanting around Paris and the battlefront, Natalya was left to run a household with two small children under wartime stringencies. She remembered these Paris years in depressing terms. "We lived in a densely populated district. Walks through Paris were our only amusement," she wrote later. "There was so much mourning [for soldiers killed on the front] that black had become the latest fashion; even the streetwalkers wore black." As for her husband's newspaper, she described it as a constant struggle to stay solvent. "*Nashe Slovo* was run on the devotion of a few militants who contributed their labor as well as what little money they could spare," she wrote. "Payment for paper and printing was a daily worry."[18] She recalled her husband often staying up past midnight to write articles, then dropping them off at the printer the next morning when he took Sergei to school.

Despite all these tensions, French authorities mostly left Trotsky alone. They let him enjoy his cafés, his leftist friends, and his travels.

They even gave him a passport in 1915 to leave France altogether for a trip to Switzerland. Here, Trotsky would attend a small conference of socialists in the resort town of Zimmerwald that would cast a long shadow over the future. Beyond everything else, it would feature the last major pre-1917 clash between Trotsky and his then-leading rival in the small world of Russian émigré socialists, the intense bearded man who would lead the Russian Revolution, Vladimir Ilyich Ulyanov, or Lenin.

TODAY, A CENTURY later, Americans mostly think of Lenin and Trotsky together, as the inseparable coauthors of the 1917 Bolshevik Revolution, famous partners in crime. Modern Russians see them differently, swayed unavoidably by the bloodstained later efforts of another rival, Joseph Stalin, to vilify Trotsky, kill thousands of his backers, and literally erase him from the country's history. For Russians today, Trotsky is a vague blank figure, largely missing from civics books.

But the lives of these two men, Lenin and Trotsky, grew so intertwined in the years around 1917 that it is near impossible to explain one without the other. And in 1915, two years before their famous collaboration, the state of the Lenin–Trotsky relationship was clear to anyone who looked: Already the two most prominent figures in Russian émigré socialism, they despised each other, or at least acted that way.

Trotsky had first become aware of Vladimir Lenin in 1902 during his first exile in Siberia. Copies of Lenin's magazine *Iskra* (Spark) and his pamphlet "What Is to Be Done?" reached him there. Trotsky read the tracts and became a convert. Lenin, nine years older than Trotsky, had already established himself as leader of the emerging Russian Social Democratic Party. He had built *Iskra* into both a tabloid and a movement, with followers across Europe and Russia. Trained as a lawyer, a veteran of Russian jails and Siberian exile like Trotsky himself, Lenin as a teenager had seen tsarist police hang his older brother, Alexander, for joining an antigovernment plot. A friend described Lenin around 1915 as "the lean, tallish man, with large fierce eyes and large, sensual, irregular mouth, perched on the platform like a 'bird of prey.'"[19]

Trotsky, after his escape from Siberia in 1902, decided he must meet this Lenin and become his protégé. As the story goes, it took Trotsky weeks to secretly cross Siberia and Europe, meeting members of the anti-tsarist underground along the way, including a two-month stop in Paris. He reached London, where Lenin had set up operations, and took until well past midnight to finally locate Lenin's apartment at 10 Holford Square near King's Cross. Trotsky left his cab driver unpaid at the curb, came inside the apartment house unannounced, bounded up the stairs oblivious to the late hour, and knocked three times loudly at the door, the signal for strangers. When Lenin's wife, Nadezhka Krupskaya, got out of bed to answer it, she found a disheveled young man excitedly telling her of his journey. She woke her husband, who recognized the stranger as the young writer he had recently heard about, and said, "The Pen has arrived!"

Krupskaya described the friendship that blossomed between her husband, Lenin, and the brilliant, outgoing young stranger, Trotsky. "Leaving them together I went to see to the cabman and prepare coffee! When I returned I found Vladimir Ilyich still seated on the bed in animated conversation with Trotsky on some rather abstract theme."[20] Over the next few days, Lenin took him on long walks through London, showing him the sights. "This is their Westminster" or "their British Museum," he told Trotsky. They spoke about Russia, about socialism, and about Lenin's plans for *Iskra,* both the magazine and the movement. Lenin decided to nurture the young man's talent. He included Trotsky on *Iskra*'s small board of editors, despite objections from some older members, and sent him on propaganda fund-raising missions to Europe.

However, this budding friendship between the older Lenin and his protégé Trotsky lasted only a few months and came to a quick end. The very next year, 1903, they had a falling-out, part of a larger, major split within *Iskra* and the Social Democratic movement that would leave Trotsky and Lenin on opposite sides: the famous schism between Bolsheviks and Mensheviks.

The rupture occurred at a 1903 party conference that started in Brussels but moved to London after Belgium police began harassing delegates. Typically, it was Lenin who started the argument. And just as typically, it was Lenin who won the key vote and seized the chance to call his faction Bolsheviks (Russian for "majority"), even though most people in the group actually disagreed with him. As Bolsheviks, Lenin and his followers insisted that socialism could be achieved in Russia only by a party tightly controlled by a tiny leadership elite, its members limited to active revolutionaries serving as vanguard of the working class. Workers could not be trusted to do it themselves.

Years later, dedicated Bolsheviks would honor Lenin by giving the concept a deeper, more profound aura, a distinction "between the 'hard' and the 'soft,' the 'workers' and the 'talkers,' the 'fighters' and the 'reasoners'—between Bolsheviks and Mensheviks—which was [Lenin's] great psychological contribution to the science of revolution," as one put it.[21] But in 1903, most people, even his friends, saw it more narrowly.

Opposing Lenin at the 1903 conference was Lenin's friend and *Iskra* cofounder Julius Martov, another Russian émigré. Martov, more bookish and soft-spoken, argued the opposite point, that socialism, like any political movement, could succeed only if backed by an open, inclusive mass movement. His group became known as Mensheviks (Russian for "minority"), even though it had more people on its side.

Trotsky attended the 1903 conference and, much to Lenin's chagrin, sided squarely with Martov. Trotsky at the time shared a London apartment with Martov and other friends and happily turned his acid pen to their defense. Trotsky ridiculed Lenin's entire concept of "dictatorship of the proletariat" as amounting to "dictatorship over the proletariat,"[22] a pinnacle of concentrated power with Lenin the self-appointed dictator.

Lenin and Trotsky never healed the wound over this argument. By 1915 their rivalry had become a high-profile, seemingly permanent fixture in émigré Russian politics, complete with name-calling and finger-pointing. Among other things, Trotsky had called Lenin a "terribly egocentric person," a "master-squabbler," and a "professional exploiter," preoccupied with "bickering" and power mongering.[23] Lenin, for his part, called Trotsky a "cur," a "judas," "always evasive, cheating, posing," his views "vacuous and unprincipled," his writing littered with "puffed up phrases" to support "absurd" arguments.[24]

Trotsky later claimed to find the whole Bolshevik–Menshevik quarrel petty, which irritated his Menshevik friends as well.[25]

The 1915 Zimmerwald conference, called originally by Swiss socialists, was intended to bridge this gap and address a new crisis created by the world war. Its attendees included a who's who of socialist celebrities, Bolsheviks and Mensheviks alike, including many destined to become top figures of the post-1917 Russian communist government: Trotsky, Lenin, Grigory Zinoviev (future Politburo member and Comintern chairman), Karl Radek (future vice commissar of foreign affairs), and others.

The problem they faced was this: Up until 1914, socialists, as a basic element of their creed, all pledged their belief in the solidarity of the international working class. This, they claimed, could always be counted on to prevent wars among nations. Why should workers in France or Germany pick up guns to kill each other, they argued, when their common enemy was the bourgeoisie? But the outbreak of world war in 1914 shattered this belief system. Instead of opposing the war, workers in Germany and France were among the first to join the war hysteria sweeping their countries and enlist in their respective armies. Worse still, leading socialist politicians across Europe, including elected members of parliaments, one after another abandoned their principles to support their national war efforts.

Lenin and Trotsky both considered this betrayal unforgivable and considered these "social patriots"—their derisive term for the turncoat socialist leaders—cowards and scoundrels. Denouncing "social patriot" traitors became just as important to them as opposing the war itself.

But faced with this immediate problem, Lenin came to Zimmerwald with a more aggressive idea, stunning in its counterintuitive boldness.

Lenin proposed that socialists must reject peace for its own sake. Instead, he argued, the world war had created an opportunity. Instead of peace, they must demand the defeat of their own countries. Russians must support *defeat of Russia*, Germans *defeat of Germany*, British *defeat of Britain*. These defeats would discredit the capitalist ruling classes and set the stage for revolution. The world war must be transformed into smaller civil wars in each country, leading to victory for the working class.

Trotsky actually agreed with Lenin on most of this bold concept. He detested "social patriots," and his exposure to the French and Balkan battlefronts had already convinced him that the war had destroyed public faith in governments, setting the stage for uprisings. But Lenin's defeatism—insisting that socialists make themselves traitors in their own countries—seemed needlessly confrontational. And Lenin's call for national civil wars could hardly attract the support of war-weary Europeans. Even the assembled socialists at Zimmerwald found it excessive. This was no way to achieve unity.

Trotsky ended up working with moderate delegates to forge a compromise, a manifesto calling for peace without victories or annexations. Lenin thought it much too weak but, finding himself outnumbered, voted for it anyway. Two later Zimmerwald conferences, with Trotsky absent, would produce manifestos much closer to Lenin's original idea. Still, the split between "Zimmerwald left" (pro-Lenin) and "Zimmerwald right" (anti-Lenin) added an entire new layer of division to the already fractured movement.[26]

After Zimmerwald, Lenin returned to his own wartime refuge in Switzerland, like everyone else, to wait.

BACK IN PARIS, Trotsky finally reached the end of his rope with French officials in mid-1916, when Russia decided to send a small navy squadron to the French port of Marseilles. Mutiny broke out on one Russian ship, the *Askold,* where Russian soldiers murdered one of their officers. When police searched the murderers, they found some carrying copies of Trotsky's newspaper *Nashe Slovo*.

Russian diplomats, long irritated at Trotsky's anti-Russian articles, now insisted he be expelled from France. Trotsky complained bitterly. He claimed that a Russian agent provocateur had framed him by placing the copies of *Nashe Slovo* on the soldiers. Besides, Trotsky argued, French censors had approved the newspaper edition. He asked political friends, including high-ranking socialist ministers, to intervene, but to no avail. After a few weeks, the French interior minister, Louis Malvy (who himself would be exiled from France in 1918 on charges of treason), bowed to Russian pressure and issued the expulsion order. "On 30 October [1916] the [Paris] Prefect invited me, pointed out that my time of grace had long ago run out, and suggested my going to Spain," Trotsky confided in a letter to a friend. "I refused," he said.

"Then what is left for us to do?" the police prefect asked.

"Cart me out in your own way,'" Trotsky told him, meaning at the prefect's expense.[27]

Sure enough, that night, a pair of plainclothes French detectives came to the apartment on rue Oudry and took Trotsky away, leaving Natalya and the boys behind. They escorted him under arms to the Spanish border—no hearing, no formal charges, no day in court.

Things went no better in Spain. Trotsky spoke no Spanish and found the country, as he put it, "lazy," "provincial," and corrupt.[28] He spent his first few days wandering the coastal town of San Sebastian, where, as he later recounted, "I was delighted by the sea but appalled by the prices."[29] In Madrid, he spent days at the famous Prado Museum, discovering masterpieces by painters Rembrandt, Hieronymus Bosch, and Jan Miel. But this leisure ended abruptly. Spanish police, acting on a tip from the French, soon arrested him. They stuck him in jail first in Madrid, then in Cádiz, where they threatened to deport him to Cuba, where Trotsky had no friends and presumably could do no harm.

"I won't go voluntarily," Trotsky told the officials.

"Then we shall be compelled to place you in the hold of the vessel," the officials snapped back.[30] As with France, Spain gave him no hearing or formal charges.[31]

Trotsky begged to stay in Europe.[32] He sent panicked appeals to Spanish politicians and socialist friends across Europe. Switzerland, Britain, and Italy each denied his request for sanctuary or passage. "All my correspondence about going to Switzerland was confiscated by French authorities," he complained.[33] Natalya, sitting in Paris, clamored for help to free her husband. With Trotsky behind bars, it fell on her alone to raise money, care for the boys, take them out of school, pay the bills and bribes, track down political friends, negotiate with steamship companies, and pack up their Paris home.

Spain finally decided to end this headache by sending Trotsky away, not to Cuba but to the United States of America, a country far across the ocean willing to take him and where Trotsky was willing to go. Who exactly made the decision? Did bribes get paid? The full truth may never be known, but the list of behind-the-scene players was long, including top Spanish officials such as Count Alvaro de Figueroa de Romanones, Spain's Liberal prime minister at the time; a Republican deputy named Roberto Castrovido; a Spanish insurance official named Dupre; future Spanish parliamentarian Julian Besteiro; and the Russian-born Spanish bohemian novelist Ernesto Barc, all mentioned by various sources.[34]

However it happened, Trotsky quickly grew sanguine with the idea of America. He knew people in New York City. Many Russian socialist friends, including some he'd shared prison time with back in Saint Petersburg, had already congregated there. Trotsky had written articles for their newspaper, *Novy Mir*. In New York, he would have a platform. Natalya and the boys could live in a stable place. Still jailed in Cádiz, he began studying English, a language totally new to him. "Received two English books," he wrote one friend from his cell. "Thank you. The English pronunciation now absorbs my attention and makes the waiting painful for me."[35]

With arrangements finally set, Natalya brought the family to Barcelona. Here they enjoyed a day or two of sight-seeing before police detectives came to escort them to the *Montserrat* and place them aboard.

One last complication: At the *Montserrat,* the ship's officers claimed to discover a problem with their tickets. Natalya, using cash she had raised from friends and family, had purchased four second-class fares for seventeen hundred pesetas, but the ship's officers now told them they had no second-class cabins left, only first-class cabins and third-class steerage. To get on board, they would have to pay the difference for first class.

Was this a shakedown? A rip-off? Probably.

Natalya balked. She insisted she didn't have the money. Trotsky claimed to be down to his last forty francs at that point (about $160). "The family was ready to pay for their second class fare," she argued, but not more.

What to do? Spain came to the rescue. "Madrid was so anxious to get rid of [us] that it paid [our] full fare for first class," Natalya later explained.[36] And so the family got its first-class cabin with its plenty of fresh air, windows, and light. "It was just about [our] only deluxe travel in [our] whole lives," Natalya recalled.[37] Or, as Trotsky put it to a friend in Madrid, "We 'enjoy' the first [class], that is to say, we are conducting a continuous struggle to receive the water to wash in the morning and not receive it in the face during the night, when they wash the boat."[38]

All that, and Natalya managed to keep in her pocket some $500 cash (more than $10,000 in modern value), money she apparently failed to mention to the ticket agent.

"The last act of the Spanish police is superb," Trotsky wrote mockingly to yet another friend. "In Valencia and Malaga, [Spanish] agents and gendarmes surround me on the boat to keep me from leaving with my wife and my children."[39]

ONCE AT SEA, they watched the last green hills of Spain sink below the horizon with little hope of returning anytime soon. "The door of Europe shut behind me in Barcelona," he sighed.[40] To a socialist friend in London who had helped in the crisis, he confided, "I press your hand warmly. . . . I hope that we may meet once again in the ranks of fighters for the common cause."[41] To yet another: "This is the last time that I cast a glance at that old canaille [a French curse meaning "vulgar dog"] Europe."[42]

As days went by at sea, Trotsky seemed to dislike most of the people he met aboard the *Montserrat,* chafing at being on this ship at all. "The population of the steamer is multicolored, and not very attractive in its variety," he wrote. He couldn't help but notice the many young men fleeing Europe to avoid military service. "There are quite a few deserters from different countries, for the most part men of fairly high standing," he noted, pointing to an artist carrying away his paintings, a billiard champion, and a few respectable older gentlemen. "The others are much of the same sort: deserters, adventurers, speculators, or simply 'undesirables' thrown out of Europe. Who would ever dream of crossing the Atlantic at this time of year on a wretched little Spanish boat from choice?"[43] He ventured below deck to explore the squalid, smelly steerage compartment, where the poorest immigrants stayed, and found the mood there sullen. "It is more difficult to make out the third-class passengers," he wrote. "They lie close together, move about very little, say very little—for they have not much to eat."[44]

One person on the ship Trotsky apparently did strike up a conversation with was a twenty-nine-year-old artist and boxer named Arthur Cravan. Cravan, telling the story years later, claimed he had just fought a one-round match in Barcelona against American world champion Jack Johnson. Johnson had knocked him out, Cravan said, but the fight was rigged. Now, like the others, Cravan had booked passage on the *Montserrat* to flee Europe and avoid serving in the war. Trotsky later described him this way: "Boxer who is also a novelist and a cousin of Oscar Wilde, confesses openly that he prefers crashing Yankee jaws in a noble sport to letting some German stab him in the midriff."[45]

By Cravan's account, Trotsky sat him down one night and told him about his work as a socialist agitator. "In New York, I hope to find support—and funding—for our cause," he quoted Trotsky as saying. "Think of it: An international movement! War will be outlawed! People will achieve economic justice!"[46]

Cravan recalled listening to Trotsky and shrugging him off as a sincere lunatic. He warned him to be careful, saying, "You will surely be betrayed by your comrades," to which Cravan recalled Trotsky saying, "Thanks for the warning, my friend, but I am not so cynical."[47] The two apparently never met again.

Snow fell the night the *Montserrat* finally reached the other side of the ocean and slipped into New York Harbor. Excitement grew among the passengers when the engines stopped throbbing at 3 AM and the crew told them to prepare for arrival. Finally, after seventeen days, they could all get off that cramped, slow, uncomfortable little ship.

The *Montserrat* passed directly under the Statue of Liberty as it steamed toward lower Manhattan, though Trotsky made no mention of it. If he or the boys actually did see Lady Liberty through the fog and dark, they might have noticed shrapnel and debris defacing her on the side facing New Jersey. In July, an explosion at the nearby Black Tom military depot had destroyed two million pounds of ammunition awaiting shipment to Britain and France, including one hundred thousand pounds of TNT. The explosion had killed seven men, shattered windows on Times Square, and shaken people out of bed as far away as Connecticut. It damaged Lady Liberty so severely that tourists still were being kept outside six months later.

New York police had determined that the Black Tom explosion was no accident and focused their suspicion once again on German saboteurs. One step closer to war.

Trotsky and his family never had to set foot on Ellis Island, New York's huge processing center for immigrants built on a small sandbar in the harbor. For first-class passengers, immigration inspectors came to the ship and examined them privately in their cabins. Natalya wore a veil that day and reportedly gave one doctor a withering stare when he tried to lift it to examine her eyes for disease—a standard check for new arrivals. Natalya, like her husband, had little patience for policemen.

The ship waited until Sunday morning, January 14, to unload its passengers on Pier 8 at the bottom tip of Manhattan Island. Looking out from the railing, Trotsky had to marvel at what he saw. On land, at the end of the pier, he saw rising abruptly before him a giant mountain range, jagged square buildings, some with spires and towers, shooting up so high that locals called them "sky scrapers." One, the Woolworth Building, stood almost eight hundred feet, the tallest building on earth. Another, the Metropolitan Life Insurance Tower, stood almost as high at seven hundred feet, the clock face on its dramatic tower covering more than four stories. Dozens more of these behemoths stretched for miles beyond.

Looking up along the East River, he saw more giant things. The massive Brooklyn Bridge arched across the sky above them, crossing the entire harbor. And two newer bridges, just as huge, stood nearby: the Williamsburg (1903) and the Manhattan (1909). The harbor itself buzzed with movement from hundreds of ships, boats, tugs, and schooners of every size and description.

Looking down at the pier, he saw a crowd of people shivering in the cold, waiting for friends and family. He and Natalya scanned them for familiar faces. Finally they saw someone wave back at them.

VLADIMIR ILYICH LENIN, sitting now in Berne, Switzerland, with his wife, Krupskaya, running his Bolshevik network with a firm grip, kept tabs on his rival Trotsky. Through letters from friends across Europe, he followed Trotsky's latest expulsions from France and Spain and finally to North America. And not without concern.

These were difficult days for Lenin. "Never, I think, was Vladimir Ilyich in a more irreconcilable mood than during the last months of 1916 and the early months of 1917," Krupskaya recalled.[48] Chronically short of money, he found himself isolated in Switzerland. Most of his Bolshevik followers were scattered abroad. He had no direct contact with Russia.

Letters and papers had to be smuggled through Scandinavia, wasting time and losing information. Britain denied him permission to publish journals and pamphlets there, cutting him off from a major source of possible support. He sensed the war going badly for Russia and heard tremors of discontent there, but the waiting seemed endless. Revolution could come tomorrow or next week, or maybe not for another ten years. It all made him impatient and agitated.

Lenin knew all about the colony of Russian socialists in New York City. He read their newspaper *Novy Mir* but complained that it reached him with "devilish irregularity."[49] Lenin saw opportunity in America. Americans had money and power but were neophytes at politics. America had a Socialist Party, but it seemed uninformed and disconnected.

Lenin had taken steps to plant his own flag on US soil. Recently, he had sent an envoy, a Scandinavian comrade named Alexandra Kollontai, with instructions to contact American leaders, raise money, sell them on his Bolshevik ideas, and get his tracts published in English, for free if possible. In addition, one of his Bolshevik circle, a talented young intellectual named Nikolai Bukharin, had recently settled in New York City after being expelled from his perch in Norway. Bukharin had established himself as an editor at *Novy Mir,* giving Lenin a direct pipeline into their central organ.

Lenin had no intention of letting Trotsky interfere with his plans for America. Kollontai and Bukharin would keep him posted.

2
TIMES SQUARE

"I am truly a fatherland-less chap and I am grateful to have found a country that is accepting me within its boundaries."

—Leon Trotsky, *New Yorker Volkszeitung*, January 15, 1917 (translated from the German original)

WHAT A GREETING! They could not have treated him better if he were the King of England! Bounding down the gangway to the pier, Trotsky found himself a center of attention, and in the best way. No one came to arrest him, harass, argue, or give him a hard time. No one challenged his paperwork, his politics, his religion, or his writings. No interrogations, no extra inspections, no snooping. Not by the police, the customs officials, or even the ship's officers.

Instead, they all smiled and acted politely, treating him like a guest. What a difference an ocean makes!

The landing of a transatlantic liner those days always attracted a carnival, and the *Montserrat* was no different. People came to watch and wave at the ship, even on a freezing cold Sunday morning like this. How many had come specifically for the great socialist Trotsky? Apparently quite a few. His friends in New York had been busy. LEON TROTZKI KOMMT HEUTE! (Leon Trotsky Is Arriving Today!) the *New Yorker Volkszeitung* had shouted from its front page that morning, urging its fourteen thousand readers to see "our much persecuted comrade" and "courageous fellow combatant."[50] So too the Russian-language *Novy Mir*.

29

At least four newspapers sent reporters to the *Montserrat*'s land-ing that morning, looking for celebrities or politicians to interview, any speck of gossip or news. Trotsky easily fit the bill. When three English-speaking newsmen approached him, Trotsky saw a man suddenly appear at his side to help. His name was Arthur Concors, a senior staff official at the Hebrew Sheltering and Immigration Aid Society, or HIAS, the well-known charity that helped Jewish refugees fleeing Eastern Europe. One of Trotsky's New York friends knew Concors and appar-ently asked him to come as a personal favor,[i] an on-the-spot expert to help untangle any last-minute customs issues and deal with the English-speaking newsmen.

Concors knew his business and came prepared with what press-savvy people today call talking points, designed to give a story the right spin. As a result, all the English newspapers got the same line—EXPELLED FROM FOUR LANDS—that was headlined the *New York Times*. Its story, appearing the next morning, portrayed poor Trotsky as kicked out of Europe for nothing more than "preaching peace."[51] The *New York Tribune* took the drama further: WITH BAYONETS FOUR LANDS EXPEL PEACE ADVOCATE.[52] The *New York Herald* touted Trotsky's four years in Russian prisons and his battle with long-arm tsarist harassment even in France. Earlier, another English-language paper, the *New York Call*, had described Trotsky as "pursued with a particular vendictiveness [sic] by authorities of the capitalistic order" and now "penniless."[53]

Both the *Times* and *Tribune* also stressed Trotsky's identity as a "Jewish" writer editing "Jewish" journals in Russia and France. A mil-lion and a half Jewish people lived in New York City then and bought newspapers, though mostly their own half dozen written in Yiddish. Trotsky himself never wrote Yiddish, barely spoke the language, was not raised in a shtetl (small Jewish Eastern European town), and never

---

i HIAS records contain no mention of the organization's involvement in the incident, nor any mention of Trotsky (by any spelling) in its voluminous lists of immigrants it assisted. Concors apparently acted on his own, most likely contacted by *Novy Mir* editor Gregory Weinstein, who had once applied for a job at HIAS.

practiced the Jewish religion. He didn't hide his Jewish background. In fact, he had spoken out eloquently against pogroms and anti-Jewish oppression in Europe, often at personal risk. But asked about it, he normally gave his religion simply as socialist or internationalist.

Still, this was Trotsky's spin for the English-language press: man of peace persecuted by European autocrats, a Jewish victim of the hated anti-Semitic Russian tsar, finding refuge in kindhearted America. A fine human-interest story: simple, sympathetic, poignant.

Only Trotsky, hearing himself portrayed as a helpless "pacifist" bullied by Europeans, seemed embarrassed by the characterization, a far cry from his own preferred self-image as revolutionary fighter. He soon found a chance to set the record straight, or at least to add his own spin. A German-speaking reporter for the *New Yorker Volkszeitung* came by to talk, and at last Trotsky had someone he could address directly in a language he knew. Even better, the reporter called him "comrade." He was a socialist. Bubbling in good humor, Trotsky quickly befriended the man and took the opportunity to recast his recent fights with the French and Spanish governments. "You know, I made myself impossible in France as editor of *Nashe Slovo*," he told the reporter. "Honestly, this [expulsion from Europe] isn't surprising in light of the fierce opposition we posed to the 'socialist' and the 'capitalist' war warmongers." Trotsky had picked this fight, he insisted, not anybody else.[54]

"In Comrade Trotsky, America gains a resolute fighter for the Revolutionary International," *Novy Mir* reported after talking with him.[55] That's the way they wanted him: Trotsky the fighter.

He must have marveled at the whole circus, this claque of newspapermen who actually listened to him and accepted his stories almost without question. His friends had done a wonderful job. Within two days, at least six New York newspapers with more than half a million readers would announce Trotsky's arrival in the city. Three put the story on the front page, and two, the *Forward* and the *New York Call,* included front-page photos.

Who were these friends arranging Trotsky's greeting in New York? The news accounts didn't specify who exactly came to the pier other than Arthur Concors, but Trotsky would spend all that day and the next shaking their hands, grabbing their shoulders, kissing their cheeks, giving them well-deserved thanks. By the time he finished the greetings at the pier, he was exhausted. He, Natalya, and the boys had been wide awake since 3 AM, and the boys whined impatiently. Arthur Concors, their expert guide, again took command. He claimed their bags and grabbed a car to take them uptown.

Trotsky's friends had arranged a hotel for their first night in America. To reach it, Concors led them on a tour through the densely packed streets of lower Manhattan.

No riverfront highways yet existed to take them around the crowded South Street waterfront or the sprawling Lower East Side. Traveling uptown, they would have seen elevated railroads erected right down the middle of traffic-clogged streets. It being Sunday morning, they heard church bells chiming over the din of motorcars, horses, and pushcarts. Out their car windows, they would have seen a cacophony of humanity—rich, poor, and homeless—peddlers and police; garish mansions, filthy tenements, and all the towers; all squashed together in vivid confusion. Trotsky would have recognized Wall Street from photographs of the famous capitalist stronghold. At Union Square, they would have passed Tammany Hall, the city's ultimate cathedral to politics. On lower Broadway, they would have seen huge shopping emporiums, stores with names like Macy's, Gimbels, and Lord & Taylor, where women searched for fashions and bargains.

Finally, they passed Forty-Second Street and reached their hotel, another eye-popping wonder. The Astor House on Times Square, opened in 1904, easily matched in luxury anything Trotsky had seen in Paris or Vienna. Its arched doors led into an opulent lobby under enormous ceiling frescoes and crystal chandeliers, a Flemish smoking room, a Pompeian billiards room, and, upstairs, an exotically landscaped rooftop garden. Piano music played by day, dance music by night. Valets in uniform opened doors and carried bags. The building dominated the full block on Broadway between Forty-Forth and Forty-Fifth Streets, its eleven stories housing one thousand guest rooms.

Trotsky must have gasped at the sight. Who picked such an elaborate, expensive place? Could they possibly afford it? Did some unidentified benefactor pay the tab? Could Natalya cover it with the $500 cash in her pocket? Would they have anything left? Neither he nor Natalya ever mentioned the Astor House in their memoirs, as if embarrassed by the splurge. It hardly fit their new image as victimized refugees and voices of the working class. But there is little doubt they stayed there. Trotsky specified the "Astor Hotel, 42nd Street" in the *Montserrat* manifest as his first stop in New York City, and the location matched their activities that day.

Once inside, the greetings continued, in the lobby, the hallways, the room. A parade of faces kept introducing themselves, the friends who had arranged his arrival in New York. Trotsky greeted them all, clapped their shoulders like any seasoned politician. He recognized many from Europe. The Russian socialist underground by 1917 numbered thousands of people scattered around the world, and Trotsky, a leading figure since the start, knew almost all of them, or they knew him.

For instance, there was Lev Deutch with his bushy gray beard, a grand old man of Russian socialism. Now sixty-two years old, Deutch had settled in New York in 1915 as an original editor of *Novy Mir*. He had earned his first arrest in Russia back in 1875—before Trotsky was even born—and described his ordeal in a book called *Sixteen Years in Siberia,* published in Europe and America. It made him one of the most recognized Russians of the era. Deutch had known Trotsky in London as part of the *Iskra* crowd and had joined Trotsky as a Menshevik in the famous 1903 split. Like Trotsky, he too had returned to Saint Petersburg for the 1905 uprising and had landed with Trotsky in the same prison. Trotsky had considered it a great coming-of-age moment when Deutsch, behind bars, finally agreed to stop calling him "the youth" and started addressing him by his actual name.[56]

Most recently, Deutch, typically obstinate, had quit *Novy Mir* in an argument over the world war and now edited his own tiny pro-Ally competitor called *Svobodnoye Slovo* (Free Word).

Then came Moissaye Olgin, a friend from Copenhagen and Vienna who also had left Russia after several arrests. In New York, Olgin landed not at *Novy Mir* but instead at the city's largest socialist voice, the *Forward*. "When I met him here, he looked haggard," Olgin recalled of Trotsky that day. "He had grown older, and there was fatigue in his expression. His conversation hinged around the collapse of international socialism. He thought it shameful and humiliating."[57]

All these reunions had to be a thrill for Trotsky, seeing these people from his past, still alive and healthy, here to support him. But the biggest greeting that day came as a surprise, from a comrade Trotsky knew only slightly in Europe. He hadn't seen him since before the war. He was a Bolshevik, Vladimir Lenin's friend, making him, what . . . ? A rival? An adversary? Still, he had suffered just like Trotsky. Norway had arrested and deported him, and he had landed in New York just two months earlier, still finding his way.

Natalya remembered the moment distinctly, perhaps because it seemed out of place. "Bukharin greeted us with a bear-hug," she wrote. Added Trotsky, he "welcomed us with the childish exuberance characteristic of him."[58] This was New York. Here they could all be friends.

NICOLAI IVANOVICH BUKHARIN had a destiny much like Trotsky's. Bukharin too would become a top leader in Bolshevik Russia after the 1917 revolution, editor *of Pravda,* chairman of the Comintern, member of the Politburo, leading theoretician, and later a close ally of dictator Joseph Stalin. Like Trotsky, he too would suffer when Stalin turned against him; had him purged, tortured, and forced to confess false charges and denounce friends he knew to be innocent (including Trotsky); and finally had him murdered. But this was all still far in the future.

For now, in January 1917, Bukharin embodied "vivacity itself, has an open, smiling face, is affectionate and a lively conversationalist with a touch of humor," as Natalya described him.[59] His red beard, balding head, ready laugh, and unassuming manner made him easy to like. Just twenty-eight years old, ten years younger than Trotsky, Bukharin had grown up in Moscow as an academic, his parents both schoolteachers. His father, a Moscow University graduate and later a government civil servant, had nurtured his son's interests in nature, botany, birds, literature, and art.

Bukharin had joined the socialist underground as a student at Moscow University back in 1905, when anti-tsarist protests had erupted across Russia. Barely sixteen years old, he found himself absorbed in the excitement, the mass meetings and crowds singing "The Marseillaise" and cheering the hot rhetoric. The experience drew him like a moth, he said, and "completed" him as a revolutionary. During those heady days, he followed the exploits of the movement's charismatic leader, the head of the Saint Petersburg Soviet who talked back to the tsarist judge at his trial, the man Trotsky.

By 1910 Bukharin had risen to the Moscow Bolshevist Party's Central Committee, making him a target for the tsar's secret police. They arrested him, and he spent six months in prison before being exiled to Siberia. Like Trotsky, he escaped. He then made his way to Hanover, Germany. After a year, he arranged an audience with the movement's leader, the great Lenin, then living in Cracow.

Lenin's wife, Krupskaya, remembered her husband's first meeting with Bukharin. They had "quite a long talk," she recalled.[60] But Lenin and his new devotee hit a sore spot when Bukharin mentioned a police informant he believed had betrayed him in Moscow, a fellow Bolshevik committeeman named Malinovskii. This same Malinovskii had since risen high in the party, heading the Moscow Bolshevik Committee and representing them in the Russian Duma, or parliament. Lenin considered Malinovskii a friend and grew indignant at Bukharin's accusation. Lenin later accused Bukharin of being "credulous toward gossip."[61]

Events ultimately proved Bukharin right about Malinovskii. A post-1917 Bolshevik tribunal would convict Malinovskii of being a police spy and sentence him to death by firing squad. For now, though, Bukharin stayed in Cracow several weeks, contributed to Lenin's newest magazine, and became a regular member of the circle.

After Cracow, Bukharin moved to Vienna, Austria, where he married a fellow Moscow refugee named Nadezhda Mikhailovna Lukina. They set up housekeeping not far from the Trotskys, though the two couples never became close. At Lenin's request, Bukharin also helped another young Lenin protégé, a Georgian who recently had started calling himself Koba Stalin. Lenin had sent Stalin to Vienna to research a paper on Marxism and the National Question. Since Stalin spoke no German, Bukharin acted as both his translator and his academic guide.

With the world war, Bukharin left Vienna and moved to Switzerland. He tried to start an independent Bolshevik journal there, but Lenin objected. In 1915 he moved to Sweden, a key link in the underground smuggling route for messages between Russia and the outside world. Here he wrote his second major book, *Imperialism and World Economy;* his *Economic Theory of the Leisure Class* had been completed in Vienna. But relations between him and Lenin continued to deteriorate.

Each time Bukharin tried to assert independence, Lenin resisted. When Bukharin asked that he and his Swedish group be appointed a "special commission" to keep contact with allies in Russia, Lenin sniffed disloyalty and forbade them from any direct contact with Russia at all. When Bukharin and his friends complained, Lenin accused them of having an "anti-party attitude" and called Bukharin himself "unstable in politics" with "semi-anarchistic ideas."[62] Bukharin also clashed with Lenin on ideological issues, such as the role of nationalism and popular self-determination.

Even Lenin's ally Alexander Shliapnikov, watching from Russia, lamented that "both sides began to display pettiness."[63]

Swedish police arrested Bukharin in April 1916 for antiwar activities and then deported him to Christiana, Norway (renamed Oslo in 1924). A German agent had tried to involve Bukharin in an espionage plot, which had infuriated Swedish authorities. The last straw between

Bukharin and Lenin came in September 1916 when Lenin rejected an essay Bukharin had prepared for him as "decidedly incorrect."[64] As the argument escalated, Lenin complained to Zinoviev, "I am now so ill-disposed toward Bukharin I cannot write."[65]

By then, Bukharin had had enough. He too complained to Zinoviev: "You simply do not want me as a collaborator. Don't worry. I won't be troublesome." To Lenin himself he wrote that his vendetta had caused rumors that "I am being kicked out because 'you Lenin cannot tolerate any other person with brains.'"[66] Bukharin decided he needed distance and booked passage to America. His biographer Stephen Cohen concluded: "The deterioration in his relations with Lenin was probably a major factor."[67]

Despite these arguments, Bukharin and Lenin never broke ties. They managed somehow to keep the door open between them. Before leaving Europe, Bukharin bared his feelings to Lenin in an emotional letter: "At any rate, I ask one thing: If you will polemicize, etc., preserve such a tone as not to force a split. It would be very painful to me, painful beyond my strength, if joint work, even in the future, should become impossible. I have the greatest respect for you and look upon you as my revolutionary teacher and love you."[68] Lenin responded in kind, telling his young protégé, "We all value you highly."[69] The two continued to write back and forth, Lenin asking Bukharin to use his new perch in New York to help the cause by raising money and finding English publishers for Lenin's articles.[70]

On reaching New York, Bukharin and his wife slept on a friend's sofa the first few nights. Then he started his new post on the editorial staff of *Novy Mir*.

Now, seeing Trotsky standing in front of him in New York City, Bukharin seemed happy to forget politics. He and Trotsky apparently said not a word about their common headaches with Vladimir Lenin that first day. Instead, Bukharin had found something in New York City that he felt Trotsky, as Europe's foremost socialist writer, would surely appreciate. It wasn't the theater or the skyscrapers; not the subway, the cinema, or the fancy stores. Instead, "[We] had hardly got off the boat when he told us enthusiastically about a public library which stayed open late at night and which he proposed to show us at once," Natalya recalled. "At about nine o'clock in the evening we had to make the long journey to admire his great discovery."[71]

THE FRONT LOBBY of the Astor House led directly out onto Times Square. New Yorkers had named this spacious, five-block-long intersection for the building at its south end, constructed by the New York Times Company, yet another behemoth skyscraper at four hundred feet tall and with twenty-five stories. Already this square had become the heart of New York theater. Giant advertising posters covered the walls, though Trotsky could barely comprehend their garish colors and oversize English words. Al Jolson? Zeigfeld Girls? Cohan? Bukharin, just five feet tall and half a head shorter than either Trotsky or Natalya, led them down the sidewalk past crowds of people laughing, singing, or talking, off to a show, a concert, or a restaurant. The voices competed with noise from taxis and horses on the street. At Forty-Second Street they turned east into a canyon between tall buildings, which whipped the wind in their faces and made them shiver. At the next block, they passed under a singularly ugly structure, the Sixth Avenue elevated train line with its metal trestles blocking the sidewalk, frustrating traffic, and hiding the streetlights. Their teeth rattled as trains passed overhead, though at least the belching smoke of coal-burning steam engines had recently been eliminated with new electric cars.

Across the street they passed the giant Hippodrome Theatre on one side, featuring that week an enormous ice ballet with more than a thousand performing skaters. On the other side they passed Bryant Park, cluttered with shanties and huts. At Fifth Avenue, Bukharin led them around the corner until they stood in front of a great white marble building, an architectural marvel opened just a few years earlier, in 1911. Two white marble lions guarded the front entrance from either side. Overhead, etched in stone, was the name New York Public Library.

Bukharin knew Trotsky would adore this site. He and Trotsky shared a passion as deep as politics, what today would label them "wonks" or "nerds" or "geeks." In every European capital either of them visited, one of their first stops had been the library, be it in Vienna, Paris, Madrid, or Copenhagen. Trotsky had loved libraries since his teens. In his first prison in Nikolaev, he had sought out the prison library for solace. As writers, they craved the long days spent doing research in the stacks, especially in an age before TV, radio, talking movies, or the Internet became distractions.

Bukharin took them inside and led them up marble stairways to the building's top floor, then through a small foyer to the library's main reading room. This too was magnificent, a vast open space almost three hundred feet long and seventy-seven feet wide, larger than the entire ship *Montserrat* on which they had just crossed the ocean, with ceiling paintings and sculptures and flooded with light. And books! The library's seventy-five miles of shelves held more than a million of them, plus newspapers and magazines from around the world! For anyone! For free! To just come and read! Till almost midnight! Even on a Sunday night!

Neither Trotsky nor Bukharin had any idea that this library was actually a monument to capitalism, largely financed by three great American fortunes: those of real estate mogul John Jacob Astor; corporate lawyer Samuel Tilden; and in particular that widely reviled enemy of the working class, Andrew Carnegie. No matter. For the Russians, it would become a second home.

They didn't stay long. The walk back to the Astor House was just five blocks, but it could seem endless on a freezing cold night like this. "On the way back we got to know the exhausted faces of the New Yorkers," Natalya recalled.[72] Walking in Times Square, one could forget totally that, across the ocean, a world war was still being fought.

At some point that night, Bukharin told Trotsky something else. The very next night, a small group of determined American leftists was planning to hold a secret meeting. Their ambition was no less than to change the future of American socialism. They had asked Bukharin to come.

And certainly, Bukharin told his new friend, they would want to hear from the great Trotsky. The meeting would be over dinner at the home of a prominent American socialist, an editor at the German-language newspaper *New Yorker Volkszeitung*. His name was Ludwig Lore, and Trotsky must come.

To get there, Bukharin went on, they would have to venture outside the island of Manhattan, cross the East River, and enter a part of New York not normally seen by tourists or visitors, called Brooklyn.

3

SAINT MARKS PLACE

"To be a Soviet Commissar one must first have swept the offices of the Novyi Mir."[73]

—Morris Hillquit, circa 1920

"His personal life? What should I know about his personal life? . . . Every day Leon Trotsky worked with me, all day long at that desk where you sit. What should I care if he had one wife or two, two children or a dozen? Or that he lived in the Bronx and drank tea? Read his books, find out what he thinks—then you will know Leon Trotsky."[74]

—Gregory Weinstein, *Novy Mir* editor, speaking in late 1917

EARLY THE NEXT morning, his first full day in America, Trotsky took the subway, his first chance to rub elbows with the local working class. Before Brooklyn, first he had to spend a day at his new office.

A New York friend doubtless joined him to make sure he didn't get hopelessly lost along the way. Leaving the Astor House, he would have grabbed the Sixth Avenue elevated train at Forty-Second Street. After seven stops of bone-rattling twists and turns on the screeching rails, watching rooftops and third-story windows sweep by at eye level, Trotsky would have reached West Eighth Street in Greenwich Village. From here, West Eighth became East Eighth at Fifth Avenue. It changed names again after Broadway to become Saint Marks Place. At Second

Avenue, Trotsky would have passed the garish marquees of the Yiddish theaters and the popular Monopole Café. Back then, this spot began the vast Jewish Lower East Side, which stretched to the East River and south beyond Grand Street toward the Brooklyn Bridge.

After Second Avenue, Saint Marks Place changed personality and became quietly residential. Old four-story brownstones lined the sidewalks on both sides. Near the end of the block came number 77, a modest row house with signs for a dentist's and a doctor's office upstairs and mail slots for a few private apartments. Stairs led down to a basement, and by the door hung a sign on a cast-iron railing that said новый мир (*Novy Mir*). Here, hidden in quiet obscurity, beat the robust heart of American Bolshevism.

This is where Trotsky came that morning. Opening the door, he found himself immediately surrounded by all things Russian: Russian voices, Russian smells, Russian papers, Russian posters on the cracked walls. The whole cellar consisted of three cramped rooms and a hallway crammed with desks, cabinets, a telephone, and piles of paper. A plaque of Leo Tolstoy decorated a wall over a fireplace. Thick cigarette smoke clouded the air. Ashtrays overflowed onto the floor, and teacups cluttered any empty space. From a back room came the clicking of a linotype machine and the hum of a small printing press. Three small windows barely peeking above the sidewalk provided the only trickle of daylight.

Novy Mir sold only eight thousand copies each day, eight flimsy pages. The penny apiece it cost on New York street corners and two cents elsewhere didn't come close to covering expenses: rent, overhead, and the $20 a week it paid a few full-time workers. Most contributors wrote for free. The paper sold advertisements to cover the difference, and it welcomed any capitalist who paid good money. Budweiser beer, Piedmont tobacco, the International Phonograph Company, the American Line shipping company, and even a few local banks all advertised in *Novy Mir*.

But those eight thousand copies made *Novy Mir* arguably the most impactful Russian journal in the Western Hemisphere, easily overshadowing the city's three larger-circulation Russian dailies, *Russkii Golos, Russkoe Slovo,* and the reactionary *Russkaya Zemla. Novy Mir*'s readers included Europeans like Vladimir Lenin and Menshevik leader Julius Martov, plus comrades in Chicago, Boston, and Philadelphia. Its contributors would read like a who's who of future leaders of post-1917 Bolshevik Russia, starting with Trotsky and Bukharin. The paper's editorial slant teetered between Bolshevik and Menshevik, though Bukharin's arrival in October had tipped the balance decidedly toward Lenin's faction.

Trotsky needed no introductions here. He knew every face in the room. In a few minutes, he and they all chatted away in Russian. They called him Lev Davidovich, or just "comrade."

Gregory Gdaly Weinstein, an old friend from Europe and now *Novy Mir*'s editor in chief, sat at the largest desk.[75] Trotsky knew Weinstein from having shared the excitement of the 1905 uprising in Saint Petersburg. Born in Vilna and a public schoolteacher at the time, Weinstein had ended up, like Trotsky, getting arrested, jailed in Brest-Litovsk, and sentenced to four years of "penal servitude" in Siberia, prison slave labor rather than simple exile. He escaped after ten days, reached Paris and then Switzerland, where he earned a degree at the University of Geneva. Then he moved to New York.

Weinstein hardly looked the radical fugitive. Mild mannered with a slight frame and scraggly beard, he had what one friend called a "humorous way of meeting embarrassing situations—he would simply smile them away."[76] He was trained as a statistician, and even the United States government had trusted Weinstein enough to once hire him to study conditions at Ellis Island. He had also applied for a job doing charity work for the Hebrew Immigrant Aid Society (HIAS).

Bukharin sat at another desk and, near him, twenty-six-year-old Grigorii Chudnovsky, one of Trotsky's protégés from Paris and his newspaper there, *Nashe Slovo.* Chudnovsky, like Bukharin, had joined the revolutionary cause as a teenager during the 1905 Saint Petersburg uprising. Like the others, Chudnovsky had won himself a tsarist arrest and Siberian exile and had escaped. Most recently, he had left Paris for Copenhagen, then made his way to America and *Novy Mir*. Natalya described Chudnovsky as "an overgrown boy with a bad complexion and somewhat curly hair, a student who was perhaps too talkative for our taste and quick to flare up."[77] Trotsky himself considered him "impressionable and hot-headed." But here, in New York, he was a friendly face in a foreign country.[78]

Others scampered in and out, but these four now comprised the paper's core staff: Weinstein, Bukharin, Chudnovsky, and Trotsky. And what a rarified group they made: four escaped jailbirds, convicted Russian radicals, veterans of Siberian exiles and the failed 1905 Soviet uprising, all now marooned in America until . . . when? The end of the world war? The revolution? And if revolution never came? Their profession in the meantime: to theorize, proselytize, and lay groundwork for achieving their life's goal of overthrowing the tsar and establishing socialism. It was good steady work.

Weinstein gave Trotsky a desk in a corner—no private offices here—surrounded by mountains of papers and manuscripts. They quickly came to terms. Weinstein would pay Trotsky $20 each week. Trotsky would deliver two or three columns, plus he could write more for any other newspaper he pleased and give all the speeches he wanted. Already Trotsky planned to contribute to at least three others: the *Call*, the *Volkszeitung,* and the *Forward*. For Weinstein, it was a bargain. With Trotsky, he got not only a celebrity writer but someone who actually could help him run the newspaper—someone who understood publishing, deadlines, and budgets, the need to fill column inches with catchy prose.

Trotsky dashed off a quick column for the next morning's edition titled "Да здравствует борьба!" (Long Live Struggle!), mostly a spoof of his adventures on the *Montserrat*. For the first time, New Yorkers would see the soon-common byline Н. Троцкий.[79]

But more important that first day, two other newspapers had asked to interview Trotsky. These weren't ignorant American English speakers who knew nothing about their movement but rather the two leading voices of American socialism, the *Forward* and the *New York Call.* These were people Trotsky actually cared about.

Weinstein didn't bother to clean the office for these guests. The Yiddish-language *Forward* sent both a reporter and a photographer for the job. The photographer asked Trotsky to step outside onto Saint Marks Place for the picture, the street making a nicer background than the cluttered basement. Trotsky ignored the cold and took his coat off for the photo, appearing in suit, vest, and tie. *Forward* readers wanted to see this man's face, this Trotsky, this Russian Jew who defied the tsar. The large bulk of New York's immigrant Jews, who now packed the Lower East Side, making it the most densely populated place on earth, had come fleeing violence and organized anti-Semitism from a Russian Empire that still included Poland and Ukraine.

Hatred of Romanovs, Cossacks, and tsarist bureaucrats ran thick here. The *Forward* would put Trotsky's photo on its front page.

The *Forward* in 1917 held a unique place in both this neighborhood and America as a whole, largest by far of New York's half dozen Yiddish newspapers and also the largest daily socialist publication in the country. The *Forward*'s founder, Abraham Cahan, a Russian himself, had come to New York in 1882 and become fluent in English. He considered himself second to none in launching American socialism. His paper had backed Eugene V. Debs, the Socialist Party presidential candidate, in every race he ran since 1900.

But Cahan also had good business sense and had built the *Forward* into a powerhouse, combining socialism with worldly advice to Jewish immigrants. With its two hundred thousand–plus circulation, rivaling any English-language daily in the city besides Hearst's *American* or Pulitzer's *World,* the *Forward* had grown rich and recently moved into its own new skyscraper, a ten-story building that towered over the Lower East Side from its perch on East Broadway, facing Seward Park.

Normally, newspapers this big affiliated with one of the country's dominant political parties, the Democrats or Republicans. But Cahan knew better. His *Forward* readers had no love for either. In 1917 New York's Democratic Party was still controlled by Tammany Hall, the venerable organization rife with corruption and limited room for greenhorn Jews. True, Tammany had backed a few labor-reform laws after the ghastly 1911 fire at the Triangle shirtwaist factory had killed 146 employees, mostly young women, a tragedy traced to locked doors, rotted fire hoses, and other safety lapses.[80] But Tammany had come late to the cause, and Republicans, for their part, had little room for left-wing views that immigrants either brought from the Old Country or learned working in sweatshops.

For Trotsky, this should have been the friendliest possible interview. But as he sat down with the *Forward* reporter (the paper didn't print a byline, so we don't know his name), the conversation took an odd turn. Could Comrade Trotsky speak to us in Yiddish? It seemed only natural for a Jew speaking to a Jewish newspaper. Yiddish, after all, was the street language of Jewish shtetls across Europe and now the dominant tongue of the Jewish East Side with its Yiddish theaters, Yiddish cafés, Yiddish street signs, Yiddish books, and Yiddish newspapers.

But no. To their apparent surprise, Trotsky demurred. He knew a few words and phrases, he conceded, but little beyond that. For all his fluency in Russian, German, and French, Trotsky had never mastered his own people's language. In fact, Trotsky had grown up on a farm, not in a shtetl. His parents at home spoke Russian and Ukrainian, barely practiced religion, and gave him only bare minimum religious schooling. In Vienna, Trotsky had enjoyed frequenting two popular cafés where they spoke Yiddish as much as German, the Café Central and the Café Arkadian, where he enjoyed haggling over politics, drinking tea, and playing chess. But he never knew enough Yiddish to give a speech or write an article in it.

The *Forward* reporter took this down politely, putting it this way: "[Trotsky] had even applied himself once to the study of Yiddish in order to be able to understand Jewish revolutionary literature [and] even had a greater desire to master Hebrew, but unfortunately he had no time for that." As a result, his knowledge was "not deep. We don't tell you this as something to be proud of. We only pass over the facts."[81] Trotsky tried to make a joke of it. "I have never sweated like now when I am under the crossfire of masters of the [journalistic] trade," he told the reporter, "not even when the political police would give me the third degree."[82] After that, they changed the subject.[83]

Just as curious was his performance with the *New York Call*. The *Call* too had a special place in New York City, as the semiofficial arm of the Socialist Party, giving it a prominence beyond its fourteen-thousand-copy circulation. It was a staple for political opinion leaders. The *Call* apparently brought a translator so that Trotsky could chat away comfortably in Russian, and it took a photograph of him for its front page. Trotsky sat at his desk, they at his side, as they peppered him with questions. This time, though, the talk turned to politics, and Trotsky chose to jump right in with a slam at his new country.

"I do not like to criticize a nation that extends the hospitality that the United States has afforded me," he told them, "but"—a significant *but*— "it does not seem possible that President Wilson's efforts toward peace and intervention in the European war can bring results."[84] Why? Because America was capitalist and ruled by its moneyed class, which had no interest in stopping the gravy train of rich wartime weapons contracts. Woodrow Wilson's meddling in Europe looked two-faced, Trotsky went on, like "the smug, middle class merchant who exploits the poor on weekdays and then goes to church on Sundays, piously asking absolution for his sins."

He went no easier on the Europeans. Why do France and Germany keep fighting? "They fear the day of reckoning," Trotsky told them. With peace, "they must give accounting to their subjects for the wastage of human life and money." And the result? After the war, "social unrest will eclipse anything the earth has ever seen. The workers will demand a heavy accounting of their masters, and the future alone can tell what forms their protests will take."[85]

Only the United States, still a noncombatant, fell outside Trotsky's grim prophesy, at least so long as it stayed out of the war. The reporter from the *Call* seemed not at all surprised by the diatribe. He knew the socialist line. He read *Novy Mir*.

Late in the day, they finished setting up the next morning's *Novy Mir,* sent it to the printer, and then set out for Brooklyn and the dinner meeting that night at Ludwig Lore's apartment. Trotsky's new colleagues Bukharin and Chudnovsky joined him for the ride, and two other *Novy Mir* contributors would meet them there. One was a fellow Russian named V. Volodarsky coming in from Philadelphia. The other, coming from New Jersey, was Alexandra Kollontai. They all knew Kollontai from Europe, their elegant comrade from Saint Petersburg. They spoke to her often. These days she was the only one, it seemed, who still got along well with Vladimir Ilyich Lenin.

ALEXANDRA MIKHAILOVNA KOLLONTAI came from aristocratic stock. Born in Saint Petersburg in 1872, she was the daughter of a Russian general, with Cossack military officers decorating the family tree. But her father taught her liberal ideas. He favored a constitutional monarchy over an absolute tsar and sent her to Western Europe for schooling. At home, the family spoke French and English, and Finnish to the servants. Alexandra married a young military student and had a son with him, Mikhail (Misha), born in 1894, but the marriage collapsed and she left her husband to travel and raise the son on her own.

A generation later, in the 1930s, after Kollontai became world famous as Bolshevik Russia's foremost women's advocate, its people's commissar for social welfare, and its ambassador to Norway, she often would be fingered as the inspiration for Greta Garbo's character in the 1939 film *Ninotchka*. But the real Comrade Kollontai was far more formidable than any fictional movie character.

She first joined the socialist underground on a European trip, agreeing to smuggle letters from radicals in Switzerland to allies back home. Back in Saint Petersburg, she joined the local Bolsheviks. But her real initiation, the shock that glued her to a lifetime cause, came on January 5, 1905, the day she witnessed Bloody Sunday. Kollontai had decided that day to join the crowd, behind militant Russian Orthodox priest Father Georgy Gapon, that marched on the Winter Palace to ask Tsar Nicholas II for a constitution. Kollontai later described the scene, how she stood watching the tens of thousands of neatly dressed peasants carrying crosses, religious icons, and portraits of the tsar himself, whom they still worshipped as God's appointed leader. She recalled the white snow, the brilliant sun, the hours of waiting, then her surprise as gunshots rang out, soldiers on horseback charged with drawn swords, and bodies began to fall. She ran for safety with the others. Before it was over, the soldiers had killed an estimated five hundred unarmed, peaceful marchers, including women and children, the spark that set off a year of strikes, protests, and demands for reform.[86]

Seeing the massacre, Kollontai had immersed herself in the subsequent turmoil. She volunteered to raise money for strikers and served the local Bolshevik organization as its treasurer. In October workers declared a general strike in Saint Petersburg. More than two hundred factories joined the protest, led by the workers themselves through a unique new body called the Saint Petersburg Workers Soviet. Bolshevik and Menshevik leaders ridiculed the idea, but not Kollontai. She joined friends from a local factory to attend one of the soviet's first meetings. Here she met the soviet's articulate young leader, the man called Trotsky.

Trotsky had spent much of 1905 hiding in nearby Finland. After returning to Russia in January with a false passport, he had retreated after Natalya had been arrested and police began looking for him too. But hearing about the general strike, he rushed to Saint Petersburg, started speaking out at meetings of the soviet, and soon won himself a leadership post as deputy to the chairman. Kollontai met Trotsky, heard him speak, and saw how he mesmerized the crowd. She appreciated how he, unlike other party functionaries, "instinctively grasped [the soviet's] significance, outlining with graphic clarity the tasks of this new organization of workers unity."[87]

Trotsky would lead the soviet in different capacities for fifty-two days, making himself one of the most visible radicals in the country. In late October, Tsar Nicholas II issued a manifesto promising constitutional rights, but Trotsky denounced it as a fraud. Police arrested the soviet's chairman in November, so it tapped Trotsky to take his place. To win public support, Trotsky pressed for an eight-hour workday and called on citizens not to pay taxes until the government kept its political promises. As government crackdowns grew increasingly violent, Trotsky moved that they end the general strike.

Finally, on December 3, police came and arrested all the remaining soviet leaders in one clean sweep. But the drama didn't end there, and Kollontai had a ringside seat for the finale. The tsarist government decided to place fifty-two leaders of the Soviet on public trial as a single group, an attempt to discredit them all. The weeks-long proceeding became a public spectacle. Threatened with eight years of hard labor and a lifetime exile in Siberia, the defendants chose Trotsky to speak for them in open court on the most serious charge against them, that of insurrection, or threatening violence against the Russian state.

Trotsky's chance to address the court came on October 4, 1906, and he gave a memorable speech widely reported at the time. Rather than deny the charge, he embraced it to denounce the regime. He quoted recent disclosures that tsarist officials had planned anti-Jewish pogroms to distract attention from the workers movement. He then asked the court what it meant to oppose the existing "form of government":

> And if you tell me that pogroms, the arson, the violence . . .
> if you tell me that Kishinev, Odessa, Bialystock [places where
> recent violence had killed several hundred Russian Jews] repre-
> sent the "form of government" of the Russian Empire, then—
> yes, then I recognize, together with the prosecution, that in
> October and November we were arming ourselves against the
> form of government of the Russian Empire.[88]

It was perhaps the most admirable moment of his life to that point. The court cleared the defendants of insurrection but sentenced Trotsky and a dozen others to lifetime exile in Siberia, leading to Trotsky's second escape.

Alexandra Kollontai, having seen this drama play out in her city, became a Menshevik for the next decade, until the world war. She kept contact with Trotsky, writing occasionally for his Paris newspaper *Nashe Slovo*. She was living in Berlin in 1914 when war broke out. As a Russian, she had to flee. She landed in Sweden but soon found herself in trouble again, this time arrested for antiwar agitation and expelled from the country. Finally she settled in Norway, where she helped build a network to smuggle messages between radicals into and out of Russia. It was in this process that she became a friend and pen pal to the Bolshevik leader, Vladimir Ilyich Lenin.

As pen pals, Kollontai and Lenin argued at first over pacifism and disarmament. She supported both; Lenin thought the ideas nonsense. She wrote a propaganda pamphlet called "Who Needs War" that ultimately would be translated into multiple languages and would reach millions of German and Russian soldiers on the front, urging them not to fight. But even more important, Kollontai decided to back Lenin on his proposal for the watershed 1915 Zimmerwald conference, helped him refine it, and persuaded Norway's delegation to support him, earning her wings as a Bolshevik. "For it is completely clear now that no one is fighting the war as effectively as Lenin," she wrote.[89] When the chance came to help Lenin in America, she jumped at it.

It was Ludwig Lore, editor of the *New Yorker Volkszeitung,* who invited Kollontai to visit the United States for a four-month speaking tour in 1915. Their common friend Karl Liebnecht, a German socialist, had recommended her to Lore as a speaker, and Kollontai was thrilled. "This is so incredibly good that I am gasping with joy and am afraid to believe it," she told one friend on receiving the invitation.[90]

Lore, for his part, had no regrets. Traveling third class to save money, he and Kollontai crisscrossed the country that year, from New York to

San Francisco, Denver to Milwaukee, giving ten speeches to packed halls in Chicago alone. He saw her dazzle crowds whether she spoke English, German, French, Russian, Finnish, or Norwegian. "A very lively and emotional personality," one critic wrote after watching her address more than a thousand rowdy leftists in New York "with fiery improvisation . . . wit and animation."[91]

Along the way, she and Ludwig Lore became friends, sharing hours together on trains, waiting for meetings, grabbing quick dinners at cheap hotels. Her "attractive and polished exterior at once betrayed her aristocratic origin," Lore wrote admiringly about Kollontai. She was "a simply friendly creature, too intensely interested in the 'revolution' to care what she ate or wore."[92] By the time they finished, Kollontai had addressed some 123 meetings in eighty cities.

Vladimir Lenin had quickly grasped the opportunity presented by Kollontai's American trip and urged her to go. It was a chance for her to raise money, spread propaganda, and basically be his eyes and ears in the New World. As soon as she told Lenin about the invitation in early 1915, Lenin jumped on the bandwagon. "We have built not a few hopes on that trip," Lenin wrote to her from Switzerland, including first and foremost "securing financial help which is extremely important to us for all those urgent matters."[93]

Kollontai agreed. "On my trip to the States I want to spread your ideas as widely as possible," she wrote back. "I've no time for myself now."[94]

Americans had money, everyone knew that, and Lenin hoped to tap some of it. But he had no idea what Americans thought, where they stood on big issues, or if they even knew about his Bolshevik ideas. He peppered Kollontai with questions. "And what is Eugene Debs? Occasionally he writes in a revolutionary manner. Or is he another milksop, a la Kautsky?" Lenin asked, referring to Karl Kautsky, a German socialist who in 1914 had refused to oppose German war funding.[95] But usually Lenin just stuck to the main point: "Concerning money, I saw with regret from your letter that so far you have not succeeded in collecting anything for the Central Committee"—that is, for Lenin's committee.[96] Beyond all the fund-raising, Kollontai in fact had met in Chicago with left-wing publisher Charles Kerr to ask if he would publish Lenin's latest pamphlet, "Socialism and War," but Kerr had declined.

Back in Norway after the trip, Kollontai learned that her son, Mikhail, now twenty-two years old, had moved to Paterson, New Jersey, to take a job at a car factory. Having not seen him in more than a year, she decided to board a ship back across the ocean in August 1916, this time to be with him. Once in New Jersey, she started visiting New York and involved herself again in causes, such as the growing movement among immigrant housewives protesting sky-high food costs, and she began writing occasional articles for *Novy Mir*.

Now, in January 1917, Alexandra Kollontai sat on a train, making the long commute from Paterson, New Jersey, to New York City on a cold winter afternoon. On reaching the city, she would first have to fight the crowds at Penn Station, squeeze herself into a grimy, packed subway car, and ride it all the way out to Brooklyn, all for a simple dinner party. Normally, she would have ignored the invitation. But the invitation had come from her favorite American, Ludwig Lore, who had asked that she join a meeting at his home over dinner to discuss the future of American socialism.

Kollontai loved spending time with Lore and his wife, Lily. Lily's German cooking alone made the trip worthwhile, and Lily had even translated a novel Kollontai had written. And Kollontai understood why Lore considered her essential to this meeting. During her 1915 speaking tour, Kollontai had gotten to know America far better that any of the other Russians, most of whom never set foot outside New York or, at best, Philadelphia. In Chicago Kollontai had shared a stage with Eugene Debs, the party's leading personality and three-time (to that point) presidential candidate. She adored Debs. "I almost hugged him I felt so happy," she wrote after the event. She met "Big Bill" Haywood, leader of the Industrial Workers of the World (IWW, or Wobblies), whom Socialist Party leaders had recently expelled for espousing sabotage as a tactic in labor strikes. In Los Angeles she had joined a group mourning

Joe Hill, a popular IWW organizer recently executed for a Salt Lake City murder, widely considered framed.

Kollontai enjoyed meetings Americans. "They come up and say, 'a splendid speech,'" she gushed. "It's just what we want; more revolutionary spirit in the movement."[97]

Like many young activists, she grew to despise the American Socialist Party's establishment leaders, conservative older men, as she saw it, preoccupied with elections and piecemeal reforms—crumbs from the capitalist table—instead of revolution. "I am suffocated with such things," she complained.[98]

She, like the others, had heard that Trotsky had come to town and wanted to see him, but she was suspicious as well. Kollontai knew perfectly well how much Vladimir Lenin distrusted Trotsky. Anyone who read the acid back-and-forth polemics saw the bad blood that existed. As a result, she would have a larger assignment this night at Ludwig Lore's dinner table: to keep an eye on Trotsky and to keep Lenin informed. If nothing else, she needed to take good notes.

4

BROOKLYN

"When about 14 years of age I entered the gymnasium of Chernigov.
. . . Here in America schoolboys spend most of their time in sports,
baseball and football. In Russia, the boys—and girls, too, for that
matter—use their leisure for reading books. . . . Our pastime was
chiefly attending underground socialist meetings and spreading
propaganda among workingmen in the city and peasants in the
country. I was no exception to the rule."[99]

—Leon Trotsky, writing in March 1917

TROTSKY TOOK THE subway again that night. He, Bukharin, and
Chudnovsky each paid their nickel and then followed the signs to
the line called BRT (Brooklyn Rapid Transit, later renamed BMT).
After a few rattling stops, the train glided out from Manhattan onto the
Brooklyn Bridge. High over the East River, Trotsky could look out the
window and see January darkness broken on either side by a dramatic
sight. Lights from thousands of building windows, offices, apartments,
and skyscrapers, all powered by electricity, shot high in the air, creating
stark panoramas under the black sky.

Brooklyn lay at the far end, a separate city until 1898, just twenty
years earlier, when it had joined Manhattan, Queens, and Staten Island
to form Greater New York. (The Bronx had become part of the city in
1874.) Now three giant bridges connected Brooklyn to lower Manhattan,
each an engineering marvel in itself, hung by cables strung from massive
towers. The bridges suddenly made Brooklyn an easy walk or train ride

away, causing its population to triple in just three decades. With its two million people, Brooklyn alone would qualify as America's third largest city in 1917, just behind New York and Chicago.

Once there, the train stopped again and again, lurching Trotsky and the others back and forth as its steel wheels screeched in the darkness, at Fulton Street, Saint Marks Avenue, Prospect Park, and Green-Wood Cemetery. Had they stayed on, the BRT would have taken them all the way to Coney Island, already famous for its boardwalk, Luna Park, roller coasters, and summer hot dogs. Instead Trotsky got off at Fifty-Fourth Street, a part of Brooklyn called Borough Park, a quiet place—at least quieter than Lower Manhattan—with shops, schools, synagogues, and apartment houses, populated largely by German and Russian immigrants, mostly Jewish, who had managed to scrape together money enough to leave the squalid Lower East Side.

On Fifty-Fifth Street, they found Ludwig Lore's building, came in from the cold, and walked up to the second floor. From there, they just followed their noses.

Lillian (Lily) Lore loved to bake, and the apartment must have smelled delicious that night as her husband greeted guests at the door. He led them to the dining room, navigating the toys and clutter from their two young sons, Karl and Kurt.

Ludwig Lore and Trotsky seemed to hit it off right away, two European men with Old World manners. "I was captivated at once, with the charm of [Trotsky's] personality and the brilliance of his intellect," Lore recalled.[100] For Lore, politics came second. Food and company came first. "He was a jolly man whose political and aesthetic inclinations fit no prescribed categories," historian Paul Buhle wrote years later.[101] Born in Germany, Lore had studied at Berlin University and had established his journalism credentials there before leaving for America in 1905. In the United States, Lore settled first in Colorado, but he couldn't resist the lure of New York City and the *New Yorker Volkszeitung,* one of the country's top left-wing dailies, with a formidable audience of twenty-three thousand readers. Now, in 1917, Lore, "stocky, quick-witted, with black curling mustache and an overgrown mass of unruly dark hair,"[102] as Theodore Draper described him, ran the newspaper as associate editor and soon-to-be editor in chief.

He and Lily, whom he had married in 1909, made their home-cooked dinners legendary. Twenty years later, in 1938, a young communist recruit named Whittaker Chambers—who would make headlines in the late 1940s by denouncing government lawyer Alger Hiss as a communist agent—would visit Lore's apartment and describe Lily as "remarkable," producing massive German meals to feed an "endless procession of guests."[103] Another guest during the 1930s, an FBI informant, described Lily's lunches as "delightfully memorable."[104] Beyond hosting Alexandra Kollontai on her 1915 American speaking tour, Ludwig and Lily Lore had helped Nikolai Bukharin and his wife get settled in America two months earlier, insisting the Bukharins sleep in their apartment until they found a place to live.

Lore was the obvious choice to host the dinner. He had arranged it weeks earlier and invited a wide mix of New York leftists, about twenty altogether—Russians, Americans, Dutch, Italians, and Japanese, a mini League of Nations speaking six different languages. What drew them together, though, was their view of the world war. As one, Sen Katayama, would explain, these people all "stood against defense of the fatherland" as "anti-patriotic Socialists," making them the most avidly antiwar faction in the country.

Ludwig Lore knew something else about these American radicals: that they were "astonishingly out of touch" and "intensely ignorant" of global affairs.[105] To accomplish anything, they needed to learn from experts. And now an unexpected surprise: A celebrity had agreed to join them, none less than Leon Trotsky, fresh off the boat from Europe.

We don't know the identities of all the people Lore invited to his home that night. Besides the Russians, only a handful of names appear in any accounts. Most of the Americans probably asked to stay anonymous, given the anticommunist, anti-German witch hunts that would break out over the following few years. But the names we do know paint a clear picture.

The Russians—Trotsky, Bukharin, Chudnovsky, Volodarsky, and Kollontai—made up the biggest faction. These five all stood on the verge of destiny. Each would return to Russia later in 1917 and play a lead role in the revolution and Bolshevik regime. It was these seasoned activists that Lore hoped could teach his American friends how to properly structure a movement.

Of the non-Russians, Louis Boudin easily ranked as the most prominent, a well-known lawyer, writer, and speaker. Short and plump, Boudin had come from Russia as a child twenty years earlier but since then had shed his accent, graduated from New York University Law School, and made a pile of money as an attorney representing labor unions and workers. Boudin had run for various judgeships in New York City five times between 1910 and 1916, always on the Socialist ticket, and he planned to run again in 1917. He never won, but he spoke and wrote extensively; he had two recent books on Marxism and the world war. Boudin claimed to see no conflict between Marx and what one biographer called his belief in "the genius of the United States Constitution."[106] For this group, that made him a conservative.

Then came another wealthy foreigner, Sebald J. Rutgers of the Netherlands. Trained in Delft as a construction engineer and one-time city engineer in Rotterdam and Medan, Rutgers had come to America on business and decided to stay. But he had a passion for socialism, and that's where he invested his fortune. Back home, he wrote for the *International Socialist Review*. In the United States, he financed the recently formed Boston-based Socialist Propaganda League and its new publication, the *Internationalist*. Vladimir Lenin had read the magazine in Switzerland and sent Rutgers a note complimenting him for it.[107]

Rutgers brought two friends with him that night. One was John D. Williams, one of his staff at the Propaganda League in Boston, who edited the *Internationalist*. The other was sixty-year-old Sen Katayama, founder of Japan's socialist movement in Tokyo. Katayama had made a splash in radical circles for breaking ranks with his own country and shaking hands with Russian socialist leaders at a 1903 conference just before the Russo-Japanese War. Country came second! The International Working Class came first!

Finally there was Louis C. Fraina, the youngest face at the table. Fraina too stood on the verge of destiny. In 1919, two years in the future, Fraina would chair the founding convention of the American Communist Party in Chicago with such aplomb that another early leader, Benjamin Gitlow, would complain of his acting like "the Lenin of America."[108] A few years after that, Fraina would quit the party, falsely accused of being an FBI spy. By the 1930s, he would renounce communism, change his name to Corey, and become a noted economist, writer, and professor, before federal Red hunters would catch up to him in the early 1950s.

He would also become one of Leon Trotsky's closest friends in New York City.

For now, though, Fraina was just a twenty-five-year-old upstart with no political affiliation. He had earned his living editing a magazine called *Modern Dance* that covered ballet, poetry, theater, and the arts. Small, with bushy eyebrows, a high forehead, and a clipped mustache, he had come to New York as a five-year-old from Italy and had grown up in stark poverty, polishing boots on street corners and rolling cigars to help feed the family. His parents sent him to Catholic school, but he quit after a nun slapped his brother. At public grade school, he graduated as valedictorian. When his father died, he dropped out and found a job with the Edison Company. Already by then, he had read Karl Marx and hated capitalism for crushing the poor.

All this led to journalism and socialism. Precocious and curious, Fraina would sneak into theaters when he couldn't afford tickets, and he read voraciously. At eighteen, he won election to the New York Socialist Labor Party's General Committee. In 1912 the *Daily People* sent him to Lawrence, Massachusetts, to cover the textile strike there led by IWW leader Bill Haywood, one of the most successful mass labor actions in America before or since. By 1915 Fraina had won paid staff positions at both *Modern Dance* and the *New Review,* where his name appeared with top writers such as John Reed, Walter Lippmann, and W. E. B. DuBois.

By late 1916 the *New Review* had closed and *Modern Dance* would close in a few months, leaving Fraina unemployed. It was around this time that he met Rutgers, and already Rutgers had suggested that Fraina join his Boston project as editor of the *Internationalist.*

These were the faces around the table that night in Ludwig Lore's apartment, at least the ones we know. Two of them, Lore and Katayama, would write accounts of what happened next, but these were painfully brief. We don't know who exactly said what. But on the main points, the accounts all agree.

Lily's dinner apparently set the tone. It's easy to picture this odd gaggle of guests mingling and laughing over their food, calling each other comrade while stumbling over each other's languages. Some drank tea, some drank vodka, some probably drank too much. Cigarette smoke filled the air and loosened tongues. Among the Russians, Kollontai chatted with Trotsky while nibbling down Lily Lore's pastries, Trotsky probably regaling the table with funny stories about bumbling Spanish police and bad food on the *Montserrat.* Among the Americans, Rutgers chatted with Louis Fraina, and Louis Boudin doubtless pontificated over the corruption of local city politicians.

We don't know who first broached the serious topic, but Lore as host probably did the honors. Why had he called them together? Lore had heard his friends' complaints that, with America possibly on the verge of entering the world war, their Socialist Party—which should be the strongest voice of dissent—seemed lethargic and hopelessly unfocused. How deep was the problem? How urgent the crisis? What, realistically, could they do?

They started talking, and complaints came pouring out. And one name apparently came up again and again, a symbol of all the things the people in this room saw wrong with the established American Socialist Party: the party's leader in New York City, Morris Hillquit. Katayama, in fact, wrote his own account of the dinner as part of a diatribe called "Morris Hillquit and the Left Wing," a wide-ranging slam against the party leader.[109]

To this jury, Hillquit's crimes were many. As a lawyer, Hillquit represented labor and radicals, but he charged too much money, making him a "parasite" of the working class. (Lawyer Louis Boudin, of course, often heard the same complaint.) Hillquit and his crowd cared more about winning elections, placating the capitalist press, than fighting the class struggle. Worst of all, in 1912 it was Hillquit's crowd that had engineered the expulsion of Bill Haywood from the party's executive committee for publicly endorsing sabotage as a labor tactic. Louis Boudin had blasted Hillquit at the time for his "bourgeois notion of legality" (Marx had never opposed violence or lawbreaking on any ethical principle, so what gave Morris Hillquit the right?) and for his readiness to compromise just because "it was popular or seemed to be popular with the masses of people."[110]

Alexandra Kollontai particularly despised Hillquit. She described him in her diary as a "vile revisionist," too cozy with the trusts and "terribly afraid [he'll] be excluded from the International."[111] Kollontai probably mentioned the run-in she had had with Hillquit during her 1915 speaking tour at a meeting in Milwaukee, where she and Ludwig Lore had proposed a resolution endorsing Lenin's Zimmerwald platform. Hillquit had jumped in to squash it. After "heated debates," as she described it in a letter to Lenin, "Hillquit and Romm [another moderate] defeated our proposal."[112]

Before long, they all agreed on the problem, and the issue came down to a choice: Should they quit the Socialist Party and form their own new group? Or should they stay and try to change it from within? That, of course, meant getting rid of Hillquit and his crowd.

Leon Trotsky, if he were any other person, hearing all this on his first day in America, probably would have said little. He knew none of the non-Russians in the room, knew none of the people they were talking about, knew nothing about their local Socialist Party or their country other than what he'd read. Still exhausted from his trip, Trotsky barely spoke English, barely knew where Brooklyn was, and barely knew even how to ride the subway. He had no concept of the brewing passions in America over joining the European fight and no idea how politics worked in New York City. But he and Bukharin both heard one thing that struck a chord, an echo of the same argument they'd fought repeatedly in Europe: the question of unity or split, straight from the classic Bolshevik–Menshevik breakup of 1903.

They both spoke up, and within a few minutes, their two shrill voices dominated the room. And when they talked, especially once they got their juices flowing, every head leaned closer. We don't know what words they used or even what language they spoke, Russian, German, or something else. But by all accounts, Trotsky and Bukharin soon had the group riveted.

Bukharin the Bolshevik went first. He had given this question some thought. He insisted they split. That's what Lenin would do. Lenin always insisted on splitting away from any faction that might slow him down or compromise the ultimate goal of revolution, be it Mensheviks, the Second International, or anyone else. To win power, a party needed discipline, committed cadres dedicated to decisive action. There was no room for doubters or hangers-on. Kollontai spoke up too, taking Bukharin's side.

But then came Trotsky, who likewise responded instinctively. He, the Menshevik, disagreed totally. Unity was best, he argued. Their small movement needed strength from numbers. Political parties like the Socialists had organization and assets. Lenin's tactics might work in a backward place like Russia, where seizing power inevitably required violence or coup d'état. But did it really make sense anyplace else? Bukharin, he lamented, was acting like a "typical Leninite."[113]

"The Russians were in their element," Ludwig Lore wrote in describing the scene, with Trotsky and Bukharin staging "long drawn-out but intensely interesting theoretical discussions."[114] As Draper put it: "Twenty four hours after Trotsky's arrival, he and Bukharin were able to carry on their European feud in terms of an American move-ment almost wholly foreign to both of them."[115] They were fighting out their Menshevik–Bolshevik split right there in the middle of Ludwig Lore's Brooklyn apartment. But unlike in Europe, the argument here never grew unfriendly, part of its mesmerizing appeal. Bukharin, as a biographer noted, believed that "political differences need not influence personal relations," and apparently he showed it that night.[116]

They took a vote, and someone suggested a sweetener: that they stay in the American Socialist Party but also launch a separate new magazine. The motion carried. The decision was made. They formed a subcommittee.

Hearing about this entire episode a few weeks later, Bertram Wolfe, another young leftist recruit, was apoplectic. How could these Russians, "knowing next to nothing about America and even less about the American Socialist Party," come together "with complete insouciance" and tell American socialists how to run their business?[117]

But so it went. Something profound had transpired in that room. The Americans—Fraina, Boudin, and the rest—found themselves transfixed by the Russians and their esoteric argument, their animation and excite-ment, the integrity that oozed from their jail terms and Siberian exiles, their brilliant minds challenging each other with passion and focus. Some, like Katayama, refused to be stampeded. The Trotsky–Bukharin colloquy left him "bewildered and dazzled . . . rather than convinced," a biographer explained.[118] But even Katayama recognized leadership. He summarized the group's feeling this way: "We intended to organize the Left Wing under the direction of Comrade Trotzky, and Madam Kollontai, who was going to Europe, was to establish a link between the European and American Left Wing movements."[119]

As they said their good-nights and headed out into the winter cold, the first American Trotskyists had been christened, and the American far left had linked its destiny to the Russians. And Trotsky, after one day in the country, had picked his first fight in New York City, with the leaders of the American Socialist Party. Soon he would have to meet this Morris Hillquit and find out what he was made of.

5

RIVERSIDE DRIVE I

"Hillquit was a type [of socialist] more common on the Continent or in England. . . . My last meeting with him revealed his pragmatism. He said as he walked me to the door, 'Comrade Recht, don't you think it's high time we ceased being a religion and became a political party?'"[120]

—Lawyer Charles Recht, undated

MORRIS HILLQUIT CERTAINLY read the *New York Call* and would have seen Leon Trotsky's interview on the front page. In fact, Hillquit's own name had been plastered all over the *Call* that January for his own high-profile life in New York City. He probably glanced at Trotsky's snapshot, saw the headline "Driven Out of Europe, He Takes Up Work as Radical Writer Here," but didn't think twice about it.

Hillquit soon would become Trotsky's leading political nemesis in America, and the high-profile, often bitter personal clash between them would define the country's left wing for a generation. But for now, the two remained total strangers.

Just that weekend, Hillquit's own snapshot had dominated the *Call*'s front page. Dressed in a crisp white shirt and a suit and tie, he had a handsome face, clean-shaven, with sharp eyes, a small mustache, and smooth dark hair. Morris Hillquit saw nothing wrong with good grooming. He agreed with a friend's remark that "a necktie can be tastefully tied and lying as it should, without breaking the principles of proletariat socialism, God forbid!"[121] The photo had appeared under the headline HILLQUIT COUNT ENDED; FRAUDS CLEARLY SHOWN: SOCIALIST CHEATED OUT OF SEAT IN CONGRESS.[122]

Morris Hillquit had run for the United States Congress in November from a district covering New York's Upper East Side and Harlem, populated mostly by immigrants like himself, Jewish, Italian, and Irish. By an honest count, he probably should have won. But honest counts didn't come cheaply back then.

On election night, Hillquit's poll watchers had reported a good turnout, and early numbers gave him a narrow lead. But then something fishy happened. Around midnight, officials at two Hillquit-leaning precincts had stopped counting votes. Word reached Hillquit that local Republican and Democratic leaders had met there and cut a deal. He ran over to the voting place at the public school on 104th Street near Madison Avenue and demanded the counters get back to work. They refused. "They sat there impassively and cynically, chinning, smoking, spitting, doing everything but counting the vote," he recalled.[123] Hillquit complained to nearby policemen, but they just shrugged.

It took until 4 AM for the precinct to report and until 4 PM the next day for the other slow precinct to finish. By then, the damage was done. The ballots had been fixed. In the three-way contest, the count showed Hillquit beating the Democrat by about 200 votes but losing to the Republican, an incumbent named Isaac Siegel, by 459.

Hillquit complained to a judge and demanded a recount. It took two months for a bipartisan panel (excluding Socialists) to study the ballots, and its final announcement had come just that weekend. The panel found plenty of dirt: more than 150 blank ballots stuffed into boxes and counted for Siegel, sixty perfectly good Hillquit votes tossed out and marked "void," plus undercounts here and overcounts there. It came to 255 net documented additional votes for Hillquit, and no one doubted there were plenty more like them. But it wasn't enough to change the outcome.

Unlike fresh-off-the-boat Russians like Leon Trotsky or Bukharin over at *Novy Mir,* Morris Hillquit knew exactly how politics worked in

New York City. Tammany Hall, the venerable club that had dominated New York's Democratic organization since the mid-1800s, still ran city hall, city jobs, and most everything else in its neighborhoods. Republican bosses ruled whatever Tammany hadn't nailed down. On election days, the two sides cheated prolifically, paying for votes—$2 apiece was the going street price—and using "repeaters" and "floaters," staples since the days of Boss Tweed. When not fighting each other, Tammany and the Republicans happily joined forces to crush anyone else.

Hillquit had learned this lesson the hard way. This was his third run for the US Congress and probably the second time he actually won, except for being, as they put it back then, "counted out." In 1906 he had won an outright plurality in a district on the Lower East Side, getting more votes on the Socialist line than either the Republican or Democratic tickets. But Tammany Hall had cut a last-minute deal with William Randolph Hearst, the newspaper mogul running for governor that year on his own, self-created Independence League line. With Hearst's blessing, Tammany had added its candidate's name to Hearst's Independent ticket and used the extra votes it got that way to defeat Hillquit. Two years later, in 1908, Hillquit again ran strong before election day. This time, it was Republicans who cut the deal, telling supporters to vote against their own candidate to beat the Socialist.[174]

These disappointments aside, Morris Hillquit counted himself lucky. By 1917 his Socialist Party had reached a remarkable status in America. Its candidates had won elections all across the country. Two Socialists had sat in the US Congress. Socialists held mayor's offices in fifty-six towns and cities, including Milwaukee and Schenectady. They held more than thirty seats in state legislatures, from Minnesota to California to Oklahoma and Wisconsin, plus dozens of city council and alderman seats. The party had more than 110,000 dues-paying members and about 150 affiliated newspapers and magazines. Its flagship national magazine, *Appeal to Reason,* reached almost seven hundred thousand readers each month, and its presidential candidate, Eugene Debs, had won almost a million votes in 1912, about 6 percent of the total, running head-to-head against Woodrow Wilson, Theodore Roosevelt, and William Howard Taft.

In New York City, Hillquit's friend Meyer London, a popular labor lawyer, had finally captured the US congressional seat from the Lower East Side for the Socialists in 1914. Building this organization had taken twenty years of painstaking work, and Morris Hillquit had sweated the details at every step.

That winter, to top it all, Hillquit, as Socialist Party leader, had waged a public campaign against the world war. In January he had traveled to Washington, DC, and met with none less than President Woodrow Wilson at the White House, leading a Socialist Party peace delegation. They asked Wilson to keep America out of the war and mediate the conflict along lines fair to all sides: no indemnities or reparations, no annexations of territory, independence for colonies that wanted it, and an international tribunal to arbitrate disputes. These items all would appear later in President Wilson's Fourteen Points.

Hillquit recalled sitting down with President Wilson that day and finding him "preoccupied and tired," though as they spoke, he became "interested and animated." The president made no commitments but promised support in the vague way politicians do.[125]

All this work—the travel, the politics, the high-profile legal cases— made Morris Hillquit in 1917 one of the best known Socialists in America, second only to Eugene V. Debs. Debs was the party's popular face, its presidential candidate, but Morris Hillquit was its leader, the workhorse.

Born in Latvia, Hillquit came to New York as a teenager in 1886 and quickly learned enough English to get a job teaching it to immigrants at a night school on the Lower East Side. By day he stitched garment cuffs in a sweatshop for a year, but he got his first real break when the Socialist Labor Party hired him as a $4-per-week office clerk. Here, Hillquit had the rare chance to learn politics and journalism. In 1890 he joined another sharp young writer, Abraham Cahan—future editor of the *Forward*—in starting the city's first Yiddish-language newspaper, the *Arbeiter Zeitung,* then he worked his way though NYU Law School.

As a young lawyer, Hillquit wore well-tailored suits, changed his family name from Hilkowitz to Hillquit, and changed his given name from Moishe to Morris. But he didn't hesitate to take on the most radical leftists as clients, often for free. In 1901, when police arrested Johann Most, a notorious anarchist and promoter of assassinations—what he called "propaganda of the deed"—for publishing a seditious article after the assassination of President McKinley, it was Morris Hillquit who defended him before a darkly hostile New York courtroom. Hillquit argued free speech, but the judge sentenced Most to a year at the Blackwell's Island prison for the offense.

In 1900 Hillquit quit the Socialist Labor Party and led a splinter group to join the Midwest-based movement led by Eugene V. Debs, the hero and charismatic leader of the 1894 Pullman strike in Chicago, an epic standoff pitting Debs's American Railway Union against the largest railroad companies in America. It had taken President Grover Cleveland sending federal troops to finally break the Pullman strike and Debs's union. The government prosecuted Debs for conspiracy over the strike and jailed him for six months for contempt. Debs used his time behind bars to think and study, and here he discovered socialism. It was this combination—Debs's Midwest group and Hillquit's from New York—that would form the new Socialist Party of America.

The new party transformed Marxism into a distinctly American brand. Its platform soon brimmed with ideas that later would become staples of modern life: a right to strike (anti-injunction laws), a graduated income tax, limits on child labor, school lunches, mine and factory inspections, public works jobs for the unemployed, a limited workweek, a minimum wage, public defenders, public ownership of key industries like streetcars and subways. The party still preached revolution, but increasingly more as a metaphor. To Hillquit, revolution meant fundamental change through hard work, winning elections, and passing laws. "Mass action," another favorite radical term, to him meant big industry-wide strikes conducted cleanly and legally, with no room for fighting, bombings, assassinations, or violence.

Just that winter, for instance, Hillquit had helped lead one of the largest labor strikes in New York's history, a walkout by forty-five thousand members of the Amalgamated Clothing Workers of America, a union he had helped form in the 1890s and now represented as its top lawyer. The strike had closed more than 150 coat manufacturers, who in turn had locked out another twenty-five thousand workers. The workers demanded better pay, sanitation, and union recognition, this at a time when garment workers typically logged sixty-hour weeks—longer if they worked "by the piece"—for a dollar or two a day. They had no insurance, no bank accounts, no access to credit, no government programs, and few charities to help them.

After months of street picketing, in December the dispute had gone to an arbitration panel, resulting in a settlement: better pay, better conditions, and union recognition, though not a fully closed shop. The workers returned to their jobs, and the union, after years of strife, had won its point.[126]

Winning elections, though, was tougher. It required public support, and for socialists, that meant overcoming the prejudice most Americans still felt against both them and immigrants generally. Just a few weeks earlier, the New York Times had labeled voters in Hillquit's congressional race "uneducated, highly emotional foreigners, most of them, who have much to learn before they can be regarded as worthy American citizens."[127] Americans had feared anarchy and socialism—few bothered to recognize the difference—ever since the 1886 Haymarket bomb incident, which had killed seven Chicago policemen and sent four anarchists to the gallows. It didn't help that Leon Czolgosz, the assassin who had killed President William McKinley in 1901, was a recent Polish immigrant and anarchist. The obvious hypocrisy—companies used violence against striking workers repeatedly—didn't seem to make a difference.

Socialists could never hope to win big elections until they had conquered this stereotype, and this demanded ridding their party of elements—anarchists, radicals, extremists—who threatened to destroy its credibility. That's why Hillquit had insisted on the expulsion of IWW leader Bill Haywood for publicly supporting sabotage as a labor tactic. Hillquit even fought Eugene Debs, the party's most beloved figure, over this issue, and he tried to block Debs's presidential nomination in 1912 and 1916 when he thought Debs's rhetoric had turned too radical.

Meanwhile, as a lawyer and politician, Hillquit became wealthy. By early 1917 he and his wife, Vera, owned a home on New York's Riverside Drive, an exclusive street just a tree-shaded park away from the Hudson River. He operated two law offices, one at 30 Church Street near city hall and another on the Lower East Side. "I can see nothing wrong in principle for a socialist to practice law in a capitalist system or to engage in other capitalist activities," he explained.[128]

But the one insult that still rankled him was if anyone questioned his loyalty to the country. When an interviewer from the *New York Times* suggested to his face that his supporters had "no patriotism and are glad of it," Hillquit barely contained himself: "Mr. Hillquit's eyes are very blue and his hair very black," the reporter wrote. "Generally the contrast is arresting, but as he turned to answer the challenge, he eyes blazed almost as black as his hair."

His terse response: "You're wrong there. Quite wrong."[129]

Hillquit knew his attitude didn't sit well with radicals, including many of the Russian crowd. He knew all about Vladimir Lenin in Europe and the platform he'd pressed at the 1915 Zimmerwald conference—that socialists should urge defeat of their own countries in the war. How preposterous. He had met Lenin at a socialist conference in Stuttgart, Germany, in 1907 but wasn't overly impressed. He had also met Alexandra Kollontai during her 1915 American speaking tour, and he made no apology about having stepped in to block a proposal she'd made in Milwaukee to endorse the Lenin Zimmerwald platform, linking good patriotic American socialists with Lenin's anti-patriotic line. Hillquit didn't mind criticism from radicals. He had a bigger purpose.

6

PATERSON

Alexandra Kollontai took the train back to Paterson, New Jersey, after the Monday night dinner at Ludwig Lore's Brooklyn apartment. During the ride and the next day, she stewed over what she'd heard. Besides the pleasant company, the chance to chat with Lily Lore and her Russian friends, the argument between Bukharin and Trotsky had dominated the night and it bothered her. Kollontai took her Bolshevism seriously. She didn't view ideological arguments as simple games, intellectual sparring for its own sake. She had agreed strongly with Bukharin, that American leftists should split from the conservative American socialists and form their own new party. She had seen the American leaders like Morris Hillquit; they were no revolutionaries.

And Trotsky had stood in the way. Trotsky had undercut Bukharin, contradicted him in front of the entire group. It was Trotsky's fault. Trotsky, it seemed, always felt as if he had to win the debating point, whether he understood the issue or not.

Kollontai had grown cynical with America during her two trips and looked forward to leaving soon for Norway. Looking at the New York skyline, she now described it not as towers of wonder but instead as "huge, twisting, relentlessly upward-thrusting lines." In the Statue of Liberty she saw disappointment, "an old and forgotten legend, a fairy tale of pre-capitalist times which can only be recounted from the reminiscences of our grandfathers." In her writing, she lamented strikers beaten by police, starving housewives, corrupt courts, and a "servile" press.[130]

Much of this was the usual stuff of socialist propaganda, but from Kollontai it rang tired and resigned.

She saved her worst criticism for New Jersey. "New York City is surrounded by the Styx," she wrote in one letter, conflating the American slang for rural areas with Dante's famous river, across which lay the inferno. "We're living in an area [Paterson] at the edge of town, divided by straight little streets lined with maple trees. Along these streets stretch identical rows of clapboard houses with porches, where women freed from their house work in the evening sit on rocking-chairs and chat. They look so bored."[131]

After a day or two back in Paterson, Kollontai finally put pen to paper and addressed a letter to Vladimir Ilyich Lenin in Switzerland. She quickly got to the main point, the meeting at Ludwig Lore's apartment and the blowup with Trotsky: "The Dutch Comrade Rutgers (a Tribunalist), Katayama, and our group have taken a step toward the 'Zimmerwald left,'" she wrote. "However, Trotsky's arrival strengthened the right wing [always the enemy in Lenin's eye] and by the time of my departure the platform had not yet been adopted."[132]

In her letter, she also told Lenin about Bukharin, how he had won acclaim at *Novy Mir* since settling in New York City, but that Trotsky's arrival threatened to eclipse him there.

She knew Lenin would be angry. Did Bukharin push her to write her letter? Probably not. Bukharin showed no sign of having been cross with Trotsky over their argument/debate at Lore's apartment. If anything, he and Trotsky both seemed to enjoy it. Either way, she felt duty-bound to keep Lenin informed. She sent the letter off to Switzerland, not knowing how long it would take to get there, maybe weeks. By then, she might be out on the ocean on a ship herself, headed home.

7

THE BRONX

"'The beautiful Bronx'—that's what we called it. It was an unusual and exciting place to live in those Days. Millions of people—hardworking, family folk—poured out of the congested tenements of the Lower East Side, East Harlem, and other crowded sections of Manhattan . . . to make a better life for themselves in the Bronx. Why did they come? Because it was 'like country.'"[133]

—Lloyd Ultan, *The Beautiful Bronx: 1920-1950*

"I don't need bodyguards. I grew up in the South Bronx."

—Al Pacino, actor

A GAIN, TROTSKY AND his family took the subway. From the Astor House, they left Times Square and navigated snow-crusted streets across Fifth Avenue to the East Side. Here they grabbed the Third Avenue Elevated. At the Forty-Second Street Street Station, Trotsky, already a budding subway veteran, would have led them up the narrow stairs, plunked down four nickels for the four of them—himself, Natalya, and the boys—and followed signs to the platform marked "Uptown."

Subway cars back then had a single long bench along each side, so sitting passengers faced each other, leaving the middle for people to stand packed together, holding leather straps hanging from the ceiling. As the train rumbled down its steel tracks, the boys could stare out at rooftops and windows that flew by. Watching the view, they'd have hardly noticed the crowd, pushing, shoving, some smoking cigarettes in the tight, stuffy space. Jammed subway cars already had become a dreaded part of New York rush hours.

It took twelve stops to reach 129th Street, the last station in Manhattan. Then the train lurched right onto a steel bridge. Here they could see water out the window, a narrow muddy channel lined with docks and warehouses and clogged with barges. This was the Harlem River, and on the far side lay the Bronx.

The boys probably giggled at the name. It came from a Dutch settler named Jonas Bronck who had bought land here back in the 1600s. Bronck named a local stream after himself, Bronck's River. Other settlers started calling his farm Bronck's land, then just the Bronx. Few people lived here until the subway lines, elevated and underground, came to connect it with Manhattan. Then came a flood of transplants from New York's packed downtown tenements. This caused the population to explode, rising from 200,000 to 732,000 between 1900 and 1920 and hitting 1.2 million by 1930.

As a result, much in the Bronx in 1917 was still new and fresh—the train tracks, the houses, the trolleys, the streets and stores, the parks. Farms and dirt roads still covered most areas east of the Bronx River. Once in the Bronx, the family sped past a commercial district called the Hub, with shops, office buildings, and department stores, then past rows of backyards behind homes and apartments, then a courthouse, then blocks and blocks of neighborhoods. They finally got off at 174th Street, descended to Southern Boulevard, and then walked two blocks to Vyse Avenue, a small side street with trees.

While Trotsky had kept himself busy at *Novy Mir* and over Ludwig Lore's dinner table, Natalya Sedova had spent her first day in America finding the family a place to live. How exactly she did it is unclear. A New York friend must have helped, sifting real estate listings and haggling with landlords. But she liked the result. On seeing the three-room apartment at 1522 Vyse Avenue, a relatively new, clean building with wide halls and stairways, Natalya snatched it up.[134] She paid a deposit of three months rent at $18 per month and arranged for furniture to come. A neighbor, the writer Sholem Asch, agreed to guarantee payment for the furniture on the installment plan.[135]

So out they moved from the Astor House with its sky-high prices to what Trotsky later described as a "workers district,"[136] though two or three days in the plush Astor House may have skewed his standards. Not all his new Bronx neighbors actually worked in factories or did hard manual labor. Shop owners, writers, clerks, and craftsmen—immigrants who had climbed the first few pegs toward middle-class life—filled many nearby apartments, petit bourgeois as much as proletariat.

Still, the boys loved it, and Trotsky marveled at the modern features. This was how Americans lived. "The apartment," he wrote, "was equipped with all sorts of conveniences that we Europeans were quite unused to: electric lights, gas cooking-range, bath, telephone, automatic service-elevator, and even a chute for the garbage."[137] Just as good was the location. The apartment stood just four blocks from the Third Avenue Elevated, a direct shot to his job in Lower Manhattan. Crotona Park, a beautiful landscape of green trees, snow-covered lawns, and a small lake, sat a short walk away. Cinemas and vaudeville theaters dotted nearby Tremont Avenue, with plenty of groceries and diners. A few blocks farther north was the new Bronx Zoo. Yankee Stadium, unfortunately, would not come to the Bronx for another five years.

The Trotskys also had neighbors. Moshe Olgin of the *Forward* lived nearby, as did Louis Fraina, the young socialist Trotsky had met at Ludwig Lore's dinner party. One neighbor, though, made a special impression. Trotsky kept the man's name secret. He never revealed it, referring to him only as "Dr. M.," a wealthy physician. Natalya in one interview called him "Dr. Mikhailovsky,"[138] though no such Mikhailovsky existed in the city directory for 1916 or 1917, under that or any similar spelling. Dr. M. had a car, a chauffeur, and money for the finest downtown restaurants. A Bronx historian later narrowed down the likely Dr. M. to one real-life physician who lived at 1488 Washington Avenue, just across Crotona Park from the Trotsky family's new apartment.[139] His name was Julius Hammer.

Dr. Hammer spoke the same languages as Trotsky and Natalya. A Russian émigré educated in Odessa and fluent in Russian and German, Hammer had come to America in the 1890s and worked his way through Columbia University College of Physicians and Surgeons. In addition to his medical practice, he owned eight drugstores by 1917 and a supply business called Allied Drug and Chemical. Hammer's son Armand was following in his footsteps, himself a Columbia medical student at the time.

But Hammer also counted himself a dedicated socialist, having learned his politics back in Russia. In America Hammer had joined the Socialist Labor Party and married a party comrade named Rose. He had traveled to Stuttgart, Germany, to meet Vladimir Lenin at the 1907 Congress. Hammer steeped himself in party affairs and often picked up legal bills and dinner tabs for the cause. Hammer even enrolled his son Armand as a Socialist when the boy turned sixteen. With thinning hair and a slight build, Hammer easily could have been one of the unnamed guests at Ludwig Lore's dinner party that week, especially with Louis Fraina living just a few neighborhoods over on Kingsbridge Road. Maybe the two came together. When word had gone out for local comrades to help make the Trotskys feel welcome, Julius and Rose Hammer had happily stepped forward.

In many ways, their new Bronx home could have been the nicest Trotsky had known in his life up to that point—the clean modern apartment, the friendly neighborhood, the school for Leon and Sergei, the friends and neighbors for Natalya. At work, Trotsky had a steady paycheck, a platform for his radical articles and speeches, plenty of fans and followers, and freedom from censors or harassment. As a Russian, he would not have known the concept of the American Dream, but he was quickly finding it in New York City.

8

COOPER UNION

On Russia:

"Our history his not been rich. Our so-called 'national originality' consisted of being poor, ignorant, uncouth . . . the kingdom of stagnation, servitude, vodka and humbleness."[140]

—Leon Trotsky, *Novy Mir*, January 20, 1917

On America:

"The economic life of Europe is being blasted to its very foundations [by the world war], whereas America is increasing in wealth. . . . Will [Europe] not sink to nothing but a cemetery? And will the economic and cultural centres of gravity not shift to America?"[141]

—Leon Trotsky at Cooper Union, January 25, 1917

A ND NOW, ON January 25, 1917, he finally enjoyed a big welcoming party. And what better place for it than the Great Hall of Cooper Union, a room that oozed with history. Since it opened in 1859, with its graceful arches, columns, and chandeliers, Cooper Union had hosted a litany of the American great and near great: Abraham Lincoln, Mark Twain, Susan B. Anthony, Elizabeth Cady Stanton, and now Leon Trotsky.

We don't know how many people actually came that cold Thursday night to see Trotsky give his first major public address in America. The Cooper Union hall held nine hundred seats, and the *Forward*, an event sponsor, reported a "large attendance to salute the Russian fighter for freedom."[142] The left-wing press spent days publicizing this "GREAT RECEPTION AND MEETING," though one witness remembered seeing plenty of empty seats.[143] Tickets sold for twenty cents at the door and fifty cents for reserved stage seats, the cost of a vaudeville show.

No big-name celebrities apparently came, no movie stars or Broadway actors. Not the governor, not the mayor, no senators or even a congressman. None of the big English-speaking newspapers sent a reporter. Not even the Justice Department, its Bureau of Investigations, US military intelligence, or the New York City Police bothered to send detectives. By the end of 1917, police forces on three continents would be scrambling to find any scrap of information about this same Leon Trotsky. By then he would have seized power in Russia and threatened the world. But now, in January, he remained a nobody. They had him right under their noses, and they all missed it.

The people who did come to hear Trotsky that night were his natural friends, immigrants and radicals, a crowd that needed speakers in four different languages—Yiddish, German, Russian, and English—just to understand a single speech. These people mostly hated the Russian tsar, dreamed of socialism, and expected to love anything this Trotsky had to say.

One exception, though, was an old Russian acquaintance who came more out of curiosity. Grisha Ziv had known Trotsky as a teenager. He and Trotsky had both belonged to the same small circle of young radical friends in the town of Nikolaev. They had been arrested together in 1898 after their group helped organize a workers union there. These days, Ziv, now a New York doctor, had grown conservative. He supported the world war, a very odd duck among this Cooper Union crowd. Having read Trotsky's interviews in the Forward and the Call, he fully expected to disagree with the speech. Still, he came late and found a seat.

Typical for these events, Trotsky had to wait on the podium as the other speakers went first. Algernon Lee, director of the Rand School for Social Research, speaking in English, welcomed Trotsky to America on behalf of American socialists and complimented him on his stead-fastness during these "times that try men's souls." Ludwig Lore wel-comed Trotsky in German as a fellow fighter and "dearest teacher." Max Goldfarb, a *Forward* editor, joined the welcome chorus, this time in Yiddish.[144]

Trotsky had been in the country just ten days by the time of his Cooper Union event, still absorbing all the newness. Wherever he looked, he still marveled at New York City, its wealth, its technology, its energy. But so much still seemed strange to him.

Take, for instance, this American concept of free speech. Yes, Trotsky could write his *Novy Mir* columns as he pleased. No censors or police came to bother him, a welcome change from wartime France, let alone Russia. But it had peculiar limits. Just that week, the New York Police had arrested and indicted a woman named Margaret Sanger for operat-ing, of all things, a birth control clinic. The charge: obscenity. Talking about women's hygiene through the US postal system constituted a fed-eral crime in America in 1917. Newspapers made the affair a high-profile cause célèbre. Sanger's sister, Ethel Byrne, had been convicted earlier of working at the clinic and was conducting a hunger strike from her prison cell at the Tombs.

An outsider like Trotsky had to find this puzzling. This was why they put people in prison in America? For providing medicine? You could talk about revolution but not sex or feminine hygiene?

Or take the other big local controversy that week. A group called the Anti-Saloon League drew five hundred ministers and clergymen to the Metropolitan Building to complain that the city's mayor, John Purroy Mitchel, had failed to enforce a New York law requiring saloons to close their doors on Sunday. The ministers also criticized the New York Central Railroad, not for cheating customers or exploiting its workers but instead for selling alcohol on its trains while passing through dry states, even if the trains didn't stop there.

This was free speech? A man could talk socialism or anarchy, but he couldn't spend his own nickel to buy a sip of schnapps on a train?[145]

Or take the workers going on strike for better pay against big companies like Standard Oil or the railroads. Police routinely beat and jailed them. The companies used private detectives like the Pinkertons to break their unions, and the federal government intervened using court-ordered legal injunctions. This too was free speech?

Now at Cooper Union, sitting in the Great Hall, Trotsky heard his name finally announced, heard the applause, and calmly stepped to the podium. He would show this crowd, his friends, what it meant to have free speech. Had police detectives decided to come and listen, they would have heard plenty of what the law would soon call "sedition."

Normally, a featured guest speaker would let the crowd cheer, whistle, and stamp its feet for a few minutes to enjoy the adulation. But Trotsky had no patience for this "American treatment," as Ziv put it.[146] Instead, he ignored them and launched right in, talking right over the applause. He started with President Wilson, "a tool of the capitalist class," then shifted to his main theme: revolution. "The Socialist revolution is coming in Europe," he announced, "and America must be ready when it comes. Socialists were caught napping when war started [in 1914], but they must not be nodding when revolution comes. In France, the soldiers who come out of the trenches say, 'We will get them.' The French think that the soldiers mean they will get the Germans, that they want to kill the workers in the other trench. But what they really mean is that they will 'get' the capitalists."[147]

Of course, revolution—the real kind made by men with guns—was a few steps beyond simple socialism, at least for Americans. But this didn't bother Trotsky. On he went.

The war had ravaged France, England, and Germany, he explained. Countries had bankrupted themselves, and people had lost their illusions. They had grown excited, ready to be daring, to demand change, to fight—all the ingredients for an uprising.

Grisha Ziv, Trotsky's old friend from Europe who fully expected to hate the speech, instead found himself enthralled. He "absolutely rejected" the content, he insisted later in his own account of the night.

But, he said, he appreciated with "aesthetic pleasure" the "artistry" of the talk. Trotsky spoke in Russian with a "crisp" and "definitive" tone, Ziv explained, using "no rough demagogic methods." Instead, he "bombarded the audience with a great number of facts." He "thrilled" them, "depressed" them, aroused them with his "burning resentment and high-minded pathos" through his descriptions of wartime Paris, the hardships, the frontline combat, the abuses, the heroics.[148]

The war had been foisted on Europe by "a gang of highway robbers called diplomats," Trotsky went on. Now, after an ocean of blood, society could never be the same. "Revolution is brewing in the trenches and no force can hold it back."[149]

The crowd loved it, giving him "loud applause," the *Forward* reported.[150] Even Ziv called it a "high success."

But not everyone agreed. Somehow an argument broke out in the Great Hall, right there with Trotsky at the podium. The setting was close enough for people to shout catcalls, heckle the speaker from their seats, hurl insults, argue, shake their fists. That, apparently, is what Trotsky started. "Instead of a declaration of welcome," as Ludwig Lore gently described it afterward, the affair somehow degenerated into a "fierce, though outwardly polite, battle of conflicting opinions."[151]

What did they argue over? Nobody quite said. But hearing him go on, it's not hard to guess. A few people probably wondered: Just what revolution was this Trotsky talking about? For Russia, it sounded fine. They all hated the tsar. Even for Europe. But here in New York City? Here in America? Did he really want revolution here too?

Trotsky had no doubt in his own mind what he meant by revolution. To him it was no metaphor. In 1905 in Saint Petersburg he had seen hundreds of thousands of factory workers rise up and seize government powers. That to him was revolution: taking power and keeping it.

Trotsky also had no doubt about the Russian side of this equation. He saw the latest headlines. Russia's military defeats continued nonstop. London and Paris now suspected the tsar of cavorting with German spies. In the Russian Duma, Deputy Paul Miliukov, head of the Kadet

(Constitutional Democrat) Party, had openly criticized the tsar, calling his failures "treason or incompetence." The tsar in turn had banned the Duma from holding any more meetings. Even the assassination of the Mad Monk Rasputin in December had failed to settle nerves.

The war had changed Russia profoundly, and even non-socialists predicted an explosion. A University of Petrograd economics professor named Ivan Chezal, reaching New York that week, had told reporters "The Russian people are demanding peace, and unless they get it there will be a revolution."[152]

As for New York, Trotsky concluded his speech with this: "Here, in America, I welcome you under the banner of the coming social revolution!"

Whatever shape the squabble took, Trotsky seemed to enjoy it thoroughly. Ludwig Lore, sitting on the podium with his new Russian friend, described Trotsky's reaction as "glee," fitting for someone "accustomed to party strife."[153] It is easy to picture Trotsky standing there, grinning at the hecklers, trading insults, giving as good as he got. Most of the crowd loved him. A few despised him. But no one in the Great Hall walked away unprovoked.

Within a year, the New York state legislature would pass a law making talk of revolution like Trotsky's a penal offense, criminal anarchy, subject to five years in prison and $5,000 in fines. Many in the Cooper Union Great Hall that night would see the insides of jail cells as a result. But for now, free speech still reigned in New York City.

NATALYA TOO FELL into a pleasant routine those first few days in the Bronx. With Trotsky off to work at the office, she enrolled Leon and Sergei in a Bronx public grade school to learn English and make friends. During the day, she began taking sight-seeing trips into Manhattan with Rose Hammer, the wife of their wealthy neighbor Dr. M. They took the Hammers' car. Traffic in Manhattan back then was a nerve-shattering mix of horses, pushcarts, wagons, trolleys, elevated trains, and motorcars. Natalya and Rose happily let the chauffeur navigate the way.

When not in school, the boys often came too, always sitting up front. They marveled at the sights and made a game of counting things, the streets, the cars, and the floors of the skyscrapers, amazed at how high they went. We don't know the chauffeur's name, but he became their favorite new friend. They considered him a magician. Trotsky's sons had never seen the inside of a car before, and it fascinated them to watch how the chauffeur could control the machine, make it obey his slightest touch of the steering wheel or tap of his toe on the gas.

Rose Hammer enjoyed stopping with Natalya for lunch at a favorite restaurant. The boys found it strange that when they went inside to eat, their friend the chauffer, the magician, had to wait outside with the car. Why couldn't he join them? It seemed unfair.[154] They complained to their parents but never got a good answer. Trotsky marked it down as just one more blind spot in this odd American "freedom."

Then something even stranger happened. Back at the Bronx apartment, one day the landlord came to Natalya and told her there was a problem with the rent. The money Natalya had paid, the three-month down payment, had disappeared. Natalya soon heard the story from other tenants. The building's housekeeper, an African American gentleman, had taken the money, plus some items she had given him for safe storage, without giving her a receipt. Other tenants had also given him their normal rent money. Then he ran off.

The panic ended quickly. Natalya soon found the property she had given the housekeeper. (She never explained what it was.) It had been in the apartment the whole time, hidden in a wooden box with cookware. And she found the rent money too, carefully wrapped up in paper. As for the other tenants, it turned out the housekeeper had disappeared with the rent money of only those to whom he had given a receipt, so they wouldn't be forced to pay it twice.

It didn't take long for Trotsky and Natalya to figure out the mystery. This housekeeper, in walking off with the cash, had been careful. He "did not mind robbing the landlord, but he was considerate enough not to rob the tenants," Trotsky wrote about the incident. "A delicate fellow, indeed. My wife and I were deeply touched by his consideration, and we always think of him gratefully."[155]

Trotsky had never met an African American person before, or any kind of African, except perhaps in Paris. Certainly not in Russia. He knew that racial prejudice existed in America, knew about the history of slavery, but only from books in an abstract, theoretical way. Now he saw something he didn't understand. "This little episode took on a symptomatic significance for me—it seemed as if a corner of the veil that concealed the 'black' problem in the United States had been lifted."[156] What was the "problem"? How did he define it?

Years later, Trotsky would devote considerable effort trying to understand this issue. In Russia he would meet with Claude McKay, the American black novelist, leader of the Harlem Renaissance, and founder of the African Blood Brotherhood, and would urge the recruitment of black propagandists in the United States. He would criticize his own American Trotskyist movement for failing to grasp the seriousness of the problem. "But today, the white workers in relation to the Negroes are the oppressors, scoundrels, who persecute the black and the yellow, hold them in contempt and lynch them," he told an American visitor in Turkey in 1933.[157] Years later, his analysis of black nationalism would reach a rising young leader named Malcolm X and shape his thinking in the 1960s.

But that was for the future. For now, Trotsky simply marked the incident to study later.

GRISHA ZIV HAD not waited around to speak with Trotsky after Trotsky's address at the Cooper Union Great Hall. Ziv seemed shy about approaching his old friend, describing Trotsky as "arrogant" for "refusing to mingle with audiences after a talk." Still, after a few days, Ziv had the chance to slip Trotsky a message through an acquaintance, a newspaper reporter they both knew. "When Trotsky visits you, tell him I say hi," he told the man.[158]

Sure enough, a few days later, the telephone rang at Ziv's home. "Grisha, is that you? Do you recognize me? It's me—Trotsky."

Ziv seemed surprised at the telephone call, that Trotsky actually had "long wanted to see me" and "did his best to find me," as he later explained. "In one word, he wanted to see me and asked to set up a good place and time."

Ziv agreed. He could hardly say no. "We shared too many old memories and old moments to simply ignore it." Ziv had known Trotsky far longer than any other person in America, certainly longer than any of Trotsky's new socialist hangers-on. Their relationship dated back to 1896, when they were both teenagers. They belonged to a commune, a group of young radicals that met at a garden near the industrial town of Nikolaev on the Black Sea. This was before Trotsky's first arrest, before his first exile to Siberia, before his first escape, before his discovery of Vladimir Lenin.

From this period, Ziv also knew the woman Alexandra Lvovna Sokolovskaya, with long hair and big eyes, who had charmed the young men in Nikolaev and become Trotsky's first and only legal wife. Ziv had been a witness at the wedding, the proper one that they held in a Moscow transit prison in 1890 with a rabbi. Ziv also knew about the two daughters they had together in Siberia, Nina and Zina, and how Trotsky had abandoned all three of them—his wife and his two infant daughters—when he escaped by himself to follow his destiny.

Fair or not, politics aside, perhaps that was why Grisha Ziv had an attitude toward Trotsky that often oozed with resentment. But now in New York City, Ziv apparently felt obliged to put aside this history and make a social visit. Maybe he and Trotsky could rebuild an old bridge.

9

RIVERSIDE DRIVE II

"Our descendants . . . will spread their hands in horror when they learn from history books about the methods by which capitalist peoples settled their disputes."[159]

—Leon Trotsky as a journalist covering the Balkan Wars, 1913

A FEW DAYS AFTER Trotsky's speech at Cooper Union, Morris Hillquit gave a dinner party at his home on Riverside Drive. Like Ludwig Lore, who had hosted Trotsky in Brooklyn his first day in America, Hillquit liked to entertain. But in a different style. Instead of vodka, tea, and cigarettes for a roomful of plotting radicals, Hillquit offered French wines, servants, and a small, intimate roomful of distinguished company.

He didn't send Trotsky an invitation, but the guest list did include the next best thing, Algernon Lee, director of the Rand School and one of Hillquit's closest friends in New York. Lee had shared the stage with Trotsky at Cooper Union, introduced Trotsky to the crowd, and praised him as a steadfast rebel. Lee certainly would have enjoyed describing the affair to his friends that night over Hillquit's dinner table, entertaining them with a few choice quotes from Trotsky's speech (or some of the heckles from the crowd). But Trotsky was still a newcomer to New York society. His chance to hobnob with the finer elements would come soon enough.

The faces around Hillquit's table that night, about a dozen people, included socialites, artists, and politicos. In addition to Algernon Lee and his wife, guests included Samuel and Clara Packard, he a prominent lawyer, she a well-known women's activist. Louis Gruenberg, the piano virtuoso and opera composer, came with his wife, as did Hermann Schluter. Schluter, a seventy-year-old German and one-time personal friend of Karl Marx and Friedrich Engels, still held the editor in chief post at the *New Yorker Volkszeitung,* Ludwig Lore's newspaper, though Lore now did the lion's share of the work. A Mr. Chadburne, agent of an American relief group recently returned from Belgium and France, also joined them.

Hillquit had invited a special guest, a European fresh from the war front. His name was Victor Basch from Paris, a Sorbonne professor and member of the French Socialist Party. Basch in Paris had been an outspoken Dreyfusard (supporter of French colonel Alfred Dreyfus, falsely accused of treason in 1894) and leader of France's League of Human Rights. Tonight Hillquit had asked him to defend France's view of the world war.

Morris and Vera Hillquit knew how to please friends: good food, gracious talk, the clinking of wineglasses, friendly toasts, and a warm fire. Never mind that these people easily could chat in a dozen different languages. At Morris Hillquit's table, they spoke English.

Some fellow Jews resented Hillquit's self-conscious Americanism and cringed when he sometimes dismissed Jewish-specific causes as "special interests."[160] They saw it as snobbery; to Hillquit it was simple ideology. His Marxism gave no special place for Jewish workers, or those of any other ethnic group, over any others.

This night they had barely finished their aperitifs when Hillquit tossed the floor to his guest Professor Basch with a simple question: How could America best help Europe?

Basch had a dark beard, dark hair, a high forehead, and his own ideas on how to charm Americans. He answered quickly: "Not by what you, Mr. Hillquit, have done in conjunction with Meyer London [the

Socialist US congressman] the other day," he said, referring to Hillquit's meeting with Woodrow Wilson in the White House, where Hillquit had urged the president to end the war.

Basch, carefully polite, had not meant to pick a fight. He had a purpose. That week, Woodrow Wilson had shocked Europeans with a remarkable speech calling again on the warring parties to stop fighting. This time Wilson had demanded a "peace without victory" and, to back it up, the creation of a World League for Peace—later the League of Nations—to settle international disputes. Already, England and France had denounced the idea. After two years of fighting and millions dead, they bitterly resented Wilson's premise that they didn't deserve the satisfaction of triumph. Even worse, peace without victory could leave Germany in possession of Belgium, parts of France, and other occupied territories.

Americans deluded themselves, Basch told the candlelit faces looking back at him around the table. France would never accept President Wilson's peace terms. France must win this war. France had justice on its side. And any talk of mediated settlements bordered on treason. "To speak of peace now is to help Germany," he argued.[161] And more. Germany only pretended to want peace, he explained, because it feared losing the war. England and Russia had just begun to fight. "The allies will win because they must win," he insisted. "It is mathematically certain. They have twice as many men."

Basch knew he faced a skeptical audience. Hillquit and his left-wing friends represented some of the foremost antiwar pacifists in America. If fact, they had all heard these arguments before and rejected them. Algernon Lee, writing in a long diary entry that night, said he found Basch's discussion "rather hideous." He described how Basch mechanically counted off the six or seven million men lost so far, plus the million permanently disabled on each side, as utter abstractions.

Skeptical questions flew at Basch from all around the table. Someone asked about Alsace and Lorraine, the former French provinces seized by Germany in 1870 and now pointed to by France as central to the conflict.

Why not just let the people there vote? Let them decide if they want to be German or French? Basch didn't flinch. No, he said. Alsace and Lorraine must be restored to France, and the inhabitants must not be allowed to choose. Why? "They would vote to remain German," he said.

This last answer drew a few nervous laughs. Lee glanced at Hermann Schluter, who rolled his eyes. But Basch went on: "Alsace and Lorraine do not belong to the people who live there now, but to the sons and grandsons of the Alsatians of 1870—many, many, many of whom emigrated after the 1870 conflict." Lee found this answer "astonishing." Is this what France was fighting for? Did they really expect Americans to spill blood over a French territorial grudge from fifty years ago?

Finally someone mentioned Russia. How could America, a free country, possibly fight for France and Britain when they allied themselves with Russia, perhaps the single most autocratic, bigoted, anti-Semitic, backward, and hated regime on earth, especially among New York's million and a half Jewish immigrants, many of whom were direct victims of tsarist persecution. Basch treaded carefully, and Algernon Lee recorded his answer carefully in his diary: "B[asch] insisted on his hatred for the Autocracy [in Russia]," Lee wrote. "But, as soon as the war ends in victory for the Allies, there will be a revolution in Russia. 'We know it.'"

To Lee this sounded bizarre. Usually it was the Germans who insisted that their victory against Russia would end tsardom, not the Allies. Was France prepared to betray its Russian comrade-in-arms?

If Professor Basch had hoped to win converts this night, he failed miserably. Nobody said it to his face. Morris Hillquit thanked Basch for his graciousness and eloquence, and then the servants brought coffee, dessert, and another round of drinks. Algernon Lee, in his diary notes, said he found Basch's whole presentation "depressing," showing how once a country got caught up in war fever, even an intellectual like Basch could fell prey to "the infection of chauvinism."

Morris Hillquit too found nothing new in Professor Basch's arguments, nothing to change his view of the world war. The war was a pointless catastrophe, and American intervention would only make it worse. Germany had not attacked the United States and never could. Misguided patriots like Professor Basch, their minds warped by the fight, had lost their capacity to think. Still, he appreciated hearing the argument. Hillquit had decisions to make, and accurate information from Europe had become scarce. Censorship and exaggerations had made most newspaper accounts barely credible. Basch at least was a fellow socialist; Hillquit could trust him to speak his mind.

If America entered the war, what would he do? Hillquit knew he and his Socialist Party must oppose the war. They had no choice. On principle, the war was indefensible. And politically, his Socialist Party would insist on a strong stand. And this, in turn, could destroy everything they had worked to build over the last twenty years. Hillquit knew the pattern repeated in country after country. When war hysteria hit, people began to look for scapegoats, traitors, and spies. And the first accused of disloyalty were always the same: immigrants and socialists.

10

WILSON

"I have, therefore, directed the Secretary of State to announce to His Excellency the German Ambassador that all diplomatic relations between the United States and the German Empire are severed, and that the American Ambassador at Berlin will immediately be withdrawn."[162]

—President Woodrow Wilson, February 3, 1917

H OPES THAT AMERICA might avoid being dragged into Europe's war suffered a major blow on Wednesday, January 31, 1917, when Germany declared its intention to resume unrestricted submarine warfare. In practice, this meant that German submarines were instructed to attack without warning any neutral ship, including American-flag vessels, armed or unarmed, sailing into German-defined war zones. The announcement contradicted direct promises Germany had made after the sinking of the *Lusitania*. It also represented the final collapse of President Woodrow Wilson's effort to mediate the conflict. England and France had rejected his formulae of "peace without victory," and now Germany had pledged a brutal no-holds-barred fight to the finish. "Thus begins the long-feared campaign of ruthlessness, conceived by [German military chief of staff Paul] von Hindenburg, a starvation blockade of England, the likes of which the world has never seen," reported the Hearst-owned *New York American,* a war opponent up until that point, but no longer.[163]

Three days later, President Wilson announced his response. Appearing before the United States Congress, he declared an immediate break of diplomatic relations with Germany, stating, "This government has no alternative consistent with the dignity and honour of the United States." Within the day, Germany's ambassador in Washington was given his passport and told to leave the country. But Wilson still held out an olive branch. "I refuse to believe that it is the intention of the German authorities to do in fact what they have warned us they will feel at liberty to do," he told Congress. "Only actual overt acts on their part can make me believe it even now."

But that said, should Germany carry out its attacks, Wilson pledged to "use any means that may be necessary for the protection of our seaman and our people."[164] Congress responded immediately by beginning the process of approving $500 million in war bonds. The path to war had begun.

These actions shook Americans as if from a stupor. From peace-loving neutrality, the country's trajectory lurched sharply toward panic and fear. Within hours of President Wilson's speech, a barrage of security measures reshaped the landscape of New York City. Five hundred guards armed with rifles and bayonets came out from the naval reserve station and took posts on the five bridges connecting Manhattan with Brooklyn, forcing all cars, wagons, and trolleys to stop and be searched. Tugboats began prowling the East River, stopping any vessel from approaching within fifty feet of the bridge piers. Cannon and machine gun nests appeared at the base of the Brooklyn and Manhattan Bridge towers. Police detectives began positioning themselves at all subway stations, and police blocked entrances to all public buildings, demanding identification from anyone trying to enter.

And that wasn't all. The Port of New York sent inspectors to seize all German steamers in the harbor, ordering that German crewmen, about two thousand of them, be confined to their ships. They boarded all five of the Hamburg-American ocean liners in port and ordered them to remain in place until officials could decide whether to impound them.

At the Brooklyn Navy Yard, tugboat crews worked overtime to install a steel cable measuring more than a mile long and six inches in diameter to block any vessel from approaching. Three thousand New York National Guardsmen were sent to protect the city's water supply, including its upstate reservoirs and aqueducts.

Why? What was the danger? One simple word: sabotage. That same day, a machinist mate in Philadelphia was caught trying to scuttle the torpedo boat *Jacob Jones* in Philadelphia Harbor by opening a water drain and flooding it. Two feet of water had already leaked into the hull before military police stopped him. All the pent-up fear over explosions at munitions plants, all the rumors about German agents, now came out. Spies, radicals, lawbreakers, troublemakers could be any place. "Tonight it has been brought unmistakably home to us that we are unprepared," New York mayor John Purroy Mitchel announced, urging immediate, mandatory military training for all American young men. He denied directing his actions against "any group in the city." But he added this: "We must assume the loyalty of the citizens of German birth," recognizing the hint of character assassination that already polluted the air.

All that week, newspapers featured stories of ship sinkings by German submarines and steps to prepare for war. With subways, bridges, docks, ferries, public buildings, aqueducts, and elevated railways all now under armed guard, "all that was lacking in this city yesterday was the knowledge that a state of war existed between the United States and Germany," declared the *New York American*.[165] Any New Yorker who wasn't convinced already about the threat of German subterfuge had plenty of reason to think again.

Fortunately for Woodrow Wilson, he had been given several hours' advance warning of the initial German announcement on unrestricted submarine warfare. Aides had described the president as "incredulous" on hearing the news, insisting on seeing the official German document. They described Wilson as reading it closely that night while sitting alone in his study in the White House until after 11 PM. This gave him a few extra hours to think and sleep before having to make decisions.

The advance warning had come from a new friend. Wilson's aide and confidante Colonel Edward House had received a tip from a young British army officer who had been gassed in Europe in 1915 and had been reassigned to New York City on behalf of the British Secret Intelligence Service. The young officer seemed to have the deepest network in North America for unearthing German spies. His name was Sir William George Eden Wiseman, and he had a particular eye out for Russians.

THE DAY WILSON announced that America was breaking diplomatic relations with Germany, Trotsky scribbled out a column for *Novy Mir* called "A Repetition of Things Past."[166] In it he recalled living in Vienna, Austria, in August 1914, when the Great War had first broken out. Trotsky recalled the excitement, how the passions had affected people, broken the monotony of their lives and given them a sense of urgency. He recalled walking the streets and seeing a "most amazing crowd" fill Vienna's fashionable city center, "porters, laundresses, shoemakers, apprentices and youngsters from the suburbs" who now felt themselves "masters of the situation in the Ring."[167]

Trotsky also recalled from Vienna how his younger son, Sergei, barely six years old at the time, came home from school that day with a black eye and bruises. All over town, graffiti on walls and chants on the streets had shouted, "Alle Serben mussen sterben!" (All Serbs must die!) Young Sergei, to be contrary, had stood on a street and shouted back "Hoch Serbien!" (Up with Serbia!) A few tough older boys had run over, chased him down, and punched him in the face.[168]

Hearing that the outbreak of war might affect his legal status in Vienna, Trotsky had gone to visit the Vienna police prefect to ask what to do. The prefect, a man named Geyer, had told him that Russians and Serbs could be arrested the next morning as enemy aliens. "Then your advice is to leave?" Trotsky asked.

"The sooner, the better," the prefect said.

"Good. I will leave with my family for Switzerland tomorrow."

"Hm . . . I should prefer that you do it to-day."[169]

By 6:10 that night, after living in Vienna the better part of eight years, Trotsky, Natalya, and the boys had become refugees, passengers on a night train leaving Austria for Zurich, Switzerland.

That was in August 1914. Now, in 1917, the world war had followed him across the ocean to New York City. America stood on the verge of following the examples of Austria and France, two countries that ultimately had forced him to flee.

ACT II:

OF WAR

11

SPY VERSUS SPY

"It is common knowledge that the Germans are counting on their propaganda to bring about a separate peace with Russia; but the details of their intrigues are not so well-known."[170]

—William G. E. Wiseman, May 1917

"The interests of the German government are identical with those of the Russian revolutionaries."[171]

—Alexander Israel Helphand, or Parvus, January 7, 1915

WILLIAM GEORGE EDEN Wiseman[172] looked every bit the stylish young English gentleman. He wore tweed suits and striped ties and kept his mustache neatly trimmed. Son of a British navy captain, grandson of a rear admiral, and tenth in a line of English baronets (a hereditary title) dating back to King Henry VIII in the 1600s, he had received proper British schooling at Westminster College and Cambridge. At school he had earned a spot on the "Fighting Blue" college team as a bantam-weight boxer. He floundered after graduating, tried journalism at the *London Daily Express,* wrote satirical plays, and then dabbled in business, traveling to Canada and Mexico on behalf of British financiers.

But then came the world war, and Wiseman, twenty-nine years old with a wife and two small children, found his calling.

He enlisted as an artillery lieutenant and rose quickly to captain of the Sixth Battalion, British light infantry. They stationed him in Flanders, where his unit joined a multinational force defending the small Belgian town of Ypres on the Western Front. When German infantry attacked in April 1915, Wiseman saw violence at its worst. He found himself at the center of an ugly bloodbath that killed or wounded more than one hundred thousand young men in just three weeks. But what most terrified the soldiers and shocked the world about Ypres was the chlorine gas.

This was Germany's first major use of poison gas in the war, and it caught the Allies by surprise. In their first attack there, German troops emptied six thousand canisters of chlorine into the wind. It formed an enormous green cloud that drifted silently over French lines and quickly crippled or killed some six thousand soldiers. The gas formed hydrochloric acid on contact with water or soft tissue—lungs, eyes, lips, throats, noses, or exposed skin. The acid burned whatever it touched, causing suffocation, blindness, bleeding, coughing fits, and scars. Most died of asphyxiation, suffocating from clogged lungs.

Wiseman experienced one of these gas attacks in Flanders. It damaged his body so severely that he had to be evacuated from the front and required months of hospitalization. His eyesight never fully recovered.

But William Wiseman, the tough college boxer, refused to let chlorine gas knock him out of the war. While recuperating in England, he found another way to participate—espionage. One day a friend sent him to see the leader of a British unit recently created to fight the Germans behind the lines. They called it the Secret Intelligence Service, "a department of the Foreign Office," or MI1c (later MI-6). Its commander, George Mansfield Smith-Cumming, walked on a wooden leg, the result of a car accident, and relished disguise and secrecy. His agents referred to him in code as C, and sometimes he had them write in invisible ink. Smith-Cumming also had an eye for talent and found invalid soldiers like Wiseman ideal for undercover work: committed, idealistic, and smart. Add to this Wiseman's prewar business background, his North American travels, and his upper-class breeding (and bank account). It made him perfect for planting in the United States. Wiseman jumped at the chance.

MI1c's prior New York chief had been a washout, and Wiseman, after a first visit, decided to ask for the top spot himself. "Let me try it, Sir," he'd said after hearing Smith-Cumming complain about his predecessor. "You?" the chief laughed. "Why not? You couldn't do worse than the others."

With that, Wiseman landed in New York City in late 1915 and opened a small office for MI1c, first in the Woolworth Building and then downtown at 44 Whitehall. He assembled a small staff, including Norman Thwaites, another injured combat veteran with experience as a New York newspaperman, a one-time private secretary to *New York World* publisher Joseph Pulitzer. As cover, they grafted their operation onto the British naval attaché's office and called themselves the American and Transport Department of the Ministry of Munitions.

Early on, their work consisted mostly of chasing down rumors, arranging protection for munitions ships, and watching: people, groups, vessels in the harbor, local politics, anything suspicious. It could be tedious. Wiseman's staff once spent days trying to discover who had stolen a pair of binoculars from a ship under their watch, then checking on a British socialite, a Duke of Morny, who had been accused of spying for Germany. The Morny charge, they decided, was "utter piffle." In another case they hired guards to watch weapons being loaded onto a Russian ship called the SS *Visigoth* only to find that five of the hired men came drunk and, after enough whiskey, started harassing the Russian soldiers.[173] In another job, Wiseman's agents had to discover the identity of the German ambassador's latest mistress.

The guard work alone soon had Wiseman managing more than two thousand private detectives. Wiseman also elbowed into politics, nurturing a relationship with Colonel Edward House, the close political confidante of President Woodrow Wilson. Wiseman and House would soon become a primary back channel for war contacts between London and Washington.

But the hardest, riskiest part of the job was finding German spies and stopping them. With America still neutral, the US government barely bothered with spy catching. Wiseman worked closely with New York City's rough-and-tumble bomb squad, but he found Washington's naval and military intelligence units still "amateur operations."[174] Wiseman, looking out at New York from his downtown office, saw threats everywhere, and no place more than among New York's bulging masses of immigrants: Germans, Irish, and all the Russians and Jews.

Wiseman developed a knack for spying. He and his team built a network of sources that soon opened windows all over the city. Wiseman didn't mention source names in his papers, but Thwaites wrote about his adventures years later, and occasional names popped up in cables. They included Russian commercial attaché C. J. Medzikhovsky; Sidney Reilly, the future "Ace of Spies" from books and the popular 1980s PBS/BBC television series; and even a Russian businessman named Alexander Weinstein, possibly a relative of Gregory Weinstein, editor of *Novy Mir*.

These sources only confirmed the dangers. German and Irish immigrants posed the most obvious threats. New York's German neighborhoods teemed with active German agents, and its German-language newspapers routinely printed propaganda from Berlin. And the city's two hundred thousand Irish virtually seethed with hostility. Just months earlier, Britain had crushed Ireland's latest demand for home rule, the 1916 Easter Rising, an armed insurrection in Dublin that British troops had battled for six days of urban warfare. The fight had killed 318 rebels and civilians, 116 British soldiers, and sixteen Dublin policemen. British officials had sent sixteen Irish home rule leaders to death by firing squad. Calls for vengeance sounded on both sides of the Atlantic.

But even this blood feud paled in comparison to the threat posed by New York's Russians and Jews. The danger here went beyond mere sabotage or propaganda. They threatened Britain with losing the war. All because of the tsar.

Britain needed Russia as a military ally in 1917. Its own army, even combined with France's, stood badly outnumbered by Germany's massive war machine on continental Europe. But Russia, with its five million soldiers, its Cossacks and vast spaces, had created a second front in

Europe that forced Germany to split its forces, giving Britain and France a combined advantage in the west. But Russia's involvement came at a steep price. The tsar had enemies.

For instance, virtually every single one of the million and a half Jews and Russian émigrés in New York City had known tsarist persecution. Russia's history of violent anti-Semitism; its targeted, abusive military conscription; its bans against Jews attending universities, owning land, or even living in most cities; its waves of pogroms killing thousands of innocents and openly backed by tsarist officials had spawned deep resentment and been a principal cause behind massive Jewish emigration from Russia to New York since the 1880s. As a result, Jews flooded into every anti-tsarist movement and represented the large bulk of Russians (which then included Poles and Ukrainians) who had left for America.

Now in New York, these Jews and Russian émigrés stood ready to block any American attempt to enter the European war, seeing it as helping the tsar. It wasn't just radicals or socialists who felt this way. Take Jacob Schiff, New York's most prominent Jewish leader at the time. Schiff, seventy years old, chaired Kuhn, Loeb, and Company, one of Wall Street's leading investment banks, and proudly used his bank's muscle to protest Russian anti-Semitism. When Count Sergius Witte, Russia's finance minister, came to New York in 1904 seeking financial support for Russia's then-brewing war against Japan, Schiff met with Witte and told him to his face that so long as the tsar persecuted Jews, he would block any American loans.

Writing years later, Witte still shuddered at the encounter. "[Schiff] banged the table with his fist," Witte recalled, "and declared that a government which indulged in massacres and inhuman persecution on religious grounds was not to be trusted."[175] Russia lost its war to Japan, and tsarist officials still fumed over the incident with typical bigotry. Said Russia's finance minister in 1911, "Our government will never forgive or forget what that Jew, Schiff, did to us,"[176] as if Russia's own generals and Japan's fleet had less to do with the defeat.

Since the outbreak of world war in 1914, Schiff again had refused to lend money to Britain and France so long as they supported the tsar, even if his Kuhn Loeb bank lost business and he was personally vilified as pro-German. Instead, he contributed to groups sending anti-tsarist literature to Russian soldiers at the front.

And then there was Trotsky. Wiseman had no special reason to think Trotsky the most dangerous Russian in New York City in February 1917. Most likely, Wiseman personally had never even met or seen Trotsky at that point. Still, for Wiseman, Trotsky's type of radical, incendiary rhetoric set off loud alarms. The fact that so many Jews and Russians supported radical movements—Bolsheviks, Mensheviks, even American socialists—fed into Britain's worst nightmare. All their talk of Marxist revolution raised an obvious question. What if one of these groups ever actually managed to pull the job off, topple the tsar, and lead Russia to sign a separate peace with Germany? Britain and France would then be left to fight Germany alone. To Wiseman and Britain, this outcome had to be stopped at all costs.

Wiseman's MI1c organization had left nothing to chance and already had a file on Trotsky, starting with the first warnings about him from French officials in July 1915. The file contained all the reports about how they had caught Trotsky snooping around French military installations, about Trotsky's Paris newspaper *Nashe Slovo,* and about his ties to a suspected Austrian agent. This was enough for MI1c to tag him for his "revolutionary and socialist tendencies."[177]

If any Russian or Jew in New York City, be it Trotsky or anyone else, tried to overthrow the tsar or lead Russia out of the war, Wiseman and his team intended to find out first and use the vast resources at their command—the combined might of the British Empire and its allies—to stop them.

ON THE OPPOSITE side from Wiseman stood a man usually called by his friends simply Parvus. And this Parvus could not have been any more different from the Brit who ran MI1c's operation in New York.[178]

Based in Denmark, Parvus enjoyed big cigars and drinking champagne at breakfast. Older, softer, chubbier than Sir William, with a goatee and a balding head, Parvus spoke a Russian-accented German interspersed with Turkish and enjoyed the company of attractive women. None of his three marriages lasted. Far from nobility, Parvus came from a poor Jewish home in southern Russia, grew up in Odessa, worked his way through school in Switzerland, and then moved to Germany to establish himself as a left-wing radical theorist. His money, and he had plenty, he had made through war-related business and speculation.

Just as Wiseman had devoted himself to the British cause, Parvus had dedicated himself to Germany, and in a special way. Parvus never joined the army, not for Germany or any other country. But it was Parvus who conceived the idea that Germany could win the world war quickly by helping revolutionaries achieve their dream of socialism in Russia. And now he had committed himself to making that plan reality.

And one more difference: Wiseman knew Trotsky only by reputation, but Parvus could truthfully claim to have once been Trotsky's closest collaborator and friend.

His real name was Alexander Israel Lazarevich Helphand (or Gelfand). Parvus (Latin for "small," perhaps a joke on his large appetites) was the nom de guerre he had chosen on joining the radical underground in the 1890s. Up until the war, Parvus had counted himself one of Europe's leading leftist thinkers, equal in stature to Lenin himself. Trotsky had called Parvus "unquestionably one of the most important of the Marxists" of the era, but he tempered this praise with caution. Parvus had a rogue side, Trotsky wrote, "always something mad and unreliable" about him, including an "amazing desire to get rich."[179]

Parvus's early radical polemics had irritated German officials so much that they banished him from Prussia and Saxony. Settling in Munich, Parvus, who was three years older than Lenin and twelve years older than Trotsky, joined the early socialists, often siding with another rising young prodigy, Rosa Luxemburg, among the fringe "hotheads" and "firebrands."[180] But he always kept an eye out for profit. Parvus ran a Dresden newspaper, started a publishing house (where he apparently cheated novelist Maxim Gorky out of a large royalty payment), and helped Lenin launch *Iskra,* his journal for the budding Social Democratic movement.

Trotsky's special friendship with Parvus began after his 1903 break from Lenin over the Bolshevik–Menshevik split. He and Natalya had traveled to Munich to ask Parvus for advice, and the two immediately became so friendly that Trotsky and Natalya moved into Parvus's house in Munich's Schwabing District, a popular bohemian neighborhood with plenty of bars and cafés, artists and writers. Over the next few months, Parvus and Trotsky worked together on what became one of Trotsky's signature contributions to Marxist theory, his "theory of permanent revolution," basically the notion that a backward country like Russia could skip over the liberal capitalist phase in its development and proceed directly to proletarian socialism, a key theoretical bridge for Russia's 1917 Bolshevik Revolution.

When Trotsky returned to Russia in early 1905 to join the antigovernment uprisings in Saint Petersburg, Parvus came too. Parvus saw the 1905 revolt as validating his stance on the importance of political mass strikes and the potential for "permanent revolution." Like Trotsky, Parvus was arrested by police, served a prison term, and escaped.[181] Back in Europe, he, Trotsky, and Natalya had spent the next summer on what Trotsky called a "tramp through Saxon Switzerland," drinking, hiking, and enjoying the mountain air till the money ran out and they went separate ways.[182]

This cozy friendship ended abruptly, though, with the world war. Its outbreak in 1914 found Parvus in Constantinople, where he had settled and established himself as a financial adviser to foreign investors. Parvus used his commercial ties to win a key role in Turkey's war mobilization. This allowed him to speculate financially on government decisions. He quickly became wealthy.

Around this time, Parvus had his epiphany. After so many years living in Germany, he had grown to appreciate German culture, music, food, and literature, though always as a political radical. Now he suddenly grasped the connection between these two strands in his life. German militarism posed no conflict with his socialism. Just the opposite. Germany's war had created the best possible chance for his long-held Marxist aims for Russia. A German military victory over the tsar could open the door to a lasting socialist regime. And Germany's best hope to win a quick victory in the world war—by forcing Russia out of the contest—could come from supporting Russian revolutionaries like his friends Trotsky and Lenin. If Lenin's Bolsheviks toppled the tsar, it would save Germany the trouble.

Parvus used his new access to top German leaders, first in Constantinople and then in Berlin, to press the idea, and the German officials agreed. In fact, they found Parvus so convincing that in 1915 they gave him an account of one million marks (about $6 million in modern times) to promote Russian radicals wherever he thought best.

The opportunity seemed fantastic, and Parvus rushed to spread what he thought was wonderful news. It came as a surprise, then, when his radical friends not only disagreed but also denounced him as a pariah. They assaulted him with their worst insult, calling him a German "chauvinist."

Parvus couldn't believe it. He decided to take his case directly to Lenin. He traveled to Zurich in mid 1915 and went to a restaurant where Lenin was having lunch with his wife, Krupskaya, and friend Inessa Armand. He interrupted them and then followed Lenin home to his apartment. By all accounts, the meeting went badly. According to a friend who spoke to Lenin after the encounter, Lenin heard Parvus out and then called him a German agent, asked him to leave, showed him the door, and told him not to return.[183]

Trotsky, hearing about Parvus's conversion to German militarism, also immediately denounced him. Trotsky wrote a column for his Paris newspaper *Nashe Slovo* titled "Epitaph for a Living Friend," calling Parvus a "political Falstaff," a "joke and a chauvinist" who "we now have to place on the list of the politically deceased."[184] Their friendship was over.

Fortunately for Parvus, he had a thick skin and an even thicker bank-roll. Instead of giving up, he kept looking for ways to conjure his Russian Revolution. He started spending German money to help radical friends. He even pumped some into Trotsky's *Nashe Slovo,* using as his vehicle a mutual friend named Christo Rakovsky, the one identified in French military police reports as an Austrian agent. Trotsky happily accepted Rakovsky's money, apparently not knowing that it actually came from Parvus.

Early 1917 found Parvus in Copenhagen running a small conglom-erate of new ventures, all backed financially by Germany, all designed to nurture revolution in Russia. He had founded an upright-sounding Institute for the Study of the Social Consequences of the War, plus a newspaper called *Die Glocke.* He created an import–export business that gave him an excuse to send agents into Russia and create pools of strategically located cash. To staff these ventures, Parvus tried to recruit friends from his former radical circle with Trotsky, including two who by January 1917 had already resurfaced in New York City and shared the small office with Trotsky at *Novy Mir.* One was Nikolai Bukharin, who turned Parvus down only after Lenin advised him to stay away. The other was Grigorii Chudnovsky, who actually had joined Parvus's Copenhagen operation for a few months before reaching New York.

To hear recent news about his old friend Parvus, Trotsky only had to look up from his desk at *Novy Mir* and ask across the room.

But if Parvus still hoped to reconcile with his former friends, Lenin seemed to hammer a final nail into the idea. Seeing a copy of Parvus's new newspaper, *Die Glocke,* Lenin publicly panned it as an "organ of renegades and dirty lackeys," a "cesspool of German chauvinism" in which "not a single honest thought, not a single honest argument, not a single straightforward article" could be found.[185]

Despite these public denunciations, Lenin kept open a discreet back channel. He gave approval for a friend, Polish socialist Jakob Furstenberg (or Ganetsky), a skilled smuggler who had lived with Lenin near Cracow before the war, to join Parvus's business operation in Copenhagen.

Parvus made Furstenberg managing director of his trading company. As a result, Furstenberg knew all about Parvus's German funding, his network of agents inside Russia, his strategically placed cash accounts, and the rest. And, by every indication, he kept Lenin appraised.

Parvus refused to take no for an answer. He bided his time in Copenhagen, building his fortune and indulging his appetites. Russia would rise up sooner or later, and when it did, he would be ready.

12

CARNEGIE HALL

"And who will lead this revolution? Perhaps Mr. Bronstein [Trotsky] sitting over there at the Café Central?"[186]

—Count Leopold Berchtold, foreign minister of Austria-Hungary, on being told that war could spark revolution in Russia, 1914

"My first contact with these people [the leaders of the American Socialist Party] was enough to call forth their candid hatred of me. . . . To me they seemed the rottenest part of that world with which I was and still am at war."[187]

—Leon Trotsky, in his 1930 memoir

WAR FEVER ONLY accelerated in the days after February 3, the day President Woodrow Wilson declared his break in diplomatic relations with Germany. Armed soldiers now guarded every public place in New York—bridges, street corners, buildings, subway platforms—as people hung American flags and draped hundreds of buildings with patriotic banners. Students and other young men signed up for military training so fast that the army couldn't supply enough rifles. Men marched instead with broomsticks or shovels. Police boats patrolled the harbor now with machine guns. In Washington, DC, Congress began approval of war appropriations totaling almost $900 million (about $30 billion today), enough to finance rapid initial deployment of three million men at the president's command.

Adding to public outrage, in the first week after Wilson's declaration, German submarines sank thirty-six more Allied and neutral ships, mostly British, leaving dozens of sailors killed or missing at sea, including at least two Americans. In one case, of the British steamer *Eavestone*, a German sub reportedly opened fire on the lifeboats, killing the captain and three others. Nations in South America, Asia, and Europe all raced to denounce the kaiser. War talk infected even the movies. New York's Broadway Theater, showing that week the epic silent film *20,000 Leagues under the Sea*, now packed the house three times a day with its new big print advertisement: "You can see what happens when a submarine hits an ocean liner," a gory allusion to the *Lusitania*.[188]

With Americans preparing to fight Germany, suddenly they started seeing things differently. Being German, speaking German, even having a German-sounding name—all became suspect. And being pro-peace began to sound even worse, like cowardice. The *New York Times* put the issue as simply this: "professional pro-Germans" versus "instinctive Americans," and whether the country would demean itself to "take orders and bread from Berlin."[189]

But the same war talk that inspired "instinctive Americans" to sign up for the army also alarmed the suddenly energized ranks of war opponents, who saw the door now rapidly closing on any chance to prevent American intervention in Europe. And no place in America had more peace activists than New York with its bulging German, Russian, Jewish, and Irish immigrant neighborhoods.

Just hours after President Wilson's anti-German declaration, leaders from New York's biggest antiwar groups—socialist, pacifist, churchmen, the Woman's Peace Party, the American Neutral Conference Committee, labor groups like the Amalgamated Clothing Workers and United Hebrew Trades, and others—met and agreed to unite in a common front, a new Keep Out of the War Committee. Its chief demand: Let the people choose. Put the question to them in a war referendum. Only ten weeks earlier, voters had decisively reelected Woodrow Wilson president because he "kept us out of war!" Wilson hadn't even been inaugurated yet for his second term. To reverse course now without a new vote, they argued, made democracy a joke.

To press their case, they decided to hold a mass citywide rally bringing all the different coalition partners together at New York's most distinguished venue for arts and politics alike: Carnegie Hall.

In most ways, city life went on as before. The rich enjoyed their money. Colonel Jacob Ruppert, beer tycoon and future owner of the New York Yankees, lit up the American Art Gallery auction that week by spending a record $2,500 (about $80,000 in modern money) to purchase a single green jade Japanese vase with a crescent neck and two dragon-head lip handles. "Every day, in New York City, 4,000,000 Mecca Cigarettes are smoked,"[190] bragged the tobacco company. Pushcarts peddled their wares, men went to work, children not working went to school, and traffic clogged the streets.

But beneath the surface, deep forces gnawed at the city's social fabric, reshaping it in ways not yet visible.

LEON TROTSKY RELISHED the excitement. During these early days of war fever, he went on a tear of speaking and writing, making himself a public figure in this strange new country where he knew so little and didn't speak the language. He became one of New York's leading voices against entering the world war. "I was up to my neck in work," he recalled, "and consequently I did not feel at all like a stranger."[191]

In early February, Trotsky addressed packed crowds at the Brooklyn Lyceum, Manhattan's Beethoven Hall, the Labor Temple near Union Square, and similar venues. His articles ran three or four times each week in *Novy Mir*. At least four appeared in Yiddish translation in the *Forward,* with others in German in the *New Yorker Volkszeitung* and the socialist *Die Zukunft*. Day after day, in speeches, columns, and talks around café tables, he pressed his case, giving vivid accounts of Europe. In one column he described a zeppelin bomb attack on Paris, in another the plight of French soldiers in filthy, disease-ridden trenches living under constant gunfire as "billions in profits" flowed to corporate war profiteers. In yet another, he decried the cowardice of European politicians who talked peace but then justified killing on grounds of "patriotism" and "national self-defense," concepts Trotsky considered meaningless in an age of global capitalism.[192] Trotsky became "one of our most popular speakers and writers," Ludwig Lore wrote.[193] Trotsky's name increasingly guaranteed a crowd.

On stage, Trotsky could mesmerize groups with his intensity, his sharp eyes and disheveled hair, his spitfire delivery in Russian or German. "I found his platform technique remarkably effective," wrote socialist politician Louis Waldman, who saw his performances. "He had an extraordinary sense of the dramatic," Waldman recalled. "There was nothing of the peasant or the worker about the man. He was an intellectual with a nervous system pitched to the highest degree of tension."[194]

For all his effort, though, the loud splash Trotsky was making sounded only in a small, obscure pond: the immigrant, foreign-language socialist subculture of Manhattan, a tiny sliver of the American body politic. For the rest of the country, it was as if he didn't exist. Nobody saw him. Nobody heard him. Since he never spoke in English, mainstream newspapers ignored him.

And for Trotsky, as for just about every other left-leaning activist in New York, the highlight that month promised to be the great antiwar rally at Carnegie Hall.

Organizers had scheduled the Carnegie Hall event for a Monday night, February 5, and a blizzard hit New York that day. Fierce winds and blinding snow clogged Manhattan streets and even disrupted the subways and elevated trains. Hospitals treated dozens of twisted ankles and broken arms caused by people slipping on the sidewalk. All that day, Trotsky could have seen girls and young women dashing about town, wearing white ribbons reading "Keep Out of the war" pinned to their winter coats, handing out leaflets and hanging posters for the rally. Snow or no snow, thousands jammed Seventh Avenue around Carnegie Hall hours before the doors opened. All twenty-eight hundred seats inside the great auditorium filled early. After that, people packed themselves tightly into any available standing room, aisles, and boxes.

It is easy to picture Trotsky, elbowing through the crowd for good seats, perched up front with his *Novy Mir* cronies—himself, Bukharin, Chudnovsky, and Kollontai, all chatting away in Russian—and a row or two behind his new friends, thin-haired Dr. Hammer, young Louis Fraina, and Ludwig Lore with his bushy mustache. The scene would have thrilled him—the noise, the chants and cheers echoing off high ceilings. Each faction—pacifist, socialist, anarchist, religious, labor, Irish, Germans, Jews—seemed to have its own cheering section with posters and banners, mostly red. They sang "The Internationale" and the Yiddish anarchist anthem "In Ale Gasn" (Everywhere You Look) in loud voices and dreamy harmonies, plenty of women among the men.

Trotsky had a fine eye for revolutionaries, and seeing the assembled radicals here, he doubtless compared them in his mind to the crowds he had seen in Russia, especially the ones in 1905 who had led the Saint Petersburg uprising, who had ignored army bayonets to defy the tsar by shutting down factories and forming the Petrograd Soviet. How strong were these Americans? Did they have backbone like the Russians? Would they stand and fight when soldiers and police came? And what about these pacifists, the women and churchmen? Could he trust them in a fight as well? Or would they turn coward like the European socialists, hide behind "patriotism" and "national defense"?

Leon Trotsky had prepared his whole life for revolution, and the situation here in America now fascinated him in a new way. If war was coming, would it lead to uprisings? Would American socialists really fight, not just with words but in the streets? And if it came to a fight—as it must have seemed here surrounded by these thousands of New York's most fervent radicals—would he, Trotsky, have the chance to lead?

Then he and his friends settled in for the night's main speaker: Morris Hillquit, the moderate leader from Riverside Drive.

"DO THE WORKERS of the United States want war?" Morris Hillquit shouted, his face red from straining to reach the far corners of the vast hall.

"NO!" came the ear-shattering answer. They waved red banners, cheered and laughed. "Down with war! Long live Peace!" came the deafening chants, even from mouths of fresh-off-the-boat immigrants who hadn't a clue what the words meant.

By the time Hillquit had taken the podium at Carnegie Hall, more than four thousand people packed the cavernous auditorium, filling every inch and all four levels of balconies. Hundreds more had to be turned away. Hillquit knew this place well, its red plush seats and curtains, its gold trimmings and magnificent arches and high ceilings, its precise lighting and acoustics. He had spoken here before. Carnegie Hall had opened its doors in 1891, with Russian composer Pyotr Ilyich Tchaikovsky conducting the philharmonic in performing his grand *Marche Solennelle,* with steel king Andrew Carnegie—who personally put up the first $2 million to build this grand edifice—leading the applause. Now it offered its luxurious stage not just to musical virtuosos like Spanish cellist Pablo Casals, Polish pianist Ignacy Jan Paderewski, and New York's own Philharmonic Orchestra but to political figures. Just that month, Margaret Sanger had spoken here to raise money for her criminal trial on charges of promoting birth control.

Hillquit himself had appeared here in 1915 to debate war preparedness with United States congressman Augustus Gardner of Massachusetts. After the war, in 1924, he would share this stage with British writer-philosopher Bertram Russell to debate socialism in England. Hillquit had refined his speaking skills over twenty years in politics, from street corner crowds to saloons to debate halls to national convention stages. He combined a loud voice and strong lungs—essential before electronic microphones—with a sense of timing and a talent for simple rhythmic phrases easily understood across the divides of language and culture.

Hillquit spoke with urgency that night to this vast sea of faces. Ever since President Wilson's February 3 breaking of relations with

Germany, he had dropped everything to focus on forging this anti-war coalition. He was one of the first to insist on forming a united front and sponsoring this Carnegie Hall event. He had helped on all the political grunt work, lining up speakers and sponsors, drafting resolutions, pushing and prodding party bureaucrats. Hardest of all was keeping his own socialists in line. Already the labor movement had fractured over the issue, with conservatives like Samuel Gompers, president of the large trade-oriented American Federation of Labor, supporting war preparedness. Twelve high-profile socialists would soon join them by publicly breaking from the party to support national defense. They included novelist Upton Sinclair (author of *The Jungle*); muckraking journalist Charles Edward Russell; social activist J. G. Phelps Stokes (scion of the Phelps-Dodge fortune); his wife, Rose Pastor Stokes; and suffragette Charlotte Perkins Gilman (author of the popular 1892 short story "The Yellow Wallpaper" about medical maltreatment of women and niece of *Uncle Tom's Cabin* author Harriet Beecher Stowe).[195]

Even worse, Hillquit saw how quickly police and businesses had started using the war emergency as an excuse to crack down on labor and the left. Just that week, a squad of navy militiamen guarding the Williamsburg Bridge had turned their rifles against twenty-five factory workers picketing outside the giant Havemayer (later Domino) sugar refinery in nearby Brooklyn, part of a general strike by twelve thousand employees against sugar refiners in New York, New Jersey, and Philadelphia. The navy guards had chased the strikers away with fixed bayonets and then escorted fifteen strikebreakers to the plant, no different than if they were Pinkertons paid for by the factory owners.

Across the country, local police and Justice Department agents had begun rounding up members of the IWW, the hard-edged labor group led by Big Bill Haywood that openly matched violent company union busting with its own strong-arm tactics. Seattle police had arrested seventy-three IWW members that week and charged them with murder from an earlier run-in with deputies.

Faced with these challenges, Hillquit had practiced his message all week in speeches and newspaper interviews. He needed to excite his political army before it disappeared. Even at this late date, free speech still ruled in America, and meetings like this could go on without harassment by police or vigilantes. Who knew how much longer that would last?

Already the crowd at Carnegie Hall that night had unanimously approved resolutions decrying war with Germany as a sop to the "masters and exploiters, the capitalist class" who would profit on weapons sales while saddling workers with the actual bloodshed. It had denounced "police dictatorship, martial law, and suppression of rights" at home.[196] For tonight's speech, Hillquit decided on a trope older than the American Civil War: "A rich man's war but a poor man's fight."

"They tell us this war is self-defense," he now shouted at the packed throng of men and women in Carnegie Hall. "But we know! We know better!" Whatever wrongs America might suffer from German submarines, he argued, were nothing compared to the devastation of full-scale war. "Never was a war threatened on a more shallow pretext," he insisted. "They say the German submarine policy is criminal. It is. I affirm it. But so is the war, so is every part of it, so are both sides to it!"

They cheered again. And with the crowd riled and loud, Hillquit now delivered his best punch. Standing at the podium, all eyes on him, he rustled some papers in his hands, then proceeded to read out loud a list of names, pronouncing them clearly, enunciating each syllable, prompting murmurs of recognition at the likes of Du Pont and United States Steel, J. P. Morgan and John D. Rockefeller. These, he said, were the biggest munitions makers in New York City, the capitalists poised to profit should America enter the war. "It is you workers who will have to pay for the patriotism of the parasites and the exploiters," he told them, pointing a finger.

Then Hillquit took another paper, a copy of a report recently issued by the mayor's own Commission on Preparedness. Hillquit opened it to the part that talked about who should be conscripted into the army,

pulled from their normal lives, and forced to do the actual fighting.[ii]
Clearing his throat, he read aloud as the report pointed to "the injustice
and economic unwisdom of calling into service men with heavy business
or family responsibilities." The auditorium erupted in hisses and boos.
Family responsibility people could understand. But business responsibilities? Businessmen should be allowed to stay home—safe and warm far
from the bullets and trenches—to tend their profits?

"But their patriotic ardor goes even further," Hillquit yelled, barely
hiding a smirk. "These highly patriotic gentlemen urge that only those
men 'economically available' be sent into service." Nobody mistook
whom this meant. It meant workers and the underemployed, people like
them. "There you have it, in black and white," Hillquit said.[197] It would
be a war for business, with workers forced to kill and die.

The crowd stood and applauded for five full minutes after he finished the harangue. Hillquit enjoyed the moment. But after twenty years
in politics, he knew that winning an audience was easy. The real fight
would start tomorrow.

TROTSKY APPARENTLY STILL had not met Morris Hillquit personally by the time he heard him speak at Carnegie Hall. But he certainly
knew Hillquit's reputation. Since arriving in New York, radical friends
had told him repeatedly how they considered Hillquit the enemy, dam-
aging their cause despite his leadership post atop the New York Socialist
Party. They complained that Hillquit was too conservative, too compro-
mising, too interested in his own status, too anxious to win elections, not
a real revolutionary.

Now Trotsky, watching the excitement at Carnegie Hall, thought he
saw the problem too, and he decided to insert himself by taking the great
Hillquit down a notch.

---

ii America would end conscription and replace it with an all-volunteer army in 1973 in response to protests during the Viet Nam War. As a result, young Americans today cannot fully appreciate the immediate life-or-death import that questions of war and peace acquired in these earlier periods. Intervention
in Europe was no abstract question for the young men in Carnegie Hall that night.

It wasn't what Hillquit said. Trotsky actually liked the speech. Writing about it the next day, he called the whole Carnegie Hall affair "impressive" and praised the roomful of cheering radicals. The "vast majority," he wrote, "consisted of the revolutionary working class"— high praise in his book. He even applauded the resolution they adopted. Its nice phrasing pleased his writer's ear. The world war had been waged to protect "the sacred right of the American capitalists to fatten up on the misfortune of war-struck Europe," it read—to Trotsky a "clear, simple, and honest formula."[198]

What bothered Trotsky was not the words. Instead it was the company Hillquit kept, all those people sharing the Carnegie Hall stage with him, the members of his coalition: the churchmen, women's groups, unions, and the rest. They reminded Trotsky of the people he hated most, the cowardly "social patriots" of Europe who talked peace before 1914 but turned colors and backed their countries' war efforts once the hysteria hit.

None struck him worse than the pacifists. Two had addressed the hall that night: the Reverend Frederick J. Lynch of the New York Church Peace Union and Elizabeth Freeman, a well-known suffragette representing the Women's Peace Party. Hearing their gauzy paeans to nonviolence, Trotsky pegged them both as phonies. Their type, he wrote, talk lovingly about peace today, but then "when they hear the first shot, will gladly call themselves good patriots [and] start supporting the governmental machine of mass murders, persuading the crowds that in order to reach 'fair peace,' 'lasting peace,' and 'eternal peace,' it is necessary to fight the war until the end."

To Trotsky, this was dishonest nonsense. Which brought him back to Morris Hillquit. It was Hillquit, putting aside his fine speech, who had made the decision to connect their perfectly good socialist revolutionary movement to these weak-kneed pacifists.

This was Trotsky's gripe, and he decided to attack the way he knew best, with his pen and his platform at *Novy Mir*. *Novy Mir* produced only eight thousand copies, but its message could spread fast and far, repeated in the wider socialist press. Sitting at Saint Marks Place the next day, hot tea staining his fingers in the cramped basement office, he took pen in hand and scribbled a title across the page: Большое Обязательство: По Поводу Резолюции Митинга В Карнеги-Голл. (Great Commitments: Resolution from the Meeting at Carnegie Hall.)[199]

Trotsky had remarkable discipline about his writing. Beyond the sheer volume of words and pages he produced—columns three and four times a week for five different tabloids, plus speeches and letters—he had an ability to focus despite distractions from all sides. As war commissar in Russia after the 1917 revolution, he would earn a reputation for punctiliousness, bringing order to chaos. His meetings started promptly, finished quickly, his decisions and orders clear and crisp.

Now, pen in hand, he began his surgical dissection of Morris Hillquit. His revolutionary friends had seen their big Carnegie Hall rally hijacked, he argued. Why had the Socialist Party—Hillquit's crowd—agreed to share the stage with "bourgeois, priest-like pacifists"? From an "organizational-political" view, he insisted, it made no sense. "The reason for that, as they said, was 'circumstantial,'" Trotsky explained, tongue firmly in cheek, "the only suitable venue, Carnegie Hall, had already been rented out by the bourgeois pacifists, and our party found it impossible to delay the meeting any further." Not exactly true, but that wasn't the point. The "price for the opportunity," he went on, was "too high." Standing with pacifists had weakened the message.

Trotsky actually had a point on this. The *New York World,* one of the city's two largest newspapers, had sent a reporter to the rally. He described it as a "protest against all war," pointing out that "police had made preparations for a hostile demonstration, but it was seen evident that the men and women who filled every available space in the auditorium were for peace under any circumstances."[200]

No. To Trotsky, this was totally wrong. This depiction of docile peace-loving fawns missed the point. It denied the "revolutionary aspect" of the meeting, the willingness of radicals to fight capitalism. What they needed instead was "clear class consciousness" and vigilant distrust of anyone who stood for "civil peace," those "backsliders, defectors, and people with no sense of honor and consciousness." Socialism involved "organized uprising against the bourgeois society," he wrote, not mindless "peace under any circumstances" or "ambiguous pleasantries toward the traditions of the bourgeois republic." The rally's resolution against capitalist war had been crystal clear. "We will watch that this obligation is fulfilled to the very end—without any weaknesses, compromises, and doubts!"

After he finished scribbling out the column, Trotsky would have passed its messy, ink-smeared pages around the office to his fellow editors. Bukharin, sitting at the next desk with his red beard and friendly face, would have approved, noting how his new comrade had changed. Trotsky's attack on Hillquit sounded far more Bolshevik than Menshevik. Instead of a big tent, it urged splitting away from talkers and foot draggers, limiting the movement to the doers and true believers. Vladimir Lenin certainly would approve. Maybe Bukharin even took credit for influencing his comrade's new direction.

Gregory Weinstein, *Novy Mir*'s chief editor, also would have read the column and given final approval. All told, Trotsky's piece was a subtle, discreet dagger, never mentioning Morris Hillquit by name but leaving no doubt of the target. *Novy Mir* ran it on Wednesday morning, February 7. Copies circulated all across the city, and the United States mail service carried it to Philadelphia, Boston, and Chicago. A few copies even went to Europe.

One of the first addresses to receive it would be right there in New York City, on Riverside Drive.

MORRIS HILLQUIT SPOKE English whenever possible, but he could read Russian perfectly well. Seeing the *Novy Mir* article, he didn't need a translator, either for the language or the politics. He reread that last line, referring to the Carnegie Hall resolution: "We will watch that this obligation is fulfilled to the very end—without any weaknesses, compromises, and doubts!" He glanced again at the reference to "backsliders" and "defectors." He had no doubt who this was aimed it: him.

And then the byline: Н. Троцкий. Trotsky.

Hillquit had seen this type of sniping before. He knew his Socialist Party had plenty of big egos and radicals threatening to discredit it. More than angry, Hillquit was incredulous at the column. What gave this Leon Trotsky the right to criticize? Here was a man exiled from his own country, Russia, for more than ten years and in America for barely three weeks. Did he understand anything about America?

Still, *Novy Mir* had a wide following. He had to take it seriously.

"Socialism assumes an organized uprising against the bourgeois society," this Trotsky had written. Really? Did he not notice that socialists in America comprised a tiny fraction of the public, a small and deeply mistrusted minority? Did he not understand that any "uprising" would cause the United States government, Pinkertons, the National Guard, and the New York Police Department to throw them all in jail? And that threats of violence would hasten a government crackdown, alienate potential supporters, and empower intolerant bullies? Did he not notice the armed guards at every public bridge and building ready to stop troublemakers?

How easy for this Trotsky to tell other people to go fight—risk their jobs, their lives, their freedom—as he amused himself writing articles down in Greenwich Village. In America you changed things by winning elections, passing laws, or bargaining collectively for union rights and better pay. That, to Hillquit, was politics. It took hard work, building coalitions, nurturing allies, convincing the public. And in any political fight, he would need those pacifists in his corner—their votes, their organization, their networks.

Hillquit had already thought hard about how he might fight this battle in an American way. He knew his coalition could never stop Woodrow Wilson from intervening in Europe once Wilson made up his mind. Still, Hillquit took seriously the idea of putting the question to the people in a war referendum. The next presidential election would not come until 1920, and the next congressional election not until 1918, both too late. But a very important election would be held in New York

City in 1917, for mayor. That could be his battlefield, and prospects there looked surprisingly good.

Not only was New York the most antiwar city in the country, but its current incumbent, John Purroy Mitchel, elected in 1914 as a thirty-four-year-old "boy mayor," looked glaringly vulnerable. Mitchel was the strangest of political animals: an anti-Tammany reformer running as a Republican and backed by an anti-graft Citizens Municipal Committee. In his first years, Mitchel had tried to burnish his reform credentials on the police department, firing hundreds of hacks. All this made him a weak candidate with plenty of enemies.

But Mitchel also was a military reservist who carried a pistol and had begun recruiting a twenty-two-thousand-volunteer civilian defense force for the city. Just that week, he had denounced a group of pacifists visiting him to complain about forced military training in city schools. Shooting and marching, Mitchel insisted, provided "essential elements of general public education," including "good citizenship" and "respect for authority."[201] If Mitchel ran for reelection, he certainly would make the war central to the debate.

This, to Hillquit, was a race worth running, a chance to put the war to a direct vote in the largest city in the country. And winning as a Socialist, even coming in a close second, would make it all the sweeter.

But first he had to deal with Trotsky. More out of irritation than thought, he wrote a short note about this man: that Trotsky had no right to advise others to pursue revolutionary tactics when he himself had not been prepared to stay in Russia to do likewise.[202] He sent it out through his channels, then tried to stay above the fray.

Unfortunately for Hillquit, this Leon Trotsky had no plan to go anyplace soon, and he did not react well when anyone told him be to quiet. Just ask Grisha Ziv.

13

ZIV

"Many traits in [Trotsky's] character also involuntarily thrust one towards such a suggestion: his sharply exaggerated egotism, his over-developed confidence, his extreme and sickly vanity, his proclivity for extravagance in speech, writing and demeanour, a kind of teasing pedantry . . . exhibited even in his precise, careful handwriting."[203]

—Grisha Ziv, on why he thought Trotsky was epileptic, 1920

"I imagine there were enough romances in Trotsky's life to occupy a really conscientious biographer for several chapters."[204]

—Max Eastman, 1926

TROTSKY HAD QUALMS about seeing Grisha Ziv, his old contact from Russia. Ziv and he had been friends twenty years before, but not since. Ziv had participated in the 1905 uprising in Petrograd and sent Trotsky occasional notes, but they had drifted far apart. Ziv now lived in New York as a settled, conservative, middle-aged physician. On politics, the glue that once connected them, they now disagreed totally. Trotsky had seen Ziv at some of his speeches, but he knew Ziv disapproved. Ziv made no secret of opposing Trotsky's antiwar stance and his anti-patriotic socialism.

But politics didn't matter today, and Trotsky refused to let it spoil things. He had invited Ziv to his home out of courtesy and nostalgia.

Facing each other in the doorway to his small Bronx apartment, shaking hands, perhaps sharing a hug and Russian greetings, Trotsky and Ziv must have startled to see the age in the other's face, the lines and the traces of gray.

Trotsky made sure that he and Ziv had the apartment to themselves, except for Leon, his eleven-year-old son, who puttered about the room. Natalya apparently had gone out with the younger son, Sergei. Trotsky would have served tea and for Ziv maybe schnapps or hot borsht. Newspapers doubtless cluttered the floor along with the boys' toys and piles of books. Sitting near a window, they would see snow clogging the street and tree branches shivering in the wind.

We know only bits and pieces of the conversation, though Trotsky and Ziv each remembered it years later. They didn't make much small talk: The weather was cold, the apartment messy, Ziv's medical practice busy. They side-stepped any mention of current events. "Both of us, as if we had a silent agreement between us, avoided any discussion on hot political topics,"[205] Ziv recalled.

Ziv asked Trotsky about some of his celebrity-socialist friends. How was Parvus? Ziv had met Parvus in Petrograd in 1905. "Working on his twelfth million," Trotsky answered with a laugh. And Georgi Plekhanov, a prominent writer and one-time *Iskra* editor? Ziv had read Plekhanov's books as a young radical. Trotsky knew Plekhanov well. He had recently denounced Plekhanov publicly over Plekhanov's decision to return to Russia and back the country's war effort, making him a hated "social patriot." Trotsky apparently mentioned the fact and made a joke of it.

"Does that mean that he is a counter revolutionist, Daddy?" little Leon asked in a squeaky high voice. Ziv recalled Trotsky just smiling at his son but ignoring the question.

Tensions soon melted, and they turned the conversation to the real connection between them, old times. For Trotsky and Ziv, old times had a special, more private meaning.

Trotsky had just turned seventeen when Ziv had first met him in 1896—brash, fresh-faced, jostled hair, eyes already intense behind pince-nez glasses. Trotsky had just graduated from the Realschule in Odessa (less prestigious than Odessa's Gymnasium, which limited attendance by Jews), where his family had sent him to study. He had moved to the nearby industrial town of Nikolaev for more classes. But in Nikolaev, Trotsky found his schoolwork boring and irrelevant. He skipped classes, even after being visited by a truant officer. Instead, Trotsky that year befriended a man named Franz Shvikovsky, who lived nearby. Shvikovsky, a gardener by trade and unusually well read, kept a cabin by the garden he tended. Here he enjoyed hosting people he found interesting: students, exiles, local radicals, free thinkers. Trotsky—Bronstein back then—became a regular.

Ziv, also a teenager back in 1896, was a regular at Shvikovsky's garden as well, though he attended medical school in Kiev most of the year.

Together, Trotsky, Ziv, and their circle at Shvikovsky's cabin spent time reading books by leading liberal thinkers—John Stuart Mill, writers on the French Revolution, Russian dissidents—plus the underground newspapers. Over time they started living together as a commune. They ate and slept in Shvikovsky's cabin and joined in projects such as a protest against a fee hike at a local library. Trotsky remembered these as happy times, summer evenings spent sharing a samovar prepared by the landlady's daughter, along with bread and sausage (no, he didn't keep kosher) they'd scrounged up during the day. And on politics, they talked into the late night hours.

Two brothers named Sokolovskaya also joined the group, along with their sister, Alexandra Lvovna. She—tall, attractive, and educated, with long dark hair—held a special place. The only woman, older and more serious than the boys, she easily held her own in debate and she alone had read Karl Marx, then a new voice to Russian radicals, who still mostly followed the Narodniki, the peasant-based anarchists behind the 1881 assassination of Tsar Alexander II. Trotsky relished these arguments, but his debating tactics sometimes turned mean-spirited. He especially teased Alexandra. "Marxism is a narrow teaching that splits the personality," he argued, needling her and calling her obdurate and narrow-minded.[206]

Ziv remembered how Trotsky's insults could startle the group, make "everyone turn to stone" as he put it. She responded in kind. "I will never, never stretch out my hand to that little boy!" she confided once to Ziv.[207] Another friend, watching these arguments, said of Trotsky, "He will either turn out a great hero or a great scoundrel."[208]

Then came the blowup with Trotsky's father, David Bronstein, who was still paying the bills for his son's schooling in Nikolaev while running his farm back home in Kherson province. When Bronstein learned that his son was skipping classes and hanging around with troublemakers, it infuriated him. He raced to Nikolaev to confront him. One of Trotsky's friends recalled Trotsky's father showing up at the garden unannounced one day: "this big-whiskered farmer" shouting, "Hello! You run away from your father too?"[209]

Trotsky often quarreled with his father. The family had settled in Kherson province—a rural area far from the Jewish shtetls of Eastern Europe—in the 1850s, during a brief time when Tsar Alexander II allowed Jews to leave their crowded pale of settlement and try farming. It was an attempt to draw Jews into mainstream Russian culture, and, at least for the Bronsteins, it worked. At home they spoke no Yiddish and barely bothered with religion. Instead Trotsky's father worked hard at building his farm business. He bought additional land and saved money.

But his son, instead of admiring the accomplishment, belittled it. He identified his father with the Russian propertied class—what future Bolsheviks/Communists would call kulaks—and routinely sided with workmen and townspeople whenever they argued with him. When young Trotsky once tried to explain to his father his democratic ideals over the family dinner table, his father dismissed him as ridiculously naive. "This will not pass even in three hundred years," he thundered back.

Now in Nikolaev, Trotsky and his father argued again. "We had several stormy scenes," Trotsky recalled. His father insisted that Trotsky at least finish school before dabbling in politics. "I uncompromisingly defended my independence," Trotsky wrote. "It ended with my refusing to accept material aid from home."[210]

Trotsky would never bridge this gap with his parents. They would reconcile briefly after 1905, when his mother and father came to Saint Petersburg to attend his public trial for leading the 1905 Petrograd Soviet. Trotsky remembered the awkwardness they created, this "old couple," as he called them, his mother crying during court sessions that "she could scarcely understand," his father sitting there "pale, silent, happy and distressed, all in one."[211] His mother had died in 1912, and he hadn't seen his father since leaving Vienna. After the 1917 revolution, the Soviets would confiscate his father's farm (as they did with all large landowners), forcing David Bronstein, by then seventy years old, to reach Moscow and take a post his son had arranged managing a small grain mill. He would die of typhus in 1922.

But for Trotsky and the Nikolaev commune, the most fateful step came in 1898 when they decided to help local factory workers organize a union. Trotsky (still just eighteen), Ziv, and Alexandra Lvovna all happily joined the project and made it a big success. Ziv even conceded Trotsky the "lion's share" of credit, pointing to his "inexhaustible energy, skill in plans and contrivances of all sorts and resistance to fatigue."[212]

Local factory owners, however, had no intention of allowing a union in their city. They complained to the police, who quickly came and arrested some two hundred union members and organizers, including Trotsky, Alexandra Lvovna and her two brothers, Shvikovsky, and Ziv. A Nikolaev court sentenced all of them to Siberian exile, with four years apiece for Trotsky and Alexandra.

This is where the story became more personal. While waiting in jail in Nikolaev, Trotsky surprised friends by asking Alexandra Lvovna to marry him, and she agreed. All the bickering back in Shvikovsky's garden had apparently sparked something between them. But Trotsky was still a minor under Russian law and needed his parents' consent to marry. His father, hearing the news, immediately objected, calling Alexandra Lvovna, this older woman and Marxist troublemaker, a bad influence on his son.

Once again, Trotsky refused to take orders from his father. It took him months to figure it out, but he finally found a way to bypass him. Moved to a prison in Moscow to await final transit to Siberia, Trotsky quietly convinced the officials there to conduct the ceremony. They produced a chaplain-rabbi, and a prison guard lent him a ring. Ziv attended the wedding.

By the time Trotsky's father found out, it was too late to stop the marriage.

As a married couple, Trotsky and Lvovna had the legal right to live together in Siberia. For political crimes like theirs, exile meant being taken to an isolated place and forced to stay there, with police periodically checking to make sure they hadn't moved. The government even paid a small subsidy for food, rent, and cleaning. Far from being locked inside a prison cell, Vladimir Lenin famously went duck hunting in Siberia. Trotsky used the time to read, write, and start a family.

The authorities sent Trotsky and his wife first to a tiny peasant village called Ust-Kut on the Lena River in Central Asia, so remote that it took three weeks to get there—by train, wagon, and then river barge. Cockroaches infested their tiny hut, and temperatures outside fell to thirty degrees below zero. Still, in Siberia they found a network of fellow radical exiles eager to connect. They won permission to move upriver to another village, Verkholensk, where Trotsky worked briefly as a merchant's clerk, but mostly he read and wrote. He studied history, politics, and Marxism; wrote for journals like the Irkutsk-based *Eastern Review*;[213] and met other young activists such as Felix Dzerzhinsky (the future "Iron Felix," founder of the Cheka, or secret police) and Moises Uritzky (future Bolshevik Central Committeeman and head of the Petrograd Cheka). Trotsky recalled pleasant times with them, such as one "dark spring night, as we sat around a bonfire on the banks of the Lena, [and Felix] Dzerzhinsky read one of his poems in Polish."

Along the way, he and Alexandra Lvovna also became parents, producing two baby daughters. By early 1902, Zina (Zinalda) was one and a half years old. Nina was just four months.

It was at this point, after two years in jails and two more in Siberia, that Trotsky grew restless and decided to leave. He had heard about exciting changes in the outside world and felt that a young politico like himself needed to be in the West with the dynamic leader Vladimir Lenin. His wife and daughters must simply stay behind. There was no room for them in an escape.

It seems only natural that Trotsky, as a father and husband, would have agonized over this decision. But here the story turns fuzzy. As he tells it, Alexandra actually pushed him to go. "You must," he quotes her as saying when he posed the question. "She was the first to broach the idea of my escape," he later insisted. "Duty to the revolution overshadowed everything else for her," he wrote. "She pushed away all my doubts."[214] By his account, Alexandra even helped in the getaway. She and Trotsky at that point lived upstairs in a two-story cabin in Verkholensk, and a police inspector came daily to check on them, barging into the upstairs bedroom. One night Trotsky told the inspector to stop intruding, and he did. He used this chance to slip away, and Alexandra hid the secret. The police didn't discover him missing until after he had been gone for five days.

How severely the police treated Alexandra and the baby girls after discovering the escape is never mentioned in any of the accounts.

Fair or not, Trotsky critics over the years have pointed to this incident, the fact that he abandoned his wife and two baby daughters in Siberia, as proof of Trotsky's bad character, his selfishness and arrogance.[215] Trotsky supporters usually respond that his decision fit the era's revolutionary code and that Alexandra Lvovna never complained about it, never publicly challenged his account, never appeared to hold a grudge. Of course, complaining would not have done her any good. Who would have believed her, taken her word against the great Trotsky? She believed in the cause and apparently chose not to make waves.

What was the private truth about their marriage, the actual face-to-face dynamic of the young husband and wife? Other than themselves, no one really knew.

In any event, when Alexandra Lvovna finally returned home from Siberia, poor and friendless, it was Trotsky's parents—his father David Bronstein, who had originally tried to block the marriage—who gave her shelter and agreed to help raise the daughters. Trotsky and Alexandra never divorced. "From abroad, I could hardly keep up a correspondence," he explained. "Then she was exiled for a second time; after this we met only occasionally. Life separated us, but nothing could destroy our friendship and our intellectual kinship."[216]

Within a few months, in late 1902 in Paris, Trotsky would meet another attractive young woman, Natalya Sedova, who would become his common-law wife, the mother of his two sons, and his life partner. Natalya certainly knew this history. Trotsky's continuing marriage to Alexandra Lvovna was the reason Natalya could never marry him herself.[217]

Grisha Ziv knew this story too. It was water under the bridge for him when he saw his old friend Trotsky resurface in New York City in 1917 and as he joined Trotsky in the Bronx apartment a good fifteen years after these events. When Ziv and Trotsky talked about old times, when they "drifted back to the mood of [our] recollections," as Trotsky's friend Max Eastman put it after hearing Trotsky's side of the story,[218] it is hard to see how they could have avoided it.

"I learned a lot about my long-lost friends and acquaintances," Ziv recalled of the afternoon. Certainly these would have included old man David Bronstein, their old circle from Nikolaev, and the girl they both knew there, Alexandra Lvovna.

At one point, Trotsky challenged Ziv to a game of chess. Trotsky loved chess and considered himself a fine player. Living in Vienna before the world war, he had enjoyed spending days at the popular Café Central on Herregasse in the fashionable Innere Stadt district, playing chess with all comers, including celebrities like Baron Rothschild. Years later, Trotsky would even be rumored to be second cousin to the Russian grand master David Bronstein, a World Chess Championship contender in the late 1940s.

But Ziv played a good game of chess too. He won the first game and noticed how Trotsky seemed to get annoyed over losing the match. "He showed himself to be a weak player and lost, which obviously upset him," Ziv wrote about it later. They played a second game, which Trotsky won. Then they stopped. Ziv insists that it was Trotsky who refused to press things to a rubber match.

Ziv left Trotsky's apartment shortly after that. He walked away offended, clearly over more than the chess game, and he stewed over it for a long time. He and Trotsky saw each other a few times more in New York, at speeches and meetings. Ziv recalled how Trotsky would "give me a friendly clap on the back" and tell people, "This is my old friend who needs to stay in France for a couple of months to become a good socialist."

Ziv would write a highly critical book about Trotsky in 1921—at the height of Trotsky's global fame—talking about their chess games that day and about the earlier times in Nikolaev. In colorful language that Trotsky himself, as a writer, would have appreciated, Ziv described him as a man who "loved his friends and loved them sincerely; but his love was of the kind that a peasant has for his horse, which assists the confirmation of his peasant individuality. But as soon as the horse becomes unfit for work, he will unhesitatingly, and without a shred of conscience, send it to the knacker's yard."[219]

Whether driven by pique, principle, or profit, Ziv's book and its many insults gave plenty of ammunition for detractors. Trotsky's friend Max Eastman would dismiss it as a "little volume of weak and ludicrous personal spite" and explain Ziv's antagonism as based simply on Trotsky's refusal to talk politics with him that day: "the manifestation of a self-seeking intellectual arrogance which [Ziv] suddenly discovered had characterized his friend's activities from the cradle."[220]

More likely, Ziv's hostility had deeper roots—in Nikolaev, in their friendship with the girl Alexandra Lvovna, and in his perception of how Trotsky had treated her.

14

ZURICH

"Dear Comrade Olga!

"Many thanks for your letter about the affairs in your local party. To tell the truth, 'pessimism' frequently takes hold of others besides yourself.

"The party here is opportunistic to the core; it is a philanthropic institution of Philistine bureaucrats.

"Even leaders who are seemingly left-minded (like Nobs and Platten) are good for nothing, especially the two mentioned. Without access to the masses nothing can be done."[221]

—Vladimir Lenin to Olga Ravich, a Geneva Bolshevik and future wife of Grigory Zinoviev, February 15, 1917

"**N**O LAME EXCUSES can conceal the fact," Vladimir Ilyich Lenin wrote in an appeal to socialist committeemen that January from his nest in Berne. "The complete fiasco of the Zimmerwald [effort] has manifested itself in Switzerland."[222] He never sent the appeal. Lenin saw little to cheer him in early 1917. His political movement appeared to be fragmenting around him, his revolution stalled, his friends scattered.

In February he and his wife, Krupskaya, left Berne and moved to Zurich, a much larger city. But the change of scenery didn't improve his outlook. Elegant and cultured, with its riverfront and lake, its theaters, cafés, and nearby mountains and spas, Zurich offered as cozy a haven from the world war as anyone could ask. Lenin spent most of his days there working in the city library on a new pamphlet called "Imperialism, the Highest State of Capitalism," which he would finish in June. He moved into a home at 14 Spiegelgasse, a narrow cobblestone lane in an old part of town, where he lived quietly with Krupskaya, busying himself writing letters by the hundreds and studying newspapers and books: Hegel on philosophy, Clausewitz on strategy, poetry by Victor Hugo. Occasionally he took Krupskaya to a lecture or concert, a restaurant or a nearby spa. To neighbors passing him on the sidewalk in his winter coat, he hardly looked like a fire-breathing revolutionary.

In his work, Lenin faced waves of frustration. He had so little cash these days that he could barely afford to print pamphlets, let alone pay for travel or books. Trying to keep touch with people brought constant headaches. His closest Bolshevist friend, Grigory Zinoviev, lived hours away in Berne. With telephones rare and service spotty, he had to rely on the mail, and letters sent abroad could take weeks to deliver, if not lost or confiscated en route. Messages smuggled in or out of Russia took longer, with even greater risk.

Worst of all, though, were the betrayals. All that winter and the prior fall, Lenin had seen one-time supporters abandon his "Zimmerwald left" line, his idea, proposed in 1915, that socialists transform the energy of world war into local civil wars of proletariat revolution. Lenin considered this principle his ultimate test of loyalty, and his list of failures grew by the week: French socialists Albert Bourderon and Arthur Merrheim (who had voted for a pacifist resolution at a Paris meeting), Italian socialist Minister Filipo Turati (who had insisted that Italy must reclaim its lost border territories), and German socialist parliamentarian Karl Kautsky (who had failed to oppose German war credits). Even in Switzerland, his long-time ally Robert Grimm, a co-organizer of the original 1915 Zimmerwald conference, had recently blocked a party meeting in Berne called to reaffirm Lenin's hard line.

Lenin complained endlessly about these turncoats. "Zimmerwald," he wrote in March, "has obviously become bankrupt and a good name again serves to cover up rot."[223]

Even his hopes for revolution in Russia took a blow that winter. Russia sat on the verge of collapse, its army in retreat, its government paralyzed, and food shortages crippling major cities. Lenin's subversive propaganda pamphlets had become popular with Russian soldiers and prisoners. But news from America threw a wet blanket on hopes for change anytime soon. If the United States entered the war against Germany, it would only strengthen the tsar and his hold on power. As Lenin saw it, Russia either had to crumble from within or be defeated in the war. There was no other way.

And when would that happen? In his lifetime? Would all his years of preparation be wasted? "We old folks may not live to see the decisive battles," he conceded in a lecture to a group of students in Zurich that January.[224] The setbacks that winter forced Lenin to rethink basic assumptions. "Ilyich considered it of the greatest importance to work out a correct tactical line," Krupskaya recalled of this period. "He thought that the time was ripe for a split on the international scale," she wrote, "to break forever with [Karl] Kautsky and Co., to begin with the [albeit dwindling] forces of the Zimmerwald Lefts to build a Third International."[225]

Amid all this pessimism, Lenin was surprised and delighted one day in mid-February 1917 to receive a letter from America. He studied the envelope and easily recognized the neat handwriting: Alexandra Kollontai, his favorite pen pal from Norway. It had taken the letter weeks to cross the ocean from New York, making it all the more confusing, since Lenin had already heard from her directly from Norway since her return. He had placed high hopes on Kollontai's trips to America, and now here was unexpected news from her second voyage. Had she raised money? Gotten his articles published? Found new allies?

KOLLONTAI HAD LEFT New York in early February and by late that month had reached her home in Holmenkollen, a small rural town just north of Kristiania (Oslo), Norway, known even back then for its beautiful mountains, skiing, and ski jumpers. It had been a nervous passage.

British sailors again had stopped her ship and searched the passengers. Now in Norway she found her family scattered. Her son, Misha, had stayed behind in Paterson, New Jersey; her estranged husband, Vladimir, still in Russia, had enlisted as an officer in the tsar's army; and her occasional lover Alexander Shliapnikov had moved on to Petrograd.

At home, back in what she called her "little red house above a fjord,"[226] Kollontai was happy to reconnect with local socialists and resume her duties managing the smuggling of messages in and out of Russia. By now even her views on Trotsky had softened. She complimented him in a letter: "A week before my departure Trotsky came, and this raised the hopes of Ingerman and Co. [the Mensheviks on the *Novy Mir* board of directors]," she wrote to Lenin on her return. "But Trotsky clearly disassociated himself from them and probably will carry on his own line, which is by no means clear."[227]

Lenin had barraged her with letters of his own, asking her to keep him posted on the local infighting among Norway's radicals and directing her to organize loyal followers in Stockholm and Copenhagen, as well as Kristiania. She was glad to rejoin the fold and would have been surprised to know her letter from America had only now reached Zurich.

LENIN READ THE new letter, shared it with Krupskaya, and sat down to answer it the very same day. He began with "Dear A.M.!," his shorthand for Alexandra Mikhailovna, as he liked to call her. "Today we received your letter and were very glad to have it. For a long time we did not know that you were in America and had no letters from you except one with news of your departure from America [the prior summer]. I wrote you on January 7 or 8," he went on, but "the French intercept everything that is mailed directly from here to America! [It] obviously missed you in New York."

Beyond the gossip and pleasantries, though, Lenin saw little good news in what Kollontai had shared with him. In a few terse sentences, she had told Lenin about an incident in New York City during which she and Nikolai Bukharin had tried to convince a group of key leftists there to split from their conservative American Socialist Party and endorse Lenin's Zimmerwald left line. But they had failed, she told him, losing the argument to an old rival fresh off the boat from Europe. Lenin saw the name: Trotsky.

Did he roll his eyes at the story? Or maybe stifle a laugh? How typical of Trotsky, Lenin must have thought, this Menshevik straddler with his "sheer false pride,"[228] who always, it seemed, had to interfere and insist on winning an argument, even in America. "I am sorry about the news of Trotsky's bloc with the 'Rights' for a struggle against Nikolai Ivanovich [Bukharin]," Lenin wrote. "What a swine that Trotsky— Left phrases [rhetoric] yet a bloc with the Right against the aim of the 'Lefts'!! He should be exposed (by you) at least in a brief letter to Sotysial-Democrat!"[229]

After these few words, Lenin turned his attention to his other wayward protégé in New York, Bukharin. He was pleased that Bukharin had established himself at *Novy Mir,* he wrote, but he then launched into complaints. He had asked Bukharin to send him materials on local New York politics but hadn't received them yet. "I have begged Bukharin to do so, but apparently the letters get lost," he wrote. As for Bukharin's latest theoretical writings, Lenin again found plenty to criticize. They were "much better than Kautsky," he wrote, but "Bukharin's mistakes may destroy the 'just cause'" in arguments with Kautsky's followers.

Then he turned to his bigger problems: disloyal followers and lack of cash. "How sad—we have no money!" he wrote.[230] He finished the letter to Kollontai, one of many he had scribbled from his desk that day in scenic, cultured, comfortable Zurich, waiting for the world to change. "Please reply at least briefly, but quickly and accurately, since it is terribly important for us to establish a good correspondence with you," he ended it. Then he took all the letters to the post office.

Lenin, by all indications, had no idea how much he and Trotsky, thousands of miles apart, were coming to see the world much the same way: resentment toward "social patriots" (socialist politicians who backed their own countries' war efforts), fear of America entering the world war, impatience at affairs in Russia, even their mutual dislike of Morris Hillquit (whom Lenin had met in Stuttgart in 1907). As long as they remained separated by an ocean, they would never bridge the gap. But this too would change in not so many weeks.

15

EAST BROADWAY

"I lived as an emigre in Vienna for several years, and there they use a word which, it seems to me, cannot be found in any other language— 'kibitzer.' Remember this word—it will prove useful to you. The word designates a man who, seeing two people playing chess, takes without fail a seat nearby and always knows the very best move. But if you sit down to play a game with him, he proves after the first move to be an ignoramus."[231]

—Leon Trotsky, speaking in Moscow about Western interference in Russia, October 1922

O N   T H E   S U R F A C E at least, Trotsky by now had settled into what looked like a conventional lifestyle in New York. He rode the subway to work each day, between the Bronx and Greenwich Village. He ate breakfast at the same small Bronx delicatessen on Wilkins Avenue, a place called the Triangle Dairy Restaurant. His boys spent their days at public school as Natalya kept house or went shopping with Rose Hammer, the wealthy doctor's wife. "They had a complex life of their own there," Trotsky wrote. "My wife was building a nest, and the children had new friends."[232]

Working at *Novy Mir,* Trotsky now regularly held court at the nearby Monopole Café on Second Avenue, a popular hangout for artists and writers, with chess and card tables sprinkled among gaggles of men debating books and politics, a place that made Europeans homesick for similar haunts back in Vienna and Paris.

On free nights he sometimes joined Bukharin at the New York Pubic Library. Or else he indulged a new passion he had discovered in Paris, the cinema. What did he see? Favorites that season, beyond epics like *20,000 Leagues under the Sea,* included Mary Pickford's *Poor Little Rich Girl* and two new releases by Charlie Chaplin, *Easy Street* and *The Immigrant.* As they were silent films, Trotsky easily could have followed the clever stories, even with his bad English. And silent movies or not, cinema houses back then offered plenty of noise, thick with crowds, cigarette smoke, wisecracks from the audience, and live music from a piano or organ. It's easy to picture Trotsky laughing out loud at Charlie Chaplin in his Little Tramp costume in *The Immigrant,* kicking a customs officer in the pants, a nice radical touch. (Fittingly, Chaplin himself would later earn a thick FBI file as a suspected communist.)[233]

Trotsky even took time that month to enjoy *Novy Mir*'s annual fund-raising gala at McKinley Square Casino in the Bronx, with dancing, music, and three one-act plays performed by the Russian Stock Company. He gladly paid the seventy-five-cent door charge, including hat check, for the night out with Natalya.

But even in these normal parts of life, his Marxism colored everything, and his impatience let nothing pass. At the Triangle Dairy Restaurant, for instance, Trotsky deliberately refused to tip the waiters who served him breakfast. Socialist purists considered tipping a bourgeois insult to honest labor. As a result, the waiters refused to serve him. Some even mocked him behind his back, calling him Leo Fonfatch (meaning Leo the Nose, because of his high nasal voice). They finally made peace only after Trotsky agreed to eat and leave quickly, so the waiters could clear his seat for regular tipping customers.[234]

His contempt for "social patriots," including ones around him in New York, grew increasingly strident. Local lawyer Louis Waldman, a friend of Morris Hillquit's, happened to run into Trotsky one night at the Monopole Café, gabbing with friends over a round of schnapps or tea. Trotsky usually attracted an entourage of young radicals. Waldman dared to challenge him on the "social patriot" point, and he remembered the rant he received in response: "Of all the species of political fauna, none was lower, none more contemptible, none more dangerous," Waldman recalled Trotsky telling him, "than the Socialist who defended his country in time of war." He remembered Trotsky "shaking his finger at me" and saying, "Yes, the victorious proletariat will know how to deal with you social-patriots."[235]

Trotsky even snapped at Bukharin once around this time. Bukharin, his affable young *Novy Mir* coeditor, had spent days organizing a *Novy Mir*–sponsored International Conference of Socialist Organizations and Groups in New York City. But despite all his work, Bukharin managed to attract only nine delegations, mostly small local clubs like the Manhattan and Brooklyn Lithuanians and the Socialist Party's Russian and Lettish branches. Just one delegation, the Boston-based Socialist Propaganda League, included any native-born Americans. The conference's main achievement after hours of meetings was a motion to support the Zimmerwald movement as "the embryo of a Third International."[236]

Trotsky, hearing the story—Bukharin's meaningless conference producing a tepid resolution—couldn't help but make a snide joke. "Have you got a Zimmerwald Left Wing in the North Pole?" he snapped.[237] Bukharin repeated the line almost a decade later during a debate in the Kremlin. It had stung enough to still hurt even after ten years.

Perhaps the strangest of all the esoteric ideological fights Trotsky picked that month was his attack on the Red Cross. Yes, this was the same Red Cross that provided medical care to frontline soldiers and handed out sweaters and knitted clothes to needy refugees. The Nobel Committee would award it the Peace Prize in 1917 for its humanitarian work.

Why would anyone attack it? One day a woman named Anna Ingerman—she and her husband both physicians—happened to speak up at a Socialist Party meeting in New York. Attendees were debating a resolution stating that, should war come, any young man who voluntarily enlisted in the army or navy should automatically be considered to have resigned from the Socialists. Everyone agreed: Socialists should not join the army. But Anna Ingerman argued that they should make an exception for those joining the Red Cross. The Red Cross was different, she said, because of its medical work. In stating her case, Ingerman invoked the name of Klara Zetkin, a celebrated German socialist and women's advocate, then being detained in Berlin for publicly denouncing the kaiser's war.

Anna Ingerman won the argument that day, and the party agreed to the Red Cross exception.[238] But Trotsky, who happened to attend the meeting, heard Ingerman and decided to make a stink. In a brief note for *Novy Mir,* he criticized her for implying that Klara Zetkin, a good socialist, would collaborate with a quasi-government, military-supporting body like the Red Cross.

That could have been the end of it. But Ingerman, taking umbrage at the criticism, quickly wrote back to *Novy Mir* claiming that Trotsky must have misunderstood. She had met the famous Klara Zetkin in Germany, she explained, and Zetkin in fact had told her, "My husband and my son, doctors, will certainly join a medical organization: it is their duty." Trotsky had gotten it wrong, she insisted. "It is possible to disagree with you, Mr. Trotsky, and all the same remain an internationalist."[239]

Anna Ingerman dropped the whole issue after that, but not Trotsky. He decided to write two more columns on it. No, he argued, the Red Cross was a "governmental militarist organization." If socialists wanted to help soldiers, they should use their own private groups, and Ingerman was an "intermediary element" for suggesting otherwise.[240] When another reader, Mary Rogov, pointed out that no socialist medical organization like the Red Cross actually existed, Trotsky again refused to back down. The Red Cross's mission was to heal soldiers and send them back to the front, he argued. Socialists should stick to publicizing soldiers' rights, sending them books and tobacco, and the like.[241] And so it went.

But all these quirky, obscure, minor irritations paled next to Trotsky's break with the *Forward,* a loud, messy, first-class feud that would cast a long shadow over both of them, sparked by the event that finally decided the issue of American intervention in Europe: the Zimmermann Telegram.

TENSIONS BETWEEN WASHINGTON and Berlin had been mounting ever since Germany's resumption of unrestricted submarine warfare and President Wilson's breaking off of diplomatic relations. Wilson, after seeing German subs continue to sink Allied and neutral ships, finally on February 26 announced a new policy called armed neutrality, under which he asked Congress for authority to arm American merchant vessels so they could defend themselves on the high seas. On Capitol Hill, sixteen pacifist senators, led by Republicans Robert La Follette (Wisconsin) and George W. Norris (Nebraska), decided to filibuster Wilson's Armed Ship Bill in a last-ditch effort to stop the approaching war. In speeches, they used language sounding very similar to the New York socialists, claiming that war would only fatten profits for weapons makers. Or, as Senator Norris put it, "We are about to put the dollar sign on the American flag."[242]

However, La Follette, Norris, and the other pacifist senators had not grasped just how drastically public attitudes had changed. Feelings against them turned ugly and intense, particularly in the East. Newspapers called them disloyal. President Wilson personally denounced them as "a little group of willful men [who] have rendered the great government of the United States helpless and contemptible." Speakers at a packed Carnegie Hall rally called them traitors, evoking chants of "Hang them! Hang them!" Former president Theodore Roosevelt called their action "unpardonable."[243] Within a few days, Congress, in an emotional session, adopted a cloture rule to silence dissent, and President Wilson claimed legal authority to bypass Congress altogether on military matters.[244]

Stoking public passions even further, the Department of Justice in Washington, DC, announced that one hundred thousand foreign spies were now operating inside the United States, "mostly Germans," it said, located all over the country but concentrated around weapons plants.[245] New York and New Jersey police a few days later announced that they had raided the Hoboken hotel room of a man named Fritz Kolb, a German chemist. After arresting him, they found two high-explosive bombs in his room and a third near completion, plus stocks of exotic

chemicals and powders. His plan, they said, was "blowing up ammunition cars stored in the Jersey railroad terminals." Hoboken police chief
Patrick Hoyes went further and told reporters that he had evidence connecting at least six prominent local German Americans to the plot.[246] The
witch hunts had begun.

Then, in late February, British secret agents informed the White
House that they had intercepted and deciphered a coded message from
Arthur Zimmermann, Germany's foreign minister in Berlin, to the
German ambassador in Mexico. President Wilson released it to the
public on March 1. The Zimmermann Telegram, one short paragraph,
instructed the German ambassador to tell the Mexican government that,
should America enter the war:

> We make Mexico a proposal of alliance on the following basis:
> make war together, make peace together, generous financial
> support and an understanding on our part that Mexico is
> to reconquer the lost territory in Texas, New Mexico, and
> Arizona. The settlement in detail is left to you. . . . Signed,
> ZIMMERMANN.

There was only one way to read the cable: as a direct, official
German threat to dismember the territorial integrity of the United States.
It wasn't lost on Americans that, just two months earlier, four thousand
US Army soldiers had been stationed on the Mexican border hunting the
Mexican revolutionary general Pancho Villa, who had recently killed
eighteen United States citizens during a raid into New Mexico. Threats
on that front were no abstraction.

Any remaining pretense of civility between the two countries disappeared. War now was only a matter of time. The only remaining hesitation on the American side was the public's deep dislike of Russia's tsar
and, to a lesser extent, England's arrogance.

AT THE *FORWARD,* the managing editor on duty that day was Baruch
Charney Vladeck, a Russian-born socialist who had served two prison

terms before fleeing to America in 1908. On reaching the United States, Vladeck had gone west and spent four years traveling, taking odd jobs before landing in Philadelphia, where he joined the *Forward* as manager of its bureau there. He moved to New York in 1916 and, like Trotsky, had settled his family into a small apartment in the Bronx near Crotona Park. He took the subway to work each day.

Unlike Trotsky, though, Vladeck had grown enamored with his new country. He appreciated it as a far better place than autocratic Russia. Out west he marveled at America's natural wonders, describing Yellowstone Park as "God's laboratory." He described how, on his first trip to Philadelphia, he "prayed silently and without a hat in front of Independence Hall."[247] He found New York "large, damned, wild and magnificent." In America, he wrote, "for the first time I felt free to explore the world as I want to see it. . . . I don't love it only as an artist for its colors, but as a citizen feeling that it is mine."[248]

The *Forward* in 1917 operated from a ten-story building it had opened a few years earlier on East Broadway, facing Seward Park, an architectural gem literally towering over the Jewish Lower East Side, twice as tall as any nearby building. Its beaux arts design; its terra-cotta, marbled stone, and stained-glass accents; the bas-relief portraits of Marx, Engels, and German liberal Ferdinand Lassalle on its sides made it a neighborhood landmark. Today, a century later, the building houses luxury apartments valued at more than $1 million apiece. More than a newspaper, the *Forward* used its building as a community center. Before radio or television, people from nearby streets made a point to check its public bulletin boards for news and local gossip. On election nights, crowds of up to forty thousand people congregated there to follow the returns.

Vladeck never let his patriotism interfere with his socialism. He opposed the world war and shared Morris Hillquit's view that Germany could not possibly attack America from across the ocean. But seeing the Zimmermann Telegram cross his desk that day forced him to question these assumptions. Vladeck at first could not quite believe what he was seeing, this purported secret cable from the German foreign minister.

What confounded him most about it was not the deceit it showed but the stupidity. Did the German government really think it could hatch a plot like this and keep it secret? Did it really think that Americans, once they found out, would fail to respond? How arrogant! How European!

Vladeck took pen to paper and wrote a headline in Yiddish: "קען דאָס זיין אז דייטשלאַנד אין ווירקליך בעגאַנגען אזא אידיאָטסקע שטיק דיפּלאָמאַטיע" (Can this be so that Germany is actually performing such an idiotic diplomatic schtick?[1])[iii] He then wrote an article consisting of two sentences:

> If this is true what is being announced today about a German
> plan to unite with Mexico and Japan against the United States,
> it is not only something idiotic, it smells of the worst militarist
> darkness. Every inhabitant of the country would fight to the last
> drop of blood to protect the great American republic against the
> monarchies of Europe and Asia and their allies.[249]

Vladeck told the typesetters to place his brief editorial in a box on the front page where nobody could miss it. He tried to find Abraham Cahan, the *Forward*'s chief editor, to check with him first before finalizing the paper, but Cahan apparently wasn't in the building. So Vladeck ran it regardless, feeling certain Cahan would approve. By the time he finally saw Cahan the next morning and showed him the front page, boys and trucks had already started delivering copies to newsstands and street corners all across New York City.

Trotsky would not have understood the Yiddish script upon seeing copies of the *Forward* being sold on the street that morning. A friend would have pointed it out to him. But once he heard it translated, he erupted. This was no ordinary mistake. Here was the *Forward*, the most widely read socialist daily voice in America, suddenly reversing course and endorsing war with Germany, even encouraging young men to join the army.

---

iii The work "schtick" has no exact English equivalent. It generally refers to a comic routine, its humor often unintentional to the performer.

How could this be? The *Forward* had been one of Trotsky's friendliest outlets since reaching New York City, happily printing his columns and sharing his public stages, giving him a platform to reach hundreds of thousands. It had impeccable socialist credentials. Trotsky even knew managing editor Vladeck and his record of arrests in Russia. Vladeck had joined Trotsky on stage at several of his speeches, translating them into Yiddish for the polyglot crowds. He saw Vladeck in his Bronx neighborhood at the local delicatessen and subway station. Trotsky's own latest Yiddish-language column in the *Forward* had told American workers to choose between internationalism and patriotism, explaining how the two directions were incompatible, "especially [for] the Jewish American workers."[250] Now, seemingly overnight, the *Forward* itself had chosen the wrong way, making itself a "social patriot," no better than the European species.

If this was so, it was an enormous betrayal. Trotsky decided he had no choice but to find out immediately! He would demand an explanation from the man who held ultimate control over the *Forward*, its founder, chief editor, and public face, Abraham Cahan.

There are two versions of what happened next. According to Vladeck's own account, the telephone in Abraham Cahan's office started ringing early that morning, within minutes of the paper hitting the streets, with Trotsky on the line.[251] Another contemporary, writer David Shub, who would spend almost fifty years at the *Forward*, remembered it differently. According to him, Trotsky that morning stormed out of *Novy Mir* on Saint Marks Place, made his way to East Broadway on the Lower East Side, walked into the *Forward* building, found Cahan's office, and barged in.[252]

However it went, by phone or face to face, both versions agree on what happened after that: The exchange degenerated into an angry, high-decibel shouting match, their voices shrill and passionate, faces red, and tempers lost. Trotsky asked Cahan about the front-page box, and Cahan told him that, yes, he had seen it, he had approved it, and it was now the official policy of the *Forward*. At that, Trotsky told Cahan that

he would never again write for the *Forward* and demanded that Cahan
return a draft article he had submitted a few days earlier. But this was
just the start, the bare-bones outline of the conversation.

Abraham Cahan was no pushover. Twenty years older than Trotsky,
Cahan too had a formidable presence and little patience to take lectures
from anyone. As editor of a big-city newspaper, Cahan had plenty of
practice dealing with big egos and prima donnas.[253] Standing several
inches taller than Trotsky, his thick gray hair swept back behind a high
prominent forehead, bushy mustache, and large eyes, Cahan knew from
twenty years of speech making how to raise his voice, shout over hecklers, and demand attention. Beyond that, Abraham Cahan took considerable pride in his credentials as a socialist, journalist, and multilingual
member of the literati, let alone as leader of the Jewish community.
Cahan had been present at the creation of American socialism along
with Eugene Debs, had fought its battles and used his newspaper to
help elect dozens of Socialist candidates from alderman to congressman. His English-language novel *The Rise of David Levinsky* had won
accolades from literary lights including William Dean Howells and
Lincoln Steffens.

And who was this Leon Trotsky, a newcomer editor of a puny
Russian tabloid, to tell him, Abraham Cahan, how to run his newspaper? To question his managing editor? To question his socialism?

Trotsky too was hardly someone to back down. He had his own
impatience with these smug American politicians like Cahan and
Hillquit. "Big shots," they called them, with their comforts, their egos,
their fancy buildings and compromises. They talked socialism, but, push
come to shove, they retreated to cheap patriotic flag waving.

The confrontation lasted no more than a few minutes, but that was
long enough to burn bridges. Trotsky stormed back to his desk at *Novy
Mir*, doubtless sputtering curses along the way. He was not going to
let this affair sit. Over the next three weeks, he wrote five articles for
Novy Mir about Abraham Cahan and the *Forward* and why he had
broken with them. He would accuse Cahan of being an autocrat, out of

touch, encamped in his ten-story building, failing to report party decisions, and being a "social patriot" of the worst order. He would insist that Cahan be expelled from the party, that he had no credibility as a revolutionary.[254] When staffers at the *Forward* apparently claimed that the argument had stemmed from a misunderstanding over a bad translation, Trotsky shot back with the headline не правда! (It's Untrue!)[255]

Twelve years later, writing his memoirs in 1929, Trotsky would still carry the grudge, going out of his way to mention the *Forward,* "with its fourteen-story palace," as "a newspaper with the stale odor of sentimentally philistine socialism, always ready for the most perfidious betrayals."[256]

For Cahan too, the honeymoon was over. On a personal level, the *Forward* would no longer give Trotsky the effusive coverage he had enjoyed to that point, no more interviews or columns. For the longer term, the incident would give Cahan a special insight into the new Russian far left. Cahan would be one of the first major American socialists to denounce the Bolsheviks after they seized power in Russia later in 1917. Speaking in 1923 at a Socialist Party conference, he would denounce Trotsky as a "bombastic windbag" whose physical ailments were "undoubtedly due to his earlier moral collapse" and denounce Lenin as a "muddle head lunatic."[257] When Moscow sympathizers later tried to pressure him to soften his criticisms, he would declare, "I would rather see the *Forward* go under than weaken the struggle against the communists."[258]

More importantly for the near term, Trotsky's courting of the New York socialist world had reached its apogee and hit an abrupt ceiling. No longer was he winning new friends. His rigid ideology had collided with American pragmatism. But Trotsky was no quitter. If he couldn't fit their mold, he would break it.

ONE DAY AROUND this time, Morris Hillquit convened the New York Socialist Party's governing committee for a private meeting to face an important question: If the United States declared war on Germany suddenly, without warning, what would they do? Its members opposed war, but the party, like any large organization, had internal rules and procedures. To act in a pinch, it needed to have a clearly stated policy formally ratified by the members with a proper vote. Once war was declared, it might be too late to adopt one. Government interference might make it impossible.

To fix this problem, they decided to appoint a special committee to meet as soon as possible and draft a resolution. They would then call a public meeting and put the resolution to a vote. To help the committee work quickly, they decided to limit its members to a small working group of seven, representing the diverse wings of the party. It would include Hillquit himself plus two other lawyers, Jacob Panken and Nicholas Aleinikoff; Algernon Lee of the Rand School; and the Finnish journalist and parliamentarian Santeri Nourteva. And to represent the party's left wing, they chose Louis Fraina and Leon Trotsky.

Why Trotsky? No record explaining how or why they made this choice exists. Louis Fraina had no track record in party affairs, but Hillquit knew him as an accomplished journalist and activist. Trotsky spoke for Russian radicals and had built a following with his articles and speeches. Had pressure been applied behind the scenes? Had someone demanded Trotsky be included? Had Trotsky himself insisted on it? Most likely, Hillquit came up with the idea himself as an olive branch, a goodwill gesture to build unity. Excluding them would only risk a party split at the worst possible time. Trotsky might be unreasonable and extreme, but he gave every sign of being a permanent new fixture in New York City. Hillquit would have to find a way to live with him.

These seven, the Resolutions Committee, would meet behind closed doors to hammer out a position.

16

THE COMMITTEE

"You are pitiful, isolated individuals! You are bankrupts. Your role is played out. Go where you belong from now on—into the dustbin of history!"[259]

—Leon Trotsky, to the Mensheviks as they marched out of the Second Congress of Soviets in Petrograd, letting the Bolsheviks prevail, November 7, 1917 (or October 25 on the Russian calendar then in use), the day of the Bolshevik Revolution

"The dance is the earliest form of art because it responds spontaneously to instinct and feeling. . . . The Greeks were a free, joyous people, and their dances swayed to the spirit of the joy of life."[260]

—Louis C. Fraina (writing as Charles Louis) in *Modern Dance*, August–September 1914

TWO REVOLUTIONS HIT New York that week—one uptown, one downtown. As a welcome break, only one involved the world war, and neither directly involved Leon Trotsky.

Downtown, riots broke out, led by mothers and housewives protesting the high cost of food. Meat, onions, potatoes—staples for poor immigrant families—all grew scarce and expensive that winter, a symptom of worsening shortages as the war began paralyzing trade and monopolizing basic goods. Average food prices in America had skyrocketed

44 percent since late 1913, and daily shipments of basic stocks like potatoes and chickens into New York City had dropped precipitously, down 90 percent for potatoes and 50 percent for onions from just a year earlier.[261] Mothers and housewives looked for convenient villains and found plenty to choose from; they accused railroads, grocers, even kosher butcher shops of hoarding food and gouging customers.

Mothers by the thousands began picketing local stores in mid-February, often carrying babies and young children in their arms, first on the Lower East Side and then in the Bronx, Harlem, and Brownsville. Frustration led to violence. Five hundred marched on city hall shouting "Bread! We starve!!" Others threw rocks and bottles at neighborhood grocery stores. Police arrested twenty-five women in the first few days. Protest leaders declared a citywide boycott, shutting down groceries by the dozens, which only worsened shortages. A crowd of fifteen hundred women stormed one shop on Rivington Street, assaulting police with trash cans and showering them with rotten vegetables.

Store owners brandished revolvers and threatened to shoot troublemakers while demanding that Mayor Mitchel call out military reserves. Some even called the women German spies. Grainy photographs of starving mothers and babies in the streets began to appear on newspaper front pages across America and Europe, hardly the image for a country girding for war.

The other revolution occurred uptown, where the Metropolitan Opera House opened its stage for a limited engagement to Isadora Duncan, sensational diva of dance. With flowing silk scarves, sensually athletic barefoot leaps, and exotic sets, Duncan had revolutionized dance on both sides of the Atlantic in the early 1900s. Her mix of fantasy, improvisation, and natural movement broke the mold of classical ballet and traditional stage shows, shocking Victorian-era prudes while fascinating the Greenwich Village avant-garde. Living in London and Paris before the war, she found inspiration at the Louvre and the British Museum, studying paganism, ancient Greek vases, and modern impressionist paintings. Back in New York since 1914, she performed regularly at the Century Theater and was booked to travel on the *Lusitania* on its ill-fated 1915 crossing until financial pressures made her change plans.

For her debut at the Met, Duncan had conceived a new production consisting of what she called "interpretations" or "dance-narratives," a story of struggle set to the music of Caesar Frank's *Symphonic Fragment of the Redemption,* selections from Tchaikovsky, and "The Marseillaise." The show threw reviewers for a loop. Her talent "seems far removed from dancing," one wrote, though he conceded its "obvious and pleasing" visuals.[262] Audiences flocked to her performances, though many walked away more confused than inspired.

Given the choice, Leon Trotsky certainly would have made his way to the dance. Not only did Isadora Duncan appeal to him as an atheist and socialist, but Trotsky also had the best possible guide to her art: his new friend Louis Fraina, now his partner on the Socialist Party's Resolutions Committee. Beyond political work, Fraina until December 1916 had been editor of *Modern Dance* magazine, and he adored Isadora Duncan.

Since meeting him at Ludwig Lore's Brooklyn apartment in January, Trotsky had grown a friendship with Louis Fraina. Fifteen years older, Trotsky took on Fraina first as a protégé. Fraina lived in the Bronx with his common-law wife, Jeanette Pearl, at 3246 Kingsbridge Avenue, an easy subway and streetcar ride from the Trotskys. Seeing each other on the subway, at speeches and party affairs, or with the crowd at the Monopole Café, the two found much in common. Fraina, slim, with a pale mustache and boyish face, was the rare political bird who appreciated popular culture as much as socialist theory. His interests ranged to ragtime, jazz, and the arts; his writing included short stories and reviews of Robert Frost's poetry. Despite his impoverished childhood in the New York slums, he and Trotsky shared passions as writers and cultural savants, including cinema, music, and novels.

But it was politics where their minds truly came together. After *Modern Dance* had ceased publication in late 1916, Fraina started a new job editing the *Internationalist,* the new journal published by the Boston-based Socialist Propaganda League. Its print run, barely one thousand copies, reached a rarified audience. Vladimir Lenin subscribed to it from Europe and paid it a rare compliment: "I have already received No. 1 of The Internationalist," he wrote to Alexandra Kollontai that month from Zurich, "and was very glad to get it."[263] They paid Fraina $100 to start the magazine and a $35 weekly salary, nice money for a left-wing activist in 1917.

When Trotsky tossed out concepts like "mass action" or "dictator-ship of the proletariat," Fraina grasped them intuitively. In 1912, as a twenty-year-old reporter for the *Daily People*, Fraina had traveled to Lawrence, Massachusetts, to cover the epic textile strike there, one of the era's premier labor confrontations in America. Twenty thousand work-ers, mostly Italian and led by IWW leader Big Bill Haywood, had walked off the job, shutting the entire textile industry in eastern Massachusetts, including dozens of companies and factories. They held out for two months without pay. To avoid hardship, striking workers sent their small children to live with volunteer families in New York and Boston, winning waves of public sympathy. Ultimately, they won an industry-wide settlement that included better pay and work rules.

Fraina, already cynical about established politicians, marveled at the discipline of the strikers and recognized their revolutionary potential. "The non-skilled are solid to a man," he reported from the scene. These workers, he wrote, organized, radicalized, and properly "molded in shape," were the ones who could "make a new socialist world."[264] This, to Fraina, was "mass action," his concept similar to what Trotsky him-self had experienced in 1905 Saint Petersburg, the spontaneous revolt of hundreds of thousands of workers and soldiers, a tide strong enough to threaten even the Russian tsar. Fraina had no trouble envisioning an expanded model, a worker-led revolution seizing power in America. All it needed was planning, education, and the right moment.

And again like Trotsky, Fraina saw that potential spark in the fight over American entry into the world war.

With this shared ideology, Fraina and Trotsky also saw eye to eye on one other key point: their mutual impatience with Morris Hillquit and his conservative crowd atop the New York Socialist Party. Fraina resented their nice homes, their profitable law offices, their cars and nights at the theater. To Fraina, these were self-satisfied petit bourgeois appeasers. Hillquit might win a law for an eight-hour workday after enough elections, but he would never be bold enough to actually seize power for the working class. To Fraina, this bordered on treason. Why bother with elections when you can win through revolution or "mass action"?

Hillquit had given an interview to the *New York Times* in mid-February that, to Fraina, showed the whole problem. Talking about possible American entry into the war, Hillquit had told the *Times:* "If our armies are to be recruited by volunteer enlistments, the Socialists, as a whole, will refuse to enlist," but "if the armies are raised by conscription [a mandatory draft], of course we will have to serve as other citizens. I do not believe that the Socialists will advocate any general industrial strike to handicap the country in its war preparations. And I do not believe there will be any such strike."[265]

This, to Fraina and Trotsky alike, sent exactly the wrong signal. As socialists, they would never agree to be docile good citizens if war came. They would fight, strike, resist, refuse to serve, and not hesitate a minute to handicap the country. They owed their loyalty to the working class, not to an American government ruled by its capitalists. Jail was a small sacrifice for the cause.

These two talented men now recognized the opportunity handed them at this pivotal moment. The Socialist Party, by placing them on its Resolutions Committee, had given them the chance to throw a monkey wrench into its own establishment, to expose the Morris Hillquits and Abraham Cahans as frauds, show them as out of touch with the rank and file. And in pressing this case, Fraina brought strengths that Trotsky lacked, especially his ability to write and speak clear English. Fraina could take Trotsky's vision from Europe and translate it for the New World.

This was an opportunity they would not let go to waste.

MORRIS HILLQUIT CONVENED the Resolutions Committee at least three times in late February and early March 1917 to draft the proposed policy statement.[266] The committee met privately. No record exists of what happened inside. No notes or minutes, no newspaper accounts, no descriptions in letters or memoirs—just the fact that they met.

Normally, a committee like this would gather at the Socialist Party's office on East Fifteenth Street, a plain row house near Union Square. The seven committee members, all men, would have sat around a wooden table smoking cigarettes, the door closed against intruders, a noisy steam radiator exacerbating the stuffiness, the winter air too cold for them to open the window more than a crack. Somebody would have brought hot tea. If they had arranged themselves by ideology, Hillquit in his suit and white shirt would have sat alongside Algernon Lee, with Trotsky and Fraina directly opposite, and the three others in between—lawyers Jacob Panken and Nicholas Aleinikoff and Finnish journalist Santeri Nourteva.

On entering the room and before sitting down, they probably tried to act friendly, smiled, shook hands, shared small talk, maybe a laugh or two, maybe clapped each other's shoulders like politicians. But if Hillquit thought this would make things go easier, he hadn't bargained on Leon Trotsky.

Hillquit had been busy in the two weeks since President Wilson had declared armed neutrality in response to Germany's sinking of neutral ships. As part of a group called the Emergency Peace Federation, he had joined a whirlwind trip to Washington, DC, where he and the others visited dozens of congressmen and senators, asking them to block Wilson's ship armament bill or any other attempt to "stampede Congress" into war, as they put it. He had then rushed back to New York City to support the housewives protesting high food costs, speaking at a rally and offering free legal representation to some of the women arrested in the riots. In the middle, Hillquit agreed to yet another public debate on the war, this time with a Columbia law professor for Columbia University students.[267]

At each stop, he made the same point of insisting that socialists remained good American citizens, loyal to the country, not traitors or subversives. Now he wondered if he might need to make the same plea to his own membership.

Once the seven committeemen settled in behind closed doors, there was no avoiding the tensions, even on something as basic as language. Hillquit normally insisted they speak English at party meetings, which should have been no problem this night, since the men in the room spoke excellent English. All but one, that is, Trotsky, who spoke almost none. But Trotsky was not about to shut up while the others talked. He had his translator—his young English-fluent sidekick Louis Fraina—and Trotsky also knew that at least four of the other men spoke Russian perfectly well. Panken, Aleinikoff, and Hillquit had all been born in Russia, and Santeri Nourteva had spoken Russian back home in Finland (then part of the Russian Empire). Only one of the group—Algernon Lee of Dubuque, Iowa—had any excuse not to understand him.

English or not, Trotsky would speak whatever he pleased.

From here, things apparently only got worse. Typically, for a project like this, Hillquit or Lee would have prepared a first draft of a resolution and then shared it with the others to start discussion. In this case, the seven committeemen had plenty on which they all agreed: They all opposed the war, despite German submarine attacks on American ships, and wanted the party to speak out against it. They all agreed that the war benefited capitalists, bankers, and weapons makers while victimizing workers and the poor. They all opposed conscription and crackdowns on dissent. These points alone made them, as socialists, stick out as extremists in the American body politic, dangerous enough given the hysteria against German sympathizers and pacifists. People already had been jailed for less.

But to Trotsky and Fraina, the consensus points barely scratched the surface. No, they said. They wanted more. They insisted on it.

Once Hillquit gave them the floor, Fraina and Trotsky presented their demands, Fraina speaking English in his clear, soft voice; Trotsky interrupting with an occasional Russian comment. Altogether, they wanted to include four points in any resolution on the war: (1) The party must denounce statements like Hillquit's promising loyalty to America in case of war in "bourgeois media" like the *New York Times*. (2) The party must denounce the concept of "national defense" as an excuse for war. They were internationalists, not patriots, and stood for the working class. (3) In all antiwar agitation, the party must separate itself from pacifists unwilling to fight for socialism when the time came. (4) Finally, in case of war, the party must commit itself not only to voicing dissent but also to "mass action" in the way Trotsky and Fraina understood those words: general strikes and street protests designed to physically block conscription, troop movements, and war industries.[268]

As Hillquit and the others listened, it is easy to picture the icy silence and shifting chairs. Hillquit may have anticipated the demands, but hearing them presented to his face by this youngster Fraina and this foreign radical Trotsky—just seven weeks off the boat from Europe—must have given him chills. For Hillquit, they represented his worst fears, a direct challenge to him personally as leader and also to his vision of a Socialist Party, one that could function as a full, equal player in American life. Trotsky and Fraina's demands committed socialists to breaking the law. To Hillquit, this violated bedrock principle. How could they ever get the American public to trust them, to elect a Socialist United States senator or governor, let alone a Socialist president, if they allowed the party to become a criminal syndicate plotting treason against the country?

No, Hillquit told them once he got the chance. He could not accept the demands.

And so it started. They argued and argued some more. All the men spoke up, though the contest ultimately fell onto the two largest personalities in the room, eyeing each other across the table: Hillquit the pragmatist and Trotsky the revolutionary on the cusp of history. "[Trotsky's] verbal duels with Morris Hillquit," Ludwig Lore wrote, hearing about the exchanges later on, "were epic in their violence."[269]

The storm raged for two weeks. The committee would meet behind closed doors and argue over precise wording, trying to forge a resolution that could win a majority vote both inside the room and later from the full party membership. Hillquit would prepare a new draft, Trotsky and Fraina would object, they'd argue again, then a next draft and more objections, each time narrowing the distance by some small amount.

Finally, to break the deadlock, Hillquit and his majority swallowed hard and agreed to accept three of the Trotsky–Fraina planks. Their final resolution would reject the concept of "national defense," reject working with pacifists, and, most painful for Hillquit, "fiercely [condemn] all members of the party who are making patriotic promises in the capitalist press," calling them "enemies of the socialist movement who should not be tolerated as members of the party any longer."[270]

On this last point, this official condemnation stopped short of naming names, but Trotsky left nothing to chance. His *Novy Mir* would fill in the blank and specify the target of this language as Hillquit's own statement to the *New York Times* that "socialists would be loyal in the event war was declared."[271]

But if Morris Hillquit thought he could buy peace with these concessions, once again he hadn't bargained on Leon Trotsky. Trotsky had no interest in peace. He wanted a fight. Why such a hard line? Opportunism? Arrogance? Envy? Looking at Hillquit's crowd, did he simply see the European "social patriots" he resented, the same ones Vladimir Lenin was railing against from Zurich?

A change had taken place. Back in Europe, Trotsky had often cast himself as a reconciler between Bolsheviks and Mensheviks. Just two years earlier, at the 1915 Zimmerwald conference, he had rejected Lenin's hard line on the war for the sake of unity. Now Trotsky no longer cared about unity. Compromise bred weakness. He was becoming a Leninist.

Trotsky and Fraina still had one last demand, their call for illegal "mass action" in case of war, and now they insisted on it. Hillquit finally drew the line. No, he said. If the two radicals wanted to push the American Socialist Party off a cliff by committing it to sabotaging the United States war effort and guaranteeing prison terms for its members, they were on their own, and the rest of the committee agreed with him.

They had reached the end of their rope. There was only one proper way to settle the argument: an open, public meeting where every member of the Socialist Party in New York could come, listen to a debate on the draft resolution, and then express themselves by voting on it, up or down. This was democracy, what they all still claimed to believe in.

For the public meeting, Trotsky and Fraina went to work. Putting their heads together, probably at Trotsky's apartment in the Bronx as Natalya watched the boys, they set about preparing a minority report, basically an alternative to the majority resolution, covering the one last issue. As literature, the minority report would combine Fraina's flowery English with Trotsky's hard line. It committed the party to resist any American war effort, military recruitment, or mobilization with mass meetings, street protests, aggressive propaganda, and preemptive strikes. "We shall not allow the class struggle to relax," it said. "The general revolutionary class struggle shall proceed with new vigor and increased intensity during the period of war." It ended with a call to action, as dramatic and seductive as any prancing leap across the stage by their favorite Isadora Duncan: "No 'civil peace'! No truce with the ruling class! War does not change the issue, but emphasizes it. War against capitalism! On with the class struggle!"[272]

Then they both signed their names to the bottom: Leon Trotsky and Louis C. Fraina.

They tried to assess their strength. Behind the scenes, friends worked the different immigrant factions: Ludwig Lore lobbied the Germans; Weinstein the Russians. "The Letts [or Latvians] were with us to a man," Trotsky wrote. "The Finnish federation gravitated toward us. We were penetrating by degrees into the powerful Jewish federation."[273]

The announcements went out: The New York Socialist Party would hold a general membership meeting to decide how to respond if war were declared. Notices appeared in the *Call*, the *Forward*, the *Volkszeitung*, and all the other socialist papers. Everyone should come to listen and vote. They set the meeting for the next Sunday afternoon—the most convenient time of the week for working people—which happened to be March 4. After they announced the date, though, someone noticed a problem. Trotsky had a conflict. He had agreed to speak that day in Newark, New Jersey, at the Newark Labor Lyceum. Announcements for his Newark speech too had already gone out and appeared in newspapers. Sponsors had started selling tickets at ten cents apiece. He couldn't back out now without great embarrassment.[274]

Had Hillquit deliberately set up this conflict to embarrass Trotsky and keep him away? It's highly doubtful. But even if it was an innocent mistake, Trotsky could not be in two places at once. His young protégé Louis Fraina would have to make the case in his absence. Fraina spoke better English; he understood the issue; and, as the younger partner, he represented the future.

To draw the best crowd, the party picked one of its favorite venues, as easy to reach from Lower Manhattan as from the Bronx, or even by subway from Brooklyn: the Lenox Casino in Harlem.

17

LENOX CASINO

"We should be asses to tell members of Local New York that they must risk death and imprisonment rather than join the army!"[275]

—Morris Hillquit, March 4, 1917, from his address at the Lenox Casino

"Trotsky was convinced—he learned to see his mistake later—that the United States was ripe for the overthrow of the capitalist order, and urged the calling of general strikes against war as a means of undermining the proud structure of our decaying civilization."[276]

—Ludwig Lore, undated

A BLIZZARD HIT NEW York on the day of the big meeting. Sixty hours of snow, sleet, and rain left streets ankle-deep in slush. Crowds jammed the subway, but dripping water caused short circuits that plunged underground stations into fits of darkness. On the surface, horses, cars, and trolleys snarled themselves into gridlock.

But that didn't stop more than two hundred voting members of the New York County Socialist Party from trekking miles across town to have their say on the most important issue in the country: what to do about the world war.

Lenox Casino, a squat, three-story redbrick building, had sidewalk storefronts and big windows letting sunlight into its main upstairs auditorium. The building still stands at the corner of Lenox Avenue (now Malcolm X Boulevard) and 116th Street, just north of Central Park and west of Morningside Park. It is known today as the Malcolm Shabazz Mosque or Masjid, the place where Malcolm X preached for the Nation of Islam until his split from its leader, Elijah Muhammad, in 1964. The building added its signature green dome, arches, and other Islamic touches after that period.

In 1917 the casino still held itself out as a popular neighborhood haunt for music, drinking, card playing, and gambling, still legal in New York. To make extra cash, the owners sometimes rented space to left-wing political group like the Socialists. Hillquit had spoken here two weeks earlier for the women protesting high food prices.

This day the casino buzzed with anticipation as men and women tramped in from the snow; pulled off wet boots, shabby wool coats, scarves, gloves, and fur hats; came upstairs; and warmed themselves with hot tea. All the talk was about the big party split, Trotsky against Hillquit, the radicals against the leaders. They all had opinions. Upstairs, people congregated in small circles between card tables and chairs, talking, laughing, scheming. Hillquit and his friends took one corner; Fraina's friends took another across the room. Russians gathered at a side wall. Ukranians there, Germans here, a Yiddish caucus formed near a window.

It's easy to picture the faces huddled around Fraina that day. He had plenty of friends in the room: Ludwig Lore, his host from the Brooklyn dinner in January; Bukharin, Chudnovsky, and Gregory Weinstein from *Novy Mir;* his Bronx neighbor Dr. Julius Hammer. Only Alexandra Kollontai was missing, having left New York earlier for Norway.

Soon the room filled with smoke from cigarettes and a few pipes and cigars, plus voices in a chaotic mishmash of languages and dialects. At least half a dozen newspapermen joined the crowd, smelling a good story. The only ones missing, it seemed, were police detectives and government spies. America was still at peace, and people remained free to say what they wanted.

As the crowd mingled and bickered over seats, Morris Hillquit, in tie and suit, stood up at the front of the hall and called the meeting to order, shouting to be heard. He, Algernon Lee, and the other party leaders quickly got down to business. Everyone knew what they had come for. Hillquit would have thanked the Resolutions Committee for its hard work, then walked the crowd through the proposed resolution on the war, explaining its key parts, the compromises and clashing points of view, taking questions shouted from around the room, stopping now and then to translate a comment into Russian, German, Yiddish, or some other language.

It didn't take long in this fractious group, though, for things to get complicated. Soon after the introductions, somebody moved for a vote. Just adopt the resolution as is and get it over with. A few people cheered. But at that point, Louis Fraina, surrounded by his claque of friends, rose and announced that he had a minority report to present on behalf of himself and his friend Leon Trotsky. Cheers rose from his part of the room, boos and hisses from other corners. All Trotsky's work speaking and writing in New York over the past few weeks now paid dividends here at the Lenox Casino. His name on the proposition carried weight, his new followers well represented among the hardcore zealots who had braved blizzard and cold to be there at this moment.

But before Fraina could get the words out of his mouth, Morris Hillquit too stood up and demanded the floor. He moved that the minority report be "laid on the table." Quizzical stares shot his way. What did this mean? Somebody had to explain. A motion to table meant putting the report aside. If the motion passed, they would never actually vote on Fraina's minority report, as if it didn't exist.

More questions. Whispers and grumbling. It didn't seem fair. Why stop members from voting? What was Hillquit doing? Didn't he have the votes to win? Hadn't he taken a count? Had the bad weather, the snow and slush, kept his own friends away? Whispers grew into a dull roar, what one reporter described as "the barely covered outrage of part of the assembly."[277]

Seeing this reaction, Hillquit decided to drop the point. He withdrew the motion in a friendly way, but that didn't stop the wrangling.

Somebody else stood up and objected to the absence of a quorum. There weren't enough party members in the room, he argued, to make the meeting official. Someone counted the people present—about two hundred—and in fact, under party rules, they were a few bodies short. Any vote taken that day could be challenged. The point made, nobody seemed to care very much, and they went on regardless.

And so the debate actually began in the packed casino auditorium, a gray winter sky looming outside the window over 116th Street. Fraina, finally given the chance to talk, basked in the attention. He laid out the minority report he had written with Trotsky, speaking with bravado, reading parts aloud and translating sections into other languages so people could understand. When he reached the stirring finish—"War against capitalism! On with the class struggle!"—the crowd this time erupted in loud clashing yeas and nays; cheers, boos, and hisses from different parts of the room. A few friends patted his back and shook his hand. All the noise made it impossible to tell which side, pro or con, had more support.

To oppose Fraina, Hillquit had lined up six speakers, including four members of the Resolutions Committee—himself, Santeri Nourteva, Nicholas Aleinikoff, and Jacob Panken—plus lawyer Louis Waldman and party vice chairman Simon Berlin. Berlin led off the barrage and set the tone. He made no effort to defend the war, defend the country, or even criticize Fraina's goals. Instead, he focused on only one point. Fraina's program of illegal actions meant prison. And no committee of any political party—Socialist or any other—had the right to demand this sacrifice of life or liberty from its members. Any person's decision to break the law was personal, not a matter of party doctrine.

By all accounts, once it started, the debate lasted all day, "protracted" and "passionate,"[278] to one participant "the stormiest meeting I ever witnessed."[279] Fistfights broke out at one point, walkouts, tantrums, shouting and more shouting, speakers interrupted with cheers and boos, catcalls and insults. Two different chairmen had to step aside for failing to keep order.[280]

Louis Waldman, who spoke late in the day against Fraina's proposal, kept the most detailed account of his own speech. "Martyrdom should not be imposed on anyone by the fiat of the Socialist Party," he recalled telling the crowd. "Should the country declare war, should the draft become law, neither this meeting nor the Socialist Party could stop the war nor stop the draft by resolutions or otherwise. Is it democratic for this meeting, composed overwhelmingly of men over military age and those who because of noncitizenship are not subject to the draft, to tell our American young men to resist the draft at the risk of being shot?" Like the others, Waldman ignored the boos and hisses thrown his way to insist that Socialists obey the law. "It is against American and Socialist tradition to tell others to do what one is not called on to do himself," he argued. "Our young men will obey the draft laws."[281]

To this, one draft-age young man named McAlpern shouted back in German that it was "better to sacrifice yourself for your own cause than to be sacrificed by your enemies for an enemy's cause."[282] The crowd cheered again.

Where was Leon Trotsky during all this excitement? The reporter for the *New Yorker Volkszeitung* wrote that Trotsky missed the entire meeting because of his commitment to speak that afternoon in New Jersey.[283] No account of the Lenox Casino debate mentions Trotsky making any public statement that day, highly out of character both for Trotsky personally and as a cosponsor of the minority report. But at least one eyewitness participant remembered seeing Trotsky in the room. Louis Waldman, who spoke for the majority, recalled the nasty look Trotsky gave him after his speech. "As I sat down," he wrote, "Trotsky, who was sitting in front of me, turned and sneered: 'Chauvinist!'"[284]

Could Trotsky possibly have finished his Newark speech early, caught a train back to Manhattan—half an hour away—and then raced up to the Lenox Casino to catch the last hour or so of the meeting? Could the *Volkszeitung* reporter have gotten it wrong? Could Trotsky have started toward Newark but found his train blocked by the blizzard? Could the Newark meeting have been canceled over the bad weather?

There is no mention of Trotsky actually speaking that day in New Jersey in the Newark or New York newspapers. But Trotsky was still a nobody to the larger world in March 1917. Who would have noticed? Who would have cared?

Or could Louis Waldman have simply concocted the scene years later when he wrote his memoirs, either from bad memory or in trying to embellish his story?

Morris Hillquit spoke last, and by the time he stood, night had fallen outside over 116th Street. Inside the casino, people had grown tired of shouting and anxious to finish. Hillquit, long practiced at political contests, didn't waste time repeating all the arguments others had already made. Instead, he made his appeal brief and personal. He pointed to Fraina across the room and, whether there or not, to his senior partner, Trotsky. He probably gave Fraina a compliment for the good fight. But these two, he told the room, were asking everyone else to risk life and liberty to defy the law, not the Russian tsar's arbitrary decrees but the laws of the United States government. And who were these two—Fraina and Trotsky—to make this demand? As one reporter described it, Hillquit turned first to the younger partner. Fraina, just twenty-five years old, "had yet to prove that he was willing to be the martyr he wanted to turn the worker i.e. the party comrades into."

And as for his mentor, Hillquit went on, "Leon Trotsky had ample opportunity to prove what he was talking about and therefore was acquainted well enough with the prisons of Europe. [But even] Trotsky did not remain abroad to be shot for his opinion. Instead he came here," to America.[285]

Finally they called for a vote. After all the hours of speeches and huddles, nobody in the hall misunderstood the implication. They were about to decide whether to turn their Socialist Party into an illegal organization committed to defying the United States government in time of war. Those in favor of the Trotsky–Fraina minority report raised their hands. They counted carefully: 79. Then those opposed raised their hands. Again they counted carefully: 101. Cheers and boos went up from different parts of the room. The minority report was rejected.

Hillquit had won the day. He still controlled his party. His members had refused to see themselves as Russians, their president as a tsar, or to follow a zealous radical to an American Siberia. But his victory was strikingly narrow, a difference of 22 votes out of 180.

It was an accomplishment. "When Trotsky landed here his name was known only to his countrymen and to a handful of German socialists," Ludwig Lore recalled.[286] Now the seventy-nine who had cast their lot with Trotsky and Fraina that day at the Lenox Casino would form a nucleus, a cadre of leftists that would continue to grow until the next major confrontation with party leaders, after the war. By then the world would have changed. Trotsky would be back in Russia, as commissar of war in a Bolshevik government. His American followers would be stronger and no longer cater to establishment socialists. They would win easily. Trotsky, in his few weeks in New York, had nurtured the embryo of what would become the American communist movement.

As for the socialist leader he had just defied, he had little sympathy. Trotsky would write sarcastically of him: "A Babbitt of Babbitts is Hillquit, the ideal Socialist leader for successful dentists."[287]

Hillquit, in his own ample memoirs, in talking about those days in New York City, would not bother to mention Trotsky's name at all.

18

RUSSIA

"We are provincials no longer. The tragic events of the thirty months of vital turmoil through which we have just passed have made us citizens of the world. There can be no turning back. Our own fortunes as a nation are involved whether we would have it so or not."

—President Woodrow Wilson, March 5, 1917

O N MONDAY NIGHT, the Socialist Party leaders celebrated. They met for a theater party, planned long before their victory in the Lenox Casino. The *New York Call* and the Rand School jointly had reserved the entire auditorium for that night's performance of the Washington Square Players at the Comedy Theater at New York University. It was a fund-raising gala, and at $2 per ticket (about $60 in modern money) for about five hundred seats, they made a fine haul.

During the play's intermission, the lobby swarmed with smartly dressed couples laughing and joking, clinking glasses of wine or champagne. The Hillquits, the Algernon Lees, the Abraham Cahans, the Louis Boudins all came. Even Anna Ingerman, the woman who had stood up for the Red Cross, came with her husband. "Everybody knew everybody," the *Call* wrote in describing its own affair. "All good friends of both these socialist organizations" made an appearance, it reported, with the mood "a tide of comradely spirit."[288]

But read the long list of attendees, and two names fail to appear: Leon Trotsky and Louis Fraina.

In the small esoteric world of New York socialists, Leon Trotsky had walked away from the Lenox Casino with his celebrity only increased. Whether he actually reached the casino on time for the vote, had shown up for the tail end or not at all, newspapers the next day, from *Novy Mir* to the *New York Times,* all described the pivotal contest as being over the Trotsky–Fraina minority report, with its dramatic 101–79 vote. Trotsky had stood up to the party leaders, argued them to a standstill, and come within two dozen votes of beating them.

The socialist establishment might have "proclaimed a blockade against me," as Trotsky put it later—no invitations to theater parties or fancy dinners—but this only made him more popular with the rank and file.[289] Now, in the aftermath, the controversy had won him a new friend, by far the biggest socialist celebrity in America, far more prominent than Morris Hillquit or any of the other local power brokers: Eugene Victor Debs.

Debs had come to New York that week to give three speeches against the world war, culminating in a mass rally at Cooper Union on Thursday night, March 8. One of his first calls in Manhattan was to Leon Trotsky. Debs wanted Trotsky to stand with him on the podium at Cooper Union.

Eugene Debs held a special place in the pantheon of American politics of that era. He had won more than nine hundred thousand votes— 6 percent of the popular vote at the time—running for president of the United States as the Socialist candidate in 1912, against a crowded field including Woodrow Wilson, Theodore Roosevelt, and William Howard Taft.[iv] He had reached all wings of the highly fractious socialist world— radicals and moderates. Tall and lanky, with an exotic speaking style, with arms flailing like windmills, he appealed with both his personality and his record. Lawyer Clarence Darrow, who had defended Debs against conspiracy charges after the Pullman strike, called him "an intelligent, alert, and fearless man,"[290] and Debs could match Trotsky almost point by point on his record of facing down authorities.

---

iv By comparison, Ralph Nader won 2.7 percent of the popular vote running as an independent for president in 2000, Ross Perot won 18.9 percent in 1992, George C. Wallace 13.5 percent in 1968, Strom Thurmond 2.4 percent in 1948, and Henry Wallace 2.37 percent, also in 1948.

Debs, from Terre Haute, Indiana, had learned his cynicism toward American capitalists in the 1890s organizing the American Railway Union, the country's first successful industry-wide union, and leading it on the epic 1894 Pullman strike, ultimately a boycott of all trains carrying Pullman cars. At its height, Debs's union, together with sympathy strikers, had managed to engage more than two hundred thousand workers and to shut down virtually all rail traffic around Chicago and points west, with minimal violence until the United States government intervened to break the strike on the pretext of protecting postal service. Once troops arrived, including some twelve thousand US Army soldiers backed by marshals and local police, riots, fires, and gunfights ensued, killing at least thirty strikers. Afterward, local prosecutors jailed Debs, charging him with conspiracy and contempt.

But much like Trotsky after the 1905 uprising in Saint Petersburg, Debs, with Clarence Darrow leading his defense team, used the trial as a platform to expose the railroad owners and their own conspiracy to crush the union. He would spend six months in prison for the episode.

As founding leader of the Socialist Party, Debs often feuded with Hillquit's New York circle on policy and tactics. Debs had sat out the 1916 presidential election, but now the world war had energized him all over again. As Debs saw it, the prospect of the country entering Europe's bloodbath, forcing workers to kill and be killed for no good reason other than to protect financial interests, was an outrage. To him, this was no time to moderate. He liked the fight he saw in this Leon Trotsky.

Reaching Cooper Union that night, Trotsky had to fight his way through the dense crowd packing the hall, paying fifteen cents apiece to sit or stand in the aisles. He found a seat reserved for him on the stage among party headliners such as Executive Secretary Julius Gerber and westerner Joseph D. Cannon. There were no seats for Morris Hillquit, Algernon Lee, or any of their circle.

As Trotsky recalled it, on meeting Debs, the older man "embraced me and kissed me" without hesitation.

Once Debs started talking, he left no doubt where he stood on the Trotsky–Hillquit divide. "Speaking for myself," he shouted, "I shall absolutely refuse to go to war for any capitalist government on this earth. I have made my choice. I would . . . rather be lined up against a wall and shot for treason to Wall Street than live as a traitor to the working class." Debs would mount a general strike to paralyze all industry, he told them. As for timid politicians, "I implore you not to wait for your leaders to unite you—many of them have more interest in drawing their salaries than in your emancipation." Far from being afraid of being labeled a lawbreaker, he declared: "I am a traitor to a government that protects slavery."[291]

Recriminations came quickly. Moderate socialists lined up the next day to denounce Debs, calling him "grievously mistaken" to think he spoke for the Socialist Party on the issue. Socialist Congressman Meyer London of New York and writers Charles Edward Russell and William English Walling all condemned the speech; Russell sent a cable to the *New York Tribune* describing Debs's notion of a general strike as "absurd and preposterous." Walling went further and accused even Morris Hillquit of taking orders from Berlin, "being hand and glove with German socialists."[292]

But let them rant. Trotsky could not have been happier. Debs had given him clear vindication for the battle. Trotsky would later praise Debs for his "quenchless inner flame" and "captivating personality," writing, "The old man did not belong to the 'drys.'"[293] His only flaw, to Trotsky, was that Debs "succumbed to the influence of people who were in every respect his inferiors."[294]

THAT SAME NIGHT, March 8, 1917, as Trotsky stood at the podium of Cooper Union Hall sharing hugs with Eugene Debs, a chain of events began to unfold in Petrograd,[v] Russia, eight thousand miles away. They

---

v The city of Saint Petersburg changed its name to Petrograd in 1914 at the outset of the World War to sound less German.

would utterly change the course of history for Trotsky, Russia, and the world. Food riots broke out, which was not new in itself. Famine, war-induced shortages, and winter cold all had conspired to make living conditions deplorable. Tsar Nicholas II, from his military headquarters in Moghilev—about four hundred miles west of Moscow—ordered Russian soldiers to crush the protests. The tsar also issued two ukases, or imperial decrees, one immediately suspending the Russian Duma, the other suspending his own Imperial Council. Otherwise, an eerie silence prevailed. European capitals found that normal news reports and cables from Moscow and Petrograd had ceased to arrive. Large shipments of Russian gold, including some smuggled out under anonymous accounts, began reaching Western banks. Rumors spread that rail service had been cut off. Otherwise, nothing.

It would take a full week, until late on Thursday, March 16, for the full impact to play out and news to reach Western Europe and cross the Atlantic. It hit like a thunderbolt: GREAT RUSSIAN REVOLUTION; CZAR NICHOLAS ABDICATES, read the next morning's front page of William Randolph Hearst's *New York American*, in print so large that the headline covered half the page. REVOLUTION IN RUSSIA; CZAR ABDICATES; MICHAEL MADE REGENT, EMPRESS IN HIDING; PRO-GERMAN MINISTERS REPORTED SLAIN, announced the *New York Times*. "Czar Abdicates and Flees, Ministers Imprisoned and Duma Rules Russia, 1,000 Killed in Street Battle in Petrograd," echoed the *New York Call*.

Details would take days to untangle, but immediate Western reactions seemed almost universally positive. "The new national Cabinet contains the best thought and energies of the nation," commented the *New York Evening Post*. "Today the unparalleled assets of the Empire are in the hands of her honest and her ablest men."[295] Alexander Kerensky, Russia's new interim justice minister, as one of his first acts, promptly declared amnesty for political refugees.

By this time, March 1917, Leon Trotsky and his common-law wife, Natalya Sedova, had not seen their homeland in more than ten years. It was time to go home, if the powers that be would let them.

Front page of the *Forward* showing Trotsky on his first day in America. The *Forward*'s daily circulation of 200,267 made it one of the most widely read papers in New York of any language.

LIBRARY OF CONGRESS, HEBRAIC.

Natalya Sedova, Trotsky's common-law wife and mother of his two sons Sergei and Lyova.

▲ New York in early 1917, seen from Brooklyn, a city uniquely free as America had kept itself out of Europe's disastrous World War. *THE OUTLOOK, 1917.*

◀ Alexandra Sokolovskaya, Trotsky's first wife whom he married in a Moscow prison and had two daughters with in Siberian exile. Sitting in front is young Grisha Ziv. MARXIST.ORG.

Morris Hillquit, leader of the American Socialist Party in New York City. LIBRARY OF CONGRESS, PRINTS AND PHOTOGRAPHS.

Ludwig Lore, editor of the influential socialist German-language *New Yorker Volktzeitung.*

Louis C. Fraina

Boudin walks out

Louis Fraina, young leftist theorist and Trotsky's protégé in challenging the American socialist establishment.

Louis Boudin, socialist lawyer who joined Trotsky for dinner on his first night in America. These three drawings by cartoonist Robert Minor appeared in *The Liberator* as part of its coverage of the Communist and Communist Labor conventions in Chicago, August 1919.

Abraham Cahan, editor of the *Forward*, the country's largest socialist daily in 1917. LIBRARY OF CONGRESS, PRINTS AND PHOTOGRAPHS.

Baruch Vladeck, left, managing editor of the *Forward* in February 1917 who wrote the front-page editorial prompting the newspaper's historic break with Trotsky, seen with Jacob Pankin, second from right, a member of the 1917 Socialist Party resolutions committee, and, on right, Norman Thomas, its five-time candidate for president. FORWARD ASSOCIATION.

▲ Anna Ingerman, who argued with Trotsky over his criticism of the Red Cross in February 1917, with her husband, Dr. Sergius Ingerman, a board member of *Novy Mir*. INGERMAN PAPERS, TAMIMENT LIBRARY.

▶ Algernon Lee, head of the leftist Rand School for Social Research and ally of Morris Hillquit, with his wife Matilde. INGERMAN PAPERS, TAMIMENT LIBRARY.

Louis Waldman, socialist lawyer who opposed Trotsky's anti-war resolution in March 1917 and whom Trotsky berated at the Monopole Café on Second Avenue as an evil "social patriot."

Sir William George Eden Wiseman, Britain's top intelligence officer in New York City until his confusing performance in the Trotsky affair. LIBRARY OF CONGRESS, PRINTS AND PHOTOGRAPHS.

Alexander Israel Lazeravich Helphand, known as Parvus, socialist theorist turned capitalist speculator and German agent, eager to help Lenin and Trotsky with their revolution whether they wanted his help or not. SOURCE UNKNOWN.

Vladimir Lenin, Trotsky's mentor, then later his rival in Russian radical émigré circles, seen here in 1903 around the time of the Bolshevik-Menshevik split. LIBRARY OF CONGRESS, PRINTS AND PHOTOGRAPHS.

Lenin, seen after the 1917 revolution with Trotsky's other rival Joseph Stalin.

Alexandra Mikhailovich Kollontai, seen here in the 1930s as Soviet Ambassador to Sweden, who toured America in 1916 and in 1917 joined the *Novy Mir* circle with Trotsky in New York.

77 Saint Marks Place, as seen in late 1917 when its basement housed the offices of *Novy Mir*, the small Russian tabloid that Trotsky helped edit in New York City. *THE OUTLOOK*, 1917.

► Nikolai Bukharin, future top leader in post-1917 Bolshevik Russia, who worked with Trotsky in New York editing *Novy Mir*. LIBRARY OF CONGRESS, PRINTS AND PHOTOGRAPHS.

▼ Leading figures at the 1904 International Socialist Congress in Amsterdam, including Morris HIllquit (USA, front, second from right), Rosa Luxembourg (Poland, the only woman), George Plekhanov (Russia, to her front left), Sen Katayama (Japan, to Plekhanov's right), and Karl Kautsky (Germany, rear, second to right from Luxembourg). FORWARD ASSOCIATION.

ACT III:
AND REVOLUTION

19

THE WHIRLWIND

"The struggle for freedom in Russia . . . has ended at last in the complete triumph of democracy. For the first time in more than a millennium the Russian people are free from despotic control, and are at liberty to shape their future destiny with their own hands and in their own way."

—George Kennan, the *Outlook*, March 1917

"All these are facts, big facts. [They] give the bourgeoisie of Europe and America occasion to say that the revolution has been won and is now complete. . . . Yet they are all amazingly stupid when they come to deal with mass-movements."[296]

—Leon Trotsky, *Novy Mir*, March 17, 1917

THE NEWS REACHED Trotsky late Thursday, March 15, at *Novy Mir* on Saint Marks Place. That afternoon, as he, Bukharin, and the others were finalizing the next morning's edition, telephones started to ring. They heard excited knocks at the door, messengers delivering telegrams, people poking in their heads: "Have you heard?" "What do you know?" The rumors sounded incredible. Chaos in Petrograd! Ministers jailed!

From the street came excited shouts. Celebrations were erupting all across New York's vast immigrant neighborhoods: Harlem, the Bronx, Brooklyn, especially the Lower East Side. Spontaneous parades, rounds of drinks, songs and dancing spread like wildfire with the news. One parade carrying red flags grew so boisterous that it degenerated into a riot at Clinton and Houston Streets, as people threw bricks and bottles and smashed windows until police broke them up with clubs.

At the Monopole Café, Trotsky's favorite haunt on Second Avenue, a reporter found "the greatest rejoicing and enthusiasm," people drinking toasts, one after the other.[297]

Inside the cramped basement office, Trotsky, Bukharin, Chudnovsky, and Weinstein—all veterans of the tsar's prisons and Siberian exiles—must have whooped with delight. Like newsmen around the world, they had to rip up the *Novy Mir* front page they had laid out for the next morning and make a new one. Huge Cyrillic block letters would cover the top third: Революція В6 Россіи (Revolution in Russia).[298]

Reporters from English-language newspapers were among the first to besiege the small office, looking for anyone Russian who could explain what had just happened. "The American press was in a state of utter bewilderment," Trotsky recalled of that day.[299] Writing about it years later, he remembered snippets of conversation. "A cablegram has arrived saying that Petrograd has appointed a Guchkov-Miliukuff ministry. What does this mean?" Names popped up: Miliukov, Kerensky, Lvoff, the grand duke, the tsarevich. Who were these people? The phone kept ringing.

"Journalists, interviewers, reporters, came from all sides to the offices of the Novy Mir," he wrote.[300] William Randolph Hearst's *New York American* would carry analysis from the tiny socialist *Novy Mir* for two days running

From the fragmentary reports, they quickly pieced together the situation: The food riots in Petrograd, started a week earlier, had exploded during the news blackout. Street crowds had grown to almost two hundred thousand by the second day and had begun attacking government buildings, setting fire to the Ministry of Justice. Police and protesters traded gunfire in the streets, with police shooting protestors from machine gun nests mounted on rooftops. Hundreds were killed. Finally, members of the thirty-thousand-strong Petrograd garrison had mutinied, turning against their commanders. Soon soldiers and protestors roamed the streets together, calling each other "comrade." They started arresting ministers and broke into the elegant Tauride Palace, where the Duma sat, hoping to join forces. In the chaos, the Duma, which the tsar had personally suspended a few days earlier, decided to assert itself. A group of Duma deputies declared a republic and placed its own leaders in the top positions.

At the same time, a Soviet of Workers Deputies—a reincarnation of Trotsky's own Petrograd Soviet from 1905—pulled itself into existence, commandeered its own space in the Tauride Palace, and claimed to speak independently for the people. In addition to leaders from factories and workhouses, its members included several local Mensheviks and even a few Bolsheviks.

At the height of the crisis, two Duma leaders—Alexander Guchkov and Vasili Shulgin—had raced across the frontier and found Tsar Nicholas II in his imperial railroad car at Pskov, near the Estonian border. Here they confronted him. Nicholas, facing overthrow, offered to surrender the throne in favor of his thirteen-year-old son, Tsarevich Alexei Nikolaevich. But he quickly reversed himself after his son's doctors explained that young Alexei, a hemophiliac, could die from the strain. Nicholas then agreed to abdicate in favor of his younger brother, Grand Duke Michael Alexandrovich. This too failed. Grand Duke Michael, hearing the offer, refused to take power without a mandate from the people, fearing that he too could be killed or overthrown. Such as mandate was impossible though, since an elected constituent assembly could not meet for several months.

Just like that, three hundred years of Romanov rule in Russia came to an abrupt end. In its wake, power suddenly shifted to a fragile new structure, an ad hoc committee of moderate and liberal Duma deputies calling itself a provisional government.

HEARING THE NEWS, one of Trotsky's first reactions was to commandeer the telephone in the hectic *Novy Mir* office and call his apartment in the Bronx. Natalya answered the phone. She had spent the day caring for their nine-year-old son Sergei, home from school with a fever that a doctor had diagnosed as diphtheria. When he told her, she too let out a yelp. She told little Sergei, and the two of them celebrated together in his room. Sergei, after a lifetime of hearing his parents tell stories about Russia and the movement, understood instantly. "He jumped to his feet and danced on the bed," as Trotsky described it.[301]

Talking it over, it didn't take Trotsky and Natalya long to reach a decision. Thousands of Russian émigrés and their families, hearing the news, were weighing the same question that night. Ten weeks in New York had given Trotsky and Natalya time to rest, enjoy comforts, make friends, and dabble in local affairs. But their new roots could hardly eclipse the commitment of a lifetime. Trotsky had been writing about revolution in Russia, talking about it, planning for it, anticipating and encouraging it, for the better part of twenty years. It had been his consuming passion.

Besides, once America entered the world war, crackdowns against radicals like him could easily land him in prison in New York, just as they had in Europe.

If revolution finally had come to Russia, he and she both needed to be there. "We were anxious to leave by the first boat," he recalled.[302]

IN THE INITIAL glow, hardly anyone in America seemed to shed a tear for the fallen tsar. By themselves, cheers from Russian immigrants in New York, Chicago, San Francisco, and other large cities were almost deafening. Fifteen thousand people jammed Madison Square Garden that Tuesday night for a huge celebration sponsored by the Socialist Party. Morris Hillquit, *Forward* editor Abraham Cahan, Algernon Lee, and dozens of local bigwigs mounted the stage as people in the hall waved red flags. A huge banner announced, "Greetings to the New Russia!" They sang "The Star-Spangled Banner" and "America" along with a teary, nostalgic rendition of the old Volga boatman's song "Ey Uchnjem."

Hillquit too was besieged by English-speaking reporters after the news broke, and he had no trouble explaining his feelings about the revolution, which were all entirely positive: "The [Russian] people were tired of war, deprivation, and particularly of the mismanagement and graft," he said in a statement.[303] To the Madison Square Garden crowd, he predicted a quick end to the European war, as Germans too would soon "dispose of the Hohenzollerns [the German royal family of Kaiser Wilhelm] and their junkers as the Russian people has disposed of the Romanovs." And more: "The Russian Revolution is the first bright ray of light that has come to us from Europe since the dark days of August 1914."[304]

And the cheering went far beyond socialists and immigrants and far beyond just New York City. London, Paris, and Washington all joined the celebration. The new provisional government, in one of its first actions, pledged to continue Russia's fight against Germany in the world war, news that delighted British and French leaders, who had long fretted over Russia's military failures. Privately, they blamed the tsar for incompetence and considered his court riddled with German spies. Now, with cables from Petrograd reporting dozens of pro-German ministers being fired or jailed, they too applauded.

On financial markets, Russian rubles soared in value. Even conservative Orthodox clergymen seemed happy with the change. At New York's Russian Cathedral on East Ninety-Seventh Street, Archbishop Evdokim Meschensky conspicuously omitted the tsar's name from his Sunday service for the first time anyone could remember.

Alexander Kerensky, justice minister in the new Russian regime, stoked the enthusiasm even further by promising sweeping reforms. He declared immediate freedom for political prisoners, and police began releasing hundreds from jail cells in Moscow and Petrograd and from exile in Siberia.

Kerensky also declared amnesty for overseas political refugees and legal equality for Russian Jews. This last point brought a quick response from Jacob Schiff, head of New York's Kuhn Loeb banking house, who had used his fortune to protest Russia's violent anti-Semitism, even to the extent of blocking war loans and funding anti-tsarist propaganda. Schiff now sent an urgent telegram to the *Evening Post* from White Sulphur Springs, West Virginia, where he was visiting, praising the new government and pledging financial support. "With the shackles removed from a great people," he wrote, "Russia will before long take rank financially among the most favored nations in the money markets of the world."[305]

The good feeling reached all the way to President Woodrow Wilson in the White House. As Wilson saw it, not only had the tsar's overthrow removed a terrible dictator from the world stage, but it also cleared a major stumbling block for what had become his own biggest headache: how finally to bring America into the European war.

All that month, German submarines had continued to sink one American ship after another: the *Algonquin* on March 12; the *City of Memphis,* the *Vigilante,* and the *Illinois,* all on March 13; the *Healdton* on March 18; and others. Two more spy plots had exploded in newspaper headlines in early March, sparking fresh waves of public outrage. In one, rumors that German agents planned to dynamite the dam in Boonton, New Jersey, sent dozens of policemen racing to the scene. The Boonton Dam held back seven billion gallons of water for the Jersey City Reservoir; an explosion there could have flooded the entire Rockaway and Passaic Valleys, wiping out dozens of towns, villages, and munitions plants. The blast never came, but that didn't stop the fear. The panic had been based on reports from a handful of witnesses who claimed to see a German officer walking along the reservoir with a camera and one who claimed to overhear him talking about the plan in a diner.[306] The other plot, a supposed attempt to blow up Fort Totten near Bayside, Long Island, again with no actual explosion, also sent dozens of policemen scrambling to the scene.[307]

Now, with the tsar removed and a new regime promising freedom, Wilson could openly side with Britain and France in the war without having to connect himself to the odious Russian autocrat. Joining the Entente would now mean fighting for a new free Russia, a cause everyone could embrace. The White House would grant the new provisional government formal diplomatic recognition within the week.

FREEDOM, DEMOCRACY, AND a new open government. Wide global support. Possible victory in the war. Americans applauded the news from Petrograd. They saw the revolution as a rousing success and a great step for mankind. Who could complain about such a wonderful thing? Everyone seemed happy.

But not Leon Trotsky and his circle at *Novy Mir,* the radical fringe within even the small cloistered world of New York socialism. They didn't see it quite that way. They celebrated too, but for a different reason. To them, the revolution in Russia, wonderful to a point, amounted to no victory. Instead it remained incomplete, a prelude to something else, an opening scene in a larger drama.

That very first night, just hours after the first reports, Trotsky, working late with the others in *Novy Mir*'s basement office, found himself greeting yet one more English-speaking newspaper reporter who had rushed down to Saint Marks Place looking for an expert on Russia. He identified himself as from the *New York Times,* though we don't know his name. His stories ran without a byline, typical back then. He may have been the same *Times* reporter who had covered Trotsky at the Lenox Casino in the vote over the Trotsky–Fraina minority report. He seemed to recognize Trotsky, asked for him by name, and called him Leo.

Trotsky, doubtless sipping hot tea in the late-night hours, sat down with him amid the clutter of desks, books, and piles of papers. Someone translated.

What did Trotsky think of the new regime in Petrograd? Trotsky answered him flatly: They "do not represent the interests or the aims of the revolutionists." And more. Its days were numbered. It will "probably be short lived and step down in favor of men more sure to carry forward the democratization of Russia."[308]

What was the problem?

Trotsky could have talked all night on this question. He, Bukharin, and the others had been at it for hours. Yes, the people had toppled the tsar, but look who held power now. Not the workers or soldiers who had risked their lives in the streets of Petrograd, as they'd told the men from the *World*, the *American*, and the *Call*. The people had been cheated. Instead power had been snatched by a small group of bourgeois liberals, tsarist apologists who had ignored corruption for years, ignored starvation in their own streets, and already committed Russia to continue the world war despite the country's terrible losses. "The people will not be satisfied."[309]

For Trotsky, this fine revolution presented the chance of a lifetime to achieve socialism in Russia and perhaps all Europe. But so far, it had been hijacked.

Just look at the top people in the provisional government. Trotsky knew them all, and he likely ticked off the names on his fingertips sitting in the cramped office late that night, eyes flaring, words dancing from his lips in rapid Russian. Prince Georgy Yevgenyevich Lvoff, the prime minister, was a nobleman, longtime bureaucrat, and supporter of constitutional monarchy. Alexander Guchkov, the new minister of war and navy, owned an insurance company and, as a conservative Octobrist (supporter of Tsar Nicholas's October 1905 program of limited constitutional reforms), had served as the tsar's Duma speaker. And so on down the list. They were the "liberal element," composed of "industrial leaders and the landed aristocracy," as *Novy Mir* would describe them, not much better than the tsar himself.[310]

Only one, Alexander Kerensky, the new justice minister, drew any nice words from the *Novy Mir* crowd. Kerensky, as a young socialist lawyer, had defended revolutionaries jailed by police during the 1905 uprising and had spent time behind bars as a result. Kerensky still called himself a socialist and served as vice chairman of the new Petrograd Soviet, a far better credential to Trotsky than his seat in the Duma.

But Kerensky was the exception. More typical to Trotsky was Paul Miliukov, the new foreign minister. Trotsky could have spent hours talking about Miliukov alone. It was Miliukov in 1906 who had first used Trotsky's name as an "ism" and an insult, blaming the "revolutionary illusions of Trotskyism" for the tumult then plaguing Russia.[311] Trotsky had returned the favor many times, such as accusing Miliukov of hiding atrocities committed by Russian-backed Serbian militias during the 1912–13 Balkan Wars, which Trotsky had witnessed as a news correspondent.[312]

Miliukov, a gray-haired academic with a wide face, pince-nez glasses, and a distinctive bushy mustache, had himself been jailed by tsarist police during the 1890s after a student riot. He had written several books and had delivered course lectures at the University of Chicago in 1903. Miliukov had cofounded the Russian reformist Constitutional Democrat (Kadet) Party in 1905 and had represented it in the Duma ever since but had abandoned any radicalism after the tsar cracked down on political liberties in 1907. Since then, Miliukov had served as a mostly loyal deputy and strong backer of the military. On Nicholas II's abdication, it was Miliukov who had insisted that the tsar's brother, Archduke Michael, take power to preserve the Romanov line, preferring a sitting tsar—a constitutional monarchy modeled perhaps on Britain's—over anarchy.

This, to Trotsky, was the provisional government: capitalist, militarist, and royalist. Not much to like.

But then there was the other side to the story. The Petrograd revolution had set powerful forces in motion. Chaos meant opportunity. Just down the hall from the provisional government, in the same Tauride Palace, sat the new Petrograd Soviet, what Trotsky called the "genuine face" of the people, already "raising a voice of protest against the liberal attempt to rob the Revolution."[313] If Trotsky and his cobelievers could only get back in time, they could still refight 1905, but this time on the winning side.

All this revolutionary theory, though, hardly mattered to the *New York Times* reporter that night. Knowing his readers, he quickly turned to how the tsar's fall might affect the world war. He filed just a short piece the next morning: CALLS PEOPLE WAR WEARY: BUT LEO TROTSKY SAYS THEY DO NOT WANT SEPARATE PEACE.[314]

All that week, Trotsky carried the same message of incomplete revolution through a blizzard of newspaper columns and speeches. He appeared before audiences almost every night, starting Friday at Beethoven Hall. His rallies had a sentimental flavor, with thousands packing the halls to see friends and share memories of Russia and the underground. They waved red flags, shouted themselves hoarse, drank plenty of schnapps, and sang songs like the "Pochorny Marsh" and "The Marseillaise."[315] "The mothers of Russia started the Revolution with their food riots," Trotsky told the crowd at Beethoven Hall, making it a family affair.[316] Typically, his rally Tuesday at the Lenox Casino on 116th Street, pulling in more than two thousand people despite taking place the same night as Hillquit's mass meeting at Madison Square Garden, featured seven different speakers in seven different languages, including Trotsky in Russian, Ludwig Lore in German, Louis Boudin in English, and Santeri Nourteva in Finnish.

Beneath the show and rhetoric, a movement was sprouting. Thousands of Russian immigrants in America suddenly wanted to go home. Many, like Trotsky, were radicals hoping to stir revolution. But not all. With the tsar gone and freedom in the wind, Russia sounded like a changed, welcoming place. Nostalgia, longing for lost homes and separated families, the chance to build a new life in an idealistic free country drew many homesick immigrants. At every rally, whether with Leon Trotsky or Morris Hillquit, they passed the hat to raise money for Russian émigrés wanting to return. One new group, calling itself the Executive Russian Committee, announced plans to raise $2 million to pay passage for as many as three hundred thousand exiles.[317] *Russkoe Slovo,* another small Russian-language newspaper in New York, also took up a collection. Almost ten thousand ultimately made the trip back.

Looking at the crowd at the Lenox Casino rally, though, Trotsky might have noticed an unfamiliar face, a squat man with a mustache and balding head talking Russian with the others, his eyes scanning the room, noticing faces and catching names. Casimir Pilenas didn't applaud much. He came because he had a job to do. He worked for an organization in New York suddenly very interested in these radical revolutionary celebrations. American authorities might still be oblivious, but not Pilenas's employer, the head of Britain's MI1c counterintelligence bureau at 44 Whitehall.

20

SPIES AGAIN

WILLIAM GEORGE EDEN Wiseman, the stylish young British baronet with the wide face, neatly combed hair, trimmed mustache, and tweed suits who ran Britain's intelligence operation in New York City, could not have been happier at the news, both from Washington and from Russia.

Wiseman had built a formidable bureaucratic empire around his office at the southern tip of Manhattan Island. Still under cover of the British Munitions Ministry, Wiseman had now gone far beyond the usual counterespionage work of arranging guards for munitions ships and tracking suspicious Germans. He had made himself one of Britain's top diplomats in America, the chief behind-the-scenes link between his country and President Woodrow Wilson's White House, a relationship built on Wiseman's budding friendship with Wilson's New York–based confidante Colonel Edward M. House.

To make this connection with Colonel House, Wiseman, the one-time college boxer and German gas-attack survivor, had to shove aside a rival. His name was Captain Guy Reginald Gaunt, the British naval attaché and chief intelligence officer in New York since 1914 who already had the same job. Others described Gaunt, a former battleship commander originally from Australia, as a "bon vivant" and "romantic." Gaunt himself called it the "breezy sailor act."³¹⁸ He made the mistake of taking an extended personal leave over the Christmas and New Year's holidays into January 1917. In Gaunt's absence, Wiseman had stepped in and displaced Gaunt's relationship with Colonel House and restructured the office to eclipse much of Gaunt's intelligence role. Gaunt, returning to find himself shut out from much of his earlier portfolio, complained bitterly about Wiseman, but to no avail. The British brass and the American Colonel House both decided they liked the new arrangement. Gaunt, to his annoyance, had to accept it. He would carry sore feelings about the incident for years.[319]

But Wiseman, as a result, now rubbed elbows with top figures on both sides of the Atlantic: the British Foreign Office, the American president, and "C," his mysterious boss at MI1c. When British ambassador Sir Cecil Spring-Rice complained about security at his embassy in Washington, DC—loose door locks and suspicious German-speaking neighbors—he called Wiseman to come fix things. Along the way, Wiseman's team in New York had broken a major India-based sabotage ring and accumulated files on thousands of potential troublemakers, according to internal reports.[320] His paid staff soon reached between thirty and forty people.

With America now almost certain to enter the European war, Wiseman spent much of his time courting US diplomats, police, and military intelligence, passing tips on everything from German submarine sightings to British shipping procedures.[321]

And a new question had promised to expand his role even further: What to do about all these Russians?

Wiseman had no special background in Russian affairs before reaching New York City in 1915, but he could hardy miss noticing how the Petrograd revolution had galvanized local immigrants. He expected the celebrations. Wiseman knew how deeply Russians in New York hated the tsar. But beyond the rejoicing, Wiseman saw another, more troubling aspect to the reaction: the large numbers of Russian radical socialists suddenly raising money to go home, apparently to destabilize or overthrow the fragile new provisional government.

For Britain, this meant trouble, and the stakes could not be higher. Germany's unrestricted submarine warfare, designed to starve Britain of food and ammunition, had started to work, and the country feared losing any further edge against Germany. On this score, the tsar's abdication had answered a prayer. Kerensky, Miliukov, and the other new leaders all made their intentions clear. They pledged to keep Russia in the war and keep its army, still estimated at five million men, fighting for the Entente. This, in turn, would force Germany to keep splitting its own forces between eastern and western fronts.

But these New York socialists were a whole different story. One sounded more pro-German than the next. The new Russian provisional government held power only by a slender thread. What if a few of these radicals actually managed to get home and organize his comrades to topple it? Or start a civil war. What would they do next? Take Russia out of the fight? Or sign a separate peace with Germany?

Plenty of these local socialists seemed eager to make trouble, and leading the parade was that hothead over at *Novy Mir,* Leon Trotsky.

Wiseman by now knew plenty about Trotsky, or was learning quickly. He and his team had built a deep network of sources and paid agents around New York. Wiseman's intelligence officer Norman Thwaites, the one-time newsman and combat veteran, oversaw a stable of spies and informers that included Russian-born Sidney Reilly, later dubbed the Ace of Spies, then in New York arranging arms shipments for Russia while making a nice profit for himself, along with Reilly's business partner in these deals, Alexander Weinstein, the likely relative of Gregory Weinstein, editor of the radical *Novy Mir.* [322]

Through Reilly and Weinstein, the web even reached Nicholas Aleinikoff, the prominent Socialist Party leader who had served on the party's recent Resolutions Committee along with Trotsky and Louis Fraina. Aleinikoff, as a lawyer, had represented Reilly and Weinstein on several business deals. It all made a cozy little circle.

Casimir Pilenas, the one who had attended Trotsky's speech at the Lenox Casino, fit neatly in this mosaic, but with a malicious bent. As an undercover agent, Pilenas had a pedigree going back twenty years. Born in Kovno, Lithuania, in 1872, he had landed in London in the late

1890s and had quickly drawn the interests of both Scotland Yard and the Russian Okhrana, the secret police. They both recruited him as an informer. Pilenas mixed easily with German and Russian émigrés. He spoke the languages and made a specialty of penetrating radical groups and snitching on them to his bosses. When Pilenas came to New York in 1913, he used a recommendation from Scotland Yard to land a comfortable niche first with naval officer Guy Gaunt and then with Wiseman and Thwaites.

Whether Pilenas still kept touch with the Okhrana's New York operation in 1917 is far from clear. He had left its payroll, but the Okhrana had at least one New York–based agent, named George Patrick, reporting on Trotsky in the city during this period.[323] Wiseman would later insist, though, that Pilenas worked only for him.[324]

Still, Pilenas's ties to the Okhrana connected him to a deep, rich vein of yet another prominent tsarist legacy: aggressive Jew-baiting. It had taken dramatic forms. Pilenas, around this time, started palling around with another Russian transplant named Boris Brasol, a lawyer who in Russia had served on the prosecution team in the notorious 1913 blood-libel case against Menahem Mendel Beilis. Beilis, a Jewish supervisor at a Kiev brick factory, had been charged by the tsarist government with murdering a thirteen-year-old Christian boy in a ritual killing to use his blood for Jewish ceremonies. The case drew global denunciations for its ugly medieval slander. Even the local Kiev prosecutor refused to touch it. No physical evidence connected Beilis to the crime, and after a two-year ordeal, an all-Christian jury acquitted Beilis outright. But years afterward, Boris Brasol, even in New York City, still defended both his own role in the case and its premise of Jewish ritual murder.[325]

Brasol had landed in New York in 1916 as chief detective for the Russian Supply Committee. Two years later, in 1918, he and Pilenas would find themselves at the center of another notorious anti-Semitic operation, this time as chief promoters of English-language versions of the propaganda piece *Protocols of the Elders of Zion,* a document forged by the Okhrana in the 1890s that claimed to show Jewish leaders plotting world domination. Brasol and Pilenas would present the *Protocols,* rarely seen yet in the West at that point, to American military intelligence and submit written reports portraying Bolshevism largely as a Jewish plot. Pilenas himself would try to extract $50,000 from the American Jewish Committee for a copy of the *Protocols.*[326]

Now, in March 1917, this same Casimir Pilenas was plying his craft for William Wiseman of British Intelligence, keeping his eye on Russian socialists, especially Jewish ones, watching how they raised money to send revolutionaries back home to destabilize the new Petrograd regime, starting with the very prominent Leon Trotsky.[327]

Wiseman, whatever his preconceptions, soon found himself struck by the very pattern Pilenas was pushing. The largest number of immigrant radicals in New York happened to be Jewish, not surprising since Jews made up the majority of all Eastern European immigrants. Russian socialists tended to be Russian Jews. German radicals tended to be German Jews. So too of the Finns, Ukrainians, Poles, and any other group from that part of the world.

Wiseman showed no sign of being particularly anti-Semitic. Wiseman dealt with many Jewish people in his life. After the war, he would join Kuhn Loeb, Jacob Schiff's own financial house, as a partner. In the 1920s, he would be the target of anti-Semitic slurs himself based on his Jewish-sounding last name. US intelligence officials would secretly accuse Wiseman of Jewish ancestry—despite his ten generations of British peerage—as a stain on his loyalty.[328] Plenty of analysts in the British, French, and American intelligence services in 1917 viewed Jews as a distinct national group with unique views and interests.

But the innocent-sounding observation had consequences. Anti-Semitism didn't limit itself to just Russia or Germany. Many police, politicians, and military analysts at the time, even in the West, took the image further, twisted it, and overlaid it with age-old stereotypes, painting Jews as international outsiders; malcontents who lived separately with their own religion, language, food, and hostile nationalism; and manipulative money merchants or bankers with secretive global ties, with their

lower classes naturally drawn to radical causes. They described Jews as a
separate race, like the Irish, Italian, or African races—the way they used
the word back then—but with a special curse, destined to hardship for
national sins dating back to the Bible.

All these elements found their way into actual formal government
intelligence reports, including at the American War Department's own
Military Intelligence Division.[329]

Even Winston Churchill, the future British prime minister, produced
a 1920 article called "Zionism versus Bolshevism," which claimed the
existence of two types of Jews, "good Jews" versus "bad Jews," the bad
ones including "International Jews" and "Terrorist Jews" at the heart of
Bolshevism.[330]

Be it from ignorance, stereotypes, fear, resentments, religious beliefs,
or deliberate slander, the result was the same: the existence in 1917 of
a virulent ethnic profiling that, over the next three decades, would crescendo as a pretext for mass murder.

William Wiseman, steeped in this environment and trained as an
intelligence officer, could hardly ignore the fact that Jewishness seemed
the glue that connected so many New York socialists. But what should
he make of it? Few doubted that Jews had legitimate grievances against
the Russian tsar or that their hostility toward Russia was a logical reaction to decades of persecution. And yes, Jewish people might constitute
a diverse group, mostly loyal and nonpolitical, but Wiseman could say
the same thing about Germans, and that didn't change the fact they were
Britain's mortal enemy.

If nothing else, Wiseman felt obliged to report on the subject. His
colleagues in British and American intelligence—driven by their own
biases—certainly seemed to find it relevant, and some already were
stretching similar reports to remarkable lengths. For instance, one typical
file memo from the US War Department shared with Wiseman during this
period contained an update on American domestic radicals—Bolsheviks,
labor agitators, Irish and Indian dissidents—all in a section titled "Jewish
Affairs."[331] Much worse would come over the next few years.

Which brought Wiseman back to Leon Trotsky: a Jew, a Russian, a socialist, a self-proclaimed revolutionary, a talented speaker and charismatic leader with international contacts. All these danger signs Trotsky combined in a single package. Trotsky's easily topped the pile of reports on Wiseman's desk, with his recent flurry of high-profile speeches and newspaper interviews. They painted a curious picture. Wiseman had never actually met Trotsky face-to-face, but the evidence made some facts about him undeniable: This Trotsky left no doubt what he thought of the new Petrograd regime. Given the chance, he would gladly replace it. Just that week, an unnamed editor of *Novy Mir*—Trotsky or one of his friends—had told the *New York Call* that the "fighting group" from 1905 (Trotsky et al.) was "eager to go back to overthrow autocracy and establish a republic."[332] How much clearer could they have been in announcing their plans?

This Trotsky also minced no words about the world war. He despised it and said so clearly at every chance. But at the same time, he hardly sounded like a friend of Berlin. "The revolutionists, even if they had it in their power, would not make a separate peace with Germany," Trotsky had told the *New York Times* that week. "They do not favor Germany. They do not want to see Germany win, but they are tired of war and the privations of war and they wish to stop fighting."[333]

Even a superficial reading of Trotsky's speeches made it clear that his vision took a different direction: "The revolution [will] spread from Russia to Germany and Austria and result in the ending of the war," he told audiences.[334] These didn't sound like words of a defeatist. Realistic or not, this prediction was a far cry from surrender to Germany. At that point in 1917, few in London or Paris would complain in the least about a revolution in Berlin that ended the war by toppling the kaiser.

Was this Trotsky someone England actually could work with? If Russia's weak provisional regime ever fell to radicals, might this Trotsky be a better choice than some of the others?

For Wiseman, the question had consequeces. He had power over this situation. Under Britain's wartime blockade of Germany, every ship leaving New York for Scandinavia—the gateway to Russia and indirectly to Germany—had to stop at Halifax, Nova Scotia, a British port, so that British officials could search both the ship and its passengers for contraband, which they could seize on the spot. The process required each passenger to obtain a visa from the British passport control office, housed in the British consulate at 44 Whitehall, and approved by William Wiseman's own MI1c unit.

If Wiseman wanted to stop Trotsky or anyone else from reaching Russia, all he had to do was ask the consulate to deny them a visa. If he wanted to avoid publicity in New York, he could cable British officials in Halifax and have them detain the person there. It was that easy.

Britain had used this power repeatedly during the war, much to the annoyance of travelers. In late February that year, British officials in Halifax made headlines when they boarded the Scandinavian passenger liner *Frederick VIII,* which had stopped there en route to Copenhagen, and confiscated $25,000 in gold from the Hungarian countess Manfred Matuschka of Washington, DC, and smaller amounts from other passengers, claiming them as contraband under the wartime embargo. Count Johann Heinrich von Bernstorff, the former German ambassador recently expelled from Washington, DC, happened to be aboard the ship that day and actually complimented the British for their courteous search. In another case, British officials at Halifax had arrested a man off the Swedish steamer *Sven du Rietz* on charges of smuggling rubber, seized his trunks, and detained him until he could be extradited back to the United States.[335]

What would Wiseman do with this Leon Trotsky? Would he dare to interfere with the Russians and Americans if they gave him travel papers? And if he stopped Trotsky, what would he do with the others?

For now, in these heady days just after the revolution in Petrograd, William Wiseman waited. Events would force his hand soon enough.

VLADIMIR ILYICH LENIN, leader of the Bolsheviks, stranded in Switzerland, also wanted desperately to get home. He felt "corked up, as if in a bottle," his wife, Krupskaya, would write of him in those days.[336]

Lenin had first heard about the Petrograd uprising from a young Zurich neighbor named Moisei Bronski, who came bounding up the stairs at 14 Spiegelgasse having seen an early-morning newspaper. "Haven't you heard the news?" he shouted. "There is revolution in Russia!"[337] Amazed, Lenin set off with Bronski, wandering through Zurich scrounging for details. He joined scenes of celebration—Russian émigrés hugging, drinking, shaking hands, singing songs.

By the time he returned to his house, he was beside himself, pacing and mumbling. "It's staggering! Such a surprise!" He began writing letters to longtime friends. "If the Germans aren't lying, it has happened," he wrote to Inessa Armand. "I'm so excited I cannot possibly go to Scandinavia!!"[338] He cabled Grigory Zinoviev, his closest Bolshevik ally in Switzerland, telling him to come quickly from Berne. They needed to make plans.

Revolution at last! But how could they possibly lead it from Switzerland? Somehow he had to reach Russia. But how?

Getting from Switzerland to Russia seemed near impossible. Lenin could see the problem whenever he looked at a map. Switzerland had no seaports, no border with Russia, and a world war raging between them. Traveling to Russia meant taking one of three routes, each with problems: He could go north, across France to the North Sea, then by boat to Finland. But French military officials would never permit him to cross their territory. He was a known fugitive and revolutionary, and even if they did, the British navy would stop him at sea.

Or he could go south, across Italy to the Mediterranean, then by ship to the Black Sea and Odessa. But Turkey controlled access to the Black Sea through the Bosporus Straits, and Turkey too would hardly permit it.

Then there was the direct route, northeast, across Germany. But this too had problems. Crossing Germany meant getting permission from the German military, a deadly dangerous prospect. If Lenin gave any appearance of conniving with Germans, it could ruin his standing, not just among socialists but particularly within Russia, a country still fighting Germany in a war. He'd be committing treason, a capital offense. "It looks as if we won't get to Russia!" he wrote despairingly to Inessa Armand. "England won't let us. [The idea of] going through Germany isn't working."[339]

Lenin's hunger to get home drove him to consider desperate lengths. At one point, he suggested disguising himself as a mute Swede and sneaking across the border.[340] He also considered chartering an airplane to fly over Germany and the battlefront trenches, until someone explained to him that 1917-vintage airplanes didn't travel that far, often crashed, and could easily be shot down.[341]

One fellow stranded Russian, Julius Martov, leader of the Mensheviks, suggested yet another convoluted idea, that they would seek permission to cross Germany, but only if Russia agreed to release an equal number of German prisoners of war. This would recast the whole transaction as a prisoner exchange rather than treasonous collusion with Russia's wartime enemy. But this idea failed too when Russian foreign minister Paul Miliukov objected.

As days passed and details filtered out from Petrograd, Lenin heard the names of the new ministers in the provisional government—Miliukov, Lvoff, Guchkov, and the rest—and this only hardened his resolve. "The bourgeoisie has managed to get its arse onto ministerial seats," he told Krupskaya, their goal "to make fools of the people."[342] Somehow, he and his Bolsheviks had to stop them.

How? Even from far-off Switzerland, Lenin saw the answer. The key was in the other new body created by the recent revolution: the Petrograd Workers Council (Soviet). Here was their weapon. In 1905 Lenin had dismissed the soviet because it had contradicted his Bolshevik belief that revolutions must be led by committed revolutionaries. But this time he saw it differently. The new 1917 soviet had already made itself a formidable competing power against the provisional government, independent and vocal, positioned to eclipse or replace it. Lenin saw this potential immediately and seized on it.

As early as March 16—the same day Trotsky was telling the *New York Times* that the new Petrograd regime could never survive—Lenin cabled his favorite messenger, Alexandra Kollontai in Norway, and asked that she signal their Bolshevik friends inside Russia to continue their opposition to the war and resist any rapprochement with the Mensheviks.[343] Then he went further. He asked her to send a second cable, this one more direct: "Our tactics—complete distrust. No support for the Provisional Government. Distrust Kerensky above all. Arm the proletariat as the only guarantee. Immediate elections to the Petrograd city council. No alliance with other parties. Wire this to Petrograd."[344]

Over coming days and weeks, Lenin would lay out his new thinking in a series of essays later called "Letters from Afar" and in a set of precepts later called his April Theses. These would mark a striking change in Bolshevik ideology. Unlike 1905, this time Lenin would not hesitate in calling for immediate change: elimination of the provisional government and a socialist seizure of power. Within weeks of his return, the slogan on Petrograd streets would reflect the new approach: "All Power to the Soviets."

But for now, these ambitious plans had to wait. Lenin remained stuck in Switzerland, spinning his wheels. All he could do was wait.

It didn't take long for frustration finally to force him to reconsider an older, earlier-rejected option. On top of all the other messages he sent during those busy first days after the tsar's overthrow, Lenin added one more, addressed to Copenhagen, Denmark, and his longtime friend Jakob Furstenberg (or Ganetsky). "We must at all costs get back to Russia," it read.[345] Furstenberg had resources to make this happen. And the biggest of these was his relationship as business partner to Alexander Israel Helphand, known to radical cognoscenti as Parvus, the one-time brilliant socialist theorist and now well-heeled capitalist agent of Germany.

Up until now, Lenin had refused any contact with Parvus, having publicly denounced him as a traitor and pariah. But times had changed. As for Parvus, hearing the news from Petrograd, he already had a plan. He intended to help Lenin whether Lenin wanted his help or not.

PARVUS HARDLY LET his lifestyle suffer from the war. Comfortably settled in Copenhagen, he thrived like the city itself. Denmark had stayed neutral and profited from doing business with both sides. Copenhagen, its capital, brimmed with profiteers: stock traders, food hoarders, arms dealers, and the rest. Locals called them "goulash barons" for the local specialty, the 145 factories sprung up almost overnight to produce portable canned food sold at exorbitant prices to opposing belligerent armies shooting at each other across the trenches.

Parvus fit right in with this milieu, running his businesses and editing his newspaper. His every venture these days seemed to profit. His latest scheme: a business built around shipping German-mined coal into Denmark, underpricing it, and thereby stealing the market from Denmark's longtime coal provider, Britain. The venture netted him millions of Danish kroner while crimping British coal exports, which delighted Germany's military brass. Money flowed in, and Parvus used it to finance his expansive tastes in food and luxuries. It even allowed him to support a few choice charities, like his high-minded Institute for the Study of the Social Consequences of War and his paying for summer beach vacations for the children of poor German families.

"Be it far from me to justify capitalist gain by personal qualities," he bragged in 1918, still trying to dress himself up as a socialist. "But I do not see why I should not bring some of the surplus value hoarded by the capitalist class over to my side."[346]

But of all his causes, Parvus still held one dearest of all: achieving a socialist revolution in Russia tied to a German military victory in the world war. And for this, his moment had finally come. Hearing of the Russian Revolution, he exulted. "Your victory is our victory," he wrote in his newspaper *Die Glocke*. "Democratic Germany must offer democratic Russia a helping hand for the achievement of peace and for effective co-operation in the field of social and cultural progress."[347]

Parvus had been planning this opportunity for years, using his German-financed export business to plant agents and pockets of cash inside Russia. Now he visited his friend Ulrich Karl von Brockdorff-Rantzau,

Germany's senior diplomat in Copenhagen, to explain his ideas. Parvus had hatched schemes with Brockdorff-Rantzau before. Brockdorff-Rantzau was a foreign ministry veteran, having served postings in Vienna, Brussels, and Saint Petersburg before Denmark, and saw the logic at once. "These developments are a great stroke of luck for us," he told colleagues.[348] Parvus asked Brockdorff-Rantzau to cable his idea to Berlin, and Brockdorff-Rantzau agreed, telling them: "Revolution is victorious, Russia is politically incapacitated, constituent assembly means peace." To the German high command, this made good clear sense, and wheels started to spin. This done, Parvus then triggered the other side of the equation. Through his business partner Jakob Furstenberg, Vladimir Lenin's friend, he sent word to Lenin, offering Lenin a way home to Russia: travel through Germany with Germany's blessing. If Lenin wanted to make revolution and topple the new Russian government, then Parvus and Germany by all means meant to help him.

Furstenberg quickly relayed the message both by letter and by sending a personal messenger, a man named Georg Sklarz, to meet Lenin in Zurich. Lenin, though, smelled trouble. Through an ally, he telegrammed back a warning: "Letter dispatched. Uncle [Lenin] wants to know more. Official transit for individuals unacceptable."[349] When Sklarz reached Zurich and presented the plan to Lenin personally, Sklarz made matters worse by offering to pay train fares across Germany for both Lenin and his top aides, making them essentially paid agents of Germany. At this point, Lenin sent Sklarz packing and broke off the talks, determined to avoid any visible connection between himself and the German government.

Secret negotiations ensued. Parvus rushed to Berlin and, with help from his friend Brockdorff-Rantzau, managed to schedule a personal visit with German foreign minister Arthur Zimmermann, who clearly grasped the opportunity. He ended up meeting instead with the deputy foreign minister—a result of clashing schedules—but Germany approved the plan regardless. Berlin gave Parvus full authority to negotiate passage for Lenin and his zealots and began lining up money to finance their work.

Through Furstenberg, Parvus now requested a face-to-face meeting with Lenin himself, but Lenin again refused. Instead he sent his aide Karl Radek to Stockholm to act as go-between in ironing out final details. Within days, the German Foreign Ministry requested 5 million marks for Lenin's work, and the German Treasury approved it.[350]

The plan fell quickly into place. Thirty-two Russians, including Lenin, Krupskaya, Lenin's friend Inessa Armand, his Bolskevik ally Zinoviev, Radek, Martov, and a host of other prominent Bolsheviks and Mensheviks, would travel together in a railroad car, part of which would be marked off and considered neutral territory. Lenin and his comrades would pay their own fares, and they would not need to speak to a single German the entire way, keeping their hands as clean as possible. They would later call it a "sealed train," though not all the doors were actually locked.

For Germany, the plan made perfect strategic sense. It was a gamble to win the war on the eastern front in a single bold stroke, by inserting into chaotic postrevolutionary Russia the most disciplined, determined cadre of radicals available. For Lenin, it provided the chance to achieve his destiny. For Parvus, it meant possible vindication. Everyone seemed to come out a winner.

ALEXANDRA KOLLONTAI, AT her home in Holmenkollen, the picturesque ski town at the foot of Norway's snow-crusted mountains near Kristiania, had barely time to fall back into a routine since her second New York journey when she heard the exciting news from Petrograd. Of all the Western European capitals, Kristiania sat closest in earshot to Russia itself. Letters smuggled from Petrograd, refugees fleeing through Finland, and cables from Russia all stopped here first. This perch gave Kollontai a unique viewpoint, making her one of the first Westerners to hear news of the street battles in the Russian capital. "My heart began to pound. I was immediately sure this wasn't a bluff," she wrote on seeing a report as early as March 11, as the fighting still raged undecided.

She was attending meetings in Kristiania when word finally arrived that the tsar had abdicated. "I darted out into the hall; we hugged one another," she wrote in her diary of that moment. "I wanted to run somewhere. We had won! We had won! The end of the war! It wasn't even joy, but some kind of giddy rejoicing."[351] When word came next of amnesty for political refugees, local Russians in Norway immediately began snatching up train tickets to go home.

Kollontai wanted to join them. She had no family in Holmenkollen or Kristiania and had friends in Petrograd from when she had fled nine years earlier. The chance to join the long-awaited revolution drew her strongly. What's more, for her, getting back to Russia raised far fewer problems than for her comrades Lenin or Trotsky. The trip from Kristiania covered more than a thousand miles by land, endless hours on railroads across Sweden's forests and tundra, but the borders were far friendlier. No war zones or hostile countries stood in the way.

Kollontai had responsibilities in Norway, particularly her postal duties for the Bolsheviks, passing messages into and out of Russia. But she assumed that it wouldn't be difficult to arrange a replacement.

Needing direction, she wired Vladimir Lenin in Zurich and heard back within the day: "Fancy asking for 'instruction' from here, where information is so scanty," he told her. "It's in Peter [Petrograd] where all our leading comrades are now. . . . A week of bloody battles and we get Milyukov, Guchkov and Kerensky! Well, so be it. The first stage of the revolution born of the war will neither be the last nor a purely Russian affair."[352]

Postal duties would not be a problem. But as for traveling home, Lenin had a request. He asked her to wait. The announced amnesty for political refugees might be a trap. She should let others go first to see if any were arrested en route. But more important, Lenin needed Kollontai first to do him a favor. On top of the cables he had asked her to send immediately to Petrograd, he also wanted her to carry something for him back to Russia, a set of letters with instructions for local comrades to firmly oppose the provisional government. Lenin asked her to deliver them personally to the Petrograd office of the Bolshevik Party newspaper, *Pravda,* for immediate publication. He didn't trust anyone else with the sensitive mission.

Lenin knew she would reach Petrograd long before he did, no matter what complicated arrangement he worked out with the Germans. She must be his courier.

Kollontai agreed to wait—but not for long.

21

CONSULATES

"Trotsky was of medium stature, with very thick glasses and unkempt black hair. Most unprepossessing in appearance, he was the most vociferous of them all. As I saw him at these meetings, he impressed me as a definitely maladjusted personality; his speech and his gestures were those of a neurotic person. He spoke in a shrill, high pitched voice, and tried to hypnotize his listener with his myopic but intense eyes."[353]

—Pierre Routsky, 1917 Russian vice consul in New York, writing in 1948

B ACK IN NEW York, Trotsky started making plans to leave. Already, as he walked the sidewalks, ate breakfast in his favorite Bronx diner, rode the subway, played with his boys, or sipped tea at the Monopole Café, his mind had moved on, to Russia. The idea seduced him. It animated his productive hours, his speaking, his writing, his endless talks with friends. At *Novy Mir,* he continued to crank out columns and speeches, but he focused almost entirely on Russia's revolution: that it must be worker-led, socialist, and ready to sweep across Europe.

Trotsky well remembered 1905, the year of the last uprising, and it reinforced his urgency to get home quickly. In 1905 he had made himself one of the first émigrés to reach Petrograd and join the movement. This head start gave him the chance to play a crucial leading role, to meet the leaders, win their trust, and understand their demands and the nature of their soviet. Trading memories with fellow veterans, 1905 looked increasingly like a dress rehearsal for this new uprising in 1917.

But this time the tsar had been eliminated. The biggest obstacle had been removed. This time they would win.

Around him in New York, Trotsky saw the growing excitement as Americans prepared themselves for war against Germany. War talk blared at him from every street corner: the military recruitment drives with pretty girls and brass bands, the parades and rallies, the soldiers standing guard with rifles and bayonets, the daily drumbeat of newspaper headlines about German attacks. President Woodrow Wilson made his intentions clear in late March by calling a special session of Congress for April 2 to consider war. Broadway producer George M. Cohan, the tap dance and singing sensation appearing that week at the Strand on Forty-Seventh Street in his comedy *Broadway Jones,* jotted down a catchy tune while riding the train to New York from his home in New Rochelle. He called it "Johnny Get Your Gun," and soon the chorus would be one everyone's lips, be it marching down the street or just whistling around the house:

> Over there, over there,
> Send the word, send the word over there
> That the Yanks are coming, the Yanks are coming
> The drums rum-tumming everywhere.

Trotsky still followed such American events, but more at a distance. Since coming to New York in January, he had fought to radicalize the American socialists and had built a cadre of local activists. He had enjoyed the culture, the cinema, the cafés and libraries; seen the wealth and technology. But all that now took a backseat. America could take care of itself. Inside his immediate circle of Russians, they talked only about Petrograd and going home.

Just within the *Novy Mir* staff, five of them had started making travel plans: Trotsky, Bukharin, Chudnovsky, and two outside contributors, Philadelphia-based V. Volodarsky and New Jersey–based Guschon Melnichansky, who also worked as a watchmaker. In the city at large, hundreds more prepared to join them.

Compared to Vladimir Lenin in Switzerland, Trotsky's path home looked relatively simple, at least on the surface. He too needed official papers to reach Russia, but he had no reason to bother with "sealed trains" or secret deals with hostile countries. Trotsky already had a French passport from his last ocean crossing, but this new Russian Revolution demanded a proper new one. Russia had declared amnesty for political refugees, so Russia should give him a passport. All he had to do was go down to the consulate, walk in the front door, and demand it. That, at least, was what they promised.

First things first. The Russian consulate in New York City took just a few days before announcing that it was ready to greet returning exiles coming to apply for travel papers. Trotsky made himself the first—literally "the very first," according to officials—to march over and make his application.[354]

The Russian consulate in 1917 housed itself in an office building at 55 Broadway, just south of Wall Street near Trinity Church. On entering the room, Trotsky, ready to assert his rights, found chaos. He saw the consulate staff, diplomats who had spent years serving the tsar, scurrying in all directions. For days these diplomats had been bombarded by confusing, contradictory orders from Petrograd. As Pierre Routsky, the assistant consul general, recalled it, the first official cable during the crisis told them nothing about the political situation but ordered them to remove all portraits of Tsar Nicholas and his family from the walls. In response, diplomats at Russian consulates around the globe, from New York to Chicago to San Francisco to Buenos Aires, Paris, and Madrid, all raced about their buildings to strip away paintings and imperial insignia, putting them in storage or taking them home as mementos.

Despite the clamor for news, Russian consuls and vice consuls canceled speeches, meetings, and interviews all that week simply because they didn't know what to say.

On top of that, while the provisional government had made a big public fanfare over its declared amnesty for political refugees, the consulates

had no actual lists of Russian political exiles in their cities. This presented a serious problem because the foreign ministry in Petrograd had
also instructed them to deny travel papers to any person unable to prove
he was, in fact, Russian, a precaution against German spies trying to slip
into the country.[355] But few actual refugees carried Russian passports.
Many had fled the country to avoid arrest and lived under fake names
or as undocumented fugitives. Separating real émigrés from imposters
might be impossible.

Routsky remembered greeting Trotsky at the New York consulate
that day, and he recalled Trotsky's pushy attitude on meeting him, his
"shrill, slightly hysterical voice." Not knowing quite what to do, Routsky
asked his superior, Consul General Michael Oustinoff, and Oustinoff
decided to meet with Trotsky personally, out of "curiosity," as he later
put it. Trotsky's radical history had made him a minor celebrity in this
office. Oustinoff doubtless had seen Trotsky's Okhrana police file, and
they'd all seen his columns in *Novy Mir*. If this man Trotsky represented
the New Russia, then Oustinoff wanted to see it for himself.

Once they sat down, though, any friendliness quickly disappeared.
Routsky joined them, and according to a tongue-in-cheek account that
Routsky wrote years later, Trotsky began lecturing them about who now
ran their country and who didn't. He reminded them they belonged to
the "old regime" with "antiquated views" and insisted that he, Trotsky,
be entitled to travel home as a "passenger of note." Oustinoff tried to
cut him off and finally interrupted with an old Russian expression. "The
eggs do not teach the hen," he said, to which Trotsky replied: "Mr.
Consul, evidently you have not grasped as yet that the time has already
come for the eggs to teach the hen."[356]

With that, Oustinoff decided to hand the mess back to his deputy,
Routsky. Routsky, at thirty-six years old, educated at Saint Petersburg's
Imperial School of Law and Paris's École des Sciences Politiques et
Economiques, had served consular postings in Brussels, the Vatican, and
Montreal and as a special European courier to the tsar before being sent

to New York in 1913. He was a diplomatic veteran, but he also didn't quite know whom he was starting up with.

Sitting down with Trotsky, Routsky first offered him a new Russian passport printed on the standard ornate stationery Russia had used for decades, showing the imperial eagle, symbol of the regime, engraved in a bed of artistic flourishes. But Trotsky refused to take it. He wanted no tsarist symbols on his paper. That was the Old Russia. Instead, he insisted they print him a new passport on plain white stationery, simply certifying his right to enter the country.

Then came the problem of how to confirm Trotsky's bona fides, a problem Routsky knew he'd face with the whole flood of applicants he expected. For this, Routsky suggested they convene a working group consisting of representatives from each local Russian political faction—Bolsheviks, Social Democrats, anarchists, and so on—to identify Russian members wishing to be repatriated. That way, they could assemble a prioritized list of people vouched for by the leaders.

Trotsky agreed, but he had to laugh at the process. "They demand proof that we are members of the Russian revolutionary organization," he told Ludwig Lore in disbelief one night. "The crimes for which we were hounded from country to country," he said, "suddenly become a badge of service that will admit us as honored citizens."[357]

Silly or not, over the next few days, as the consulate's clerks worked on Trotsky's paperwork, Routsky convened his working committee of Russian émigrés. Trotsky and Bukharin came to represent the *Novy Mir* group,[358] with Trotsky, of course, doing the talking. Bukharin, normally friendly and outgoing, seemed tongue-tied in this strange milieu, hobnobbing with former tsarist officials. He spent the meetings in silence, looking absorbed but saying nothing. Routsky found this curious. He had thought Bukharin the more intellectual of the pair and asked one of Bukharin's friends about it. The friend explained, perhaps tongue-in-cheek as well, that Bukharin was a "true Yogi follower" who enjoyed "concentration and meditation."[359]

Finally the passports came. They had cleared the first hurdle. The next stop was to buy steamship tickets.

By now Trotsky had organized a group of sixteen fellow Russians who wanted to make the voyage with him, Natalya, and their two sons. The group included two of Trotsky's colleagues at *Novy Mir*—Grigorii Chudnovsky, his sidekick at Saint Marks Place, and Guschon Melnichansky, the contributor from New Jersey. Also traveling with them would be a carpenter named Konstantin Romanchinko, whose wife still lived in Russia, though he himself was largely nonpolitical, and a man named W. Schloima Dukhom, the only one who insisted on traveling first-class.

For tickets, all sixteen of them decided to walk en masse to the office of Henry C. Zaro, an agent for the Russian Steamship Company at 1 Third Avenue, a few blocks down the street from *Novy Mir*. Trotsky acted as their spokesman since they and Zaro all spoke Russian. With Zaro's help, they checked schedules, dates, and calendars and finally decided on the *Kristianiafjord,* a comfortable, relatively new steamship of the Norwegian-America Line, capable of carrying twelve hundred passengers at a speed of fifteen knots. Its route would take them from New York to Bergen, Norway. From there they would take trains across Scandinavia to Russia. The ship had one scheduled stop, in Halifax, Nova Scotia. As Zaro explained it, second-class tickets cost $80 apiece (today about the cost of a first-class round-trip airfare between New York and Paris). First-class cabins went for $114.50.

When time came to pay, Trotsky collected the money from each of his travel mates, each paying their own way. For the sixteen second-class cabins and one in first class, he handed Zaro a fat pile of bills coming to $1,394.50.[360] Zaro then handed him the tickets to pass out to the group. They were almost done.

Finally, one last stop: Trotsky and his group would need British visas for the ship's stop in Halifax, where British officers would inspect them for contraband under the British blockade. So down Broadway they all marched to the British consulate at 44 Whitehall. Here, once again, all went smoothly. They went inside and found the consulate staff helpful and polite. Trotsky and his friends each filled out forms and questionnaires. Then Trotsky went through an elaborate cross-check. "From the office of the British Consulate, in the presence of one of its officials, I telephoned to the Russian Consulate which assured me that I had complied with all formalities and could make my journey without any difficulties," he explained.[361] Finally, the paperwork finished, the British approved their visas. "They told me," he wrote, that they "would put no obstacles in the way on my return to Russia."[362]

That was that. They had taken all the proper steps. They had tickets, passports, visas, and assurances from all the relevant governments. The *Kristianiafjord* would leave from its dock on the Brooklyn side of the harbor at 10 AM Tuesday morning, March 27, exactly ten weeks and two days after Trotsky had first set foot in the New World.

At that point, Trotsky went back to his office on Saint Marks Place and used the telephone to call Henry Feuer, the salesman at the Bronx furniture shop that had supplied his apartment on Vyse Avenue with chairs, tables, carpets, and beds: "I'm going to Russia, Comrade Feuer," Trotsky told him. "You can have back your furniture."[363]

WILLIAM WISEMAN HEARD all about Trotsky's visit to the Russian consulate. Pierre Routsky, the veteran diplomat there, knew that plenty of his friends around New York City would enjoy the story. They included Sidney Reilly and Wiseman's spymaster Norman Thwaites.[364] Routsky doubtless gave them a good laugh, telling it over a few rounds of vodka, describing Trotsky's antics in his office, lording over the consul general and lecturing them about their "antiquated views."

Wiseman also heard all about Trotsky's visit to the British consulate at 44 Whitehall, his own building. Wiseman's group would have had to approve their visas that day.

So far, Wiseman had done nothing to interfere with Trotsky. But Trotsky wouldn't leave the city for a few more days, and Wiseman hadn't finished yet. He still had all his concerns about Jews, socialists, and revolutionaries threatening to destabilize Russia, and possible German agents behind them.

For instance, Wiseman would have heard about Trotsky's visit to the steamship ticket office. Henry C. Zaro, the agent who sold his group their cabins aboard the *Kristianiafjord,* was also part of Wiseman's network. Zaro had friends, and they had friends who spoke to Norman Thwaites, who in turn reported to Wiseman.[365] One detail in the story that apparently got highlighted was that Trotsky personally had paid for tickets for the whole group by handing Zaro a stack of bills totaling $1,340.50, an eye-popping sum of money for a supposedly poor revolutionary. Where did he get it? From rich Germans? From rich Jews? Or agents from Berlin?

The fact that Trotsky had collected it from each of the sixteen other people traveling with him, each paying their own way, seemed to get lost.

And more. Wiseman kept hearing reports of Trotsky receiving money from local Germans all over town. Wiseman would have seen the special collection being taken up by the German-language socialist daily *New Yorker Volkszeitung,* money for Trotsky and his comrades to carry home to support revolutionaries. And this was on top of all the collections at speeches and rallies, at Beethoven Hall, Lenox Casino, and the rest. All this money, certainly most of it as Wiseman saw it, came from Jews and Germans. Were German spies behind it? How much did it amount to? He had no idea and no real way to find out.

Wiseman milked his sources. He reached out to a Professor Richard J. H. Gottheil at Columbia University, known to have fears about "Russian-Jewish-Socialists," and asked him to tap his network in the Jewish community.[366] He may have also heard from a one-time official at the Russian-American-Asiatic Corporation named Nikolai Volgar, who later claimed that he could prove in court that Trotsky had received German money.[367] Through Thwaites, he may have heard more from Sidney Reilly, who heard from his business partner Alexander Weinstein, who may have spoken to his likely relative Gregory Weinstein, editor of *Novy Mir.*[368]

But then came the clincher. Casimir Pilenas, his Russian-speaking agent with the long history with Scotland Yard and the Russian Okhrana, sent him a message. No copy of Pilenas's report exists in the British Intelligence files, but the files do contain a document in which Wiseman confirms its existence and importance.[369] It apparently contained concrete allegations about Trotsky's activities in the city.

Wiseman now decided to act, at least in a cautious, initial way. He took the formal step of drafting a warning to his superiors at MI1c and sending it by secret cable:

> An important movement has been started here among Socialists
> backed by all Jewish funds, behind which are possibly Germans,
> with a view to getting back Revolutionary Socialists into Russia
> under expedited political amnesty, with object of overturning
> present Government and establishing Republic and initiating
> Peace movement; also of promoting Socialistic Revolutions
> in other countries, including United States. Main leader is
> TROTZKI who was principal speaker at a mass meeting here
> March 20th. He says he means to leave for Russia March 27th.
> Some Socialists are reported to have left on a Scandinavian boat
> on March 19th.[370]

Wiseman, ever circumspect, stopped short of asking the British navy to detain Trotsky at Halifax or even to stop him from leaving New York Harbor. He didn't directly accuse Trotsky of planning a separate peace with Germany.

Wiseman sent the cable on March 23, four days before Trotsky's planned departure, giving himself extra time to think, gather more facts, and perhaps take stronger steps later.

A thought was forming in his mind: With pro-German socialists threatening to make trouble in Petrograd, why not insert into Russia a few high-profile socialists of his own, ones who might actually help Britain or, if things went awry, at least speak out against a separate peace with Germany? Wiseman already envisioned an organized program to send prominent left-wingers back to Russia to counter anti-British propaganda. Within a few weeks, he would have $75,000 placed in his credit at J. P. Morgan to get started.

But for now, he still had his immediate problem: What to do about Trotsky?

SOON AFTER HE finished making travel plans, Trotsky took the opportunity to win perhaps one additional convert to his cause. He answered an invitation he'd received earlier from Frank Harris, a brash, Irish-born, big-mustachioed editor of one of New York's popular English-language magazines, *Pearson's*. A few mainstream progressives had started noticing Trotsky, and Harris, for one, had decided to reach out. Harris dabbled in socialism, or at least liked to talk about it. Before settling into a literary life, editing London's *Evening News* and *Saturday Review* and writing a handful of novels before landing in New York to edit *Pearson's*, Harris had done manual labor, working as everything from a boot polisher to a cowboy to a construction worker on the Brooklyn Bridge. He'd also invented a pornographic card game called Dirty Banshee, with cards showing satyrs and goddesses in various erotic poses. Harris thought that he, if anyone, could understand what this Trotsky had to say.

And so Trotsky walked the dozen blocks up Second Avenue to Harris's office at *Pearson's* magazine on East Twenty-Fourth Street, an address far more expensive than *Novy Mir* could ever afford. Harris made him comfortable, and Trotsky agreed to stay for a few hours. Harris's account doesn't mention a translator, but Harris would have needed one, since he apparently spoke little Russian or German.

Banter came easy, and the conversation wandered from politics to philosophy to world events. Harris found his guest to be "an idealist and unselfish in the main," he would say later.[371] Harris even felt relaxed enough to challenge Trotsky on his core socialist beliefs. "The Russian," he argued, "is not likely to work harder than his neighbour unless he gets something more out of it than his neighbour," he suggested, to which

Trotsky had a ready answer: "We shall all work for Russia and the future." Then "we want the complete Social Revolution, the antithesis to the capitalist state in every particular."[372]

When Trotsky at one point proclaimed, "The hour of the social revolution has struck," Harris replied, "You frighten me."

They talked most of the afternoon, until Trotsky finally had to leave. Then, as he was getting up, Harris happened to ask Trotsky about his plans to travel back to Russia. When Trotsky mentioned a stopover in Halifax, Harris acted surprised. "Good God," he asked. "You surely won't trust yourself in an English port?"

"Why not?" he recalled Trotsky's answering. "The English are our allies, you forget."

"If you think that the English government regards itself as an ally of any revolutionary Socialist and firebrand such as you, you are mistaken. [They] regard you as more dangerous than the Kaiser or Bethmann-Hollweg or Hindenberg."

"However they dislike me personally, they can do nothing; they are our allies, allies of all Russians," Harris recalled Trotsky telling him. They both laughed about it for a few minutes before Harris showed Trotsky back out onto the street.[373]

Back at *Novy Mir,* Trotsky penned a few last columns, including a manifesto for Louis Fraina to publish in the *Internationalist* after he had left the country. Then came one last complication. The telephone rang, and someone said it was for him. Trotsky picked it up and heard Natalya's voice speaking in an unusually nervous tone. Their son Sergei was missing. After days in bed, she had let him go outside alone onto Vyse Avenue for a few minutes, and the boy had wandered off.

22

MISSING

"I sit in solitary confinement. . . . My parents brought me a photograph of the girls [his daughters Zina and Nina]—I wrote you about it. They are both wonderful in their own way, Ninushka has such a face—frightened and yet slightly inquisitive at the same time. And Zinushka is so thoughtful. Someone here managed to put a smudge on Zinushka's face. If you have a spare picture, please send it."[374]

—Leon Trotsky to Alexandra Sokolovskaya Bronstein, from prison in Saint Petersburg, May 17, 1906

L ITTLE SERGEI HAD been stuck in bed on doctor's orders for more than a week with diphtheria, but the fever had finally broken during their last week in America and he wanted to go outside. The cramped three-room apartment on Vyse Avenue had started to feel like prison. He asked. He begged. He whined the way nine-year-olds do, insisting until his mother felt compelled to ignore better judgment.

Natalya told him he could go. The doctor had no objection. Just so long as he stayed nearby and came back after half an hour. After all, winter was turning to spring in New York City. Temperatures no longer plunged below freezing day after day. Mounds of snow by the curb had started to melt. People strolled the neighborhood, for errands or just to walk. The spring religious holidays, Easter and Passover, were just two weeks away, on April 7 and 8, though as socialists she and Trotsky didn't celebrate either one.

Natalya had plenty to keep her busy that day, tying up loose ends for the return to Russia. She had arranged to take the boys out of the Bronx public school where they already had learned enough English to make American friends. She didn't need to pack much for the trip. They carried no furniture, no artwork, few clothes or keepsakes. Having been in America just ten weeks, they hadn't had time to collect much clutter. As refugees over the years, she and Trotsky had learned to travel light. They would end up carrying just three bags for themselves and the boys, no trunks or boxes.

That week, Natalya probably enjoyed a final lunch and sight-seeing outing with her friend Rose Hammer, the doctor's wife, in their chauffeured car, a rare luxury just for herself. The boys, Sergei and Lyova, also felt the excitement. For them, the trip meant another great adventure, crossing the Atlantic on another big ship with sailors and smokestacks and seagulls and icebergs and strangers and endless vistas of ocean. They would finally get to see Russia, the place their parents came from.

Sadly, though, it also meant leaving New York, this city they'd barely gotten to know, where everything seemed so big and busy and exciting.

Sergei had found New York fascinating since they day they'd landed. He liked to count things, and here the numbers grew so big: so many stories in the skyscrapers, so many subway stops, so many streets. They lived in the Bronx on Vyse Avenue at 172nd Street. Papa's office was on Saint Marks Place, or Eighth Street. The numbers went up or down depending which way you walked.

Sergei, with his nine-year-old's curiosity, always wondered: If you went far enough, would you actually reach a First Street? And what came after that? Zero Street? And what after that? It might sound silly, but once his mother let him out of bed that day, dressed him in warm clothes, and sent him out to the sidewalk, little Sergei started to walk. He didn't plan to go far. It would take just a few minutes, and who knew if he'd have another chance. He went south, where the numbers got smaller. He crossed a big street, navigated the horses and motorcars, saw the buildings and shops on the other side. One block looked much like the next. He walked to the next street corner, then the next. Then he looked around.

Then something changed. Sergei noticed how streets below 172nd didn't have numbers anymore but names: Jennings Street, Freeman Street. After a while he reached 167th, but then Vyse Avenue itself disappeared and became something else: West Farms Road, then Hoe Avenue, then Westchester Avenue.

After a while, none of these streets looked familiar. He didn't recognize any of the names. He looked all around and saw apartment buildings and stores, but not the ones near his home. Where was he? Which way had he come?

He walked faster, not sure what direction to take. Then it dawned on him. He was lost.

Back in the apartment, Natalya, busy trying to pack bags and decide what items to carry halfway around the world back to Russia, noticed after a while that Sergei had not come back. Half an hour had gone by, and he had promised to return by now. At this point, she would have gone to the window and looked outside but not seen him on the sidewalk. She would have gone downstairs onto the street and walked to the street corners but not seen him there either. She'd have waited, looked around again, then gone back upstairs. But more time passed, and still nothing. She grew anxious. What to do? She picked up the telephone and called her husband at *Novy Mir,* but he didn't know either. So she waited.

Sergei, meanwhile, not the least bit shy, started asking people on the street where he was. In this neighborhood, even dozens of blocks away from his apartment, he had no trouble finding someone to understand his garble of Russian and English. Someone finally offered to walk him the few blocks to the nearest police station. Here, a nice man in a blue policeman's uniform asked Sergei if he knew his apartment's telephone number. Of course he did, he said.

It was three hours by the time the telephone finally rang and Natalya frantically picked it up. She heard a man's voice on the line, speaking in English, which she didn't understand. Then she heard Sergei. "I am here," he told her.

By now Natalya had found her older son, Lyova, and together the two of them raced over to the police station. When she walked up to the front desk and told them who she was, the officers on duty were thrilled and relieved. "She was greeted gaily," Trotsky wrote later, "like a long awaited guest."[375] Natalya found little Sergei playing checkers with one of the officers, chewing a stick of gum they had given him, having a delightful time with his new friends.

What an odd place, this America. Strangers in the street stepped up to help. The policemen were nice. They treated her like a welcome neighbor and treated her son like their new best friend. Would Russia be anything like this?

DURING THESE LAST days, Trotsky made at least one attempt to mend fences with the establishment leaders of the New York Socialist Party, though apparently not with Morris Hillquit. Hillquit, ever since his narrow victory at the Lenox Casino two weeks earlier defeating Trotsky's minority report, had continued trying to build a united peace front, even as doors now closed in his face. The country appeared days away from entering the European conflict. Hillquit had called a national emergency convention of the Socialist Party in Saint Louis on April 7 to address the crisis. He promised a strong antiwar stance, which only provoked criticism from all sides. He faced a growing revolt in his own ranks, not just from Trotsky's leftists but also among high-profile socialists who now suddenly decided to put country first. Novelists Upton Sinclair and Jack London, historian Gustavus Myers, journalists Charles Edward Russell and a dozen others all threatened to bolt the Socialists unless they gave up their pacifist line and supported going "over there."

At the same time, Hillquit insisted that any antiwar effort by the Socialists must be "strictly on American lines," no general strikes, no violence, no lawbreaking, a view certain to alienate hardliners on the left.[376]

Trotsky met a group from Hillquit's circle to talk, but it didn't go well. Trotsky still found them infuriating. He recalled how at one point he explained that the proletariat party in Russia would seize power in a second stage of the revolution, but they "took my words as a joke," as he put it. One of them told Trotsky that it was "not worth while wasting five minutes to refute my nonsensical dreams." The whole scene, he wrote, produced "the same sort of impression as a stone thrown into a puddle alive with pompous and phlegmatic frogs."[377]

With time now running short, Trotsky decided to spend his last Sunday morning in New York giving yet another speech, this time to a group of five hundred members of the National Committee of Jewish Workmen jammed into Beethoven Hall on East Fifth Street. Henry Moskowitz, then New York's commissioner of public markets, happened to share the stage with Trotsky that morning and wrote about it later. What struck Moskowitz was the connection this curious Russian had built with these immigrant workmen. Moskowitz noticed how Trotsky sat on the podium that morning "shabbily dressed" with "lines of suffering in his face," looking "unshaven," his hair "disheveled," like a "fighting agitator [with] neither the means nor the inclination to concern himself with his appearance," staring out with his "keen and blazing eyes."[378]

But when this Trotsky took the podium to speak, the impression changed abruptly. Trotsky's appearance didn't matter. His presence captured the room, "calm, sincere, and undramatic. His sharp metallic voice penetrated the hall without exertion and carried conviction."

Trotsky spoke Russian to the men, a foreign language to Moskowitz, though a friend at his side translated bits and pieces. But Moskowitz caught the room's reaction: a chuckle here, then laughter, then a round of nods, all eyes fixed on the shabbily dressed man. They "recognized him as one of their own," he wrote. The speech itself, as much as Moskowitz could decipher, had Trotsky's usual flair, painting the world war as a clash of capitalists: America's Morgans versus Germany's banking family, the Bleichroeders, and the Rothschilds of France and England.

Countries and governments took a backseat to these men of money. The common interest of workers from all lands stood on the opposite side. There was "only one war," Trotsky told them, "the class struggle; and only one enemy—capitalism."[379]

When he finished, Trotsky sat down and let the applause wash over him. There would be much to miss about America.

23

HARLEM RIVER CASINO

THE NIGHT BEFORE his ship set sail for Russia via Halifax and Norway, New York socialists threw Trotsky an enormous going-away party. More than eight hundred people jammed a gala for him at the Harlem River Casino on 127th Street, a cavernous hall that William Randolph Hearst would purchase in 1920 and convert into a film studio (called Cosmopolitan Productions) to produce movies starring his then-mistress, blond-haired comic actress Marion Davies, recently of the Ziegfeld Follies. The studio would burn down in 1923, but not before cranking out its most famous film, a historical spoof called *When Knighthood Was in Flower,* featuring Davies as a love-struck Mary Tudor in 1600s England playing opposite, among others, a promising young vaudevillian named William Powell, future Nick Charles of *The Thin Man* movies, still a struggling New York wannabe. The film grossed more than $1.5 million, making it the sixth-biggest moneymaker of 1922.

For Trotsky's gala, everyone came in good spirits. It rained that day in New York, but inside the hall a band played sentimental music, people sang, and couples danced. Red banners draped the walls as men drank schnapps and greeted old friends with hugs and shoulder slaps. A kaleidoscope of languages peppered the room. As routine for such events those days, they passed the hat and collected almost $300 in contributions for Trotsky to carry back to Russia to support the revolution.

Left-wing celebrities dotted the crowd, but none drew more attention than Emma Goldman, America's most celebrated anarchist, standing beside her lover/partner of twenty-five years, Alexander Berkman.

Goldman held a special place of adoration for these radicals, and people circled around her, wanting to touch her or catch a glimpse. Best known in early 1917 for her magazine *Mother Earth,* which drew more than ten thousand subscribers, and her frequent lectures on birth control and free love, as well as politics, labor, and socialism, Emma Goldman could be spellbinding on the stump. She had caused a riot in 1894 by urging striking garment workers in New York to attack homes of wealthy people on Fifth Avenue and seize bread off their tables. This resulted in her first prison term, a year on New York's Blackwell's Island in the East River. A few years later, Leon Czolgosz, the self-proclaimed anarchist who had assassinated President William McKinley in 1901, had claimed Emma Goldman as an inspiration, having seen her speak shortly before committing the crime. This assertion caused more arrests.

But these adventures all paled next to her long-term free-love relationship with Berkman, who had spent fourteen years in prison for his failed attempt in 1892 to murder Henry Clay Frick, manager of the Andrew Carnegie steelworks in Homestead, Pennsylvania, during the notorious 1892 strike there. Frick had hired three hundred armed Pinkerton detectives to crush a group of workers who had seized the factory. The resulting gunfight ended with ten dead and dozens wounded before eight thousand Pennsylvania militiamen intervened to restore order. Goldman and Berkman had planned the crime as an act of propaganda, hoping to spark a wider labor revolt. She defended Berkman against a storm of criticism over it.[380]

Now, she and Berkman looked like any other slightly overweight, middle-aged couple mingling politely with admirers. Emma Goldman had never seen Trotsky and, being in New York, couldn't resist the opportunity to meet him. She would remember him from that night as a plain-looking man, "medium height, with haggard cheeks, reddish hair, and straggling red beard," but dazzling from the podium.

Emma Goldman wasn't the only celebrity present. By then, even the New York City Police Department, tipped off by British intelligence, thought enough to send a detective to spy on the affair.

Looking out at the crowd that night, Trotsky had to feel satisfaction, seeing what he had accomplished during his barely ten weeks in America, here in tangible human form. "Trotsky built up a large and enthusiastic personal following," Ludwig Lore explained.[381] He had created a movement, a political faction too powerful to ignore and ready to fight. No guest list from the night survives. Newspaper accounts mention only the names of a few well-known people. Trotsky's admirers in the hall didn't yet call themselves by any special name: Trotskyites or Trotskyists or even communists. Those labels would come soon enough.

But by now Trotsky's followers had become a distinct voice in socialist circles. The group Ludwig Lore had pulled together for dinner at his Brooklyn apartment on Trotsky's first day in America had stuck with him. Lore and Louis Boudin both made speeches that night. Louis Fraina, now editor of the *Internationalist,* had become Trotsky's protégé fighting to radicalize the Socialist Party. Another new disciple, James P. Cannon, a westerner, had followed Trotsky's lead by showing up at Morris Hillquit's huge Madison Square Garden meeting on the Russian Revolution and delivering a revolutionary stem-winder: "If we can't get liberty by our votes, we will use the bayonets they put in our hands," Cannon had told the crowd that night to Hillquit's doubtless chagrin. "The house of Rockefeller and the house of Morgan will fall as has the house of Romanoff in Russia."[382]

After his few weeks in the country, Trotsky, through hard work—his dozens of speeches, columns, and meetings—had grown that small following into hundreds. Now, with the Russian Revolution, he emerged as a unifying figure on the far left. He had quarreled with local leaders and often felt like a fish out of water. Even so, on this night, Trotsky seemed at peace, and New York at peace with him. Soon he would be gone and no longer able to make trouble. On this night, Trotsky could present himself to New York as its ambassador to the New Russia. Americans, from the comfort of home, could support him by contributing a few dollars and claim their bona fides as revolutionaries.

The night's big moment finally came as Trotsky took the podium for one last harangue. He spoke for two hours, first in Russian, then repeating the entire oration in German. He was sorry he couldn't stay longer in America, he told them, but "when revolution calls, revolutionaries follow." For he and his comrades returning to Russia, "the world is [our] country, [we] live for it, fight for it, and if need be are ready to die for it."[383]

No transcript of the speech survives. Emma Goldman, caught up in the dramatics, described it this way: "His analysis of the causes of the war was brilliant, his denunciation of the ineffective Provisional Government in Russia scathing, and his presentation of the conditions that led up to the Revolution illuminating. He closed his two hours' talk with an eloquent tribute to the working masses of his native land. The audience was roused to a high pitch of enthusiasm, and Sasha [Berkman] and I heartily joined in the ovation given the speaker."[384] She found the whole performance "powerful and electrifying."

Ludwig Lore recalled an "almost religious fervor" among this multinational, multilingual radical crowd.[385]

Even the New York Police spy gave Trotsky's speech a dramatic flourish in his English translation, claiming, according to reports, that Trotsky climaxed it with a call for revolution right here in America. "I am going back to Russia to overthrow the Provisional Government there and to stop the war with Germany," he quoted Trotsky as saying. "I want you people here to organize and keep organizing until you are able to overthrow the damned rotten capitalistic Government of this country."[386]

After the speeches, the affair broke up and people walked out into the cold New York night. Emma Goldman made a point to buttonhole Trotsky, and she remembered the conversation: "He knew about us and he inquired when we meant to come to Russia to help in the work of reconstruction, she wrote. "We will surely meet there," Trotsky told her.[387]

TROTSKY, NATALYA, AND the boys left the apartment on Vyse Avenue in the Bronx early the next morning. They left the door unlocked, leaving behind whatever belongings couldn't fit into their small travel bags for neighbors to come and take what they wanted. Henry Feuer, the salesman for the Bronx furniture shop, came to collect the furniture that day and remembered finding it in "first-rate" condition, good enough to sell at auction.[388] Trotsky had been paying $2 per week for the furniture on the layaway plan, but the sudden departure left a balance. Sholem Asch, a Bronx neighbor and well-known writer, claimed that he was the one who got stuck with the remaining $200 payment. "I am honored with the burden bequeathed to me by the Russian Premier," he joked to a reporter while sitting in a Lower East Side café, telling him about the unpaid bill a few months later, in early 1918, after Trotsky had become world famous as Bolshevik Russia's new foreign minister. "His Excellency, answering the call of his country, left New York and left me with the debt—which I had guaranteed."[389]

Changes had come to New York by the morning Trotsky boarded his ship for Russia. When he had arrived in January, America still enjoyed peace, a tsar ruled in Russia, and Trotsky himself remained an obscure nobody. Now, by late March, Russia had toppled its tsar, America stood two weeks away from entering the European war, and, whether he knew it or not, Trotsky's own movements were being tracked by global intelligence teams.

New York's latest scandal that week typified the change. It involved the mayor, John Purroy Mitchel, who had found a new political voice as military booster. "I say to you in the galleries that today we are divided into two classes—Americans and traitors," Mitchel had told a Carnegie Hall crowd that week.[390] Now he had gone further and publicly smeared state senator Robert F. Wagner, a protégé of Tammany Hall boss Charles Murphy and future four-term United States senator. Wagner had been born in Germany forty years earlier, and that was enough for Mayor Mitchel to accuse him of disloyalty, claiming that Wagner had backed "German interests" by delaying a vote in the state legislature on acquiring land near Rockaway Point to build a defense installation (and doubtless earn someone a kickback). The "Gentleman from Prussia," he called him.[391] Wagner had demanded an apology, calling the charge "wickedly and atrociously false."[392]

A high-ranking public figure, Wagner survived the political attack. But with war imminent, open season for character assassination against German Americans had begun.

Riding the elevated train from the Bronx to lower Manhattan, then crossing the Brooklyn Bridge to Brooklyn, Trotsky would have passed for one last time the dizzying mix of New York, its crowds and skyscrapers and noise and traffic. Riding past the streets around Five Points and the Lower East Side, he might have glanced gangs of tough young kids on street corners, teenagers with names like Charles (later "Lucky") Luciano or Meyer Lansky, or Lansky's young sidekick, a kid named Benny (later "Bugsy") Siegel, future kings of New York crime. In Brooklyn, he would have passed rows of warehouses, grain elevators, and factories set among the tenements.

More than three hundred well-wishers came to see them off at the South Brooklyn pier jutting into the East River, as if the movable feast from the previous night's Harlem River Casino gala had simply hopped the subway and followed them. "Rain fell in torrents," Ludwig Lore remembered of that morning, but that didn't stop the enthusiasm. People waved red banners and threw floral bouquets. "When Trotsky arrived [at the pier] he was lifted on the shoulders of his admirers to the top of a huge packing box and with his beaming face and happy smile he bade a last farewell," Lore wrote.[393]

At about 10 AM, Trotsky, Natalya, and the boys left their friends one last time and walked up the gangplank to the main deck of the *Kristianiafjord*. The steamer sat five hundred feet long, with two large smokestacks bearing colors of the Norwegian-America Line. Trotsky waved a last farewell before stepping out of the rain. But Lore remembered the mood among the Americans staying behind. They stayed, watched, and continued the celebration even after Trotsky had disappeared from view, he wrote. "Down at the pier, in the pouring rain, the crowd lingered, lingered on and on, loath to leave, as if its presence there were bringing it nearer to the land of its hopes."[394]

A few minutes later, the ship cast off and tugboats steered it out into the harbor toward the Statue of Liberty. Those on deck saw the jagged skyline of buildings on Brooklyn and Manhattan recede into the distance beneath the steel-gray sky. Time had passed so quickly that Trotsky could barely process his thoughts. He had experienced something extraordinary but couldn't verbalize it quite yet. For now, aboard the *Kristianiafjord*, he could only struggle for words. "I was leaving for Europe, with the feeling of a man who has had only a peep into the foundry in which the fate of man is to be forged," he wrote. "My only consolation was the thought that I might return."[395]

What Trotsky did not know at that moment was that New York, or at least a few people at the southern tip of Manhattan, had not finished with him yet.

As the ship receded into the distance, William George Eden Wiseman could catch a glimpse of it from the window of his office at 44 Whitehall. So far, despite all he knew, he had done nothing to stop it. But Wiseman was not the only person in the building aware of who had been allowed to leave.

24

KRISTIANIAFJORD

"The passenger list was long and mysterious. Trotsky was in the steerage with a group of revolutionaries; there was a Japanese revolutionist in my cabin. There were a lot of Dutch hurrying home from Java, the only innocent people aboard. The rest were war messengers, two from Wall Street to Germany; and spies; and war business men; one war correspondent. . . . No tourists."[396]

—Journalist Lincoln Steffens, a passenger with Trotsky aboard the
  Kristianiafjord, writing in 1931

T HE NEXT DAY, after the *Kristianiafjord* had left New York and been at sea almost twenty-four hours, a second coded telegram issued from the British Intelligence office at 44 Whitehall. This time the message left nothing to chance: "URGENT. TROTZKI sailed yesterday on Board S.S. 'KRISTIANIA FIORD' accompanied by VOSKOFF, CLADNOWSKI, MUCHIN and other Russian Socialists." Then it went on: "TROTZKI is reliably reported to have $10,000 subscribed by socialists and Germans to start revolution against present Russian Government. Various Germans saw TROTZKI off. I am notifying HALIFAX, telling Authorities there to try to hold steamship until they receive direct your instructions [*sic*] regarding these men."[397]

Unlike the prior one, this second cable came not from William Wiseman, the dapper chief of Britain's MI1c intelligence operation in New York City, but rather from Captain Guy Gaunt, the naval attaché Wiseman had pushed aside in January so that Wiseman could fatten his own diplomatic portfolio. Gaunt had been nursing a grudge over the affair for weeks. Gaunt had addressed this second cable not to anyone at MI1c, Wiseman's bureau, but instead to his own direct superior officer in the British navy, Admiral Reginald "Blinker" Hall, director of British naval intelligence in London.

How had Gaunt learned about Trotsky? In raising the alarm, had Gaunt gone behind Wiseman's back, trying to embarrass Wiseman as revenge for his sharp-elbowed office politics? Had he even talked to Wiseman before sending it? Had they argued?

To this day, it remains a mystery. Up to that moment, William Wiseman gave every outward sign of having decided to let Trotsky leave New York and return to Russia without interference. He had allowed Trotsky to get his visa from the British consulate and watched Trotsky's ship sail without lifting a finger. And he had plenty of good reasons to justify this choice. The evidence against Trotsky as a German agent had been weak, giving Britain little legal basis to hold him. Wiseman also might have feared embarrassing the Russians, who had just given Trotsky a passport. Or he might have decided that Trotsky could do Britain more good back in Russia, where he might speak out against a separate peace with Germany. He even might have gotten approval for the decision from his MI1c chiefs in London. British intelligence files refer to a secret report from Wiseman to his MI1c boss "C" from around this time on "Russian Revolutionaries in New York—Activities and Movements of Trotzki Leon," but the report itself is missing.[398]

But appearances can be deceiving, especially in spycraft, and especially here, where there was another possibility. All Wiseman's approvals of Trotsky's trip could have been a trap. Wiseman might have decided from the start to put Trotsky behind bars but preferred to have him stopped or arrested in Canada, not America, and at Halifax, a British port far away from the gossipy New York newspapers. If this was the case, then Guy Gaunt might have sent the cable to help Wiseman, acting at his request.

The archival record is painfully silent on this question. Whatever went on behind the scenes, we can only speculate.

But there was something else. Gaunt's cable that morning was sloppy, riddled with errors. Nobody named Voskoff was on the ship, "Chudnovsky" was misspelled, and the man Muchin named in the cable was not part of Trotsky's group. Further, the cable claimed that Trotsky was carrying $10,000 given to him by socialists and Germans to carry out revolution. But this assertion had no visible basis. In 1917, $10,000 was a remarkable sum of money for a person to carry, worth hundreds of thousands of modern dollars, enough to buy a fleet of cars or small boats, or rifles for a hundred men. It was wildly out of proportion to any money Trotsky had been seen collecting during his time in New York: his $20-per-week salary at *Novy Mir,* the $10 or so he received for articles and speeches, even the $300 in donations that sponsors claimed from the Harlem River Casino going-away party two nights earlier.

Did the money exist at all? Had Guy Gaunt or someone else simply made up the number for dramatic effect? Or had Trotsky actually taken a secret payment from a German spy or some wealthy Jews or socialists? If they arrested Trotsky in Halifax, at least they'd have the chance to search him and find out.

On this one point, the British intelligence files do give a clear answer. One of Wiseman's superiors would later ask him to reveal the source for this tip, and Wiseman would tell him. It had come from Casimir Pilenas, Wiseman's Russian-speaking informer, with a history with the Russian Okhrana, who had heard Trotsky speak at the Lenox Casino and seen them pass the hat.[399]

Guy Gaunt's cable that day worked like a charm. It reached London and set off a bureaucratic scramble. Within twenty-four hours, British naval intelligence officials there decided to act. They issued their own coded telegram to Halifax, Nova Scotia, where the *Kristianiafjord* was scheduled to stop the next day. Following Gaunt's lead, they instructed the British naval control officer there, a Captain O. M. Makins, to stop the *Kristianiafjord,* identify the suspicious Russians on board, and have them "taken off and retained pending instructions." In case Makins failed to grasp the urgency, they explained: "These are Russian Socialists leaving for the purpose of starting revolution against present Russian Government for which TROTSKY is reported to have 10,000 dollars subscribed by Socialists and Germans."[400]

Captain O. M. Makins, a veteran naval officer, had no intention of letting such dangerous people escape on his watch.

OUT AT SEA, the *Kristianiafjord* spent its first days en route to Russia via Norway under forbidding gray skies. Following the usual route, it would have hugged the coast of Long Island past the sandy beaches of South Hampton and Amagansett, then rounded Montauk Point and Cape Cod before steaming out over the North Atlantic toward Nova Scotia. Frigid north winds blew across the open water, giving any stroller on deck a bone-chilling blast of late-winter cold.

After settling into their second-class cabin, Trotsky, Natalya, and the boys started exploring the ship and found the mood strikingly upbeat and excited. Most of the passengers, like themselves, were headed to Russia, suddenly the most interesting place on earth. People talked about the future, homecomings, revolution, and the parts they hoped to play. This time Trotsky had brought friends with him, his circle of New York radicals. One passenger, a man in first class named Robert Zhivotovskii, may have even been his cousin.

Among those in first class, Lincoln Steffens, the celebrated muckraking journalist from *McClure's* magazine and the *New York Evening Post,* probably drew the most attention. Beyond his books and lectures, Steffens had covered the recent revolution in Mexico, riding the range with renegade general Pancho Villa, and had assisted famed defense lawyer Clarence Darrow in a murder case involving the 1911 bombing of the Los Angeles Times Building. Now he hoped to witness the next great global upheaval in Russia. Steffens traveled with a quasi-political figure, financier Charles R. Crane, a former US minister to China and financial contributor to President Woodrow Wilson's political campaigns.

Steffens remembered visiting Trotsky during those first few days at sea. Steffens knew Trotsky's reputation from New York and wanted to pick his brain about Petrograd. "I called on Trotsky and his friends," Steffens wrote, "and we talked some."[401] In a letter, Steffens described this on-ship conversation, how "all agree that the revolution is in its first phase only" and that "we shall be in Petrograd for the re-revolution."[402] Steffens would keep in touch with Trotsky long after this trip. He would write a foreword to a 1918 edition of Trotsky's book *War and the International* and for a time would become enamored with Bolsheviks and Bolshevism. Back in America in 1919, after seeing the revolution in action, Steffens would remark, "I have been over into the future, and it works." This catchphrase, shortened to "I have seen the future and it worked," would become a favorite Soviet propaganda piece in the 1920s, though Steffens would sour on communism after that.[403]

After three days at sea and almost a thousand miles traveled, the *Kristianiafjord* on Friday, March 30, finally reached Nova Scotia. It rounded the lighthouse at Peggy's Cove and entered the channel connecting the North Atlantic to Halifax Harbor, the ship's only scheduled stop between New York and Norway. Halifax sat on a protected peninsula inside the harbor. Behind it, the harbor opened up into a wide, deepwater expanse called Bedford Basin. With the European war now in its third year, this spot had become a magnet for ships of all shapes and sizes. The Canadian navy based its Atlantic fleet here, and the British navy kept a sizable presence as well. Smokestacks mingled with sails and wooden masts. Tugboats worked alongside schooners and fishing boats, warships and passenger liners bearing flags from a dozen European countries, cargo and relief convoys preparing to run the gauntlet of German submarines.

Many of the vessels here carried large stocks of arms and munitions, which posed considerable danger in these tight quarters. In December 1917, a French munitions ship, the *Mont-Blanc*, fully loaded with two hundred tons of TNT and twenty-three hundred tons of explosive picric acid, would collide with a Belgian relief vessel, the *Imo,* setting off a blast that would damage much of the city, killing eighteen hundred people and destroying more than sixteen hundred buildings, the worst such disaster in the city's history.

Once the *Kristianiafjord* entered the harbor, found its mooring, and laid anchor, the ship's crew spotted a British warship approaching at high speed. Nobody panicked. This was normal procedure, and the crew instructed the passengers to come on deck for inspection. Everyone knew what to expect. Their stop at Halifax, required under the British blockade, was designed to give British naval officers a chance to come aboard, search the ship for contraband, and examine the passengers. Not routine, however, was the British officer who came personally to command the operation that day, Captain O. M. Makins, the chief British naval control officer on site, acting on orders from London.

Once aboard, the British officers started the process as usual. Passengers lined up and British sailors inspected each of them, one by one, checking papers and rifling belongings. But Lincoln Steffens, who joined the other passengers on deck for inspection that day, noticed a special intensity in the effort. "Having gone through us once and given us time to bring out of hiding whatever we had to conceal, the British searched us again—and again, and yet again," he explained. Mostly what struck Steffens was their brusque attitude. As he put it, "the British take command and order you about as if they really ruled the waves."[404]

The exercise didn't concern Trotsky until after the British inspectors had finished with the English-speaking passengers and begun processing Trotsky's own circle of friends. They "subjected us Russians to a direct examination, in the style of the old Russian Gendarmes," he recalled.[405] The strange part was that, rather than asking about their passports and visas, which Trotsky knew to be proper since he had obtained them just days earlier from the Russian and British consulates, the officers started questioning them about politics. What did they think of Russia, the world war, the revolution, the provisional government? This was not standard procedure and had not been done with any of the other passengers.

What's more, Trotsky noticed a Russian military officer suddenly appear, standing with Captain Makins to assist with the interrogations. His name was Andrei Kalpaschnikoff, a colonel traveling on the *Kristianiafjord* as a passenger in first class since New York. Looking at him closely, Trotsky probably recognized Kalpaschnikoff, perhaps had even traded pleasantries with him during the first few days at sea. Beyond his military rank, Kalpaschnikoff had been a prominent diplomat under the tsar, serving before the war as secretary to the Russian embassy in Washington, DC. In New York, where he had returned as a Red Cross purchasing agent, Kalpaschnikoff was close friends with Pierre Routsky, the Russian consulate official who had haggled with Trotsky over his passport a few days earlier.

Kalpaschnikoff later would deny any involvement with the British officers that day, claiming he had simply offered to help translate, since many of the Russian men scarcely spoke English. "I was the only [Russian] government official [on the scene] and the commander of the port asked me to help him, which I did willingly," he would explain. "Among the many emigrants questioned in my presence was Trotsky."[406]

But Trotsky, seeing Kalpaschnikoff that day, would long suspect the Russian consulate back in New York of somehow orchestrating this inquisition. In fact, Trotsky may have been right. Routsky, Guy Gaunt, or even the informer Casimir Pilenas easily could have told Kalpaschnikoff about Trotsky and the plan to have him arrested. Trotsky himself had no doubt. Two years later in Russia, in 1919, Trotsky would have Kalpaschnikoff arrested for counterrevolutionary activities.[407] When Kalpaschnikoff was freed, returned to New York, and got married later that year, he would make a point to include Pierre Routsky as an honored guest at the wedding.[408]

But for now, in Halifax Harbor aboard the *Kristianiafjord*, confronting his British questioners, Trotsky refused to answer. "My relations to internal Russian politics [are] not at present under the control of the British naval police," he told them.[409]

But the British officers refused to accept his answer. Faced with his silence, they started asking other passengers about Trotsky and his party. Had anyone spoken with them or heard their opinions? Trotsky remembered one passenger calling him a "terrible socialist." He found the whole process "undignified," as he would put it in a formal protest a few weeks later, treating Russians passengers in an "exceptional" way for citizens of a country allied with Great Britain.[410]

Still, Captain Makins and his officers kept at it and finally managed to examine each Russian passenger and identify six who seemed to fit the description contained in Makins's orders. Three of them, Trotsky, Nikita Muchin, and Grigorii Chudnovsky, directly matched the names in his cable from London. Two of the others had visible links to Trotsky—Guschon Melnichansky as a contributor to *Novy Mir* and Konstantin Romanchinko as part of Trotsky's traveling group. As for the sixth, a man named Liebe Fisheleff, he was a writer for the popular Jewish anarchist weekly *Freier Arbeiter Stimme* (Free Voice of Labor), which made him a target even if he had no apparent connection to the others.

Since these names failed to match the original list from British naval intelligence—he found no Voskoff, and Fisheleff, Romanchinko, and Melnichansky were new additions—Captain Makins decided to cable London and ask instructions. These six, he reported, were "all avowed Socialists" who "might well be in league with German Socialists in America, and quite likely to be a hindrance to the Govt. in Russia just at present." On this basis, Makins proposed to arrest them all. "It is proposed to remove also the wife and two boys of Trotski," he added, for civil detention.[411]

Meanwhile, until he received orders, Captain Makins told the passengers nothing but ordered the *Kristianiafjord* to sit in the harbor and wait. For Trotsky, the delay might have been annoying, but it still gave him no reason to think his trip had been jeopardized. He had a proper British visa and a proper Russian passport. Yes, the British officers had acted rudely, but the British consulate in New York had told him they would put no obstacle in his way. So far at least, he had no reason to think they hadn't told him the truth.

FINALLY, THREE DAYS later, on Tuesday morning, April 3, Captain Makins came back to the *Kristianiafjord,* still anchored at its mooring in Halifax Harbor, this time leading a squad of British sailors sporting rifles and bayonets. "It was a beautiful spring morning," Colonel Kalpaschnikoff, the Russian officer, recalled. "The sea was calm and when a big launch full of armed sailors came alongside we all rushed on deck to see what was going to happen."[412]

The sailors came aboard and quickly rounded up Trotsky, his family, and the five other identified Russians. Then they told Trotsky to come with them immediately to a cutter headed toward shore. Trotsky asked why, but the sailors said they could explain the situation only on land in Halifax. Once again, Trotsky refused. He insisted that the demand was illegal and that he would not leave the ship. So Captain Makins ordered that the British sailors seize him.

There are different versions of what happened next. By Trotsky's own account, the sailors grabbed him, lifted him bodily, and carried him away as several passengers shouted "Shame," this prompting his older son, eleven-year-old Lyova, to charge one of the sailors, grab him, and shout, "Shall I hit him, father?"[413] According to another version, this from a friendly German-language newspaper, Trotsky resisted and then one of the sailors shot him in the arm with his rifle. Then, as they were dragging him off, he shouted: "England is the enemy of liberty. Long live socialism."[414]

Colonel Kalpaschnikoff, standing nearby, described how Trotsky "protested and kicked but was carried by big strapping seamen who did their work calmly and methodically," removing him from the ship. Then, he wrote, "as the boat moved away, Trotsky shook his fist at the English officers and cursed England."[415]

A very different picture came from a Canadian publisher and former lieutenant colonel named J. B. Maclean. Maclean, not aboard the ship that day, wrote his version almost a year later based on conversations with unnamed police sources, who gave a less flattering account. "[Trotsky] crouched and whined and cried in abject terror" at the sailors' guns, Maclean wrote, and it was only "when he found he was not to be shot [that] his bluff returned and he protested violently."[416]

Either way, once they had him, the sailors took Trotsky and the other prisoners from the *Kristianiafjord* and placed them onto a military cutter waiting alongside. A navy cruiser joined them as added security for the ride to Halifax. Captain Makins and his men took nine prisoners ashore that day. They included Trotsky, the five other Russians, plus Natalya and the two boys. After that, Captain Makins ordered the *Kristianiafjord* to raise anchor, leave the harbor, and proceed on its way to Norway. "They held us for a week or more, an anxious week during which everybody worried," Lincoln Steffens wrote after watching the whole affair—everybody "except the Wall Street messengers to Germany."[417]

Once again, six days after leaving New York, Trotsky found himself under arrest, not charged with any crime, and denied any legal rights. And for now, other than the British and a few passengers on the *Kristianiafjord,* no one even knew about it.

DESPITE ALL THE searches by Captain Makins and his crew during their two incursions onto the *Kristianiafjord,* plus more searches after the arrests, no records from the Canadian or British Intelligence files contain any mention of Trotsky, his wife, or anyone in their party carrying $10,000 or anything close to that amount in cash, gold, or any other form of money. If Trotsky in fact had been carrying it, he would have had to throw it overboard into the ocean or the deep waters of Bedford Basin to avoid the British finding it, highly unlikely given the hundreds of witnesses on board. With the specific reference to the $10,000 in Captain Makins's orders from London, Makins certainly would have alerted his inspectors to search for it specifically and reported it immediately had they found it. Britain would have trumpeted the news around the world as a great propaganda coup. Instead, they said nothing of it, either publicly or privately.

The silence leaves little doubt that the $10,000 charge had been a fabrication from the start, at best a gross exaggeration. Still, that $10,000 figure, baseless or not, had now appeared in two formal intelligence cables from the British government, giving it a life of its own. It would soon seep into the public domain, becoming fodder, over the next century, for a range of conspiracy theories that would make people's heads spin.

BY THIS POINT in early April, the race by Russian radicals around the world to get home was well under way.

Alexandra Kollontai would be one of the first to reach Petrograd. She left Holmenkollen on March 31, carrying the letters Vladimir Lenin had asked her to hand deliver to *Pravda* on reaching Russia. Her train traversed eight hundred miles of tundra before reaching the Finnish border station of Haparanda. At Beloostrov, the last checkpoint before Petrograd, a guard greeted her by pulling from his desk an old tsarist arrest warrant for her dating back to 1908 and laughing while ripping it into pieces. As she left the garrison, he took her hand in a gallant gesture and kissed it. Reaching the city, she was mobbed by friends and relatives eager to hear about the outside world.

Kollontai's 1915 pamphlet "Who Needs War" had reached millions of Russian soldiers on the front and families back home, making her one of the best-known and best-liked Bolsheviks in Russia. Now finally in Petrograd, she found the city excited and confused. She discovered that the Bolshevik Party itself had fallen under control of two local leaders, Joseph Stalin and Lev Kamenev, both of whom had been serving exiles in Siberia when the revolution broke out and had been freed by Kerensky's amnesty. They had rushed back to Petrograd, assumed authority over *Pravda,* and taken the initiative to announce a new party line: conditional support for the provisional government.

Kollontai had to laugh. As personal courier for Vladimir Lenin, she knew perfectly well that Lenin would reject the new line immediately.

Lenin had no intention of providing Kerensky, Miliukov, and their clique any support whatsoever, conditional or any other kind. Lenin had already mapped out a radical new approach based on seizing power for the soviets. Kollontai had Lenin's letters in her pocket to prove it, and she delivered them to *Pravda* on her very first morning in the country.

Lenin started for Russia a few days after Kollontai. He led a group of Bolsheviks and Mensheviks by local train from Zurich to Schaffhausen on the German border. Here they boarded another train, this one supplied by the German government. German soldiers led them to seats in a special car set apart for them. The soldiers locked three of the car's four doors. It took them six days to cross Germany. The train stopped in Berlin, but the travelers never left the car, eating in it, sleeping in it, and even sharing its small bathroom. At Sassnitz on the Baltic Sea, they boarded a ferry for Trelleborg on the southern tip of Sweden, where Jacob Furstenberg—acting as agent for the Germans—welcomed them with a lavish banquet.

One of the first people Furstenberg contacted with news of Lenin's arrival was Alexander Israel Helphand, or Parvus, who had done more than anyone else to arrange it. From there Lenin reached Stockholm, then Finland, then arrived in Petrograd on April 16, greeted by even more fanfare and celebration.

By then, even Nikolai Bukharin, Trotsky's young fellow editor at *Novy Mir* in New York City, had started his own long trip home, traveling from New York to Vancouver, British Columbia, then across the Pacific Ocean to Japan. Bukharin was briefly detained by authorities in Tokyo and then arrested in eastern Russia by local Mensheviks before, in early May, finally reaching Moscow, where friends invited him to resume his old seat on the Moscow Bolshevik Committee.

As they all gathered in Russia—Bolsheviks, Mensheviks, Kadets, Social Revolutionaries, radicals of every stripe in new forms and combinations, plotting and scheming—only Lev Davidovich Trotsky remained missing, stuck four thousand miles away in Canada, unable to move under British detention.

25

NOVA SCOTIA

"We undersigned political refugees after declaration of amnesty by
present Russian Government returning via Norway to our country
with passports issued Russian consul General New York are arrested
Halifax on board 'Kristiania.' Held by British military authorities
without any cause and reason and interned internment station
Amherst together with German prisoners of war. We energetically
protest against such unprecedented act and demand your immediate
intervention to protect our interests of Russian citizens and dignity
of government which you represent.

Signed trotzky melnitchaniny fishleff ishoodnouski muchin
konstantin romanchenka."[418]

—Telegram from Trotsky and fellow prisoners to the Russian consul
general at Montreal, April 5, 1917

I N HALIFAX, HARBOR police immediately separated Trotsky from
Natalya and the boys and surrendered him to the Canadian military.
For his first night in captivity, they placed Trotsky and the other Russian
prisoners at nearby Fort George, what locals called the Citadel, a star-
shaped fortress that had sat on a hill overlooking Halifax since 1749,
built originally to defend it from attacks by Indians and later Americans
during the War of 1812. Recently, the Citadel had been converted into
a wartime prison for domestic "enemy aliens," primarily German immigrants suspected of disloyalty and German sailors captured in the port.

But Trotsky's stay there would be brief. After one night, they put
him and the others on a train to Amherst, a small industrial town in the

Nova Scotia interior. Here, far from public view, 90 miles from Halifax, 500 miles from Quebec, 650 miles from Montreal, and surrounded by vast stretches of wilderness, Canada had opened a larger wartime camp, this one mostly for captured German soldiers.

The Amherst camp operated inside an abandoned iron factory once run by the Canadian Car and Foundry Company. The cavernous structure stood one hundred feet wide and a quarter of a mile long and held eight hundred prisoners at the time Trotsky arrived. Most of these, about five hundred, were soldiers and sailors rescued by the British navy from German ships it had sunk, including the SS *Kaiser Wilhelm der Grosse,* scuttled off the coast of West Africa. Another two hundred were German civilians, laborers working in Canada when the war broke out and considered disloyal. About one hundred, housed in separate, better quarters at the building's far end, were German officers and wealthier German civilians.

Canada would jail some eighty-five hundred "alien enemies" during the war, and Amherst was one of its largest camps.

If the Amherst camp had a personality, it came from its strict commanding officer, Colonel Arthur Henry Morris, a sixty-six-year-old retired British military officer and veteran of colonial campaigns in India, Burma, and Africa. Born on the Isle of Wight, Morris had won medals, including the Distinguished Service Order, for bravery both in the Boer War and the Anglo-Ashanti War in modern-day Ghana on the African Gold Coast. There he'd played a crucial role in the bloody battle over Kumasi, the Ashanti capital, leading infantry columns both into and out of the strategic city, despite severe injuries. Queen Victoria's son-in-law, Prince Henry of Battenberg, had died of malaria in the campaign. After that, Morris, an avid hunter and shooter, commanded the Duke of York's military school in England before coming to Canada in 1915 to run Amherst.

Morris had a favorite line when Trotsky annoyed him. "If only I had him on the South African Coast," he'd mutter. There he could impose discipline as he pleased.

The Amherst camp sat along the railroad tracks between Park and Hickman Streets, toward the southern end of town. On bringing the prisoners inside, Colonel Morris's men greeted them with an inspection worthy of any full-security prison. They recorded Trotsky's height (five foot eight and a half), weight (137 pounds), eye and hair color (black), complexion (dark), and age (thirty-seven). They searched him, removed his clothes in front of a roomful of people for a full-body examination, and then took his fingerprints. Having seized his luggage and clothing, they gave Trotsky and his group uniforms, making them indistinguishable from the German soldier-prisoners. The guards then assigned them bunks in the main hall, where hundreds of men slept and lived cramped together, with the bunks arranged in three tiers, two deep along the walls on each side of the long room. "Men hopelessly clogged the passages, elbowed their way through, lay down and got up, played cards or chess," Trotsky would write, describing the place as "very dilapidated."[419]

They treated Trotsky and his party as prisoners of war, thereby limiting their access to habeas corpus and other legal rights accorded Canadian citizens and residents. They also assigned Trotsky a share of the daily menial labor required of captured German soldiers: sweeping floors, washing pots and dishes, peeling potatoes, cleaning the lavatory. Only the German officers and wealthier civilians apparently escaped these duties.

At his first chance, Trotsky requested a face-to-face audience with Colonel Morris, the camp commandant, to assert what he considered two key rights: learning the charges against him and being allowed to communicate with the outside world. Morris took until the next morning before finally agreeing to see him, and Trotsky didn't get far on either score.

Trotsky and Colonel Morris apparently clashed from the start. Morris appeared in his sharp military khakis; Trotsky wore prison clothes. Beyond the thirty-year age difference and Trotsky's Jewishness, Morris had made a career of fighting rebels in Burma and Africa and had little patience for back talk. Trotsky, for his part, had always despised uniformed bureaucrats like Morris.

Trotsky, by his own account, asked Morris the basis for his arrest, to which Morris told him simply, "You are dangerous to the present Russian government" and have been sent to Amherst "until such time as further instructions are received from the Admiralty."[420] Trotsky argued the point, telling Morris: "But the New York agents of the Russian government issued us passports into Russia, [and] the Russian government should be allowed to take care of itself."

At this, Morris simply shifted ground. "You are dangerous to the allies in general," he answered, and, having fled his own country, "should not be surprised" at being arrested now.[421]

Trotsky again tried to argue, pointing to the Russian Revolution as having changed things, but Morris stopped answering. Trotsky asked to see any written charges against them, but Morris had nothing to show.

As for contacting outsiders, the conversation here reached the same dead end. Trotsky had prepared telegrams for the Russian consuls in Halifax and Montreal, the Russian justice minister in Petrograd, the Petrograd Soviet, the *New York Call,* and others. He submitted them all, and Morris apparently took them but never told Trotsky what he planned to do with them. Trotsky asked Morris if he could contact his wife in Halifax, but Morris refused unless Trotsky promised not to try to send messages through her to the Russian consulate. This time it was Trotsky who refused. Trotsky was free to send letters through the normal postal system, Morris told him, but he and military censors routinely examined all outgoing mail from the camp.

In the end, Morris agreed to forward just one telegram that day, a cable from Trotsky and his group to the Russian consulate in Montreal and its consul general, I. A. Lakatscheff. Canadian archives confirm that Lakatscheff actually received the telegram in Montreal and that, on reading it, he dutifully contacted the Canadian foreign ministry in Ottawa, asking for an explanation.[422] Joseph Pope, the Canadian undersecretary of state for external affairs, responded a few days later, saying simply, "I am informed that this action was taken at the request of the Admiralty;

the persons arrested being Russian Socialists animated with the purpose of starting revolution against the present Russian Government."[423]

And that was that. The archive files contain no indication of any follow-up by Lakatscheff, and none of this exchange was shared with the prisoners.

As Trotsky languished in Amherst, Natalya and the two boys, Sergei and Lyova, settled awkwardly into their new roles as civil detainees in Halifax. Britain had not charged Natalya with a crime or even being a threat to anyone, so it had no basis to lock her up. But the authorities hardly intended to let her run loose around Halifax or, even worse, skip town to make trouble. Instead, Canadian harbor officials coaxed a local staff member into boarding Natalya in his house. David Horowitz, the port's official Russian translator, lived with his family on Market Street and, speaking Russian, could communicate with Natalya in her native language. The port officials tried at first to separate Sergei and Lyova and place them in an asylum, but Natalya refused to separate from her sons. On this point, the officials relented. They allowed Natalya to keep the boys so long as she prevented them from leaving the house without her supervision.

Natalya soon detested living with Horowitz. She described his home as "utter squalor" and him personally as "so stupid as to be comical. Having been ordered to keep a discreet watch over me, he nevertheless boasted to me of his many disguises."[424] After a week of complaints, the authorities determined she was not a flight risk and decided to let her and the boys live on their own, moving them into a local hotel, the Prince George on Sackville and Hollis Streets near the waterfront (a few blocks from the hotel's modern site on Market Street). But they insisted that Natalya continue to check in at the local police station each day to make sure she didn't run off or cause problems.

Once on her own, Natalya tried to meet people in Halifax but found it difficult. She had no friends there, didn't speak the language, and had no visible means of support. Unlike the Bronx, she found few fellow

Russians or leftists to sympathize with or understand her. Natalya did strike up a friendship with Fanny Horowitz, adult daughter of the port translator who had housed her originally. Fanny spoke Russian and remembered watching Natalya fumble with her few English phrases, such as asking people on the street, "Speek you French?"[425]

On anything political, though, Fanny found that Natalya could be just as rigid as Trotsky himself. One day, Fanny took Natalya shopping for a notepad. They happened to stop at a bookstore on Barrington Street, where a clerk showed her a pad decorated with flags of all the Allied countries. "I want none of them," Natalya complained in Russian. "I have no use for any flags but the flag of real freedom." The flag she meant, of course, was the red one.[426]

BACK INSIDE THE crowded Amherst detention camp, cut off from the outside world, Trotsky decided to turn his attention instead to the German soldier-prisoners surrounding him there. He spoke fluent German and didn't hesitate to strike up conversations. The prisoners took to him, and Trotsky, as he watched them, began to appreciate the prisoners as well. He noticed how they survived for months or years under these conditions, how some practiced crafts at their bunks, some with "extraordinary skill," and he admired what he called their "heroic efforts . . . to keep themselves physically and morally fit."[427]

Most of these captured German sailors and soldiers, homesick and lonely, cooped up during the long Canadian winter, had long since grown cynical about the war. They now despised their own government and officers even more than they hated their British and Canadian guards, making them perfect grist for Trotsky's brand of socialism. In the bunks, at meals, at work and exercise, he began to engage them, and he soon found himself giving talks to small ad hoc circles, all under the watchful eye of Colonel Morris and his guards.

The camp provided the prisoners only one newspaper, the *Halifax Chronicle*, but few could read it because it was in English. So Trotsky designated himself their collective translator. He would take the paper each day, use his own poor, broken English to interpret a few key words, and then extemporize in German on his own views of the world.

As he got to know them, he started acting like a big brother, pushing the young soldiers to use their time better. Trotsky himself had spent years in Russian jails when he was younger and had used the time behind bars to write articles and build his underground network. Now he told these German prisoners to be more productive, take pride in cleaning up the camp, even study English while there in Canada.

And he interweaved every conversation with politics. "We had constant group discussions," Trotsky recalled. "Our friendship grew warmer every day."[428] In small and then larger gatherings, he told the men about the Russian Revolution, about Lenin, about America's intention to join the war, and about how, once the war ended, they could go home and overthrow their own government in Germany, just as Russian soldiers had helped topple the tsar. They could get rid of the Kaiser and the whole capitalist crowd in Berlin that had started this pointless bloodbath in the first place.

He soon had a following. Even many of the Amherst guards found him intriguing. "He was a man who when he looked at you seemed to hypnotize you," recalled one of them, a Captain F. C. Whitmore. "He gave us a lot of trouble, and if he had stayed there any longer . . . would have made communists of all the German prisoners."[429]

Not everyone in the camp appreciated his agitation, though. Preaching overthrow of the kaiser in a British camp as Britain was fighting a desperate war against Germany hardly seemed seditious on its face. But the separately housed German officers, still loyal to their country, resented it. "The officers and non-commissioned Naval officers who had separate quarters, at once beheld us as their hated enemies," Trotsky recalled, and this created a problem for the camp's commandant, Colonel Morris.[430]

Morris watched Trotsky's antics with growing concern. "After only a few days stay here [Trotsky] was by far the most popular man in the whole Camp with the German Prisoners of war, two thirds of whom are Socialists," Morris complained to the Ottawa police commissioner.[431]

As commandant, Morris insisted on order. For now, there was little he could do about this man Trotsky and his constant talking. So he simply told his guards keep an eye on him. These were the times he'd mutter, "If only I had him on the South Africa coast."

THE NEWS FINALLY reached New York on April 9, a Monday, seven days after the Halifax arrests and two weeks since Trotsky's ship had sailed. A letter arrived at the basement office of *Novy Mir* on Saint Marks Place. Gregory Weinstein, the *Novy Mir* editor, was there to open it. Weinstein had stayed behind in New York when most of his staff left for Russia. Almost forty years old, living in Brooklyn with his family and having been a refugee before, Weinstein showed little desire to pull up stakes again. But the empty desks made it difficult now to produce a newspaper each day.

The letter came from Canada and bore the signature of Grigorii Chudnovsky, Trotsky's young sidekick and fellow editor at *Novy Mir,* who had joined Trotsky on the trip back to Russia. Chudnovsky, doubt-less with Trotsky's help, had crammed a treasure of detail into a few terse sentences:

> The British Military Authorities found that we, a group of
> Russian Socialists, are dangerous to the cause of the Allies.
> They took us off the ship and sent us to an internment camp
> for Prisoners of War in Amhurst. We protested and refused to
> leave, but in spite of all they dragged us off by force. We sent
> telegrams to the Russian Consul in Halifax and Montreal, to the
> Russian Minister for Foreign Affairs, and the Russian Minister
> of Justice, the Vice President of the Deputation, Committee of
> Workers and Soldiers, Tchkeidze, to the New York 'Call' and
> some private people. We do not know whether the telegrams
> arrived. . . . They left us without clothes and even took away
> our towels and handkerchiefs. Direct material help is necessary.
> It is also necessary to take steps to set us free.[432]

Weinstein, studying the letter, had to be amazed at what he read. No one in New York had even a hint of this story. For all anyone here suspected, Trotsky had long since reached Russia and joined the revolution. As an experienced journalist, Weinstein, holding the letter in his hand, fully recognized what he had here: a scoop, and a good one.

New York had hardly forgotten Trotsky after the splash he'd made. Weinstein had shared this basement office with him for ten weeks that winter, and with Chudnovsky even longer. They had drunk tea and worked side by side late into the night. They were friends and comrades. Trying to confirm what facts he could, Weinstein contacted the *New York Call* and asked if they had received a telegram from Trotsky or his party in Canada, but they'd seen nothing. If Chudnovsky was right, this meant someone had blocked it.

Unable to check anything else, Weinstein decided the letter had to speak for itself. His best strategy would be the most simple: sound the alarms.

America had changed in the two weeks since Trotsky had left town. Spring had come. The Easter and Passover holidays had just passed, and baseball opening day at the Polo Grounds that week featured young Boston Red Sox pitcher Babe Ruth, the "round-faced, left-handed Baltimore orphan boy," as Hearst sportswriter Damon Runyon described him.[433] Ruth threw a three-hitter to embarrass the Yankees before their home crowd on his way to twenty-four wins and a 2.01 ERA that season. But a military tone dominated the game. Army general Leonard Wood, not the mayor, threw out the ceremonial first pitch, and the pregame fanfare at the Polo Grounds featured Yankee and Red Sox players marching across the infield to patriotic songs in military drill formations, carrying bats on their shoulders instead of rifles.

Most things in New York now jangled to military tunes. Young men in crisp new army uniforms popped up on every corner. The country had crossed a bridge on April 6, when President Woodrow Wilson had finally led it into the European war, famously telling Congress in a joint session, "The world must be made safe for democracy." He asked for an army of 500,000 men to fight Germany, a number that would top 2.8 million by the time the war ended. More than 2 million would reach Europe, and of these, 230,000 would be wounded and more than 116,000 would not come home alive.

Congress had approved Wilson's proposed declaration of war by lopsided votes, 82 to 5 in the Senate and 373 to 50 in the House. New York's Meyer London, the only Socialist congressman, and Jeanette Rankin, a Republican from Montana and the recently elected first woman member of the House, both voted no.

The country celebrated war with parades and recruitment rallies, but, Wilson's rhetoric aside, the declaration also triggered immediate action. Federal Justice Department agents arrested sixty-five German residents in New York during the first twenty-four hours on suspicion of espionage. Port officials seized ninety-five German vessels and sent more than nine hundred German sailors to detention on Ellis Island, turning the immigration center into a vast prison, much like Halifax's Citadel or Amherst. And this was just the start. A crackdown would soon touch Americans from all backgrounds. In New York that week, police arrested two men for disorderly conduct in Madison Square Park simply for getting up at a street-corner rally and criticizing the president. One of them called Wilson a "dirty skunk" and "perjurer," the other called the United States "rotten." A judge sentenced them each to six months in the city workhouse, making them early victims of a new regime. Insulting politicians had now become a crime in America.[434]

Arrests would escalate over the coming days. The police would shut down an anti-draft protest in Brooklyn. Crackdowns on newspapers would follow quickly.

And it wasn't just the government enforcing patriotism. Any German or socialist insulting the flag or the president risked getting punched, kicked, or beaten on the subway or in the street. In Chicago stores refused credit to newlyweds, suspecting young men of using marriage to avoid the army. In a the favorite new expression, such men were "slackers." Demand for American flags ran so high that wholesale dealers stopped taking orders and flag manufacturers ran out of bunting.

Swimming against this tide, Morris Hillquit, New York's Socialist leader, still worked frantically to build his coalition against the war. That week he managed to pull two hundred Socialist Party leaders to an emergency conference in Saint Louis—still possible in these early weeks of mobilization. "It was a tense and nervous gathering," he recalled, reflecting the hostility and growing isolation.[435]

Unlike earlier party meetings, though, the bleak atmosphere this time helped forge consensus. The Saint Louis convention adopted a strikingly clear platform. "In all modern history there has been no war more unjustifiable than the war in which we are about to engage," it read. It denounced the war, the draft, press censorship, and limits on free speech, and it called for resistance though public demonstrations, mass petitions, and "all honorable and effective means within our power"—everything short of breaking the law.[436]

With this result, Hillquit had now unified his Socialist Party but had also set it on a direct collision course, both with federal law enforcement authorities and with his own party's left wing and its increasing embrace of Russian-style extremism. Reckonings on both scores would come soon.

All these distractions aside, the news of Trotsky's arrest in Canada still managed to command attention in New York City. Trotsky's loyalists wasted no time springing into action. At *Novy Mir,* Gregory Weinstein still had plenty of friends in the newspaper business, and he called on them now. He mobilized his remaining small staff, and within a few hours they shared copies of Chudnovsky's letter with the *New York Times,* the *New York Call,* the *New Yorker Volkzeitung,* the *Forward,* and any other newspaper he thought might help. By the next morning, each had printed large chunks of the letter verbatim. BRITISH SEIZE RUSSIAN SOCIALISTS AND INTERN THEM IN PRISON CAMP, the *New York Call* announced in a front-page headline. RUSSIAN RADICAL DETAINED: TROTZKY AND SEVEN OTHERS TAKEN OFF STEAMSHIP IN HALIFAX, echoed the *New York Times.*[437]

Weinstein also sent telegrams to top officials in Russia, including Alexander Kerensky, the minister of justice, and the leaders of the

Petrograd Soviet. At the same time, the *New York Call* used its Socialist Party contacts to reach Congressman Meyer London in Washington, DC. "Can you do anything through government? Please wire answer," it asked him in a telegram.[438]

Another idea came from Nicholas Aleinikoff, the lawyer and local socialist leader. Aleinikoff had sat with Trotsky on the Socialist Party's Resolutions Committee in its arguments over the war and had spoken against Trotsky's minority report at the Lenox Casino back in March. But despite the disagreement, Aleinikoff agreed to help.

Aleinikoff happened to know the Canadian postmaster general, a man named R. M. Coulter, whom Aleinikoff had dealt with in prior legal work on behalf of Russian newspapers, possibly *Novy Mir* itself. "Trust as champion of freedom you will intercede on their behalf," he cabled Coulter on April 11, telling him about the arrests and insisting he knew Trotsky, Chudnovsky, and Melnichansky "intimately" and considered them "true sons of Russia who should be released at once [to] contribute their share" to rebuilding the country."[439] Arthur Wolf, another colleague at 134 East Broadway, knew Coulter too and also sent him a cable that day to underline the point.

Coulter, receiving these messages in Ottawa, would tap his own contacts in the Canadian military to get to the bottom of things.[440] But this too was just the start.

EVEN IN PETROGRAD, Russia, preoccupied with war and political upheaval, Trotsky's arrest made headlines. Trotsky hadn't set foot there since his public trial a decade earlier for chairing the 1905 Petrograd Soviet, but many local socialists now playing lead roles in 1917 remembered Trotsky from those days, his escapes from Siberia, and his defiance of tsarist prosecutors. Many of Trotsky's anti-tsarist writings since then, from Vienna, the Balkans, Paris, even New York, had filtered back there. His name still grabbed attention, and politicians treated it gingerly.

The provisional government, under Paul Miliukov and Alexander Kerensky, had learned about Trotsky's arrest when it first occurred but kept the news secret. Britain's Foreign Office had notified them in early April, and Miliukov, as Russia's foreign minister, initially had asked that Trotsky be released.[441] But Miliukov changed his mind after British officials told him what they'd heard about Trotsky from New York: that Trotsky had been leading "an important movement . . . financed by Jewish (and, possibly, ultimately German) funds" aimed at overthrowing Miliukov's own provisional government.[442] That was enough to convince Miliukov to cancel his request for Trotsky's release.

All this changed, however, once word reached the city. Hiding the story became impossible. Mensheviks, Bolsheviks, and a dozen other left-wing parties all vied for support in Petrograd, and each one flooded the sidewalks with its tabloids, posters, and pamphlets. They quickly made Trotsky's arrest a sensation, sparking protests and speeches. The Mensheviks, who still considered Trotsky their own, demanded his release and accused Britain of deceit.[443] Britain's ambassador in Petrograd, Sir George Buchanan, felt so threatened by the anti-British tone of the Trotsky clamor that he complained to the provisional government. "The attacks made against us in the press . . . had taken such a serious turn," he wrote, "they were even endangering the lives of some of the British factory owners."[444]

Old rules no longer applied in postrevolutionary Russia, and now a new catalyst had come to stir the pot even more. It was the most important Bolshevik leader of all, Vladimir Lenin.

Lenin's return from exile at this moment in April 1917 would set in motion a chain of events that would reshape world history: seventy years of communism, transformation of Russian society, Stalinist purges, victory over Hitler, the Cold War. None of this, though, appeared likely at the time. Lenin's Bolsheviks in early 1917 remained a small minority even within Russia's radical left, smaller than the Mensheviks and shut out from government circles. In a democratic Russia, the Bolsheviks had little chance to amount to more than a tiny fringe.

But from the moment he set foot in Petrograd, Lenin had set about changing Bolshevism. His weeklong trip from Switzerland gave him time to refine his April Theses, a new ten-point strategy that would win him power before the year was over. For now it remained a provocative, radical departure, defying orthodox socialism. Lenin called for complete rejection of the provisional government, immediate power for the proletariat and the "poorest sections of the peasants," rejection of parliamentary democracy, confiscation of landed estates, and recognition of the workers committees, or soviets, as the "only possible form of revolutionary government."[445]

At this point, only two other figures in the socialist world had publicly reached these same radical conclusions: Trotsky and Parvus in their 1905 theory of "permanent revolution."

"Few Bolsheviks could believe their ears" on first hearing Lenin's new line, biographer Robert Service wrote about these days.[446] Lenin's April Theses set him at odds with just about everyone. At one meeting his first day back, he delivered what Service described as a "diatribe" against his own Bolshevik Central Committee for its weak stance. Later, at the Tauride Palace, he criticized any reconciliation with Mensheviks. His April Theses, when finally published, sparked heated debate. At a joint meeting with Mensheviks that day, Lenin shouted "Never" when asked about party unity. The more the Mensheviks understood Lenin's concept, the more hostile they became. "Lenin's program is sheer insurrectionism, which will lead us into the pit of anarchy," one proclaimed.[447] Said another, "Lenin will remain a solitary figure outside the revolution and we'll all go our own way."[448]

Even Ambassador Buchanan, appalled at Lenin's extremism, took comfort in its rejection by fellow leftists. Alexander Kerensky, talking with the ambassador, agreed.[449]

But Lenin finally got his way. The turning point came in late April when newspapers disclosed that Paul Miliukov, the provisional government's foreign minister, had secretly told Allied governments that he planned to continue Tsar Nicholas's aims in the world war, a wildly unpopular position in war-weary Russia. The public backlash not only forced Miliukov to quit his post, but it discredited the entire provisional government as a force for change. Lenin used this moment to raise his April Theses at a party conference on April 24. This time the majority backed him.

It was also around this time that Lenin decided to place his Bolsheviks behind another popular cause: freedom for Leon Trotsky, hero of 1905, jailed by the British in Canada.

Lenin had no special love for Trotsky, still nursing insults and quarrels with him stretching back a dozen years. But Lenin recognized opportunity. Seeing Trotsky jailed by Britain on charges of accepting German help must have startled him. After all, it was he, Lenin, who had traveled home through Germany on a "sealed train" provided by the German government and arranged by the German agent Parvus. Lenin had his own vulnerabilities on this score, and what Britain had done to Trotsky, it easily could do to him.

Besides, Trotsky was popular. Why not ride his coattails? Lenin had worked with Trotsky, he recognized his talents, and the reports he heard about Trotsky from New York, especially from friends like Alexandra Kollontai—who came regularly to Lenin's Petrograd meetings and speeches—had to affect him.

"Can one even for a moment believe the trustworthiness of the statement that Trotsky, chairman of the Soviet of Workers delegates in St. Petersburg in 1905—a revolutionary who has sacrificed years to a disinterested service of revolution—that this man had anything to do with a scheme subsidized by the German government?" the Bolshevik Party organ *Pravda* pronounced in an editorial at the height of the controversy. It was "patent, unheard-of, and malicious slander," *Pravda* added. "Six men dragged Comrade Trotsky away by his legs and arms, all in the name of friendship for the Provisional Russian government!"[450]

Finally, even Miliukov, in his last days as Russia's foreign minister, on the verge of resignation, had to bite his lip and agree. Shortly before stepping down, he reinstated his demand that the British release Trotsky.

BACK IN NEW York, Trotsky's friends hadn't finished showing their support. No movement could be complete without a mass meeting, and for Trotsky, they threw a fine one. They held it on a Sunday afternoon, April 15, and Louis Fraina, Trotsky's partner back at the Lenox Casino, took the lead arranging it, sponsored by the Boston-based Socialist Propaganda League.

In the vacuum created by Trotsky's departure, Fraina, just twenty-four-years old, had stepped up and made himself a leading voice of the American far left. He still used the offices of *Modern Dance* magazine at 562 Fifth Avenue, a few blocks from Times Square. Seeing the growing hostility toward foreigners, he had prepared papers to apply for US citizenship later that month, despite having lived in New York without it for twenty years. But Fraina saved his main energies for his two political magazines: the *Internationalist* and *Class Struggle,* which he would soon coedit with Ludwig Lore and Louis Boudin.

Within a few weeks, by May 16, Fraina would add another credential to his list: his first visit by agents of the federal Justice Department's Bureau of Investigations (forerunner of the FBI). The agents that day would come looking for the mailing list for Fraina's *Internationalist,* which Fraina easily would avoid giving them by claiming he didn't have a copy, that somebody else kept it. Fraina ultimately would be the subject of one of the bureau's thickest files from that era. Before the end of the year, he would have his first arrest and conviction on federal charges, for giving an antiwar speech in September and thus violating the Selective Service Act by encouraging young men to refuse to register.

The rally for Trotsky drew a big, boisterous crowd of mostly radical immigrants—Russians, Jews, Lithuanians, and Germans. Accounts don't mention the locale, but one of the usual favorites, Lenox Casino or Beethoven Hall, was most likely. Any good rally needed music, and this one featured a choir of children from the Ferrer School singing under a red banner, not only movement favorites such as "IWW Unite" and "The Internationale" but also the peppy 1915 tune "I Didn't Raise My Boy to Be a Soldier" (so popular that it had already spawned a prowar alternative called "I Didn't Raise My Boy to Be a Coward," sung to the same tune):

I didn't raise my boy to be a soldier,
I brought him up to be my pride and joy.
Who dares to place a musket on his shoulder,
To shoot some other mother's darling boy?

Then came speeches and resolutions in multiple languages. Fraina chaired the event and gave the major address in English. "We talk about the autocratic Governments of Germany and Austria, but the Allies are just as bad," he shouted to loud applause. "In England Lloyd George is as supreme as the Kaiser is in Germany, and here in this country they are seeking to introduce similar autocracy."[451] Then came talks from a Russian, a Dane, and a Japanese, doubtless Gregory Weinstein, Sebald Rutgers, and Sen Katayama. The crowd cheered and waved and sang and passed resolutions. They urged workers all over the world to "use all force in their possession to bring about the release of Trotzky and to bring peace."[452]

The rally probably did more to raise the morale of local socialists than to push government officials. The *New York Times* account in particular tried to paint the event as pro-German, describing the crowd as "dominated by Germans," describing the immigrants as "many apparently of German birth or extraction," and highlighting the German speeches and songs.[453] But all the efforts—the letters, demonstrations, telegrams, and newspaper stories—had a cumulative impact: Government officials in America, Canada, Britain, and Russia were now all asking questions. If William Wiseman of British intelligence had hoped to avoid an international incident by having Trotsky arrested in faraway Canada instead of New York City, he had failed badly.

BACK AT AMHERST, tension between Trotsky and the camp's commandant, Colonel Arthur Henry Morris, continued to escalate as Trotsky continued to preach revolution among the German prisoners. "The whole month there was like one continuous mass meeting," Trotsky wrote.[454] The German soldiers, bored and frustrated after months of captivity, came to appreciate the idea of overthrowing their kaiser once they got home, at least as something to talk about while stuck in Canada.

The talk became so general that the German officers, housed in nicer quarters at the opposite end of the camp, finally lodged a formal complaint with Colonel Morris. It was an insult to their country, they said, let alone a threat to themselves.

Colonel Morris, having had enough of Trotsky, issued an order forbidding him from giving any more speeches. When Trotsky predictably refused to obey, Morris ordered his guards to separate Trotsky from the other prisoners. They removed him from the crowded bunk area and placed him into an old foundry blast furnace that they'd converted into a chamber for solitary confinement.

We don't know how long Trotsky spent inside the old blast furnace, but instead of complaining, he seemed to take an almost cheerful view of it. Despite the discomfort, Trotsky saw Morris's action as a moral victory. "The British colonel instantly sided with the Hollenzollern officers," he wrote years later, as if Trotsky had forced Morris to concede a bigger point: that Trotsky had been right all along about the war and its basis in the global class struggle, a force that transcended national borders, pitting rulers (officers and capitalists) against workers and soldiers of all countries.

The rank-and-file German prisoners had come to enjoy Trotsky's daily dissertations and now came to his defense. They passed around a petition protesting Trotsky's silencing and confinement. As Trotsky remembered it, a full 530 of them, a majority of the entire camp, signed it. "A plebiscite like this, carried out in the very face of [the guards'] heavy-handed supervision," he wrote, "was more than ample compensation for all the hardships of the Amherst imprisonment."[455] Still Morris wasn't ready to let go.

THE FINAL STRAW came from inside government circles, both in London and Ottawa. Canada's postmaster general, R. M. Coulter, having received telegrams from his two acquaintances in New York City, decided to raise the issue with Major General Willoughby Gwatkin, the Canadian military chief of staff in Ottawa. Gwatkin, in turn, passed his concern along to top navy brass, warning of concerns that "an act of high-handed injustice has been done."[456] Another ranking military figure, Admiral C. E. Kingsmill, director of the Canadian Naval Service, took the point further, contacting Captain Makins in Halifax, still responsible for the prisoners, and asking him to make an early decision on their disposition. In London pressure grew too as the Russian charge d'affaires pressed the British Foreign Office on the situation, reminding them that Trotsky carried a valid Russian passport.[457]

Canada, a British dominion, still owed allegiance to the British Crown. It practiced limited autonomy, but its foreign policy emanated from London. Canada thus had no right to free Trotsky without permission from the British navy, whatever its own government ministers might think. Still, top officials in both countries, Canada and Britain, recognized a problem. Their countries' legal systems still required some legal basis to hold a prisoner. But Trotsky had broken no law, had not carried contraband (at least that anyone had found), had presented a proper British visa and Russian passport, and, as a noncombatant, hardly qualified as a prisoner of war. And the evidence against him as a German spy was thin at best.

If Trotsky ever got his case in front of a judge, any court in Canada or Britain ultimately would be hard-pressed not to release him. And now, with newspapers on three continents reporting his arrest, they were turning Trotsky into a global celebrity.

The turning point came on April 20, when British colonel Claude E. M. Dansey,[458] the senior British MI-5 official responsible for port intelligence (controlling who could enter or leave British territory), arrived in Halifax en route to Washington, DC, as part of a delegation of British military experts assigned to advise the US Army. With twenty-six years of service, Dansey ranked as one of Britain's most senior intelligence chiefs. He had learned the spy game in Rhodesia in the 1890s, practiced it during the Boer War, and spent three years in America before 1914 spying on Irish nationalists and US bankers. Sometimes known by his code name, "Z," he had been an original agent for Britain's Secret Service Bureau (forerunner to MI-5 and MI-6) when it was first created in 1909.

Dansey knew all about the Trotsky controversy before he landed in Halifax, and he sought out Captain Makins to discuss it.[459] To Dansey, the whole situation looked suspicious. "I believed the new Russian Government would at once ask for Trotsky's release," Dansey reported telling Makins when they finally got together, and "unless they [British naval authorities were] very certain of the source of the information against him, it would be much better to let him go before he got angry."[460]

Trotsky, of course, was already quite angry. Still, as Dansey remembered it, Makins promised to wire New York or Washington and "ascertain the reliability of their information."[461]

Who or what exactly had sparked Dansey's suspicions over the Trotsky affair is far from clear. The War Office in London had grown concerned over the performance of Britain's intelligence operation in New York City—Wiseman, Gaunt, Norman Thwaites, and the rest. Wiseman in particular came across to some London officials as a likeable amateur, just thirty-three years old and with barely sixteen months' experience in intelligence work at a point when America was about to enter the war.

Dansey apparently expected that he himself would be asked to take over the job of managing British intelligence in New York—perhaps as Wiseman's commanding officer—once he had finished his assignment in Washington, DC. "Dansey was obviously unimpressed" with Wiseman's work, one biographer noted,[462] including probably Wiseman's confusing signals over the Trotsky affair.

Dansey would explain his concern once he reached Washington a few weeks later. Seeing for himself the report from the informer Casimir Pilenas that had prompted Trotsky's arrest in the first place, he would shake his head in disbelief. It "looked to me like the work of a Russian Agent Provocateur," he wrote. When he finally had the chance to confront Wiseman directly in New York, he reported: "I told Wiseman that [Pilenas] had better be discharged at once, and [Wiseman] said that he was going to do so."[463]

Whatever Dansey said or did behind the scenes in Halifax, the next day, April 21, Captain Makins informed Ottawa that he had received new orders from the admiralty that the "Russian Socialists should be allowed to proceed."[464] Gwatkin, the Canadian military chief of staff, quickly informed Postmaster General Coulter. "Our friends the Russian socialists are to be released," he told him in a letter. "Arrangements are being made for their passage to Europe."[465]

Still, even with the decision made, British and Canadian officers dragged their feet. "We must permit but need not expedite their journey," one Foreign Office bureaucrat grumbled.[466] It would take another week, until April 28, for the order freeing Trotsky to reach Amherst. Canadian officials said they needed the extra time to arrange for a ship to carry him immediately from Halifax to Norway. They had no intention of allowing Trotsky even a few hours to dawdle around Halifax making trouble.

AT AMHERST, COLONEL Morris still hadn't finished with Trotsky and his Russian friends. Getting word from the British admiralty to release them, Morris at first refused to tell them. Instead, he waited until the day came. Then he ordered Trotsky and the others to pack their belongings so they could be taken back to Halifax. "We were never told, either that we should be freed, or whither we were to be sent," Trotsky recalled.[467] As a result, they assumed the worst, that the Canadians planned to send them to another prison, perhaps the Citadel again, en route to someplace else, maybe this time to the Canadian interior, even farther from civilization.

So Trotsky refused to move. He and the others sat on their bunks as soldiers came and seized their belongings and as a crowd of prisoners congregated around them to watch. Finally, facing a confrontation, Morris gave up. Standing at Trotsky's bunk, he gave him the news. "In his characteristic Anglo-colonial way [Morris told us] that we were to sail on a Danish boat for Russia," Trotsky recalled. "The colonel's purple face twitched compulsively."[468]

Trotsky remembered his departure from Amherst as bittersweet. The German soldiers and sailors came to see him off. They lined the sidewalk on both sides, and a makeshift band played socialist tunes as they shared speeches and handshakes. "In later years I received letters from many of them, sent from Germany," Trotsky wrote.[469]

It would take until May 3, a full month after his arrest in Halifax, for the British to place Trotsky, his family, and the other Russian prisoners on a Scandinavian-America Line ship called the *Hellig Olav* for the trip to Kristiania. Trotsky remembered the crossing as dull and eventless, like "going through a tunnel."[470] Natalya recalled the small ship being "pounded mercilessly by the Atlantic waves." The only entertainment came from Chudnovsky, who apparently found romance on the voyage. He "paid court to a little Russian dancer" he met on board, Natalya recalled.[471]

From Kristiania, it would take another week by train to reach Russia. But finally they had escaped beyond the reach of Britain, Canada, and America. No chains or hesitations held them back. Trotsky could now go home and join the fight he'd been itching to finish since 1905, taking the chaos in Russia and shaping it to his own unique vision of the world.

26

PETROGRAD

"An old literary lady wrote me the other day, 'Russia is like a Slav woman who loves the man in whom she finds a master and who, in the words of an old peasant song, asks her husband if he does not love her any more when he no longer beats her out of jealousy.'"[472]

—Sir George Buchanan, British ambassador to Petrograd, April 10, 1917

TROTSKY REACHED PETROGRAD on May 17 (May 4 under the Julian calendar used there until 1918), seven weeks after leaving New York City. His month of captivity in Nova Scotia had spoiled any chance to lead the parade of émigrés back home, but it gave his entrance a dramatic flourish. Controversy over his imprisonment helped Trotsky regain his celebrity status inside Russia and elevated his arrival to public spectacle. A handful of friends met him at the Beloostrov crossing. By the time they reached Petrograd's Finland Station, so many well-wishers mobbed the train they had to lift him onto their shoulders to carry him to the street.

Petrograd, Russia's imperial capital since Peter the Great, with its grand palaces, canals, and government buildings, had been transformed by the dramatic upheavals of early 1917. Tsarism shattered, the city now buzzed with excitement, capital of a Russia that Lenin called "the freest of all the belligerent countries in the world."[473] Concerts, meetings, and street corner rallies all mingled with city traffic. Banners hung from buildings, thousands of men and women wore scarlet ribbons pinned to winter coats, radicals clogged the streets, and soldiers carrying red flags sang songs while marching and jamming the trains.

Before Trotsky even found a hotel room, his friends launched him into a dizzying whirlwind of meetings and receptions. "Men and events swept by me as swiftly as litter in a rushing stream," he recalled of that day.[474] Among the first stops, they took him across the Neva River to the city's latest political mecca, the former elite girls' boarding school called the Smolny Institute. Surrounded by elegant gardens, this landmark had become the new home of the Petrograd Soviet, that odd gathering of workers' and soldiers' deputies that now stood as an independent competing government in postrevolutionary Russia.

Trotsky entered the chamber where the soviet's executive committee was meeting that day, and it greeted him with applause. The committee deputies interrupted business and made a few speeches. Then a Bolshevik formally proposed inviting Trotsky to join them as a member, in honor of his role as chairman of this same committee in 1905. But the gesture, though gracious, created an awkward moment. Trotsky had been away from Russia for more than ten years, which made him a stranger here. He represented no political group. Looking at the committee members, a motley collection of workers, radicals, and politicians—mostly socialists, many from local Menshevik and Bolshevik organizations—Trotsky didn't recognize many of the faces. Others, old friends, he hadn't seen in years.

But the deputies all knew Trotsky, at least by reputation, including his penchant for high-profile arguments with Lenin, Martov, and other top figures. Some probably even heard about his fights with Morris Hillquit in New York City. They had to wonder: Who would he support now? Who would he attack? Nobody knew Trotsky's views on the latest political twists and turns, and Trotsky himself had barely had time to figure them out. That day, for instance, as Trotsky came into the room, the committee had been debating a proposal from the provisional government, now mostly controlled by Alexander Kerensky as minister of war, to offer ministry portfolios to a handful of these soviet deputies.

Should they accept? Trotsky, asked his opinion, said no, but he kept his words brief.

After some debate, they decided to seat Trotsky, but only as an honorary, nonvoting member. For now he would have to earn his wings anew.

Natalya and the boys spent their first night in Russia at the Kiev Hostelry, one of the few hotels in Petrograd that still had available rooms. "We lived as modestly as we had done in Paris and the Bronx," Natalya recalled of those first weeks home. "Each day brought joyful or grave political news together with the constant problem of finding something to eat."[475] The boys, Sergei and Lyova, marveled at finally seeing their parents' homeland. Exploring Petrograd with their mother, what fascinated them most was how people spoke here. Not only did they all talk the same language—the opposite of New York or even Paris—but it was Russian. With Russian words on street signs, shops, and billboards, the boys, for the first time in their lives, could actually understand all the conversations around them.

Politics aside, this was a homecoming for Trotsky and Natalya. They both had family here, relatives their sons had never met, including Alexandra Sokolovskaya, Trotsky's first (and still legal) wife. She went by the name Bronstein and lived in Petrograd with her two daughters, Nina and Zina, the ones she'd had with Trotsky in Siberia during their exile together before his 1902 escape. Nina and Zina had grown into teenagers, fifteen and sixteen years old.

Trotsky brought the families together and apparently the reunion went well. Trotsky's sons became fast friends with their half sisters. The families started spending time together. That summer, when Trotsky would bury himself in politics, the wives and children would vacation as a group at the nearby beach resort of Teriyoki (now Zelenogorsk) on the Gulf of Finland.

Meanwhile, after so many years abroad, seeing his own country again had to be a shock for Trotsky. Russia had suffered terribly in the world war, to an extent that outsiders could barely imagine, making its backwardness and poverty painfully visible. Russia had mobilized

14 million young men for the fight, more than any other country in Europe, and now 3 million lay dead and another 4 million had been wounded. The war had killed more than a million civilians from disease, dislocations, malnutrition, and military cross fire. Fighting had devastated Russia's farmlands and wrecked hundreds of villages and towns. The resulting chaos had created millions of refugees.

Even before the war, Russian society had strained under vast disparities in wealth and privilege. Its economy remained predominantly agricultural, but the tsar personally owned 70 percent of the country's arable land, and nobles owed most of the rest, leaving 110 million peasants, more than 80 percent of the population, largely landless and poor. Military mobilization had dragged millions off the land and organized them into an army that now sat angry and disillusioned. Starvation plagued the cities. This, plus a growing militant urban proletariat, created a powder keg easily capable of exploding again any time.

Trotsky had recognized this dynamic even sitting far away in Paris and New York. Back in Petrograd, watching soviet deputies quibble over ministry portfolios and a provisional government trapped in a doomed war effort, he saw only one other person in the city who seemed to grasp the moment as he did, with the same impatience and single-minded opportunism. It was a returned exile like himself, his old mentor and rival Vladimir Lenin.

The Lenin–Trotsky partnership of posterity, the one that finally seized power later that year, began as a courtship starting almost the minute Trotsky set foot in Petrograd. Lenin sent an emissary to the border crossing at Beloostrov to greet him and ask about his plans. Trotsky recognized the friendly overture and reciprocated. His younger sister, Olga, whom he had not seen since before the war, lived in Petrograd and was married to Lev Kamenev, one of Lenin's close confidantes and a member of the Bolshevik Central Committee. Trotsky and Natalya made a point to meet them over dinner on one of their first nights back in Russia. Through Kamenev, Trotsky arranged to visit the Bolshevik newspaper *Pravda* and meet the local party chieftains.

For the time being, Trotsky decided to join only one political group, Mezhrayontska, the Inter-District Committee. Known by its Russian-language acronym RSDLP, it was a loose confederation of socialists who had described themselves as unifiers before the war. The group attracted many returning émigrés who simply hadn't yet decided where to place themselves in the new constellation, including many of Trotsky's friends from abroad: Chudnovsky and Volodarsky from New York, Moises Uritsky from Paris, and Adolf Joffe, whom he'd known in Vienna. Its membership, never more than a few hundred before, had risen to four thousand since March, swelled with newcomers.

Trotsky encountered Lenin face-to-face in Petrograd for the first time just a few days after arriving. Bolshevik and Mezhrayontska leaders had decided to meet and consider merging the two groups, and Trotsky and Lenin both decided to participate. Trotsky hadn't seen Lenin in more than two years, since the 1915 Zimmerwald conference in Switzerland, and it's easy to picture them, Trotsky thirty-eight years old and Lenin forty-seven, two no-nonsense, ambitious politicos, eyeing each other across the table, each trying to size up the other, curious and skeptical at the same time. There's no indication they formed any special chemistry that day. Instead, pleasantries aside, they mostly bickered.

Trotsky by now had read Lenin's April Theses, and he appreciated how closely they tracked his own thinking. But, typically, instead of seeing this as a reason to join forces, Trotsky took Lenin's new approach as a concession, as Lenin's finally agreeing that Trotsky had been right all along. That being so, he suggested, why shouldn't Lenin be the one to change sides and join Trotsky's group rather than asking the Mezhrayontska to become Bolsheviks? "I cannot call myself a Bolshevik," he insisted. "We should not be expected to recognize Bolshevism."[476]

But Lenin refused even to consider the idea. Friendly overtures aside, he had not yet decided what to make of Trotsky: friend, foe, or indifferent. Besides, Lenin had no intention of giving up his Bolshevik apparatus. Why should he? Things were going well at that moment. Not only were his calls for "Peace, Land, and Bread!" winning followers, but his party suddenly had become rich. After years of struggling on shoestring budgets, Lenin now had all the money he needed to print pamphlets and run the organization. By one count that spring, Lenin's Bolsheviks were operating as many as forty-one newspapers inside Russia, including the largest, *Pravda,* with a daily print run of ninety thousand copies, costing them some 260,000 rubles each month. And this was on top of paying salaries and other party expenses.

Much of the new funds came from an account at the Commercial Bank of Siberia that always seemed to have plenty of money. Russian government investigators had already started asking questions about the account and tracing its cash flow back to Copenhagen, Denmark, and Lenin's friend Jacob Furstenberg. And through him to Alexander Israel Helphand "Parvus," a known agent of Germany.

Trotsky, Lenin, and their followers made no decisions at that first meeting. Over the next few weeks, they continued to see each other. In the frenzy of revolutionary Petrograd—its daily rallies, speeches, and backroom huddles—early morning till late each night, they stood on platforms together and shared the excitement. Lenin spoke at Mezhrayontska assemblies and Trotsky addressed Bolshevik conferences. Lenin came to hold a unique sway over these crowds. He was "a strange popular leader," as John Reed, the American journalist, would describe him in October, "a leader purely by virtue of the intellect: colourless, humourless, uncompromising and detached, without picturesque idiosyncrasies—but with the power of explaining profound ideas in simple terms. . . . And combined with shrewdness, the greatest intellectual audacity."[477]

Trotsky, for his part, started to write articles for Lenin's newspaper *Pravda,* though he also kept doors open to other political groups, particularly the Mensheviks and their leader, his old Paris and London friend Julius Martov. His favorite venue became the Cirque Moderne, a large concert hall in the Vyborg District near the army barracks, where his speeches drew big audiences most nights. Petrograd was enjoying a moment of freedom that must have made it reminiscent of New York.

It TOOK A crisis that summer finally to cement the deal. They called it the July Days, a week of violent street clashes culminating in a harsh crackdown by Kerensky's government against Lenin and his followers. "Lenin's attitude to me went through several phases," Trotsky later explained. "First he was reserved and content to wait and see. The July days brought us together at once."[478]

That summer Kerensky, yielding to demands from Britain and France, decided to launch a major military offensive against German forces in Galicia in western Ukraine. He committed four Russian armies to the operation. It enjoyed initial success using heavy artillery to blast German lines, but then it stalled and collapsed, disintegrating into a rout. Russian forces suffered staggering losses, almost one hundred thousand men killed or wounded, in what looked like an increasingly pointless effort.

Soldiers back in Petrograd, angry at both Kerensky's military failure and worsening conditions at home, decided to launch protests against the government. But both the provisional government and the soviet, fearing violence, insisted the soldiers stay in their barracks. Only Lenin's Bolsheviks decided to support them, partly in hopes of keeping the situation under control.

By the second day, the demonstrations had grown immensely. Half a million armed military men, including a fully equipped machine gun unit and sailors from the Kronstadt naval base, plus tens of thousands of rifle-carrying workers from nearby factories, jammed the streets demanding "All Power to the Soviets," a direct challenge to Kerensky. The mob surrounded the Tauride Palace and threatened to kill government ministers. At one point Trotsky personally had to intercede with demonstrators to rescue Viktor Chernov, the minister of agriculture, when protestors surrounded him on the palace steps.

Kerensky, finally sensing public support, decided to respond with force of his own. He sent loyal troops to disperse the crowds, resulting in more than seven hundred demonstrators being shot or beaten in street battles. Through friendly newspapers, Kerensky blamed Lenin's

Bolsheviks not only for the violence in Petrograd but also for the collapse in army morale behind that summer's military disaster. In fact, all along Lenin's Bolsheviks had been sending agitators to the front lines, urging soldiers not to fight.

But this led to an even darker charge. At the height of the crisis, a popular progovernment newspaper claimed to possess evidence that Lenin had acted on orders directly from Berlin, that he was a German spy, financed by the Kaiser's general staff. In addition to the Bolsheviks' suddenly flush bank accounts, the newspaper pointed as evidence to Lenin's "sealed train" through Germany; his dealings with Parvus, the notorious German financier; and all the material assembled by government prosecutors looking into the Commercial Bank of Siberia. The charges prompted even more violence. Government troops and right-wing vigilantes broke into the Bolshevik Party's headquarters that week and vandalized the offices of *Pravda*. The charges mixed with traditional Jew-baiting, attacks in Jewish neighborhoods, and calls to "drown the Jews and Bolsheviks," the same tactic that tsarist officials had used in 1905.[479]

As icing on the cake, Paul Miliukov, now the former foreign minister, speaking through his affiliated newspaper, took this precise moment to charge Trotsky with being part of the German conspiracy. Based on what? That Trotsky in New York City had received $10,000 from German sources that he had carried with him back to Russia to overthrow the provisional government. How did Miliukov know this? He had an excellent source, he explained: the British.

It was the same old accusation from New York of a secret $10,000 payment that had started at the British intelligence office at 44 Whitehall. It had followed Trotsky across the ocean. Instead of being discredited after British officials had failed to find the money on Trotsky in Halifax, the story had lived on within British intelligence circles.[480] And now, through Miliukov, it had leaked into the wider world.

Having painted them as traitors, Kerensky's government now issued arrest warrants for Lenin and his top lieutenants. Lenin, refusing to surrender himself, decided instead to go underground, ultimately reaching

Finland.[481] "They have chosen this moment to shoot us all," he told Trotsky shortly before leaving the city.

But Kerensky chose not to arrest Trotsky, at least not yet. Trotsky, after all, was not part of Lenin's official circle—technically he had not become a Bolshevik yet—and he remained a sitting member of the soviet executive committee. The protection this gave him wasn't much, but Trotsky decided to use it, for however long it lasted, to defend himself.

What followed was a one-person publicity campaign in which Trotsky turned his pen, his popularity, his press contacts, and his seat on the soviet committee into weapons against the government. Refusing to distance himself from Lenin, he sent a public letter to Kerensky's government, printed in the widely read *Novaya Zhizn,* a newspaper edited by Maxim Gorky, tying himself directly to the Bolsheviks:

> Comrade Ministers! I know you have decided to arrest
> Comrades Lenin, Zinoviev, and Kamenev. But the arrest order
> does not include me. Therefore I think it is essential to draw
> your attention to the following facts: 1) In principle, I share
> the views of Lenin, Zinoviev, and Kamenev, and I defend them
> in my newspaper *Vpered* and in my many public speeches.
> . . . I am just as irreconcilable an opponent of the general
> policy of the Provisional Government as the above-mentioned
> Comrades.[482]

But he didn't stop there. He insisted on confronting his accusers. He marched over to the Smolny Institute and took the podium at a meeting of the soviet committee, which had backed Kerensky's crackdown up to that point. "Lenin has fought for revolution thirty years, I have fought against the oppression of the popular masses twenty years," he told the roomful of deputies, who reacted mostly with silence and a few catcalls. "We cannot but hate German militarism. Only he who does not know what revolution is can say otherwise." Privately, he made the case even more sharply. "Everybody thinks they can stab Lenin in the back," he told people. "Whoever accused Lenin of being a German agent is a scoundrel."[483]

Finally, on the $10,000 charge itself, he turned to ridicule. In the same speeches and public letters, he explained how, yes, in New York he had received small donations from local socialists at speeches and rallies—nickels, pennies, quarters, and a few dollars, totaling a few hundred altogether. The mysterious German newspaper editor identified by Miliukov, he explained, was Ludwig Lore, editor of the *New Yorker Volkszeitung,* a longtime socialist who'd taken a collection among his readers; and the crowds at the Harlem River Casino, Beethoven Hall, and other venues were simply immigrants wanting revolutions in their home countries, including Russia and Germany. That's who had given him money in New York.

"In my entire life I have not only never had at my disposal, at one time, $10,000, but even a tenth of that sum," he wrote, making a joke of the affair.[484] Besides, he added, $10,000 was a cheap price to overthrow a government. Germany would have given more if it really meant business. And it was Miliukov himself who had insisted that Trotsky be released from Halifax over the same charge.

After about a week of this, Kerensky decided he'd had enough and ordered Trotsky arrested along with the others. Trotsky found himself behind bars again, this time in Petrograd's Kresty Prison near the Neva River, rapidly filling up with Bolsheviks caught in the dragnet. But all the publicity had its effect. On the street, sympathies began to change.

Nobody found these shifting political winds more confusing than Trotsky's own sons, Sergei and Lyova. "What sort of revolution is this?" they asked their mother the morning the squad of policemen came and invaded their apartment before dawn to arrest their father, "if Dad could first be put in a concentration camp and then in prison?"[485] Natalya, working at the woodworkers trade union by day that summer to earn money for the family, kept the boys away from Petrograd to insulate them from these attacks. She sent them to Tariyoki, the beach town on the Gulf of Finland, where they mostly enjoyed being "happy, sunburnt and mad about swimming and fishing," as she put it. But when she came to visit them once around this time, she discovered the boys cowering in a corner of their room at the local boardinghouse. They had heard people call their father a German spy and had gotten into a fight. Someone had pulled a knife and thrown a chair. They hadn't eaten in hours.[486]

After that, she took Sergei and Lyova back to Petrograd. There the boys got in the habit of riding the tram to the prison to carry baskets of food to their father.

In the end, Trotsky's loud protests reached their most important audience. In early August, with both of the key leaders absent—Lenin hiding in Finland and Trotsky locked up in Kresty Prison—their followers decided to seal the alliance. Trotsky's vocal defense of Lenin had removed any doubt about loyalty between Bolsheviks and Mezhrayontska. At a party congress, the Bolsheviks formally voted to absorb them, and the Mezhrayontska formally voted to accept. Leading the congress in Lenin's absence were Nikolai Bukharin, Trotsky's fellow *Novy Mir* editor from New York and now head of the Moscow Soviet, and Joseph Stalin. On Stalin's motion, they also voted to make Alexandra Kollontai the only female member of the Bolshevik Central Committee.

They were all Bolsheviks now, committed to revolution, the full package: toppling Kerensky and "All Power to the Soviets."

THE GOVERNMENT RELEASED Trotsky from prison on September 4 during its next big crisis. This time, it was an attempted coup d'etat by Russian army general Lavr Kornilov, a leader of that summer's failed military offensive against Germany, now fed up with Kerensky's leadership. Kornilov, promising to restore military discipline, had ordered his soldiers to march on Petrograd, occupy it, and impose martial law. Faced with Kornilov's approaching army, Kerensky decided he now needed help from the Bolshevik soldiers in local garrisons, the same ones whose demonstrations he had crushed in July. And to convince these soldiers to support him, he needed Trotsky.

In the end, Bolshevik support proved crucial in stopping Kornilov by instigating dissent among Kornilov's own soldiers.

By now the winds had turned. Trotsky returned to the Smolny Institute and found that Bolsheviks, recently vilified, now controlled a majority on the soviet committee. In early October, the soviet elected Trotsky its chairman, then gave him control of its newly created Military Revolutionary Committee, a group Trotsky himself had proposed for the Soviet to defend against government attacks and that he now used to plan and execute the ultimate seizure of power. Lenin kept contact from hiding places, first in Finland and then safe houses around Petrograd. In early November, he showed himself to participate in a key meeting of the Bolshevik Central Committee, where it voted to launch its own coup d'etat. The decision came on a ten-to-two vote, with Kamenev and Zinoviev opposing the idea. Two of the Bolsheviks voting yes along with Lenin and Trotsky were Joseph Stalin and Alexandra Kollontai. Kollontai remembered the session as exhausting. "We felt hungry," she wrote of the moment after the tense vote. "A hot samovar was brought out, we fell upon cheese and sausage."[487]

By the time Lenin appeared in disguise at the Smolny Institute on November 6 (October 24 on the Russian calendar), all was ready. At that point, Trotsky was in full flower, running from speech to speech, meeting to meeting. "His influence among the workers and the revolutionary leadership was colossal," recalled fellow soviet committee member Nikolai Sukarnov. "He was the principal actor, the hero of that extraordinary page of history."[488]

The Bolshevik Revolution of November 7, 1917, was largely a bloodless coup. Operating from their command center at the Smolny Institute, Trotsky and his Military Revolutionary Committee directed Red Guards—organized groups of armed party members—and sympathetic military units, including sailors from the Kronstadt naval base, who stationed the battle cruiser *Aurora* and three torpedo boats in the Neva River. Starting before dawn, they captured strategic facilities, the central post office, bridges and railway stations, the state bank, electrical generating stations, newspaper offices, communications and administrative centers, and telephone exchanges, culminating in seizure of the Winter Palace, the ornate former home of tsars that had become the official seat of the Kerensky government. The palace surrendered well past midnight after Cossack troops, cadets, and a women's battalion protecting the building either deserted or surrendered.

In Petrograd only six people died in the clashes. In Moscow it took a far bloodier fight, resulting in deaths of about five hundred Bolsheviks and government defenders.

Seizing control, the Bolsheviks would change their name to communists and set about consolidating power. It would take three years to fully control the country after a grisly civil war. They'd move the capital to Moscow, easier to defend in case of invasion. Communists would hold power in Russia for seventy-four years, during which they would reshape both it and the power structure of the world, making their revolution a pivotal event of the twentieth century. Their legacy would include a pronounced dark side: harsh realities of life under Soviet dictatorship, gulag prisons and KGB torture, Stalinist purges and Cold War, economic stagnation, deaths and imprisonments by the millions.

Lenin and Trotsky personally would hold power only a short time. Lenin would survive two assassination attempts, both in 1918, and suffer three strokes in 1923. The strokes left him largely incapacitated until his death in January 1924, at just fifty-three years old. Trotsky, celebrated in Russia as a hero of the revolution and subsequent civil war, would lose a power struggle after Lenin's death to his rival Joseph Stalin, who would orchestrate Trotsky's ouster from the party in 1927 and expulsion from Russia a year later.

But in the flush of victory at that moment in 1917, an era when millions around the world placed their trust in a vague, seductive notion they called socialism, it seemed a modern miracle, a grand experiment, a chance for utopia. It captured imaginations and abruptly transformed its chief architects, Lenin and Trotsky, into two of the most recognized, notorious, loved, hated, and talked-about figures on earth.

BACK IN NEW York City, news of the Bolshevik takeover made headlines, but it hardly sparked the same giddy celebrations that had greeted
the toppling of the tsar the prior March. No parades or street parties
broke out this time. Applause came only from a few rarified places.
Americans mostly found the situation confusing. Russia had been in
turmoil for months, and they struggled to see much difference in one
strongman, Kerensky, being overthrown by another. Besides, who were
these Bolsheviks? Most Americans had never heard of them. Even Meyer
London, the Socialist New York Congressman, predicted the new regime
would "last but a matter of days," since Bolsheviks, he explained, "represent an infinitely small part of the Socialist Party in Russia."[489]

Americans now looked at world events through a single new lens:
How would it affect our boys "over there?" Almost a million young
men had already joined the army: husbands, fathers, sons, and neighbors from cities and towns across the country. The first large waves
of American soldiers were now crossing the ocean—braving the threat
of German submarines—to fight the kaiser. More than 180,000 of
them would reach Europe by the end of 1917. The war now touched
every walk of life in America, from conscription to what people could
eat, speak, or write. That month, the Federal Fuel Administration in
Washington issued an edict ordering Broadway itself, New York's glit-
tering theater district, to dim its lights, limiting electric signs to three
hours per night to save coal.

Would these Bolsheviks help our boys fight the Germans? Were
they on our side? Or theirs? Here too confusion. "If the Bolshevik win,
America must not make the mistake of thinking that this is a German plot
or feel that Russia is lost to the war," warned one prominent news correspondent, the *New York World*'s Arno Dosch-Fleurot, from Petrograd.
Bolsheviks, he explained, wanted to give Germany "a chance to accept
an offer of peace" without annexations or indemnities," but should it
refuse, "she will then have to be beaten by arms."[490]

This tough talk, though, didn't quite measure up to actions. Americans
had seen the midsummer accusations that Lenin, the Bolshevik leader,

was a German spy. And one of the Bolsheviks' first moves in power was to declare a temporary, thirty-day armistice with Germany to start peace talks. It hardly sent a reassuring signal.

The one place in America that saw it differently, though, was New York City, and not just its socialists and Russians. Trotsky had made a mark here, and people remembered him. Hundreds had met him; thousands had heard him speak or read his columns. Even the big-circulation English-language newspapers felt obliged to put his face on their front pages, the sharp eyes looking out from behind the signature beard and wire glasses. TROTSKY, NOW IN KERENSKY'S PLACE, ONCE LIVED HERE, headlined the *New York World*.[491] TROTZKY, NEW RUSSIAN LEADER, IS KNOWN HERE, echoed the *New York Call*. TROTZKY, WHO HELPED OVERTHROW KERENSKY, ONCE WORKED FOR NEW YORK PAPER, announced the *New York American*. TROTZKY IN EXILE LIVED IN THE BRONX, added the *New York Times*.[492]

The *Forward* carried Trotsky's photo on its front page two straight days, placing it just *above* Lenin's when they appeared together. The *Bronx Home News* made the point best: BRONX MAN LEADS RUSSIAN REVOLUTION.[493]

Slants varied. The *World* portrayed Trotsky in New York as a hot-head radical who had challenged local moderates like Morris Hillquit and *Forward* editor Abraham Cahan. The *Times* spotlighted the recent charges against him as a German agent. On the other side, William Randolph Hearst's *New York American* painted Trotsky as a good influence, almost one of the family, a friend of the newspaper who had written an article explaining how "Russia will be a republic built on the lines of the great American republic."[494]

At *Novy Mir*, Trotsky's actual base in New York, the staff virtually rejoiced. "A wonderful man," gushed Alexander Menshoy, an editor there, happy to now call himself Trotsky's "most intimate friend in America." In talking with the *New York Call*, he described Trotsky as "tall, commanding, about 40 years old with a wonderful personality and a winning smile."[495]

But all the accounts agreed on one thing. Whether they liked him or not, they all made Trotsky out as the real leader in chaotic Petrograd, as if confirming the obvious: that only a New Yorker could have pulled off this affair.

In fact, to their growing dismay, Americans were quickly learning that New York City had supplied a whole raft of leading Bolsheviks, not just Trotsky. Dozens of top new officials announced in Petrograd had names familiar to the cafés of lower Manhattan. They included Alexandra Kollontai, the new people's commissar for social welfare, and Nikolai Bukharin, the new editor of *Pravda*.[496] Grigorii Chudnovsky, still remembered as Trotsky's young Russian sidekick in New York, was identified as one of the Red Guards leading the assault on the Winter Palace. Another *Novy Mir* contributor, V. Volodarsky, emerged as Petrograd's new commissar over the press. Alexander Menson-Minkin, a *Novy Mir* linotype operator, became director of the Soviet state mint, and a *Novy Mir* advertising agent named Model became commandant of Petrograd's Peter-Paul Prison. The soviet heads of the city governments of Moscow and Kronstadt and of a key rifle factory all came from New York.

Soon the number of New Yorkers known to hold top posts in the new regime reached into the hundreds, almost all of them Russian immigrants returning since March. "The returned radicals, on account of their wider experience, are gaining the ascendency in power over the Bolsheviki," a *New York World* on-the-scene reporter wrote. Only the Russian wives of some of these American Bolsheviki seemed to miss the comforts of Broadway and New York shopping.[497] Final estimates of returning Russians from New York would range as high as ten thousand, making it the largest reverse migration in American history.[498]

Most Americans, though, hardly took comfort in this news. They had never trusted these immigrant radicals, and now, seeing the trouble they'd made in Russia, they liked them even less. "Both Trotzky and Lenin have many friends and sympathizers in New York, where they once lived," warned William Shepherd, a United Press reporter just returned from Russia since the takeover, "who, if given the opportunity will try to do the same thing in the United States."[499] Worse, they had a "direct line of communication between the Bolsheviki in Petrograd and the radicals in New York," added Robert Maisel, director of the anti-socialist American Alliance for Labor and Democracy.[500]

Within weeks, an even darker picture started to emerge. American socialists who had traveled to Russia during the revolution started coming home with stories about Bolshevik extremists ruining their long-sought Marxist state, turning it into a dictatorship not of the proletariat but for themselves. Within days of taking power, the Lenin–Trotsky regime had banned political parties, shut down newspapers (even socialist ones), and arrested scores of political opponents, including the entire Kerensky cabinet and members of a recently elected constituent assembly. "The revolution is on the verge of destruction through the excesses of its new leaders," explained Anna Ingerman, the woman who had clashed with Trotsky in New York over her support for the Red Cross and who had gone to Russia as a nurse to help wounded revolutionaries. "If the revolution is crushed," she said, "history will place the blame on the Bolsheviki."[501]

Another returning socialist, a man named S. Lovich, reported how Trotsky had confiscated printing plants, dissolved the Petrograd Duma, "arrested men who have given half of their lives to the cause of the revolution, some of them who have spent at least thirty years in the prisons of Siberia," and "placed 6-inch guns along the Nevsky" in downtown Petrograd.[502]

Trotsky himself fanned these flames with his own hot rhetoric. In a speech to the Petrograd Soviet that December after banning the Kadet (Constitutional Democratic) Party and jailing members of the recently elected constituent assembly, he laughed at their squeamishness. "You are perturbed by the mild terror we are applying to our enemies," he told them. "But know that within a month this terror will take the terrible form of the French revolution—not the fortress but the guillotine."[503]

But at that moment in late 1917, these fears too remained abstract and hypothetical, especially for Americans watching from the safe distance of New York City. Here, among socialists and well-meaning friends, optimism reigned. The revolution still seemed a wonderful event, a vindication of Marxist dogma they had recited for years. Even Morris Hillquit, as skeptical as anyone toward Trotsky after their bitter fights in New York, gave him grudging credit for the accomplishment. While they differed on many points, he conceded, "I believe [Lenin and Trotsky] have rendered a tremendous service to our movement . . . by shaking up the old world."[504]

LOOSE ENDS

"We cannot deal with Trotsky. He is an individualist."[505]

—Joseph Stalin, Soviet leader, 1924 to 1953

"[Trotsky] is the only Bolshevik worth asking the question about."[506]

—Writer Christopher Hitchens, asked in 2006 if Trotsky was a "good guy" or a "bad guy"

"You may not be interested in the dialectic [or war, or history, or the logic of events], but the dialectic is interested in you."[507]

—Leon Trotsky, 1940

TROTSKY AND THE RUSSIANS

Leon Trotsky emerged from the 1917 Bolshevik Revolution and subsequent Russian civil war as the most popular figure in Moscow after Lenin himself, the dashing hero of the day. And why not. Trotsky had led the 1918 peace talks at Brest-Litovsk ending Russia's war with Germany. Then, as people's commissar of military and naval affairs, he had rebuilt and commanded the Red Army against enemies on all sides, including White Russian armies numbering almost three million, plus a ten-nation Western expeditionary force including British, Japanese, French, and American soldiers—all despite having no prior military experience. More than a million died in the struggle, including hundreds of thousands of civilians, but it won the peace and secured the Soviet state. Socialism had prevailed.

American visitors to Russia who saw Trotsky during his glory days marveled at the transformation. Emma Goldman, deported from New York during the postwar Red Scare, spotted Trotsky at the Moscow ballet one night in 1920 and gushed at the spectacle of him in his military uniform. "What a change in his appearance and bearing!" she wrote. "He was no longer the pale, lean, and narrow cheeked exile I had seen in New York." Instead, "he carried himself with proud mien, and there was disdain in his eyes, even contempt, as he glanced at the British guests."[508]

Armand Hammer, then a young businessman on his first trip to Russia, described meeting Trotsky in his Kremlin office with its high ceiling, maps covering the walls, the desk buried under books and papers and yet in perfect order. "The place was scrupulously clean and tidy," Hammer recalled, "no cigarette stubs on the floors, no tea glasses in saucers on the desk." It was a far cry from Trotsky's cluttered corner in the basement office of *Novy Mir* in Greenwich Village. During the civil war, Trotsky had lived for weeks at a time on a special armored train, speeding from front to front, giving orders and dispensing discipline. Now, the "Red Warlord wore khaki breeches, a plain tunic buttoned up to his neck, and glasses," Hammer went on. His decorum was all business. "Though he greeted me quite cordially, his glance was cold and piercing, very different from Lenin's human and friendly attitude. Never once during the meeting did he smile."[509]

Another visitor, journalist Frederick Marcosson, found Trotsky's manner "abrupt and aggressive. He walks and talks rapidly. Nothing about him save the swiftness of his movements was more distinctive than his eyes. They seemed to burn with zeal."[510]

But appearances aside, Bolshevik Russia had shown itself a brutal place. Beyond the ravages of civil war, the regime had banned political parties, jailed opponents, shut down newspapers, and even abolished the workers' soviets. Civil war made the repression worse. It brought "war communism," a system of forced labor, mass property seizures, industry nationalizations, food rationing, and confiscation of grain production. It succeeded in feeding the Red Army but also worsened the economy, causing farm fields to be abandoned, hoarding, and famine.

At the same time, the Cheka, Soviet Russia's first secret police organization, launched a Red Terror, prompted in part by a 1918 assassination attempt on Lenin. The effort killed between 50,000 and 150,000 people considered political opponents, troublemakers, or counterrevolutionaries. Most prominent of the killings was the post-midnight execution of Tsar Nicholas II and his entire household—his wife, Alexandra; his son; four daughters; their doctor; a maid; and two other servants—on July 17, 1918.

At the time, Trotsky justified all these actions—the terror, the violence, the killings, the building of a single-party dictatorship.[511] Later he would describe them as "temporary measures dictated by civil war, blockade, intervention and famine."[512] Arguably, Trotsky himself would ultimately become their most tragic victim.

A low point came with the 1921 Kronstadt Rebellion, a movement by sailors at the Kronstadt naval base demanding more freedoms and an end to wartime repression. These same sailors had proved their loyalty by backing Lenin's Bolsheviks in 1917, both during the July Days and the November putsch. But Trotsky, with Lenin's support, ordered them crushed for insubordination. His Red Army launched a massive assault under the command of General Mikhail Tukhachevsky, one of Trotsky's best fighters against the White Russians. Some sixty thousand troops stormed the base; hundreds on both sides died during the ten-day battle. Once the base was captured, the regime executed an estimated two thousand sailors, many by drowning under the ice. Thousands more died in prisons. The incident caused even anarchist Emma Goldman to turn against Trotsky and Lenin.

After the civil war, Lenin decided to try rebuilding popular support by loosening the reins. He introduced his New Economic Policy (NEP), an effort to boost food supplies by allowing a limited space for commercial freedoms: private enterprise, market incentives, and use of cash, particularly in agriculture. NEP became popular and lasted almost a decade, creating a boom in small farming and returning food stocks to prewar levels, though along with inflation and profiteering.

Trotsky became a prominent NEP critic. He had suggested a similar idea a year earlier, but by 1921 he considered NEP a retreat from socialism. Instead he advocated the "militarization" of labor, treating workers like soldiers, forcing them to work where needed. "The very principle of labor conscription has replaced the principle of free labor as radically and irreversibly as socialization of the means of production has replaced capitalist ownership," he argued.[513] This stance not only placed him at odds with Lenin but also gave ammunition to future enemies. Trotsky came to lead a left opposition that challenged the increasing bureaucratization of the party and pressed for more intraparty democracy.

Lenin's death in 1924 sparked a fierce battle for succession. Years of tension within the Bolshevik ruling clique boiled over. Even at this point, Trotsky still enjoyed wide public support, especially from the army. Even his Jewishness didn't seem an insurmountable obstacle. Many Jews still held top Bolshevik posts, and even if it made Trotsky hesitate about taking the top job as party chairman, he still held enormous influence in picking a friendly ally as the successor.

That, at least, was how it looked on the surface. But in the new reality of postrevolutionary Russia, the advantage had shifted to a different kind of player, Joseph Jughashvili Stalin.

Stalin, a year older than Trotsky, had followed a different path to power. Unlike other early Bolsheviks, Stalin had written few articles or books. He had stayed in Russia during the world war. But his political strengths had caught the eye of Lenin, who mentored him into the party leadership. Stalin served loyally, and Lenin appreciated it. Stalin came from Gori, a small town in then-Russian-controlled Georgia. His parents had sent him for education to the Tiflis Spiritual Seminary, where he first trained for the priesthood before deciding he was an atheist and was expelled for missing exams. He read voraciously, wrote poetry, and even worked in a meteorological office. Stalin's early Bolshevik work included organizing workers but also robbing banks and pulling off kidnappings. Still, his writing and leadership claimed enough respect for him to take the helm as coeditor of *Pravda* in early 1917.

Stalin saw Trotsky, part of the international literati, as a condescending snob. As early as 1913, Stalin had described him in print as "Trotsky, a noisy champion with fake muscles, a man of beautiful uselessness."[514] Trotsky, for his part, dismissed Stalin as a mediocrity.[515] But Stalin had won Lenin's confidence, and Lenin in 1922 appointed him as Bolshevik party secretary, a position Stalin used to stack the bureaucracy with supporters.

Stalin also outmaneuvered Trotsky within the Bolshevik ruling circle. He managed to corral two key allies, Kamenev and Zinoviev, into an anti-Trotsky coalition and used it to increasingly isolate him on the Central Committee. Also, Stalin's plan for the war-weary Russia of the 1920s, what he called "socialism in one country," struck a far friendlier chord than Trotsky's own calls for exhausting-sounding "permanent revolution."

Once in control, Stalin tightened the noose. In 1926 he had Trotsky removed as war commissar and then from the party's politburo. The next year, in 1927, he had Trotsky expelled from the Central Committee and then from the party altogether, along with Trotsky's then-most-recent allies Zinoviev and Kamenev (who had both defected from Stalin, seeing themselves at risk). Zinoviev and Kamenev immediately recanted, and Stalin allowed them to return, but Trotsky refused. After that, Stalin had Trotsky exiled to Alma-Ata (now Almaty), then a remote village, today the capital of modern Kazakhstan. The next year, he expelled him from Russia altogether. Trotsky would be forced to spend the last dozen years of his life in exile, first in Turkey, then France, then Norway, and finally Mexico.

Having eliminated his rivals, Stalin now emerged as the undisputed heir to a Bolshevik/communist system conceived and won by generations of Marxists claiming to seek a better world. He ruled for almost thirty years, chairing the Soviet Communist Party until his death in 1953. He consolidated power to a stunning degree and used it to industrialize the country, defeat Germany in the Second World War, and transform Russia into a world power rivaling the United States. But the price tag in human misery was just as stunning. Stalin left a bloodstained trail of purges, famine, and domestic terror rivaling Nazi Germany. The number of deaths alone is staggering. Estimates of the killings reach into the multiple millions: eight hundred thousand executions, 1.7 million deaths in gulag prisons, almost half a million deaths during liquidation of the kulaks (independent small farmers), and between 6 and 8 million deaths from famine and violence during the forced collectivization of agriculture in Russia and Ukraine.

In the 1930s, Stalin launched a series of purges that, among others, would liquidate virtually the entire generation of Bolsheviks who had played significant roles in the 1917 revolution, including former allies Zinoviev, Kamenev, and Bukharin. But Stalin showed special venom for Trotsky, making him the chief public villain, the evil face behind a parade of alleged conspiracies detailed in dramatic confessions at show trials staged throughout the 1930s, all false. He purged Trotsky's supporters—murdering most, exiling others. He hunted down Trotsky's family, friends, acquaintances, and allies. Trotsky's older brother, Alexander (then an agronomist working at a Russian sugar mill), and his younger sister, Olga (wife of ousted Bolshevik leader Lev Kamenev), were arrested and shot. Stalin rewrote Russian history to eliminate Trotsky's very presence, removing his face from photographs and his name from accounts of key events.

After the Second World War, Stalin's Soviet Union occupied most of Eastern Europe under tightly controlled dictatorial states, acquired nuclear weapons, built an arsenal of nuclear-armed intercontinental missiles, and waged a four-decade Cold War against the West. Communism at its height covered vast portions of the globe, including movements in Africa, Asia, and South America and regimes in China, Cuba, North Korea, and Southeast Asia that survive to this day.

But the fall was just as dramatic. After Stalin's death in 1953, his successor, Nikita Khrushchev, secretly denounced Stalin's abuses and began an internal "thaw." In 1985 a later Soviet leader, Mikhail Gorbachev, launched glasnost (open discussion) and perestroika (restructuring), a set of reforms aimed at opening the Soviet system. In short order, the system collapsed. Eastern and Central European peoples one by one demanded freedom, starting with Poland, Hungary, and the Baltics, then East Germany, Bulgaria, Czechoslovakia, and Romania. The Berlin Wall fell in 1989. Inside Russia, President Boris Yeltsin faced down an abortive coup in 1991 by leaders of the Defense Ministry and the KGB, after which he banned the Communist Party in Russia.

That September, the Russian Congress of People's Deputies voted to dissolve the Soviet Union itself, seventy-four years after the 1917 revolution that had put it in place. The experiment was over.

TROTSKY AND HIS friends from New York fared particularly badly under Stalinism. NIKOLAI BUKHARIN thrived at first as a Soviet official in the early 1920s, editing *Pravda,* sitting on the Bolshevik Central Committee, and leading the Third International, or Comintern. Lenin called him "the favorite of the whole Party" for his outgoing nature and academic brilliance.[516] But after Lenin's death, the tables turned.

Bukharin had made himself a prominent supporter of Lenin's NEP, and he sided with Stalin in his power struggles against Trotsky, an NEP critic. He served Stalin as chief theoretician and helped him outmaneuver not only Trotsky but also his other top rivals, Zinoviev and Kamenev. But Stalin, after he achieved control, decided that NEP had outlived its usefulness and chose to scrap it in favor of forced industrialization and collectivization. This "great turn," as Stalin called it, placed Bukharin suddenly on the outside, tarring him with a "right deviation." Bukharin abruptly lost his position at the Comintern, was stripped of the *Pravda* editorship, and was expelled from the politburo. After a brief rehabilitation in the mid-1930s, he was arrested in 1936 and charged with conspiracy.

Bukharin was forced to confess to crimes he never committed and to testify to a nonexistent conspiracy of "wreckers" and "counterrevolutionaries," all conceived by the usual arch-demon Trotsky. Waiting behind bars for his show trial, Bukharin wrote forty-three letters to Stalin, pleading for his life. In a final one, he proposed a deal: Let him live and send him to, of all places, New York City. "Send me to American for x years," Bukharin begged, even offering to leave his wife behind as a hostage. "Arguments in favor: I could mount a public campaign about the trials, wage war to the death on Trotsky, win over large sections of the vacillating intelligentsia. I would be in effect an anti-Trotsky and I would do all this with great energy and enthusiasm."[517]

The appeal did little good. After a public trial that drew wide condemnation, Stalin had Bukharin executed in March 1938 and had his wife sent to a labor camp shortly thereafter.

ALEXANDRA KOLLONTAI likewise emerged as a popular figure in the early Bolshevik state. As people's commissar for social welfare, she led energetic campaigns for women's equality, including literacy, medical care, and liberalized marriage and family laws. She flouted convention in 1918 by having a high-profile love affair and then marrying a much younger naval officer named Paul Dybenko, whom she divorced a few years later.

Kollontai courted more serious danger in 1920, however, by cosponsoring a dissident Worker Opposition Party demanding freedoms from state controls and criticizing the party bureaucracy. This time, Lenin intervened and not only dissolved Kollontai's party but also removed her from the country. He launched Kollontai on a diplomatic career that would keep her far from Moscow most of the next thirty years, as Soviet ambassador to Norway, then Mexico, then Sweden and also as a Soviet representative to the League of Nations.

This distance ended up saving her life. Stalin, having purged the army, doctors, and early Bolsheviks, began planning a purge against diplomats in 1937 and apparently had Kollontai on his list. She was summoned to Moscow that year. Expecting to face questions about her political reliability, she decided to protect herself by publishing an article to prove her loyalty. In it she described the famous 1917 meeting of the Bolshevik Central Committee that voted to launch the November putsch. After ridiculing Zinoviev and Kamenev for cowardice, she turned her pen on Stalin's own favorite scapegoat, Trotsky, describing him as "the Judas Trotsky, future agent of the Gestapo," spinning treacheries behind false smiles.[518]

Stalin allowed Kollontai to leave Moscow and return to Sweden, where she served her country through the Second World War. Her writings on women's rights became popular during the feminist movements of the 1970s and 1980s, and her image as a sexually liberated Soviet diplomat is widely considered the basis for the Greta Garbo character in the 1939 film *Ninotchka*.

Trotsky's two sons, SERGEI AND LYOVA SEDOV, both died young, one clearly murdered by Stalin's regime, the other dying under circumstances making murder highly plausible.

Sergei, the younger, the one who as a nine-year-old got lost trying to count the streets in the Bronx in 1917, ended up studying science in Moscow. He became a professor at the Moscow Institute of Technology and published several technical papers, mostly staying far from politics. But in 1935 he was working at a gas plant when an explosion occurred. Stalin's great purges were under way, rife with accusations of "wreckers" and saboteurs. Sergei was arrested and charged with setting the explosion himself, plotting to destroy the plant and kill fellow workers. He was sentenced to exile in Krasnoyarsk, a tiny outpost in central Siberia. Here, he was freed for a time and allowed to work as an engineer, but he was then rearrested, sent to a labor camp, and executed.

Before he died, Sergei married twice. Both wives endured long prison terms. The second had a daughter, Julia, who managed to escape Russia in the 1970s and reach the United States, then Israel, where she and her family still live today.[519]

Lyova, the older son, was more like his father. A stubborn purist, he refused to live in the Kremlin as a young adult and criticized his parents for their "bourgeois" life there with its luxuries. He once refused to accept a gift jacket from the Moscow Soviet because it looked too "new and shiny," as Natalya remembered it, at a time when most Russians faced stark poverty.[520]

Lyova accompanied his father into exile and published an anti-Stalinist *Opposition Bulletin* from there. He settled in Paris, but in 1937 he suffered a routine attack of appendicitis. Instead of Lyova entering a public hospital, a Soviet agent of the NKVD (successor to the Cheka), posing as a friend, arranged for him to be admitted to a private clinic operated by Russians with NKVD ties. They operated on Lyova and the procedure appeared successful at first, but then complications, including a suspicious bruise, set in. Lyova died in the clinic shortly after. The family never doubted that Stalin had arranged the death. French authorities never fully investigated the incident, and a clear verdict was never reached.

Lyova had been forced to leave a wife and son behind in Moscow. She was imprisoned and shot; the child disappeared.

Trotsky blamed himself for the deaths of his sons, convinced they had been killed on his account. "Perhaps my death would have saved Sergey," told confided to Natalya on hearing the news. "And at moments I felt he was sorry to be alive," she wrote.[521]

Trotsky's first wife, ALEXANDRA LVOVNA SOKOLOVSKAYA BRONSTEIN, also disappeared in the Stalinist camps. Agents arrested her in 1935 and sent her to the Siberian outpost of Omsk. During her exile, she and Trotsky shared a few letters, but communication soon broke off. She survived until 1938 and vanished after that, presumably executed.

Alexandra Lvovna's two daughters, NINA and ZINA (ZINAIDA) BRONSTEIN, also both died young. Nina, the younger, succumbed to tuberculosis in Moscow in 1928 after Trotsky had been exiled to Alma-Ata, making it impossible for him to see her or attend the funeral. The older daughter, Zina, cared for her sister in her dying days. Stalin's government permitted Zina to leave Russia in 1931 to join her father in exile in Turkey but allowed her to take only one of her two children, leaving the other behind. Zina suffered from depression, tuberculosis, and possibly other ailments, and in late 1932 she traveled for treatment to Berlin. Here she learned that Russia had stripped her of citizenship and that, apparently on Soviet urging, Berlin had ordered her to leave the city. She was found dead, locked in her apartment with the gas jets turned on. Talk of her death being an NKVD job disguised as suicide persisted but was never substantiated.[522]

Zina had had two children by two different husbands, and while both husbands disappeared in the great purges, presumed executed, the two children survived. Her son Esteban (Seva) Volkow, the one she took with her into exile, was brought to Mexico by the Trotskys and raised there. Her daughter, Alexandra, stayed behind in Russia and, after her father's arrest, was raised by her stepmother and for a time by her grandmother, Alexandra Sokolovskaya. She was arrested in the 1930s and sent to a prison camp in Kazakhstan but was freed after Stalin's death and returned to Moscow.

Zina's two children—Trotsky's grandchildren—had the chance to meet face-to-face only once during their lifetimes. It came in December 1988, when Mikhail Gorbachev's glasnost briefly raised hopes for a Trotsky rehabilitation. Volkov, living in Mexico as an engineer and learning that his sister still lived and was dying of cancer, applied for a visa and was allowed to visit Moscow for the first time in fifty-seven years.

Volkov described meeting Alexandra as "a little like people from a shipwreck who meet safe and sound on the beach."[523] Alexandra, now sixty-six years old, happily lapsed into memories of their mother, Trotsky's daughter Zina. "My mother was a revolutionary," she told an interviewer. "She wore a leather coat and, I believe, a gun. She taught me geography. The revolutionaries were afraid their children would stay ignorant." Alexandra died of her cancer about a month later. Volkov returned to Mexico City, where he raised four daughters and still lives.

NATALYA SEDOVA, Trotsky's common-law wife since 1902, would outlive Trotsky by twenty-two years. After following him throughout his exiles, she defended him publicly against Stalinist attacks long after his death. Her loyalty survived even after she learned of her husband's affair with artist Frida Kahlo in the late 1930s. Natalya remained in Mexico, stayed active in communist movements, and coauthored a Trotsky biography published in France in 1951. She lived to be an old lady of seventy-nine years, helping to raise her grandson.

TROTSKY used his exile in Turkey, Europe, and Mexico to attack Stalin and his regime. In his most devastating critique, a 1937 book called *The Revolution Betrayed,* he described Soviet Russia under Stalin as a country ruled by a "greedy, lying and cynical caste of rulers," self-serving bureaucrats who "learned to fear the masses with a perfectly bourgeois fear" and who would "devour the workers state" unless they themselves were overthrown.[524] "The real danger," he wrote, "begins when the bureaucracy makes attitudes towards Lenin and his teaching the subject of automatic reverence."[525] After that, he argued, critical thought disappears.

In exile, Trotsky wrote prolifically, producing an autobiography, a *History of the Russian Revolution,* and hundreds of articles and letters. He created a new Fourth International composed of Trotskyist groups in Europe, Asia, and North America, dedicated to spreading socialism free of the Stalinist taint. He spoke out against German fascism and, into the late 1930s, kept contact with American Trotskyists, some of whom traveled to Mexico to visit him.

Trotsky continued to dabble in American affairs throughout his life, and he learned to speak English quite well.[526] In 1939 he threatened to visit Washington, DC, to testify before the Dies Committee (forerunner to the House Un-American Activities Committee) and use it as a platform to publicly defend American communism. Congressman Dies, a Democrat of Texas, quickly withdrew the offer. At the outset of World War II, Trotsky challenged his own American Trotskyist supporters over whether Stalinism and the Stalin–Hitler nonaggression pact had left Soviet Russia so "degenerate" that it no longer deserved support.

Trotsky's insistence that Russia remained a true "workers state"—even if suffering a debilitating cancer—caused the American group to splinter yet again.[527]

In 1939 Stalin, hearing that Trotsky might be in poor health, instructed NKVD chief Lavrenty Beria to hunt him down. Trotsky by this point had settled into a villa outside Mexico City with twenty-foot-high garden walls and constant guards. In May 1940 a group of Mexican communists led by an NKVD agent assaulted the house, firing Thompson machine guns, trying to kill Trotsky and his family, but guards fought them off. One American guard was captured and killed by the attackers.

Fears of another attack forced Trotsky to give up his regular walks though the Mexican countryside. Guards installed bulletproof doors and windows along with towers and barbed-wire traps, mostly financed by American supporters. "When we left the house he always went in a car, with another car behind it or in front with more bodyguards," recalled his grandson Esteban, who was fourteen years old at the time and suffered a gunshot wound to his foot in the earlier attack. Esteban also remembered his grandfather's exercise routine during these last weeks: "to look after the rabbits kept there which were eaten and the chickens which provided fresh eggs."[528]

Trotsky still carried on his busy life inside the compound, writing letters by the dozen and meeting visitors from around the world. Finally, on August 20, 1940, an NKVD agent named Ramon Mercader entered the villa, posing as a friend and writer, and as Trotsky sat in his study, Mercader attacked him from behind with an ice axe and killed him.

The news electrified the world, making headlines and deepening fears of Stalin's long reach. On hearing it in New York City, Louis Waldman, one of Trotsky's old political enemies from 1917, wrote simply: "Trotsky's career was perhaps one of the most tragic in modern times."[529] Esteban Volkow, Trotsky's grandson, still maintains the villa where his grandfather was murdered and has turned it into a Trotsky museum.

HILLQUIT, FRAINA, AND THE AMERICANS

In America, Trotsky's most lasting influence was on the people he got to know best, the American socialists. Reaching New York in January 1917, Trotsky found an American Socialist Party healthy, growing, competitive, and increasingly mainstream. It had elected congressmen, mayors, and legislators in a dozen states. Its presidential candidate, Eugene V. Debs, had attracted almost a million popular votes in 1912. Its publications drew large readerships, and it offered a program of social reforms that would become basics of American life. Anchored in immigrant-heavy cities like New York, Chicago, and Milwaukee, it stood poised to become a viable long-term force in the country, perhaps in time even rivaling Tammany Hall.

But within three years, by 1920, the bubble would burst. The Socialist Party would be wrecked, its members scattered, many behind bars, with Trotsky's fingerprints all over the collapse. From his very first day, Trotsky pushed to radicalize American socialism and transform the party into a vessel for revolution. He almost succeeded in just his ten weeks on America soil. His success would spell the party's doom.

The high point came with Trotsky's proposed minority report calling for illegal mass disruptions to block American entry into the First World War. Morris Hillquit, the moderate leader, defeated Trotsky in their showdown vote at the Lenox Casino that March, but the seventy-nine Socialists who supported Trotsky that day would come back two years later in bigger numbers, shatter the old establishment, and create a new American communism dedicated to nothing less than a full Russian-style, worker-led socialist uprising in the United States. This, in turn, would prompt a major, crippling government crackdown, remembered today as the 1919–20 Red Scare, or Palmer Raids, which would send many to prison, scare away others, and drive most of the rest underground.

Trotsky's closest New York protégés, Louis Fraina, Ludwig Lore, and Julius Hammer, would lead the new movement, at least initially. Many, including Fraina, Lore, and Hammer, would face jail terms as a result.

What remained after 1920 was a tiny, fragmented collection of feuding splinter groups: socialist, communist, Trotskyist, Stalinist, and shades in between. The Socialist Party's legislative agenda would be largely accomplished not by Morris Hillquit but by mainstream leaders like Franklin D. Roosevelt and the New Deal.

How could this happen? Hillquit himself had reached a personal high point in late 1917. He made good on his plan to run for mayor of New York City that year, making his candidacy a plebiscite on American entry into World War I. He drew twenty thousand backers to a kick-off rally at Madison Square Garden that September in an atmosphere he described later as "reminiscent of a powerful religious revival meeting."[530] "A Socialist victory," he told them, "would be a clear mandate to our government to open immediate negotiations for a general peace."[531] When election day came, Hillquit had won 145,332 votes, just short of the 155,497 for incumbent mayor John Purroy Mitchel and far more than the 56,000 for the Republican, a lawyer named William F. Bennett. But the Democrat, John F. Hylan, beat them all easily with 314,010.

"Personally, I am highly gratified," Hillquit announced. In fact, despite losing the race, he had made a remarkable showing, better by far than any prior Socialist candidate for mayor.[532] And with Hillquit's name topping the ticket, Socialists won outright victories up and down the ballot, including ten seats in the New York State Assembly, seven seats on the city Board of Aldermen, and a city judgeship—all records.[533] Even the conservative *New York Evening Post,* which backed Mayor Mitchel, complimented Hillquit for his "courage" and "good temper" in the heated contest.[534]

Said Hillquit himself: "The election has established the Socialist Party as an important and permanent factor in the politics of the city."[535] Most people agreed. But sadly for him, it was a last hurrah.

First came the wartime crackdowns. In late 1917, the *New York Call,* the *Volkzeitung, Novy Mir,* the *Forward,* the *Masses,* and even *Pearson's* magazine—virtually the entire socialist press and more—all faced charges from the United States Post Office for disloyalty or espionage, all upheld. As a result, each was either banned from the US mail entirely or lost its second-class postal status. Some, such as *Novy Mir,* found themselves subjected to repeated unannounced raids by federal agents, who ransacked their offices looking for "anarchistic literature" to use in prosecutions. In an era before TV, radio, or the Internet, barring these voices from the US mail effectively silenced them across the country outside a few large cities. It was a death knell.

Then came the arrests. Citing wartime statutes, prosecutors jailed hundreds for the sheer act of criticizing the government (construed as interfering with the war effort). Again, socialists found themselves targeted. Those put behind bars included former congressman Victor Berger, a Socialist from Wisconsin; party national secretary Adolph Germer; popular speakers Kate Richards O'Hare and Rose Pastor Stokes; famed anarchist Emma Goldman; four-time presidential candidate Eugene V. Debs; and almost two hundred members of the IWW. The IWW trials alone resulted in prison terms of twenty years apiece for fourteen top officers, including IWW president Bill Haywood. Emma Goldman got two years in a federal penitentiary, Kate Richards O'Hare got five years, and Debs got ten years, keeping him behind bars long after the war.[536]

Still, the Socialist Party survived. After peace returned with the November 1918 Armistice ending World War I, the party emerged stronger than before. Its dues-paying membership in 1919 shot up to more than 109,000, but its profile had changed. A full 53 percent of its members now belonged to separate foreign-language federations, mostly Russian and Eastern European, up from 30 percent just a year earlier. These new recruits consisted almost entirely of immigrant radicals inspired by Lenin and Trotsky and their success in Russia. They were "Bolshevik to the core," as Hillquit described them.[537]

Heading this new, radicalized mass was a younger, more aggressive set of leaders, and at its front tip was Louis Fraina, Trotsky's protégé from 1917.

Fraina, just twenty-seven years old in 1919, had spent the war years establishing himself as the premier voice in America for Russian-style

Bolshevism. After a brief jail term in late 1917 for giving an anti-conscription speech, Fraina kept personal contact with Lenin and Trotsky, published their essays in English translation, and edited the movement's two leading outlets, the *New International* and, with Ludwig Lore and Louis Boudin, *Class Struggle*. In 1918 he also published a theoretical tract called "Revolutionary Socialism" that urged American workers to launch "mass actions," meetings, demonstrations, and strikes aimed at toppling capitalism by capturing the streets.

As the go-to theoretician for the far left, Fraina in late 1918 joined other radicals to launch a new, tightly organized left-wing faction within the Socialist Party, along with a new weekly tabloid, the *Revolutionary Age,* which became its voice. Fraina took charge as editor, and his contributors included a half dozen of his old Trotsky crowd: *Novy Mir* editor Gregory Weinstein, plus Ludwig Lore, Louis Boudin, S. J. Rutgers, and Sen Katayama, all veterans of that original dinner with Trotsky at Lore's Brooklyn apartment on Trotsky's first day in America. Their goal was nothing less than an organized takeover of American socialism. "The center [Hillquit et al.] must be smashed," they declared, "as a necessary means of conquering the party for revolutionary Socialism."[538]

With the party now bulging with radicals, Fraina and the left wing soon decided to attack. After the Bolshevik victory in Russia, anything seemed possible.[539]

Morris Hillquit, after losing the New York mayor's race, had spent most of 1917 and 1918 in courtrooms defending targets of government crackdowns. He was preparing to join the defense team for Eugene V. Debs in mid-1918 when he started suffering bouts of fatigue. Doctors diagnosed him with pulmonary tuberculosis, then an often fatal disease that sent him to upstate New York for months of recuperation. But even from this distance, Hillquit watched with alarm the growing threat from Fraina and the left-wing faction, and he refused to let them damage the party he had spent a lifetime building.

Hillquit decided to strike first. From seclusion, he drafted a column for the *New York Call*, blasting the left wing for its "unrealistic" talk of revolution. "Better a hundred times to have two numerically small Socialist organizations, each homogenous and harmonious within itself," he concluded. "The time for action is near. Let us clear the decks."[540]

Within days, Hillquit pulled himself from his sickbed and traveled to Chicago for an emergency meeting of the Socialist Party's National Committee, where he still controlled a majority. Here he lowered the axe. Invoking party rules barring members who advocated crime, sabotage, or violence, Hillquit moved that the party immediately expel the seven largest foreign-language federations—Russian, Lithuanian, Polish, Latvian, Hungarian, Ukrainian, and Slavic—plus the entire Michigan state organization. Massachusetts, Ohio, Chicago, and other locals soon joined them on the chopping block. The total purge came to almost seventy thousand members, leaving Hillquit's own party left with fewer than forty thousand.[541]

The final break came in Chicago in late August 1919, when the party met to formalize the split. Two separate, simultaneous conventions convened in two separate ballrooms just a few blocks apart: Hillquit's Socialist Party at Machinists' Hall on Ashland Avenue and a new Communist Party down the street on Blue Island Avenue. In the chairman's seat for the Communists, making the keynote address, having already written the party's manifesto, sat Louis Fraina.

A third group, consisting of about eighty socialists led by journalist John Reed and a young Bronx assemblyman named Benjamin Gitlow, decided to fight. Refusing to accept their expulsions, they chose instead to storm the Socialist Party meeting, force their way inside, and demand reinstatement. When they entered the ballroom and ignored demands to leave, fights broke out and party leaders called in a squad of thirty club-swinging Chicago policemen to drag them out.

Afterward, bloodied and out on the sidewalk, the Reed/Gitlow group decided to return to the Ashland Avenue hall, take over a small billiards room downstairs, and there form their own new entity, the Communist Labor Party. Its leaders included Trotsky's other close friend in New York City, *New Yorker Volkzeitung* editor Ludwig Lore.

These two new parties, Communist and Communist Labor, both called themselves Bolshevik. Both demanded "mass action," "conquest of political power," and "overthrow of capitalist rule." Both sang "The Internationale," waved red flags, called their members comrades, and haggled over manifestoes. Within two years, on orders from Moscow, the two would merge into one.

All this infighting, however, had served to draw the attention of the United States government, which now planned its own final assault. The Justice Department in Washington, DC, had assigned agents to infiltrate all three of the conventions in Chicago: Socialist, Communist, and Communist Labor. That June, a wave of bombing attacks had panicked the country, capped on June 2 by an explosion at the Washington, DC, home of Alexander Mitchell Palmer, the United States attorney general, almost killing Palmer and his wife and teenage daughter. That fall, labor unrest reached a frightening crescendo: a Boston police strike, a strike by three hundred thousand steelworkers, and another strike threatened by half a million coal miners. With Lenin and Trotsky ruling Russia, bombs exploding in the streets, and mass strikes erupting almost daily, the public demanded tough action, and Washington obliged.

Starting in November, Palmer and his twenty-four-year-old assistant John E. Hoover (soon to change his name to J. Edgar and start a forty-eight-year reign atop the FBI) launched coast-to-coast raids aimed principally at members of the Communist and Communist Labor parties.[542] They cited the groups' violent rhetoric as legal basis to deport their entire memberships under federal immigration statutes. The Palmer Raids resulted in arrests of between five thousand and ten thousand people, most held for months in makeshift prisons at exorbitant bail, denied access to friends or lawyers. More than eight hundred of the prisoners were ultimately deported to Russia. Dozens were prosecuted on state sedition charges.

After the Palmer Raids, the movement had been effectively crushed. The old Socialist Party of Morris Hillquit and Eugene Debs lay broken, its 109,000 members down to fewer than 25,000. The Communist and Communist Labor parties, starting at about 75,000 between them in late 1919, saw their own memberships drop to fewer than 10,000.

THE SOCIALIST PARTY OF AMERICA would never regain the status it held before the First World War. Its law-abiding respectability failed to shield it from disloyalty charges during both the war and the postwar Red Scare. In January 1920, the New York State Legislature voted to expel all five of its legally elected Socialist members. The action drew protests from a parade of establishment figures, led by the New York Bar Association and Charles Evans Hughes, former New York governor, Republican presidential candidate, and future secretary of state and Supreme Court Chief Justice. Even A. Mitchell Palmer, the attorney general and author of the Palmer Raids, called the action excessive. But the state legislators refused to reconsider. They never allowed the Socialists to return.

For the 1920 presidential contest, the Socialist Party once more nominated Eugene V. Debs, still serving time in an Atlanta federal prison for his wartime conviction under the Conscription Act. Debs campaigned as Convict No. 9653 and won 913,000 popular votes. But after that, the party fell into decline. In the late 1920s, its membership dropped to eight thousand. It enjoyed a resurgence in the 1930s with its five-time presidential candidate Norman Thomas, a popular Presbyterian minister and editor of the Christian magazine the *World Tomorrow*. Thomas kept the party firmly anti-communist and lived long enough to oppose the Vietnam War and to support the Reverend Martin Luther King's civil rights crusade in the 1960s. In 1956 the Socialist Party ran its last presidential candidate, a man named Darlington Hoopes, one of the party's last elected officials, who had served in the 1930s in the Pennsylvania State Legislature. He received a total of 2,044 votes.

A successor, the Socialist Party USA, continues to field presidential candidates and remains active in politics.[543]

As for the COMMUNISTS, after the Palmer Raids, even this small remaining group faced new fractures, now driven by Moscow. As a satellite of the Soviet Third International, American communists had to follow each tortured twist and turn of Kremlin politics to see who was in or out on any given day. Their decisions on American affairs were second-guessed by apparatchiks on the opposite side of the globe.

After Lenin died in 1924, the power plays became increasingly byzantine as groups jockeyed for position in Moscow.

When Stalin finally ousted Trotsky in 1928, it caused an immediate schism in America. James P. Cannon, a dissident party leader who had shared auditorium stages with Trotsky in New York in 1917, led about two hundred members in bolting to form a new separate group following Trotsky's lead on ideology. Pro-Soviet but anti-Stalinist, they published a newsletter, the *Militant;* opposed European fascism; and briefly rejoined the Socialist Party before being expelled. They made personal contact with Trotsky in Turkey and then France. When Trotsky found refuge in Mexico in 1937, the American group supported him, providing him security guards, secretaries, and funding. Never more than a few hundred, a small minority within the small American communist world, they organized the American Committee for the Defense of Leon Trotsky during the Stalinist show trials of the 1930s and sent philosopher John Dewey to Mexico to take Trotsky's testimony on the charges. After Trotsky's assassination in 1940, American Trotskyists experienced more internal splits. "Many cadres remaining in the movement for twenty or more years sustained themselves through memories of the 'Old Man,'" historian Tim Wohlforth noted.[544]

American communism never disappeared. It waxed and waned over the decades, growing during the economic depression of the 1930s and the country's temporary alliance with Soviet Russia during World War II, then receding during a second postwar Red Scare in the 1940s and 1950s, led this time by Senator Joseph McCarthy, Republican of Wisconsin, and the House Un-American Activities Committee. The movement expanded during the antiwar protests of the 1960s, receded after the fall of the Berlin Wall in 1989, and bounced back with the global economic meltdowns of 2008 and 2009.

Today, after many schisms and reconfigurations, American Trotskyists remain active primarily as the Socialist Equality Party, still fighting his battles against capitalism, worker exploitation, imperialism, and historical revisionism. Its World Socialist Web Site (www.wsws.org) attracts some fifty thousand unique views per day.

LOUIS BOUDIN quit left-wing politics after 1919. Boudin had traveled to Chicago that August, participated in the brawl and walk-out at the Socialist convention, joined the original meeting of the Communist Labor Party, and then bolted that group in an argument over dogma, saying "I did not leave my party of crooks to join a party of lunatics!"[545] He continued to practice law and to write articles for left-leaning journals over the next three decades, but he renounced communism in the 1930s.

JULIUS HAMMER managed to avoid arrest during the First World War and the Palmer Raids. But in 1919, Bronx prosecutors charged Hammer with manslaughter for the death of a woman named Marie Oganesoff, wife of a Russian diplomat, who had died accidentally during an abortion procedure in Hammer's clinic. A judge sentenced him to three years at Sing Sing Prison. The family had little doubt that the prosecution was politically inspired. After his release, Julius Hammer returned to Russia to assist the Bolshevik regime.

His son Armand went on to a storied career in business, both as an American investor in Soviet Russia and later through his ownership of the Occidental Petroleum Company.

LUDWIG LORE, Trotsky's dinner host on his first day in America, continued to edit the *New Yorker Volkszeitung* until 1931. He then joined the *New York Post*, where he would write a popular world events column called "Between the Cables" until the late 1940s.

In communist circles, his early friendship with Trotsky gave him extraordinary standing, but Lore quickly ran afoul of Moscow. He particularly disliked Comintern chief Grigory Zinoviev and criticized him both in print and to his face. By 1924 Lore's friendship with Trotsky had become a liability, and Zinoviev decided to punish him. Acting on orders from Moscow, the American Communist Party that year adopted a resolution pledging the "liquidation" of "Loreism" as a "dangerous right wing tendency." They expelled him outright in 1925.

Lore kept contact with Trotsky through the 1920s and 1930s, though never joining the formal American Trotskyist group. Living in Brooklyn and tracked by Soviet secret police, he worried frequently about assassination plots. In the 1930s, he began working undercover for the American Justice Department.[546] Whittaker Chambers, the young communist recruit who later would make a splash by exposing State Department lawyer Alger Hiss as a Soviet agent, was sent to spy on Lore in the 1930s and remembered him fondly. Learning later that it was Lore who had denounced him to the FBI, Chambers wrote, "I respected Lore all the more for that act."[547]

LOUIS FRAINA quickly lost his leadership role in American communism. In late 1919, fellow communists accused him of being a spy for the Justice Department. An internal party tribunal in New York cleared Fraina, but the scandal followed him to Moscow, where a second tribunal heard the case and cleared him again. He was later accused of embezzling funds from the Comintern, a charge never substantiated, and he may have secretly aided the British as well.[548]

Disillusioned by these attacks and a futile assignment to Mexico, Fraina quit the party in 1922, returned to New York, changed his name to Lewis Corey, and started his life over from scratch. He and a new wife moved into a Lower East Side tenement. He did menial jobs at a dry goods store, worked as a proofreader at the *New York Times,* and then started submitting articles to the *New Republic.* His writing won him a fellowship at the Brookings Institution, a stint in the 1930s as an economist for the Works Projects Administration, and later a professorship at Antioch College.

Fraina/Corey reemerged as a leading economic theorist of the New Deal era, with his books including *The House of Morgan* (1930) and *The*

Decline of American Capitalism (1934). He attempted to reconcile with the Communist Party but broke with it in 1940 and became a founding member of the liberal Americans for Democratic Action. Though stridently anti-communist by the late 1940s, Fraina was served with deportation papers by the United States government in December 1950. In September 1953, while preparing his defense, he suffered a cerebral hemorrhage at his desk and died the next day.

"Neither I nor most of my comrades were enemies of democracy," Fraina wrote thirty-five years after first meeting Leon Trotsky. "The mistake we made was in taking democracy for granted, not realizing that the institutional proposals of Bolshevik Communism must necessarily end in the destruction of democracy."[549]

MORRIS HILLQUIT has been widely forgotten in America. But had his Socialist Party survived intact, it is easy to picture him becoming a leading figure of the era, perhaps a senator or governor. Trotsky grabbed the headlines in 1917, but Hillquit's side won a larger battle of ideas. His Americanized brand of socialism, based on legitimate electoral politics and "reforms" like our modern social safety net, financial and safety regulation, and strong civil liberties, would survive far longer than the Russian version.

Hillquit would best appreciate the fact that, in 2016, a socialist, Francois Holland, can serve as president of France and a self-described "democratic socialist," Bernie Sanders, can run a credible primary race for president of the United States.

Hillquit never made peace with the new leaders of Soviet Russia. "If Lenin had remained in Switzerland and Trotzky in the Bronx, New York," he wrote, "the Russian revolution would have gone on just as well."[550] After his defeat for mayor of New York in 1917, Hillquit endorsed President Woodrow Wilson's Fourteen Points as the best basis to end the First World War, noting how they embodied his own earlier demand of no annexations. He became a leading anti-communist voice in the socialist world, taking it as a compliment when, in the 1920s,

Moscow included him on a list of "notorious opportunists" banned from joining its Third International.

Even radical Emma Goldman came to appreciate Hillquit. She turned to him for help in 1917 when Alexander Berkman, her longtime lover/partner, faced deportation. Despite clashing politics, Hillquit agreed to suspend his mayoral campaign and lead a delegation to Albany to appeal to New York governor Charles Whitman on Berkman's behalf. "His hair was thickly streaked with grey, his face lined, and his eyes weary," she recalled of him at the time. The appeal failed, but, she wrote, "I felt closer to Hillquit than to many of my own comrades."[551]

Hillquit ran for mayor once more, in 1932, winning 250,000 votes, but he finally succumbed to tuberculosis the next year. The United States government honored him by naming a World War II Liberty Ship the SS *Hillquit*. In the next mayoral election after his death, most of Hillquit's support moved to another independent reformer denounced as being "too Red," the Republican–Fusion candidate Fiorello La Guardia.

CONSPIRACY THEORIES

Trotsky's visit to New York spawned a glut of myths and conspiracy theories. Writers and gossips have portrayed Trotsky in Manhattan as a tailor, a waiter, an electrician, a publicity hack, even a movie actor. A 1932 *Herald-Tribune* story identified Trotsky as a $5-a-day extra in a Brooklyn-filmed Vitaphone feature called *My Official Wife,* even though the grainy photo of the purported on-screen Trotsky looked little like the real-life Russian communist and the movie actually came out in 1914, three years before Trotsky's visit.[552] Another writer insisted Trotsky had composed Yiddish-language publicity copy for a New York stage producer named Morris Gest for his 1917 biblical production *The Wanderer,* despite Trotsky's poor Yiddish and his disdain for anything religious.[553]

But the conspiracy theories have been the most persistent, and Trotsky's time in New York City generated four major ones—German, Jewish, British, and American—all involving his return to Russia.

THE GERMAN PLOT: The one most widely believed, known as the German Libel, was the charge that Trotsky, Lenin, and the Bolsheviks in 1917 had acted as agents of Germany, making their 1917 revolution a mere creature of the German military effort to defeat Russia in the First World War.

For Lenin, the charge had considerable truth. Lenin had no interest in helping Germany per se, but his own wartime Zimmerwald platform urged military defeat of his own country, Russia, to set the stage for his real goal, socialism. Germany obliged with plenty of support when needed, from Lenin's "sealed train" to generous financial aid. As Lenin's German benefactor Parvus had persuaded Berlin as early as 1915: "The interests of the German government are identical with those of the Russian revolutionaries."[554]

Germany certainly saw it that way. General Erich von Ludendorff, its wartime military leader, even bragged about it in his memoirs. "In helping Lenin to travel to Russia, our government accepted a special responsibility," he wrote. "We had to bring Russia down," and Lenin's regime "exists thanks to us."[555] Lenin denied the charge in 1917—a necessity to avoid prison—but few of his followers cared. "Many would accept assistance from the devil himself and not question the source," the *New York World*'s Arno Dosch-Fleurot reported at the time from Petrograd.[556]

Parvus saw it that way too. After the revolution, he asked for an invitation to visit Moscow, apparently expecting Soviet Russia to reward him for his contributions, and he was sharply surprised by Lenin's response. "The cause of the revolution should not be touched by dirty hands," Lenin told him in a message relayed through intermediaries.[557] In response, Parvus publicly condemned the Bolshevik regime, calling it "an insult to the splendid history of European revolutions."[558]

For Trotsky, though, the issue carried more complexity. The charge against Trotsky—that he had received $10,000 from an unidentified German or Jewish source in New York City—invited speculation. Who gave him the money? The very question opened a door to link all the future sins of Bolshevism to a dizzying range of possible villains, not just Germans but Rockefellers, Rothschilds, "Jewish bankers," "global Zionism," Wall Street—take your pick.

New York State deputy attorney general Alfred H. Becker conducted a full investigation in early 1918, when the trail was still fresh, at the request of the federal Justice Department in Washington. Becker's investigators traced every dime Trotsky earned during his ten weeks in New York, including his $20-per-week salary from *Novy Mir,* the $10 to $15 he received for each article for the *New Yorker Volkszeitung,* the $280 to $300 he collected delivering between twenty-eight and thirty speeches, and the $226 collected at the Harlem River Casino at his going-away gala. The money added up to less than $1,000. Becker also confirmed that the $1,394.50 Trotsky had paid in cash for the sixteen steamship tickets he had purchased for the return trip to Russia came from the individual members of his traveling party, not Trotsky himself.[559]

"I have been unable to verify any indications of Trotsky's receiving money from any German sources," Becker concluded.[560] This, plus the failure of British and Canadian port inspectors in Halifax to report finding the money on Trotsky when they arrested and searched him there— including a full-body search at the Amherst detention camp—should have put the story to rest. But that's not how conspiracy theories work.

The issue came up at a 1919 public hearing of a United States Senate subcommittee in Washington, DC, investigating Bolshevik influence in the United States. A witness named Colonel V. S. Hurban, a Czech military official stationed in Russia during 1917, mentioned it while testifying about Bolshevik leaders. "Trotsky, perhaps, took money from Germany, but Trotsky will deny it," he told the senators. "Miliukov proved that he got $10,000 from some Germans while he was in America. Miliukov had the proof, but Trotsky denied it." The subcommittee chairman, Senator

Lee Overman, a Democrat of North Carolina, asked for details, but Colonel Hurban changed the subject and the subcommittee adjourned for the day. The Senators never returned to it.[561]

Trotsky's prewar friendship with Parvus, a fact known to British and American intelligence, also raised eyebrows. Parvus, after all, had helped channel German support to Lenin. Could he have helped Trotsky too? It's tempting to think so. After all, Parvus had contacts in New York both through his business dealings and his past ties to socialists such as Gregory Chudnovsky.[562] But here too, the practicalities speak otherwise. For Parvus, in Europe, to arrange to sneak a large sum of money into America, convince Trotsky to accept it, and figure out how Trotsky could slip it past British inspectors—all without alerting police or British agents or leaving documentary footprints—would have been daunting. Most likely, it simply never happened.

Did Trotsky raise money from German and socialist immigrants in New York to support revolution? Clearly yes. Was it a plot by the German government? Almost certainly not.

THE JEWISH PLOT: If not Germany, could the money have come from someone else? Say Jewish bankers in New York City?

On its face, the very idea—that bankers would finance a radical socialist bent on destroying their capitalist financial system—sounds ludicrous. Yes, many American companies hoped to do business in post-tsarist Russia, but Kerensky had already opened that door before Trotsky ever left Manhattan. They had no need to gamble on Bolsheviks—unless, of course, one saw more sinister forces at play.

Anti-Semitism existed well before 1917 and would have spread during the 1920s and 1930s without Trotsky or the $10,000 charge against him. Jewish people widely despised the Russian tsar, a not-surprising response to generations of persecution, and many Russians saw an element of Jewish revenge in the uprisings of 1917. Even a respected magazine like McClure's ran an article explaining the Russian Revolution as a "Jewish problem that paved the way for Jewish control of economic life."[563] With Trotsky's notoriety, talk of Jewish conspiracies could hardly be avoided.

But the Trotsky–Jewish conspiracy theory that emerged after 1917 took a very specific form, centered on Jacob Schiff, the seventy-year-old senior partner of Wall Street's Kuhn, Loeb, and Company.[564] Schiff made an inviting target. The most conspicuous Jewish financier in New York, Schiff had openly used his wealth to pressure Russia into changing its anti-Semitic policies. He had spent millions backing Japan in the 1904 Russo-Japanese War and, after that, on anti-tsarist agitation among Russian soldiers. In 1915 he refused to allow his bank to participate in American war loans to Britain or France so long as they allied themselves with Russia. All this made it easy to paint him as "pro-German," or worse.

The suggestion of a direct link between Schiff and Trotsky came from none less than the United States government and its Military Intelligence Division (MID). MID files from this period are rife with anti-Jewish slurs aimed at high-profile figures, from future Supreme Court justice Felix Frankfurter to *Forward* editor Abraham Cahan to sitting Supreme Court justice Louis Brandeis, and certainly bankers like Schiff.[565] But one particular 1918 report titled "BOLSHEVISM and JUDAISM" took it to the extreme. Written by an agent identified only as a "special confidential source," it detailed a vast conspiracy.[566] "[Jews] have already achieved formal recognition of a Jewish State in Palestine" it claimed, and they had designs on a "Jewish [that is, Bolshevik] republic in Russia" and a "Jewish republic in Germany and in Austria-Hungary."[567] The report provided long lists of Jewish conspirators, mostly Bolsheviks and bankers, wrapped around quotations from "Secret Zionist Protocols."

Then, citing no sources, it made this direct assertion:

In the Spring, 1917, Jacob Schiff, started to finance Trotzky, a Jew, for the purpose of accomplishing a social revolution in Russia. The New York 'Forward,' a Bolshevist Yiddish daily paper, also contributed certain funds for the same cause. At the same time, in Stockholm, Max Warburg, a Jew, financed Trotzky & Company, which is a Jewish firm.[568]

Then, to make matters worse, the document leaked. Though it was secret, US officials shared it with French and Allied militaries, and it seeped into the public domain. A version appeared in the *British Guardian* on February 13, 1925, and spurred copycat editions, all citing the American Secret Service as the authoritative source.[569]

But that wasn't the end of it. The Schiff–Trotsky–Jewish–Bolshevist conspiracy story spread through the 1920s and 1930s, repeated in outlets as diverse as the *London Times,* the *Brooklyn Anti-Bolshevist,* and Henry Ford's *Dearborn Independent*. It became a favorite trope of Nazi anti-Jewish propaganda. The $10,000 payment grew to $10 million, then $20 million or more.[570] In 1949 a gossip writer for the *New York Journal-American* named Cholly Knickerbocker poured fresh gasoline on the fire in a column chiding high-society "Parlor Pinks"—his term for wealthy leftists—in the emerging Cold War. "Old Man Jacob Schiff . . . boasted that his money had been one of the causes of the first Russian Revolution of 1905," he wrote. "Today it is estimated even by Jacob's grandson, John Schiff, a prominent member of New York society, that the old man sank about $20,000,000 into the final triumph of Bolshevism in Russia."[571]

The Schiff–Trotsky conspiracy theory survives even today. Just go into Google and search "Trotsky" and "$10,000" or "Schiff" to see a sampling.

But once again, even a cursory look at the facts undermines the whole idea. Jacob Schiff almost certainly never met Leon Trotsky in New York City in 1917 and almost certainly never paid him $10,000 to make revolutions or for anything else. In mid-March that year, the very time Trotsky was planning his return to Russia, Schiff was spotted hundreds of miles away, in White Sulphur Springs, West Virginia.[572]

What's more, Schiff's politics at that point directly opposed Trotsky's. Schiff's gripe against Russia had been its anti-Semitism.[573] At home Schiff had never shown any sympathy for socialism, not even the milder Morris Hillquit variety. Schiff had declared victory for his purposes in Russia after the tsar was toppled in March 1917 and Alexander Kerensky, representing the new provisional government, had declared Jews to be equal citizens. In addition to repeated public statements of support, he used both his personal wealth and the resources of Kuhn Loeb to float large loans to Kerensky's regime.

When Lenin and Trotsky seized power for themselves in November 1917, Schiff immediately rejected them, cut off further loans, started funding anti-Bolshevist groups, and even demanded that the Bolsheviks pay back some of the money he'd loaned Kerensky.[574] Schiff also joined a British-backed effort to appeal to fellow Jews in Russia to continue the fight against Germany.[575]

Finally, who was this "special confidential source," the author of "BOLSHEVISM and JUDAISM"? He has been identified as none other than Boris Brasol, the former Russian official who in Kiev had prosecuted the 1913 Mendel Beilis ritual murder case and in America had become chief promoter of the not-yet-discredited *Protocols of the Elders of Zion*, providing copies to American intelligence. Brasol had been hired by MID and authored many anti-Jewish reports.[576]

Yes, Schiff spent millions to topple the tsar, but not to insert Bolsheviks. Whatever his grandson might have said in 1949, the story dissolves in daylight.

THE BRITISH PLOT: Could Trotsky have been a pawn for somebody else? Say Britain? The strange behavior of William Wiseman, Britain's MI1c chief in New York City, inevitably raises this question. Wiseman, in March 1917, gave every appearance of having decided to let Trotsky return to Russia. He had allowed the British consulate in New York to approve Trotsky's visa and promise him safe passage through Halifax. Only the intervention of Wiseman's rival, naval attaché Guy Gaunt, probably acting behind Wiseman's back, resulted in Trotsky's arrest in Halifax.[577]

What was Wiseman really thinking? Had he intended to use Trotsky as a pawn for Britain, whether Trotsky knew it or not?

Around this time Wiseman had devised a larger strategy to slip his own spies into Russia. They included not only future British novelist W. Somerset Maugham but also friendly socialists who could speak out against German-backed propaganda.[578] "We should endeavor to do in Russia what we have done successfully elsewhere," he told his superiors in London, "namely to place Germans who are working for us among the real German agents."[579]

Trotsky, a credible leftist who publicly opposed separate peace with Germany, largely fit this profile. Wiseman seemed to suggest a connection. "One of our agents from America is a well-known international socialist," he wrote in one report. "He was at once accepted by the Bolshevics [sic] and admitted to their conferences. He challenged Trotzky to a public discussion" in Petrograd.[580] It's not impossible that Wiseman's agent was Trotsky himself, with Wiseman not wanting to state the fact directly, even in an internal memo.

Not impossible—but, alas again, not likely.

Whatever Wiseman's original plan, Trotsky's arrest in Halifax made any secret deal with him essentially impossible. After his treatment there and at the Amherst detention camp, Trotsky showed no sympathy for anything even remotely British. There is no record of Wiseman or any other British officer ever mentioning to Trotsky that he should help Britain in exchange for being allowed to reach Russia. Had they done so, it's easy to imagine Trotsky lacing his emphatic "no" with a chorus of choice Russian and German curses.

On the contrary, once in power, Trotsky went out of his way to even the score. As foreign affairs commissar, he ordered that no British subject be allowed to leave Russia until Britain had unconditionally released every Russian prisoner under its control and had recognized a new Bolshevik-appointed ambassador in London. He also ordered the arrest of Colonel Andrei Kalpaschnikoff, the Russian officer who had helped British officers interrogate Russian passengers aboard the *Kristiniafjord*.[581]

Also, once in power, Trotsky handled Russia's exit from the war in a manner that was strikingly evenhanded, neither pro-British nor pro-German. He insisted that Germany accept peace on Bolshevik terms, without annexations. As for the Allies, he publicly blasted them for refusing to negotiate peace at all, and he irritated them again by exposing embarrassing secret treaties signed by the Entente powers. In peace talks at Brest-Litovsk in early 1918, Trotsky took a hard line. When Germany demanded vast tracts of Russian territory in exchange for peace, Trotsky broke off negotiations, returned to Petrograd, and advocated instead a policy of "no peace, no war," all while calling on workers in Berlin to rise up against their own kaiser.

In the end, Germany resumed military attacks in response to Trotsky's walkout from Brest-Litovsk, making Lenin afraid they might capture Petrograd and topple his fragile government. It was Lenin who convinced the Bolsheviks' ruling committee to accept German terms harsher than the original. Trotsky abstained on the key vote.[582]

If Wiseman had hoped simply to let Trotsky return home to turn his obstinacy against Germany uncoached, the idea made sense. But if he had counted on anything more than that, on Trotsky being an actual ally, it was probably wishful thinking from the start, and certainly so after Halifax.

THE AMERICAN PLOT: Why then did the British release Trotsky from Nova Scotia? Had some deeper power forced London's hand? Even Trotsky wondered about it. "I must admit that even to-day the secret machinery of our arrest and our release [in Canada] is not clear to me," he wrote in his 1930 memoirs.[583]

Britain's decision to release Trotsky in 1917 took criticism from the start. "If the Dominion Government had held him for an indefinite period, the history of Russia might have been different," William

Shepherd, a United Press reporter in Petrograd during the Bolshevik takeover, reported days afterward.[584] Why did they let him go? When in doubt, blame the Americans. Enter the Woodrow Wilson conspiracy.

"Trotsky was released because of orders from Washington, instigated by Woodrow Wilson, who was President," *Saturday Evening Post* reporter Isaac Marcosson wrote in the 1930s, citing a British source. "Wilson had been the dupe of ultra liberals in the United States who looked upon Trotsky as the protagonist of Russian democracy."[585] Marcosson wasn't alone. Another senior journalist of the era, Arthur Willert of the *London Times*, in 1952 repeated this same story: that Kerensky had telegraphed President Wilson and that Wilson had contacted the British requesting Trotsky's freedom.[586] Another variation, from a military historian named Jennings C. Wise, writing in 1938, had Wilson personally intervening in 1917 to get Trotsky an American passport in New York City.[587]

Once again, these stories, though widely repeated, simply don't stand up. Not only do they all fail to cite documentation, but logic argues against them. Trotsky got his 1917 passport from the Russian government, not the Americans, and Britain at the time was not about to release a potential security threat like Trotsky unless its own intelligence and military brass gave the OK, regardless of any phone call or telegram from an American president.[588]

All these conspiracy theories suffer from one consistent flaw. Even his worst enemies understood it: Nobody controlled Trotsky—not British intelligence, not the German military, not international Jews, not Woodrow Wilson's White House. Call it integrity, stubbornness, or narcissism, call him a loose cannon, but Trotsky was an ideological purist. "He is absolutely unpurchaseable," insisted one of his self-described rivals in New York when asked about it. "Money would not tempt him to depart a hair's breadth from his simon-pure Marxism."[589]

LIFE IN NEW York City went on without Trotsky after he left in March 1917. Music continued to play—on Broadway, on the vaudeville stage, in the Yiddish theaters, in the Irish saloons, and in the German beer halls. The philharmonic and the opera delighted crowds at Carnegie Hall and the Metropolitan. The Yankees and Giants played baseball all that summer. The Giants even won the National League pennant, losing the World Series to the Chicago White Sox and their star outfield slugger Shoeless Joe Jackson (the same team that two years later would be accused of taking bribes to throw the World Series, the era's biggest sports scandal). By the next summer, 1918, the situation would change. Hundreds of baseball players would disappear for the European trenches, resulting in a shortened season.

America's entry into World War I changed more than just the baseball schedule. The unbridled freedom that had allowed socialism to flourish gave way to a more tempered variety. The wartime crackdowns and Palmer Raids came and went, but they produced what today we call a "new normal." New York installed its first traffic light in 1919, at Fifth Avenue and Forty-Second Street, then the busiest intersection in the country. Cars now outnumbered horses in New York. The Roaring Twenties saw flappers and jazz and sexual liberation, but Prohibition made it illegal to buy a drink, the New York Police Department kept a permanent bomb squad dedicated to fighting radicals; and Washington's new secret police forces, the FBI under its young new director J. Edgar Hoover and the War Department's MID (still authorized to act on American soil), kept an eye on subversives.

New York's flavor as a global city changed as well. The United States Congress in 1921 and 1924 passed new immigration statutes that largely cut off the flow of newcomers from Eastern and Southern Europe. The Jewish Lower East Side, the city's largest ethnic enclave, largely disappeared in three short generations as its children and grandchildren learned English and scattered across the country. Other such neighborhoods followed—German, Italian, Irish, and the rest. Of the six major Yiddish newspapers in New York, selling half a million daily copies in 1917, only the *Forward* remains, published today in English as well as Yiddish. Yiddish theater survives only as a memory.

Over time, the young radicals of 1917 grew into nostalgic old men. Radicals aged into liberals and moderates; socialists aged into Democrats, some even Republicans. But their adventures in the early socialist movement trained many for lifetime careers as lawyers, teachers, speakers, writers, community leaders, and mainstream politicians.

Trotsky's footsteps too disappeared from the city. Elevated subways tracks were torn down in Manhattan to make room for traffic and sunlight. Pier 8 on the East River, where Trotsky's ship from Spain, the *Montserrat,* landed in 1917, disappeared long ago. His apartment house in the Bronx likewise was replaced. The skyscraper buildings that Trotsky found so impressive back then today appear puny next to the newer, taller, sleeker towers that dominate the city's skyline. The transatlantic steamships he rode have been replaced by jumbo jets that make the crossing in six or seven hours instead of a dozen days.

One building that remains is 77 Saint Marks Place, home to *Novy Mir* during Trotsky's era. Today it features a Mexican restaurant on the street level. Another is the Lenox Casino in Harlem, scene of Trotsky's great confrontation with Morris Hillquit in March 1917, today housing the Shabazz Mosque. What hasn't changed at all about New York are the noise and the traffic, the busy energy, the brashness of a city in constant change.

For three months in 1917, New York offered Leon Trotsky and his family freedom, comfort, security, friends, and celebrity—a rare package in his turbulent life. He would carry back to Russia American ideas for his new Soviet state: the movies, culture, civility, and science. "We lack the technique of the Americans and their labor proficiency," he wrote in the 1920s. "To have Bolshevism shod in the American way," with technology, math, and efficient factories, "there is our task!" "Americanized Bolshevism will crush and conquer imperialist Americanism."[590] In the future, he predicted, "all the problems of our planet will be decided upon American soil."[591] Years later, Trotsky would still describe New York as a place of wonders, "of prose and fantasy, of capitalistic automation, its streets a triumph of cubism, its moral philosophy that of the dollar."[592]

Seeing Trotsky during those weeks in New York in 1917, still young and idealistic, his integrity still intact, no blood yet on his hands, one can't help but suggest what might have been. The future tragedies hardly seemed inevitable. Had Trotsky stayed in New York City, it is easy to picture him mellowing with age, perhaps teaching history at Columbia or City College, writing a best-selling book or two, or venturing out to California to try his hand at Hollywood movie scripts, or perhaps to Washington, DC, to become a minor functionary in the New Deal.

Had Trotsky won the power struggle in Moscow in the 1920s to become Lenin's successor (or perhaps placed a loyal friend atop the party leadership) instead of Joseph Stalin, might communist Russia have turned out a different, better place? This innocent-sounding hypothetical has sparked fierce debate, engaging generations of scholars and partisans. At stake is history's judgment not just of a single human being but of an entire movement. Could communism itself have worked as a fair and humane system had it been placed in better hands? Or was its descent into brutal totalitarianism inevitable, inherent in its genetic makeup, regardless of whether led by a Stalin, a Trotsky, or anyone else?

Trotsky's early zeal for repression after 1917; his easy defense of war communism, the Red Terror, and "militarization of labor"; all the mass killings and jailings have allowed critics to argue that Trotsky, had he prevailed, at best would have been a "Stalin lite" and produced his own brutal excesses. How else could he have industrialized the country and imposed socialist purity on a rural-based peasant economy? There is no denying that Trotsky helped create and nurture the very system of violent dictatorship that Stalin later pushed to extremes and used to kill Trotsky himself.

But just as undeniably, it was Trotsky who led the opposition to that system, who spoke out consistently against Stalin and Stalinism—at risk to his own life and those of his family and friends—from the early 1920s until his death. His "left opposition" inside Russia early on challenged the danger of concentrated party bureaucracy. In exile, he continued to criticize the regime, and he organized followers worldwide to create a political counterweight. In the 1930s, he spoke out against Nazi fascism as well.

Was this self-serving? Perhaps. But the question lingers. Trotsky had a worldliness and eloquence that remain central to his appeal. A person who could so clearly express the rights of the oppressed and speak truth to power, be it Stalin or the tsar, and at the same time appreciate culture and ideas, French novels, lively debates at the Monopole Café or Vienna's Café Central, a Charlie Chaplin film or an Isadora Duncan dance—could such a person commit the atrocities of a Stalin? It hardly seems likely.

The Russian biographer Dmitri Volkogonov, one of the first to publicly reassess Bolshevism's founders in the post-glasnost era, perhaps best captured the contradiction. "Trotskyism expressed the Marxist postulates in their most refined form," he wrote in 1996. "As a counterweight to Stalin it formally rejected totalitarianism, though it is not clear how the dictatorship of the proletariat could be applied to such circumstances. Thus, Trotskyism was a Utopian attempt to combine dictatorship with democracy, the monopoly of one party with political pluralism."[593]

Trotsky's status as global cultural icon has grown steadily since 1917. His assassination and brief love affair with artist Frida Kahlo in Mexico alone have generated dozens of books and two Hollywood movies, with Trotsky played by none less than Richard Burton (*The Assassination of Trotsky,* 1972) and Geoffrey Rush (*Frida,* 2002). Only Russia seems to have forgotten him. There, thirty years of Stalinist propaganda have turned Trotsky into a vague blur for young people.

Today, more than seventy-five years after his death, Trotskyist candidates and parties still compete in France, Britain, Portugal, Brazil, Argentina, and other countries. In America, his influence can be traced to political groups as diverse as neoconservatives on the right and socialists on the left, to writers as varied as Saul Bellow, Irving Kristol, and Carl Sagan.

In the 1980s, under Mikhail Gorbachev, the Soviet Supreme Court reexamined the cases of thousands of victims from the Stalinist show trials of the 1930s. The court decided to "rehabilitate" hundreds, clear them of old charges, restore their names and reputations. They included Bukharin, Zinoviev, Kamenev, and even Trotsky's son Sergei. But not Trotsky himself. Gorbachev permitted Trotsky's name to be discussed in public, a few scholarly papers were written, but no clean bill for him ever appeared. Gorbachev himself continued to repeat the old Stalinist line, calling Trotsky an "excessively self-assured politician who always vacillated and cheated."[504]

Even then, Trotsky still appeared too dangerous. He still represented the historical alternative, the possibility that things can always be different, that socialism could have worked, that ruling powers any place and any time can be overthrown by the conscious, organized will of the people. All this made Leon Trotsky dangerous to the Russian tsar in 1905, to Kerensky in 1917, to Hillquit in New York, to Stalin in the 1920s, even to Gorbachev in the 1980s. For all his faults, he remains the eternal agent of change in a world that craves stability.

ACKNOWLEDGMENTS

NO BOOK IS the product of any single person, least of all any book of mine. With *Trotsky in New York, 1917*, I am grateful to acknowledge the help of many, whom I take this opportunity to thank.

Once I began writing, I benefited from the sharp eyes of friends and colleagues who gave me feedback on the manuscript. These included my OFW Law colleagues David Durkin, Bob Hahn, and Steve Terman; historian Will O'Neal, Bronx native Al Sorkowitz; Rabbi Lia Bass; and the accomplished members of my writing critique group: Nancy Derr, Michael Kirkland, Cheryl LaRoche, Bonny Miller, Diana Parsell, Michael Scadron, Judi Latta, and Sonja Williams.

A critical element of this project involved translation of source material from Russian, German, and Yiddish, and here too I benefited from the help of many, including, with Yiddish, Alexander Lieberman; with Russian, Straker Translations and Irina Kolb, a native of Kaliningrad; and, with German, Nicola Hofstetter, a native of Munich.

I also thank David North, chairman of the Socialist Equity Party and one of the leading modern Trotskyists in America; Professor Richard Spence of the University of Idaho; and Professor James G. Hershberg of George Washington University for sharing their expertise and insights.

Researching Trotsky's New York story brought me to many of the great research centers of the country. Here, among others, I thank Gunnar Burg of the YIVO Institute for Jewish Research, Chana Pollack of the *Jewish Daily Forward*, Carol Leadenham at the Hoover Institute Archives at Stanford University, and Laura Peimer of the Schlesinger

Library at Harvard University. A particular thanks goes to Andrina Tran for her help at the Sterling Memorial Library at Yale University.

Living in the Washington, DC, area, I also benefit from being surrounded by a community of writers who are always generous in sharing knowledge and support. The Writers Center in nearby Bethesda, the Washington Biography Group, and the Washington Independent Review of Books all have been part of my life here for many years and have enriched me continually with their friendship. Part of this community includes my main research homes for this project, the Library of Congress on Capitol Hill and the National Archives research center at College Park, Maryland, two national treasures deserving all our support. Their staffs are the best in their fields, and they certainly helped me during many long hours and days rummaging through materials. I make special mention of the teams at the Library of Congress manuscript, periodical, Hebraic, prints and photographs, and rare book rooms, who humored me on countless requests over many months.

I also thank the team at Counterpoint Press, who applied their considerable skill and expertise to all phases of bringing this manuscript to market, including editor Rolph Blythe, Bethany Onsgard, Kelly Winton, Sharon Wu, Meagan Fishmann, Peg Goldstein, and many others. My publicist, Jane Wesman at Jane Wesman PR, who teamed up with me a decade ago on my book *Boss Tweed,* led me once again through the maze of the New York media market. I also thank Karin Bilich and her group at Smart Author Sites for making my website presentable for the new book.

A special thanks goes to Ron Goldfarb, my agent, who heard me explain my slightly off-the-wall idea for a book about Trotsky and his barely ten weeks in Greenwich Village while watching a baseball game one summer night at Nationals Park and saw the promise in the concept. Another special thanks goes to Jack Shoemaker at Counterpoint Press, who also saw the potential when others did not. They took the risk and made this book a reality in a tight business climate. Their support made all the difference, and I appreciate it.

I thank my colleagues at OFW Law, my law firm home for the past fifteen years, for once again giving me the freedom and support to pursue this writing adventure. Thanks too to my big sister, Arline Hershberg, for key advice on items ranging from the book cover to the dedication to navigating the Bronx. Finally, to Karen, my wife: Thanks once again for being a good sport. For the next adventure, it's your turn.

SELECTED SOURCES

MANUSCRIPTS

British National Archives: "Lev Davidovich Bronstein, alias Leon Trotsky: Russian." (KV2/502 et seq.)

Canadian National Archives: "Arrests of Certain Russians on S.S. Kristiania, 1917." (RG25-A-3-a)

Hoover Institution Archives: Albert Glotzer Collection

Library of Congress:

Communist Party papers

Morris Hillquit papers

Socialist Party of America papers

Woodrow Wilson papers

National Archives:

Bureau of Investigations, 1918–1922 (RG65 and M1085)

Military Intelligence Division (MID) (Record Group 165)

Department of State, consular files (Record Group 59)

Schlesinger Library, Harvard University: Freda Kirchwey papers

Sterling Memorial Library, Yale University: William Wiseman papers

Tamiment Library, New York University:

Morris Hillquit papers

Meyer London papers

Charles Recht papers

Algernon Lee papers

Socialist Party papers

B. Vladeck papers

YIVO Institute for Jewish Research:

Abraham Cahan papers

HIAS papers

NEWSPAPERS

Guardian

Globe and Commercial Advertiser

Jewish Daily Forward

Jewish Morning Journal

New York American

New York Call

New York Commercial Advertiser

New York Communist

New York Evening Post

New York Herald

New York Herald Tribune

New York Times

New York Tribune

New York World

New York World-Telegram & Sun

New Yorker Volkszeitung

Novy Mir

Outlook

Revolutionary Age

BOOKS

Ackerman, Kenneth D. *Young J. Edgar: Hoover and the Red Scare, 1919–1920.* Falls Church, VA: Viral History Press, 2007, 2011.

Ali, Tariq, and Phil Evans. *Leon Trotsky: An Illustrated Introduction.* Chicago: Haymarket Books, 1980.

Alpera, Sara. *Freda Kirchwey: A Woman of the Nation.* Cambridge, MA: Harvard University Press, 1987.

Barrett, James R. *William Z. Foster and the Tragedy of American Radicalism.* Urbana: University of Illinois Press, 1999.

Braudy, Susan. *Family Circle: The Boudins and the Aristocracy of the Left.* New York: Alfred A. Knopf, 2003.

Bell, Daniel. *Marxian Socialism in the United States.* Ithaca: Cornell University Press, 1952, 1967.

Bendersky, Joseph W. *The Jewish Threat: Anti-Semitic Politics of the U.S. Army.* New York: Basic Books, 2000.

Birmingham, Stephen. *Our Crowd: The Great Jewish Families of New York.* New York: Harper & Row, 1967.

Boyer, Richard O., and Herbert M. Morais. *Labor's Untold Story.* New York: United Electrical, Radio & Machine Workers of America, 1955, 1984.

Brzezinski, Zbigniew. *The Grand Failure: The Birth and Death of Communism in the Twentieth Century.* New York: Charles Scribner's Sons, 1989.

Buchanan, George. *My Mission to Moscow,* vol. 2. London: Cassell and Company, 1923.

Buhle, Mari Jo, Paul Buhle, and Dan Georgakas. *Encyclopedia of the American Left*. New York: Oxford University Press, 1998.

Buhle, Paul M. *A Dreamer's Paradise Lost: Louis C. Fraina/Lewis Corey (1892–1953)*. Atlantic Highlands, NJ: Humanities Press, 1995.

Cahan, Abraham. *The Education of Abraham Cahan*. Philadelphia: Jewish Publication Society of America, 1969.

Chambers, Whittaker. *Witness*. Washington, DC: Regnery Publishing, 1952, 1980.

Chalin, Anna Alice. *Greenwich Village*. New York: Dodd, Mead and Company, 1925.

Clements, Barbara Evans. *Bolshevik Feminist: The Life of Alexandra Kollontai*. Bloomington: Indiana University Press, 1917.

Cohen, Stephen F. *Bukharin and the Bolshevik Revolution: A Political Biography, 1888–1938*. Oxford: Oxford University Press, 1971, 1973, 1980.

Cohen, Naomi W. *Jacob H. Schiff: A Study in American Jewish Leadership*. Hanover, NH: University Press of New England, Brandeis University Press, 1999.

Deutscher, Isaac. *The Prophet Armed: Trotsky, 1879–1921*. New York: Oxford University Press, 1954.

Draper, Theodore. *The Roots of American Communism*. New York: Viking Press, 1957.

Drehle, David Von. *Triangle: The Fire That Changed America*. New York: Grove Press, 2003.

Eastman, Max. *The Young Trotsky*. London: New Park Publications, 1926, 1980.

Epstein, Edward Jay. *Dossier: The Secret History of Armand Hammer*. New York: Carroll and Graf, 1996.

Epstein, Melech. *Profiles of Eleven*. Detroit: Wayne State University Press, 1965.

Former Russian commissar. *Trotsky*. Wichita, KS: Defender Publishers, 1937.

Fowler, W. B. *British-American Relations, 1917–1918: The Role of Sir William Wiseman*. Princeton, NJ: Princeton University Press, 1969.

Freeberg, Ernest. *Democracy's Prisoner: Eugene V. Debs, the Great War, and the Right to Dissent*. Cambridge, MA: Harvard University Press, 2008.

Friedman, Saul S. *Pogromchik: The Assassination of Simon Petlura*. New York: Hart Publishing Company, 1976.

Gankin, Olga Hess, and H. H. Fisher. *The Bolsheviks and the World War: The Origins of the Third International*. Stanford, CA: Stanford University Press, 1940, 1960.

Gaunt, Guy. *The Yield of the Years: A Story of Adventure Afloat and Ashore*. London: Hutchinson & Company, 1940.

Ginger, Ray. *Eugene V. Debs: The Making of an American Radical*. New York: Collier Books, 1947, 1962.

Gitlow, Benjamin. *I Confess: The Truth about American Communism*. New York: E. P. Dutton, 1939, 1940.

Goldman, Emma. *Living My Life*. New York: Da Capo Press, 1931, 1970.

Goldstein, Margaret J. *V. I. Lenin*. Minneapolis: Twenty-First Century Books. 2007.

Gornick, Vivian. *Emma Goldman: Revolution as a Way of Life*. New Haven, CT: Yale University Press, 2011.

Hammer, Armand. *Hammer*. With Neil Lyndon. New York: Perigee Books, 1987.

Harris, Frank. *Contemporary Portraits,* fourth series. New York: Brentano's Publishers, 1923.

Hillquit, Morris. *Loose Leaves from a Busy Life*. New York: MacMillan Company, 1934.

Hood, Clifton. *722 Miles: The Building of the Subways and How They Transformed New York*. Baltimore: John Hopkins University Press, 1963.

Howe, Irving. *Leon Trotsky.* New York: Viking Press, 1978.

———. *World of Our Fathers: The Journey of the East European Jews to America and the Life They Found and Made.* New York: Schocken Books, 1976, 1989.

Jeffreys-Jones, Rhidri. *In Spies We Trust: The Story of Western Intelligence.* Oxford: Oxford University Press, 2013.

Kalpaschnikoff, Andrew. *A Prisoner of Trotsky.* Garden City, NY: Doubleday, Page & Company, 1920.

Kennan, George F. *Soviet-American Relations, 1917–1920: The Decision to Intervene.* Princeton, NJ: Princeton University Press, 1958.

King, Charles. *Odessa: Genius and Death in a City of Dreams.* New York: W. W. Norton, 2011.

Kotkin, Stephen. *Stalin.* vol. 1, *Paradoxes of Power, 1878–1928.* New York: Penguin, 2014.

Kublin, Hyman. *Asian Revolutionary: The Life of Sen Katayama.* Princeton, NJ: Princeton University Press, 1964.

LeBlanc, Paul. *Trotsky.* London: Reaktion Books, 2015.

Lenin, Vladimir Ilyich. *Lenin's Collected Works.* Moscow: Progress Publishers, 1974.

Lipsky, Seth. *The Rise of Abraham Cahan.* New York: Schocken Books, 2013.

Marcosson, Isaac Frederick. *Turbulent Years.* Freeport, NY: Books for Libraries Press, 1938, 1969.

Michels, Tony. *A Fire in Their Hearts: Yiddish Socialists in New York.* Cambridge, MA: Harvard University Press, 2005.

Miliukov, Paul. *Political Memoirs 1905–1917.* Ann Arbor: University of Michigan Press, 1967.

Morris, James McGrath, and Kevin Stillwell. *Revolution by Murder: Emma Goldman, Alexander Berkman, and the Plot to Kill Henry Clay Frick.* Amazon Digital Services, 2014.

Morton, Frederic. *Thunder at Twilight: Vienna, 1913–1914.* Philadelphia: Da Capo Press, 1989.

Nedava, Joseph. *Trotsky and the Jews.* Philadelphia: Jewish Publication Society of America, 1972.

North, David. *In Defense of Leon Trotsky.* Oak Park, MI: Mehring Books, 2010, 2013.

Porter, Cathy. *Alexandra Kollontai: A Biography.* Chicago: Haymarket Books, 1980, 2014.

Pratt, Norma Fain. *Morris Hillquit: A Political History of an American Jewish Socialist.* Westport, CT: Greenwood Press, 1979.

Radzinsky, Edvard. *Stalin: His Life, His Death.* New York: Doubleday, 1996.

Read, Anthony, and David Fisher. *Colonel Z: The Secret Life of a Master of Spies.* London: Hodder and Stoughton, 1984.

Reed, John. *Ten Days That Shook the World.* New York: Modern Library, 1919, 1935.

Reinhardt, Guenther. *Crime without Punishment: The Secret Soviet Terror against America.* New York: Signet Books, 1953.

Rosenstone, Robert A. *Romantic Revolutionary: A Biography of John Reed.* Cambridge, MA: Harvard University Press, 1990.

Rubinstein, Joshua. *Leon Trotsky: A Revolutionary's Life.* New Haven, CT: Yale University Press, 2011.

Sanders, Ronald, and Edmund V. Gillon Jr. *The Lower East Side: A Guide to Its Jewish Past in Ninety-Nine New Photographs.* New York: Dover Publications, 1979, 1994.

Schlesinger, Arthur M., Jr. *The Almanac of American History.* New York: Perigee Books, 1983.

Serge, Victor, and Natalya Sedova Trotsky. *The Life and Death of Leon Trotsky*. New York: Basic Books, 1951, 1975,

Service, Robert. *Lenin: A Biography*. Cambridge, MA: Belknap Press of Harvard University Press, 2000.

——. *Trotsky: A Biography*. Cambridge, MA: Belknap Press of Harvard University Press, 2009.

Spence, Richard. *Trust No One: The Secret World of Sidney Reilly*. Los Angeles: Feral House, 2002.

Steffens, Lincoln. *The Autobiography of Lincoln Stephens*. New York: Harcourt, Brace, 1931.

Sutton, Anthony C. *Wall Street and the Bolshevik Revolution*. West Hoathly, UK: Clairview Books, 1974, 2011.

Swanberg, W. A. *Citizen Hearst*. New York: Galahad Books, 1961.

Thatcher, Ian D. *Leon Trotsky and World War One: August 1914–February 1917*. New York: St. Martin's Press, 2000.

——. *Trotsky*. London: Routledge, Taylor & Francis Group, 2003.

Thwaites, Norman G. *Velvet and Vinegar*. London: Grayson & Grayson, 1932.

Trotsky, Leon. *The Balkan Wars, 1912–13*. New York: Pathfinder Press, 1980, 1991.

——. *In Defense of Marxism: The Social and Political Contradiction of the Soviet Union*. New York: Pathfinder Press, 1942, 1973.

——. *Leon Trotsky on Black Nationalism*. New York: Pathfinder Press, 1994.

——. *My Life: An Attempt at an Autobiography*. Mineola, NY: Dover Publications, 1930, 1960, 2007.

——. *Our Revolution: Essays on Working-Class and International Revolution, 1904–1917*. Edited by M. J. Olgin. New York: Henry Holt and Company, 1918.

——. *Problems of Everyday Life*. New York: Pathfinder Press, 1973.

——. *The Revolution Betrayed*. Mineola, NY: Dover Publications, 1937, 2004.

——. *The Russian Revolution: The Overthrow of Tzarism and the Triumph of the Soviets*. New York: Doubleday Anchor Books 1932, 1959.

——. *Terrorism and Communism: A Reply to Karl Kautsky*. Lansing: University of Michigan Press. 1920, 1961.

——. *Vingt Lettres de Leon Trotsky*. Paris: La Vie Ouvriere. 1919.

Ulam, Adam B. *The Bolsheviks: The Intellectual and Political History of the Triumph of Communism in Russia*. New York: Collier Books, 1965.

Ultan, Lloyd. *The Beautiful Bronx, 1920–1950*. New York: Bronx County Historical Society, 1979.

Ultan, Lloyd, and Gary Hermalyn. *The Bronx in the Innocent Years, 1890–1925*. New York: Harper & Row, 1964, 1985.

Vaksberg, Arkady. *Stalin against the Jews*. New York: Alfred A. Knopf, 1994.

Volkogonov, Dmitri. *Lenin: A New Biography*. New York: Free Press, 1994.

——. *Trotsky: The Eternal Revolutionary*. New York: Free Press, 1996.

Von Drehle, David. *Triangle: The Fire that Changed America*. New York: Grove Press, 1969

Waldman, Louis. *Labor Lawyer*. New York: E. P. Dutton and Company, 1944.

Willert, Arthur. *The Road to Safety: A Study in Anglo-America Relations*. London: Derek Verschoyle, 1952.

Wise, Jennings C. *Woodrow Wilson: Disciple of Revolution*. New York: Paisley Press, 1938.

Wittlin, Thaddeus. *Commissar: The Life and Death of Lavrenty Pavlovich Beria.* New York: MacMillan, 1972.

Wolfe, Bertram D. *A Life in Two Centuries.* New York: Stein and Day, 1981.

———. *Three Who Made a Revolution: A Biographical History.* New York: Cooper Square Press, 1948, 2001.

Zeman, Z. A. B., and W. B. Scharlau. *The Merchant of Revolution: The Life of Alexander Israel Helphand (Parvus), 1867–1924.* London: Oxford University Press, 1965.

Ziv, G. A. *Trotskii: Testimony as to Character.* New York: Narodoprevstvo Publishing House, 1920.

ARTICLES, PAMPHLETS, AND PAPERS

Becker, Alfred. "In Re Leon Bronstein Trotzky (or Trotsky)." NARA, RG65, M1085, File OG1980592 ("Becker Report"), Bureau of Investigations, January 1918.

Cameron, Silver Donald. "Trotsky in Amherst." *Canadian Geographic,* 1988.

Cannon, James P. "Trotsky on America," *International Socialist Review* 21, no. 4 (Fall 1960):99–105.

Churchill, Winston S. "Zionism versus Bolshevism: A Struggle for the Soul of the Jewish People." *Illustrated Sunday Herald,* February 8, 1920.

Corey, Esther. "Lewis Corey (Louis C. Fraina), 1892–1953: A Bibliography with Autobiographical Notes." *Labor History* 4, no. 2 (1963).

Feigenbaum, William M., editor. "Should Socialism Prevail: A Debate Held October 21, 1915." Rand School of Social Sciences, 1916.

Fraina, Louis. "Mass Action and Industrial Unionism." *International Socialist Review* 17, no. 9 (March 1917):556–557.

Gorenstein, Arthur. "A Portrait of Ethnic Politics: The Socialists and the 1908 and 1910 Congressional Elections on the East Side." *Publications of the American Jewish Historical Society* 50, no. 3 (March 1961):202–238.

Greene, Doug Enaa. "Nikolai Bukharin: Favorite of the Whole Party." *International Journal of Socialist Renewal,* February 13, 2015.

Griffin, Frederick C. "Leon Trotsky in New York City." *New York History* 49, no. 4 (October 1968):391–403.

Halpern, Michael D. "Trotsky Eats and Runs," *Jewish Ideas Daily,* January 25, 2012.

Hogsbjerg, Christian. "The Prophet and Black Power: Trotsky on Race in the US." *International Socialism* 121 (January 2, 2009).

James, Clive. "Leon Trotsky." Slate.com, April 2, 2007, http://www.slate.com/articles/news_ and_politics/clives_lives/2007/04/leon_trotsky.html.

Jonas, Franklin. "The Early Life and Career of B. Charney Vladeck, 1886–1921: The Emergence of an Immigrant Spokesman." Unpublished Ph.D. thesis, New York University, February 1972.

Kirchwey, Freda. "When Trotsky Lived in New York," Freda Kirchwey papers (MC280, Folder 427), Schlesinger Library, Harvard University.

Kopp, Harry W. "Trotsky in the Bronx." *Bellevue Literary Review,* Spring 2012.

Lenin, Vladimir. "What Is to Be Done?" Marxist Internet Archive, https://www.marxists.org/ archive/lenin/works/1901/witbd/, accessed May 3, 2016.

Literary Digest. "On The Trail of the Truth about Trotzky." *Literary Digest,* February 9, 1918.

Lloyd, William Bross. "Convention Impressions." *Class Struggle* 3, no. 4 (November 1919):389–394.

Lore, Ludwig. "Leon Trotsky." *Class Struggle,* November 7, 1918.

———. "When Trotsky Lived in New York," Special Collections, Browne Manuscripts, Lilly Library, Indiana University.

MacLean, J. B. "Why Did We Let Trotsky Go? Canada Lost an Opportunity to Shorten the War." *MacLean's,* July 1919.

Moskowitz, Henry. "Trotsky on the East Side." *Outlook,* January 30, 1918.

Pitzer, Andrea. "Trotsky's Canadian Holiday." *Lapham's Quarterly,* April 28, 2014.

Recht, Charles. "A World to Win." Recht papers, Tamiment Library, New York University.

Roberts, Priscilla. "Jewish Bankers, Russia, and the Soviet Union, 1900–1940: The Case of Kuhn, Loeb and Company," *American Jewish Archives Journal* 49, no. 1–2 (1997):9–37.

Routsky, Pierre. "A Page from the Past," *Russian Review,* 7, no. 2 (Spring 1948):69–75.

Schurer, Heinz. "Alexander Helphand-Parvus: Russian Revolutionary and German Patriot." *Russian Review* 18, no. 4 (October 1959).

Shachtman, Max. "Natalya Ivanovna Sedoff (Sedova)." Box 18, Folder 18, Hoover Institution Archives, Albert Glotzer Collection.

Shub, David. "Bibliography: The Russian Press in the United States," *Russian Review* 3, no. 1 (1943):120–128.

Spence, Richard. "Catching Louis Fraina: Loyal Communist, US Government Informant, or British Agent?" *American Communist History* 11, no. 1 (2012).

———. "Hidden Agendas: Spies, Lies, and Intrigue Surrounding Trotsky's American Visit of January–April 1917." *Revolutionary Russia* 21, no. 1 (June 2008):33–55.

———. "Interrupted Journey: British Intelligence and the Arrest of Leon Trotskii, April 1917," *Revolutionary Russia* 13, no. 1(June 2000):1–28.

———. "The Tsar's Other Lieutenant: The Antisemitic Activities of Boris L'vovich Brazol, 1919–1960." Part 1, "Beilis, the Protocols, and Henry Ford," *Journal for the Study of Antisemitism* 4, no. 1 (2012):199–220.

Thatcher, I. A. "Leon Trotsky in New York City." *Historical Research* 69, no. 169 (June 1966):166.

Trotsky, Leon. "Europe and America." Marxist Internet Archive, February 1924, https://www.marxists.org/archive/trotsky/1926/02/europe.htm, accessed May 20, 2016.

———. "In British Captivity, 1917." *Class Struggle* 2, no. 4 (December 1918).

———. "Our Political Tasks." Marxist Internet Archive, 2008, https://www.marxists.org/archive/trotsky/1904/tasks/.

Troy, Thomas F. "The Gaunt-Wiseman Affair: British Intelligence in New York in 1915." *International Journal of Intelligence and CounterIntelligence* 16, no. 3 (2003):442–461.

Truro, Aaron Beswick. "Leon Trotsky Forged Notable Month at Amherst Foundry-Turned Internment Camp." *Chronicle Herald* (Halifax), January 2, 2015.

Ultan, Lloyd. "The Mystery of Trotsky's Bronx Friend." *Bronx County Historical Society Journal* 36, no. 2 (Fall 1999):73.

ENDNOTES

1: MONTSERRAT

1   Trotsky, *My Life*, 269.

2   *New York American*, January 13, 1917.

3   *New York Call,* January 17, 1917.

4   Marcosson, 413.

5   *Montserrat* manifest from Ancestry.com.

6   Serge and Trotsky, 12.

7   Shachtman, 2.

8   Serge and Trotsky, 15.

9   Olgin, "Our Revolution," 3.

10   Kirchwey, "When Trotsky Lived in New York," 3.

11   Volkogonov, *Trotsky*, 33.

12   Trotsky, *My Life*, 268, and *Novy Mir*, January 16, 1917.

13   On *Palermo* sinking, see statements of Frank M. Carney and Daniel O'Connor, Barcelona consulate files, NARA, RG 59, December 22, 1916.

14   Shachtman's files, 6.

15   Trotsky, *My Life*, 269.

16   July 13, 1915. British Archives, KV2/502.

17   Telegram July 11, 1915, British Archives, KV2/502.

18   Serge and Trotsky, 28.

19   Deutscher, 70.

20   Deutscher, 57–58.

21   Eastman, *Young Trotsky*, 85.

22   Trotsky, *Our Political Tasks*, part 2. He went on, describing Lenin's Bolshevism as a system of "the Party organization 'substituting' itself for the Party, the Central Committee substituting itself for the Party organization, and finally the dictator substituting himself for the Central Committee."

23   Morton, 96.

24   Thatcher, *Leon Trotsky and World War One*, 57–75; Thatcher, *Trotsky*, 75.

25   Why create splits, he argued, when their group was so small to start with? He recalled joking upon seeing the thirty-eight delegates arrive at the 1915 Zimmerwald

conference that after fifty years of organizing, "It was still possible to seat all the internationalists in four coaches." Trotsky, *My Life*, 249.

26   Trotsky, *My Life*, 251.

27   Letter to M. Uritzky, November 24, 1916. British Archives, KV 2/502.

28   Thatcher, 191

29   Trotsky, *My Life*, 260; Thatcher, *Leon Trotsky and World War One*, 191.

30   Trotsky, *My Life*, 265.

31   Notably, Trotsky had not given a single speech or written a single article in the country. According to Trotsky, Spanish authorities said simply, "Your ideas are too advanced for Spain." Thatcher, *Leon Trotsky and World War One*, 193.

32   See letter to M. Uritzky, November 24, 1916. British Archives, KV 2/502. "At Cadiz, [Spain] they wanted to put me straight onto a steamer starting for Havana. . . . I protested . . . & then there came from Madrid permission for me to be left at Cadiz until the first steamer sailed for New York."

33   Letter to M. Uritzky, November 24, 1916. British Archives, KV 2/502.

34   See Spence, "Hidden Agendas"; Thatcher *Leon Trotsky and World War One*, 191–94; documents in British Archives, KV2/502, and Trotsky, *Vingt Lettres*.

35   Trotsky, *Vingt Lettres*, November 22, 1916.

36   Shachtman's files, 6.

37   Ibid.

38   Trotsky, *Vingt Letters*, December 31, 1916.

39   Ibid.

40   Trotsky, *My Life*, 268.

41   Letter to Tchitcherine, November 16, 1916. British Archives, KV 2/502.

42   Deutscher, 241.

43   Trotsky, *My Life*, 268.

44   Ibid.

45   Ibid.

46   Cravan, 37

47   Ibid.

48   Gankin and Fisher, 218.

49   Lenin to Kollontai, February 17, 1917, from Gankin and Fisher, 576.

2: TIMES SQUARE

50   *New Yorker Volkszeitung*, January 14, 1917.

51   *New York Times*, January 14, 1917.

52   *New York Tribune*, January 15, 1916.

53   *New York Call*, December 2, 1016

54   *New Yorker Volkszeitung*, January 14, 1917.

55   *Novy Mir*, January 15, 1917.

56   Trotsky, *My Life*, 185.

57   Trotsky, *Our Revolution*, 8.

58   Trotsky, *My Life*, 273.

59   Serge and Trotsky, 30.

60   Krupskaya, in Cohen, *Bukharin,* 18.

61   Cohen, *Bukharin,* 18.

62   Cohen, *Bukharin,* 37.

63   Gankin and Fisher, 249.

64   Cohen, *Bukharin,* 39.

65   Cohen, *Bukharin,* 38.

66   Cohen, *Bukharin,* 40.

67   Ibid.

68   Gankin and Fisher, 217.

69   Cohen, *Bukharin,* 41.

70   Gankin and Fisher, 568.

71   Serge and Trotsky, 30.

72   Ibid.

3: SAINT MARKS PLACE

73   Shub, 124.

74   Kirchwey, "When Trotsky Lived in New York," 1–2.

75   On Weinstein, see file OG177382, National Archives, RG 65, M1085.

76   Recht papers, 31.

77   Serge and Trotsky, 31.

78   Trotsky, *Russian Revolution,* 358.

79   *Novy Mir,* January 16, 1917.

80   On the Triangle fire, see Von Drehle.

81   Nedava, 36, and *Forward,* January 16, 1917.

82   Quoted in Ziv, chapter 10.

83   Nedava, 36, and *Forward,* January 16, 1917

84   *New York Call,* January 16, 1917.

85   Ibid.

86   Porter, 92.

87   Porter, 101.

88   Deutscher, 168.

89   Clements, 91.

90   Clements, 94.

91   *New York World,* October 12, 1915, in Porter, 228.

92   Lore, "When Trotsky Lived in New York," 3.

93   Lenin to Kollontai, September 1915, in Gankin and Fisher, 207.

94   In Porter, 216.

95   This was Lenin's favorite insult around this time. Lenin on Kautsky: "At present I hate and scorn Kautsky more than anyone else. What vile, cheap, self-conceited hypocrisy." Gankin and Fisher, 195.

96   Lenin to Kollontai, November 9, 1915, in Gankin and Fisher, 572.

97   Clements, 96.

98   Ibid.

4: BROOKLYN

99   Trotsky, "A Revolutionist's Career," *St. Louis Labor*, February 16, 1918.

100   Lore, "*When Trotsky Lived in New York*," 1.

101   Buhle, "Ludwig Lore and the *New Yorker Volkszeitung*," 172–73.

102   Draper, 72.

103   Chambers, 391.

104   Reinhardt, 18.

105   Lore, *Leon Trotsky*, 1.

106   Braudy, 4.

107   Gankin and Fisher, 567.

108   Gitlow, 33; Ackerman, 76.

109   Sen Katayama, "Morris Hillquit and the Left Wing," *Revolutionary Age*, July 26, 1919.

110   Pratt, 107.

111   Porter, 216.

112   Gankin and Fisher, 566.

113   Lore, *Trotsky*, November 1918.

114   Ibid.

115   Draper, 81.

116   Cohen, 44.

117   Wolfe, *Life in Two Centuries*, 183.

118   Kublin, 241.

119   Sen Katayama, "Morris Hillquit and the Left Wing," *Revolutionary Age*, July 26, 1919.

5: RIVERSIDE DRIVE

120   Recht papers, 191–92.

121   Pratt, 29.

122   *New York Call,* January 14, 1917.

123   Hillquit, 118.

124   See Hillquit, 114–16, and Gorenstein, 207 et seq.

125   Hillquit, 161–62. One more thing: Earlier that January, Hillquit had traveled to Springfield, Massachusetts, to participate in the founding of the American Jewish Congress.

126   The strike, in fact, threatened starvation for half a million workers and their families. At its height, city prosecutors, apparently pressured by manufacturers, indicted five union members for the 1910 murder of a former strikebreaker. Hillquit defended the men in court and won outright acquittals for all five.

127   *New York Times*, October 17, 1916.

128   Pratt, 29.

129   *New York Times*, June 4 and October 17, 1916.

6: PATTERSON

130   Alexandra Kollontai, "The Statue of Liberty," Marxist Internet Archive, 2006, https://www.marxists.org/archive/kollonta/1916/statue-liberty.htm.

131   In Porter, 226. See also Clements, 99.

132   In Gankin and Fisher, 576, footnote 125. This letter is usually cited as from January 11, 1917, an impossibility since that predates Trotsky's arrival in the United States. The confusion most likely stems from a simple handwriting flourish, with the actual date being January 17.

7: THE BRONX

133   Ultan, 7.

134   Apparently a "new law" tenement. See Ultan on the Bronx.

135   Moskowitz, 183.

136   Trotsky, *My Life*, 271.

137   Ibid.

138   Shachtman file, 7.

139   See Ultan, cited approvingly in Spence, "Hidden Agendas."

8: COOPER UNION

140   January 20 article included in Trotsky, *Our Revolution*, 35.

141   *New York Call*, January 26, 1917.

142   *Forward*, January 26, 1917.

143   Ziv, chapter 10, 2.

144   *New York Call*, January 26, 1917.

145   *New York Times*, January 30, 1917.

146   Ziv, chapter 10, 2.

147   *New York Call*, January 26, 1917.

148   Ziv, chapter 10, 2.

149   Speech from version in *New York Call*, January 26, 1917.

150   *Forward*, January 26, 1917.

151   Lore, "When Trotsky Was in New York," 2.

152   *New York American*, January 22, 1917.

153   Lore, "When Trotsky Was in New York," 1–2.

154   Trotsky, *My Life*, 277.

155   Trotsky, *My Life*, 272.

156   Ibid.

157   See Trotsky, *On Black Nationalism*.

158   Ziv, chapter 10, 6.

9: RIVERSIDE DRIVE II

159   March 14, 1913, from Trotsky, *Balkan Wars*, 439–41.

160   Gorenstein, 208–13.

161   Algernon Lee's diary, January 29, 1917, Lee papers, Tamiment Library.

10: WILSON

162   *New York American* and other newspapers, February 4, 1917.

163   *New York American*, February 1, 1917.

164   Wilson message to Congress, February 3, 1917.

165   *New York American*, February 4, 1917.

166   *Novy Mir*, February 7, 1917, in Thatcher, *Leon Trotsky and World War One*, 199–200.

167   Trotsky, *My Life*, 233–34.

168   Trotsky, *My Life*, 233.

169   Trotsky, *My Life*, 236.

11: SPY VERSUS SPY

170   Memorandum titled "Russia," May 18, 1917, Wiseman papers, Folder 255.

171   Zelman and Scharlau, 136.

172   On Wiseman, see W. B. Fowler, Spence, and Wiseman papers at Yale University.

173   See memorandum on Dougherty's detectives, August 8, 1916, and letter to Gaunt dated September 27, 1916, in William Wiseman papers, File 161.

174   Thwaites, 144.

175   Witte, from Cohen, *Schiff*, 138.

176   Cohen, *Schiff*, 134.

177   From Oudaille to British base, July 13, 1915. British Archives, KV2/502.

178   On Parvus generally, see Zeman and Scharlau, and Spence, "Hidden Agendas."

179   Trotsky, *My Life*, 167.

180   Schurer, 314.

181   Even here, Parvus showed flair. Parvus, a theater lover, purchased fifty tickets for a satirical play debuting in Saint Petersburg the week of the police crackdown, planning for a group night out. When police seized him, they found the tickets and spent weeks trying to figure out how they played into his schemes.

182   Trotsky, *My Life*, 204

183   Zelman and Scharlau, 158.

184   *Nashe Slovo*, February 14, 1915, in Zeman and Scharlau, 155.

185   Zelman and Scharlau, 178.

12: CARNEGIE HALL

186   A. J. Taylor, *The Struggle for Mastery in Europe*, 1848–1918.

187   Trotsky, *My Life*, 275.

188   *New York American*, February 28, 1917.

189   *New York Times*, February 4, 1917.

190   Advertisement in *New York American*, January 23, 1917, et seq.

191   Trotsky, *My Life*, 270.

192   On these *Novy Mir* articles, see generally Ian Thatcher, *Leon Trotsky and World War I*, 197–200.

193   Lore, *Leon Trotsky*, 2.

194   Waldman, 64–65.

195   See "The Question of War," letter to the *New York Call*, March 25, 1917.

196   Resolution text in the *New York Call*, February 6, 1917.

197   *New York Call*, February 6, 1917.

198   "Big Responsibility: In Reference to the Carnegie Hall Meeting Resolution," *Novy Mir*, February 8, 1917, reprinted in Leon Trotsky, *War and Revolution*, vol. 2, 379.

199   Ibid.

200   *New York World*, February 6, 1917.

201   *New York Times*, February 2, 1917.

202   Thatcher, *Leon Trotsky and World War One*, 251, note 40.

13: ZIV

203   Ziv, 33, from Service, *Trotsky*, 344.

204   Eastman, 77.

205   Ziv, chapter 10, 6.

206   Service, 44.

207   Ziv, quoted in Service, *Trotsky*, 45.

208   Ibid.

209   Eastman, 26–27.

210   Trotsky, *My Life*, 100.

211   Trotsky, *My Life*, 191.

212   Ziv, from Wolfe, *Three Who Made a Revolution*, 202.

213   Trotsky, *My Life*, 126.

214   Trotsky, *My Life*, 132.

215   Including even Winston Churchill, writing in 1937: "He found a wife who shared the Communist faith. She worked and plotted at his side. She shared his first exile in Siberia in the days of the Czar. She bore him children. She aided his escape. He deserted her." Churchill, *Great Contemporaries*, 200, from Nedava, 239, note 46.

216   Trotsky, *My Life*, 132–33.

217   Even Isaac Deutscher, perhaps Trotsky's friendliest biographer, found it difficult to believe that his separation from Alexandra Lvovna in Siberia didn't haunt him. To Deutscher, this explained why Trotsky, in his own autobiography, "devoted no more than a single sentence to the whole affair." Deutscher, 71.

218   Eastman, 21.

219   Ziv, 14, from Service,*Trotsky*, 46.

220   Eastman, 21.

14: ZURICH

221   Gankin and Fisher, 557.

222   Gankin and Fisher, 554.

223   V. I. Lenin, to Alexandra Kollontai, March 5, 1917. Gankin and Fisher, 597.

224   Volkogonov, *Lenin,* 104.

225   Krupskaya, *Memories of Lenin,* vol. 2, 196, quoted in Gankin and Fisher, 218.

226   Alexandra Kollontai, "A Giant Mind, a Giant Will," Marxist Internet Archive, 2006, https://www.marxists.org/archive/kollonta/1914/giant.htm.

227   Clements, 100

228   Gankin and Fisher, 574.

229   A few months earlier, Lenin had complimented Trotsky in one letter: "The reconciler, Trotsky, is now compelled to recognize the inevitability of a break with the 'patriots'—i.e. who are justifying the entrance of workers into the war Industries Committee." But Lenin also found something to criticize: how Trotsky, out of "sheer false pride," had defended Akakii Chkheidze, the prowar Menshevik in the Russian Duma. Lenin to Safarov, February 10, 1916, in Gankin and Fisher, 574.

230   Lenin to Kollontai, February 17, 1917, in Gankin and Fisher, 576.

15: EAST BROADWAY

231   *Pravda,* October 20, 1922, from Nedava, 237, note 26.

232   Trotsky, *My Life,* 277.

233   "I do not know whether New York or Paris possesses at the present time more cinemas or taverns," Trotsky would write after the 1917 revolution. "But it is manifest that, above everything, the cinema competes with the tavern on the matter of how the eight leisure hours are to be filled. Can we secure this incomparable weapon?" Trotsky, *Problems of Everyday Life,* 41.

234   On the Triangle Dairy Restaurant, see Halpern.

235   Waldman, 64–65.

236   Draper, 82–83. In fairness, Bukharin had made the effort in response to a request from Lenin, who had asked him in a letter from Europe to "form a small group of Russian and Lettish Bolsheviks capable of following interesting literature, writing about it," and so on. Lenin to Bukharin, October 14, 1916, published in *Bolshevik,* no. 22, 1932, from Marxists.org.

237   Draper, 83.

238   See *New York Times,* February 12, 1917.

239   Ingerman letter in *Novy Mir,* February 16, 1917, from Thatcher, *Leon Trotsky and World War One,* 201–202.

240   Trotsky responses in *Novy Mir,* February 16 and March 3, 1917, from Thatcher, *Leon Trotsky and World War One,* 202, 251, note 43.

241   Thatcher, *Leon Trotsky and World War One,* 251, note 43.

242   Norris quoted in Recht, 175.

243   *New York American,* March 6, 1917.

244   Senator Norris's stand on the issue would earn him a chapter in President John F. Kennedy's classic book *Profiles in Courage.*

245   *New York World,* February 20, 1917.

246 *New York American*, March 2 and 8, 1917.

247 Jonas, 117.

248 Jonas, 118, 133.

249 *Forward*, March 1, 1917, 1.

250 Nedava, 26.

251 Jonas, 143–44. Vladeck also gave a second account. In a late 1917 interview, he downplayed the incident, saying that Trotsky had called him personally, not Cahan, asked simply, "Did you write that article?" and "Does the paper stand for it?" When Vladeck said yes, Trotsky said, "Then send me back my last article. I am sorry but I can no longer write for you." Kirchwey, 4.

252 Shub told this story to Nedava in 1969. See Nedava, 26, and 235, note 20.

253 Emma Goldman once complained, through a business manager, "To me it seems very strange that you should devote so little space to Emma Goldman's Jewish lectures when she is by far the most popular lecturer in Jewish who ever carried on propaganda in American"; her every meeting is crowded and "intensely interesting." *Mother Earth* to Vladeck, February 8, 1917, in Vladeck papers.

254 *Novy Mir* articles of March 6, 7, 9, 14, and 20, from Thatcher, *Leon Trotsky and World War One*, 204–5.

255 Thatcher, *Leon Trotsky and World War One*, 252, note 50.

256 Trotsky, *My Life*, 275–76.

257 Lipsky, 144.

258 Ibid.

16: THE COMMITTEE

259 Reed, 94.

260 "The Spirit of the Dance," *Modern Dance*, 1914, quoted in Buhle, 44.

261 Food price and shipment data from *New York Globe and Commercial Advertiser*, March 1, 1917, and US Bureau of Labor Statistics.

262 *New York Evening Post*, March 7, 1917.

263 Lenin to Kollontai, February 17, 1917, in Gankin and Fisher, 577.

264 *Daily People*, February 17, 1912, from Buhle, 12.

265 *New York Times*, February 11, 1917.

266 On three weeks and three meetings, see *New York Call*, March 5, 1917.

267 *New York Evening Post*, March 2, 1917.

268 *Novy Mir*, March 6, 1917.

269 Lore, "When Trotsky Lived in New York," 4–5.

270 *New Yorker Volkszeitung*, March 5, 1917, and other papers.

271 *Novy Mir*, March 7, 1917.

272 *New York Call*, March 18, 1917, *New Yorker Volkszeitung*, March 5, 1917, and other papers.

273 Trotsky, *My Life*, 275.

274 *New York Call*, March 2, 1917.

17: LENOX CASINO

275   *New York Times*, May 5, 1917.

276   Lore, "When Trotsky Lived in New York," 5.

277   *New Yorker Volkszeitung*, March 5, 1917.

278   *New York Call*, March 5, 1917, and *Novy Mir*, March 7, 1917.

279   Waldman, 68.

280   Ibid.

281   Ibid.

282   *New Yorker Volkszeitung*, March 5, 1917.

283   See *New Yorker Volkszeitung*, March 5, 1917.

284   Waldman, 68.

285   *New Yorker Volkszeitung*, March 5, 1917.

286   Lore, *Leon Trotsky*, 8.

287   Trotsky, *My Life*, 274.

18: RUSSIA

288   *New York Call*, March 6, 1917.

289   Trotsky, *My Life*, 275.

290   Darrow, 58, in Ackerman, 219.

291   Debs speech from the *New York Call*, March 8, 1917.

292   *New York Times*, March 9, 1917.

293   Trotsky, *My Life*, 275.

294   Ibid.

295   *New York Evening Post*, March 16, 1917.

19: THE WHIRLWIND

296   Trotsky, *Our Revolution*, 41.

297   *New York American*, March 16, 1917.

298   *Novy Mir*, March 16, 1917.

299   Trotsky, *My Life*, 276.

300   Ibid.

301   Trotsky, *My Life*, 278.

302   Ibid.

303   *New York Call*, March 16, 1917.

304   *New York American*, March 21, 1917.

305   Schiff cable in *New York Evening Post*, March 19, 1917.

306   *New York American*, March 15, 1917.

307   *New York American*, March 14, 1917.

308   *New York Times*, March 16, 1917.

309   *New York American*, March 16, 1917.

310   *New York American*, March 17, 1917.

311 Trotsky, *My Life*, 223.

312 See, for instance, "An Extraparliamentary Question for Mr. Miliukov," January 30, 1913, from Trotsky, *Balkan Wars*, 403 et seq.

313 Trotsky, *Our Revolution*, 41.

314 *New York Times*, March 16, 1917.

315 Announcement in the *New York Call*, March 16, 1917.

316 *New York Call*, March 17, 1917.

317 *New York American*, March 18, 1917.

20: SPIES AGAIN

318 Troy, 442, 443, 459.

319 For more on the sore feelings and controversy, see generally Troy.

320 See memorandum to Colonel Murray, September 6, 1918, Wiseman papers, Folder, 171.

321 See Fowler, 23–24.

322 On Reilly and Weinstein, see Spence, *Trust No One*, and memorandum from Captain Charles Billinghar to Major Nicholas Biddle, War Department, April 13, 1918, in MID RG 165, 9140-6073. Weinstein had even thrown a dinner party in his apartment after the revolution that, according to later American intelligence reports, included several unnamed "Russians" and "Socialists," including no doubt his likely relative the *Novy Mir* editor. See Spence, "Hidden Agendas," 13, citing MID 9140-6073, August 23, 1918.

323 Spence, "Hidden Agendas," 5, citing records of the Paris Okhrana at Stanford University's Hoover Institute.

324 See CX 015649, extract of memorandum from C. E. Dansey, January 19, 1918, in British Archives KV2/502.

325 See Spence, "Tsar's Other Lieutenant," 202.

326 Generally on Pilenas, see Bendersky, *Jewish Threat*, 54–55; National Archives file OG 105638, RG 65, M1085, and National Archives MID document in RG 165 10110-9210.

327 Document CX 015649, memorandum from C. E. Dansey, "Reference PILENAS," January 19, 1918, and Document CX 625 (also numbered 169987 and 170514), "Memorandum from W. W. on Internal Conditions (Neutral Countries)," March 22, 1917, both in British Archives KV2/502.

328 See Jeffreys-Jones, 30.

329 See, for instance, (a) "Memorandum on Judaism and the Present Jewish World Movement—A Study," prepared by the Division of Russian Affairs, MID, September 1919, no. 254-3; (b) "Memorandum for the Chief, Positive Branch," from M. Churchill, director of military intelligence, October 2, 1919, no. 245-15; (c) "From Office of Military Observer in Riga, Latvia, to Director of Military Intelligence re: Jewish Immigration to U.S.A.," LS no. 593, November 27, 1920, all in MID RG 165. See also generally Bendersky, *Jewish Threat*.

330 Churchill, "Zionism versus Bolshevism."

331 Unsigned memo from War Department, Office of the Chief of Staff, Washington, Wiseman papers, Folder 173.

332 "Revolution Must Not Stop until Freedom Comes, Says *Novy Mir* Editor," *New York Call*, March 17, 1917.

333   *New York Times*, March 16, 1917.

334   *New York Call*, March 17, 1917.

335   "Memorandum to D.I.D. from Naval Attaché," March 30, 1917, Wiseman papers, Folder 165.

336   Zeman and Scharlau, 209.

337   Goldstein, 8; see also Volkogonov, *Lenin*, 106.

338   Volkogonov, *Lenin*, 107.

339   Volkogonov, *Lenin*, 110.

340   Volkogonov, *Lenin*, 107.

341   Service, *Lenin*, 255.

342   Volkogonov, *Lenin*, 107.

343   Service, *Lenin*, 255.

344   Letters from Lenin to Kollontai, from Porter, 230, and Volkogonov, *Lenin*, 108.

345   Volkogonov, 107.

346   Zeman and Scharlau, 204.

347   *Die Glocke,* March 24, 1917, in Zeman and Scharlau, 207.

348   Zeman and Scharlau, 207.

349   Zeman and Scharlau, 210.

350   Zeman and Scharlau, 219.

351   Clements, 102.

352   Letters from Lenin to Kollontai, from Porter, 230.

21: CONSULATES

353   Routsky, 69, 73.

354   Routsky, 71.

355   On precaution against German spies, see *New York Times*, March 22, 1917.

356   Routsky, 71.

357   Lore, "When Trotsky Lived in New York," 6.

358   In his account, Routsky says that Trotsky and Bukharin represented Bolsheviks, an obvious mistake since Trotsky did not join the Bolsheviks until July 1917, about four months late. Routsky wrote his account in 1948, after Trotsky's association with Bolshevism was unavoidable.

359   Routsky, 74.

360   Becker report, 3.

361   Letter from Trotsky to Russian Ministry of Foreign Affairs, attached to Trotsky article "In British Captivity," in *Class Struggle*, December 1918.

362   Trotsky, *My Life*, 279. See also Trotsky, "In British Captivity."

363   Kirchwey, "When Trotsky Lived in New York," 4.

364   Spence, *Trust No One*, 157.

365   Spence, "Hidden Agendas," 17.

366   Fowler, *Wiseman*, 111.

367   Spence, "Hidden Agendas," 11.

368   On the Weinstein relationship, see Spence, *Trust No One*, 163 et seq.

369   See Document CX 015649, memorandum from C. E. Dansey "Reference PILENAS,"
       January 19, 1918, British Archives KV2/502.

370   Document 625 (also nos. 169987 and 170514), "Memorandum from W. W.
       on Internal Conditions (Neutral Countries)," March 22, 1917. British Archives
       KV2/502.

371   Harris, 195.

372   Harris, 198.

373   Ibid.

22: MISSING

374   Volkogonov, *Trotsky*, 42.

375   Trotsky, *My Life*, 278.

376   Pratt, 124, and Draper, 92–93.

377   Trotsky, *My Life*, 276.

378   Moskowitz, "Trotsky on the East Side."

379   Ibid.

23: HARLEM RIVER CASINO

380   See Morris and Stillwell.

381   Lore, "When Trotsky Lived in New York," 5–6.

382   *New York Times*, March 21, 1917.

383   *New York Call*, March 27, 1917.

384   Emma Goldman, chapter 45.

385   Lore, "When Trotsky Lived in New York," 6.

386   From 1919 congressional testimony of New York Police Bomb Squad inspector
       Thomas J. Tunney. This account was presented at the height of the postwar Red
       Scare and thus may have been highly embellished. *New York Times*, January 22,
       1919.

387   Goldman, chapter 45.

388   Kirchwey, "When Trotsky Lived in New York," 3–4.

389   Moskowitz, "Trotsky on the East Side."

390   *New York Evening Post*, March 24, 1917.

391   *New York Times*, March 24, 1917.

392   *New York Globe and Commercial Advertiser*, March 23, 1917.

393   Lore, "When Trotsky Lived in New York," 7.

394   Ibid.

395   Trotsky, *My Life*, 278.

24: KRISTIANIAFJORD

396   Steffens, 744. See also Sutton, 26.

397   Unsigned cable from British Intelligence in New York, March 28, 1917, British
       Archives KV2/502. See also Spence, "Hidden Agendas," 17, and "Interrupted

Journey," 11, both citing Admiral Hall's April 29 arrest order crediting Guy Gaunt as the source.

398   See Document 174400, undated, in British Archives KV2/502.

399   Document CX 015649, memorandum from C. E. Dansey, "Reference PILENAS," January 19, 1918, British Archives KV2/502. Pilenas had presented it in a letter to Wiseman that Wiseman produced for his superiors, though it doesn't show up in the intelligence files themselves.

400   Cable from London to Halifax, March 29, 1917. Canadian Archives, Trotsky file.

401   Steffens, *Autobiography*, 774.

402   Steffens letter, from Sutton, 26.

403   Draper, 115–16. Draper notes that Steffens, quick with his passions, would also admire Mussolini as "historically due."

404   Steffens, 744–45.

405   Trotsky, "In British Captivity," 8.

406   Kalpaschnikoff, 223.

407   Ibid. The December 1917 arrest was based on changes that the American Red Cross, with Kalpaschnikoff's involvement, was using its charitable operations as a cover to sneak automobiles and other equipment to General Alexei Kaledin, a Cossack commander opposing the Bolsheviks. Kalpaschnikoff would plead innocence, backed by American Red Cross and diplomatic officials. See also, *New York Times,* December 28, 1917.

408   "Col. Kalpatchnikoff Weds," *New York Times*, June 5, 1919. Kalpaschnikoff, apparently unknown to Trotsky at the time, had connections to William Wiseman's British Intelligence circle back in New York City as well as to Russian consulate officials, raising suspicions that Wiseman or the Russians had asked Kalpaschnikoff to keep an eye on Trotsky during the trip.

409   Trotsky, "In British Captivity."

410   Trotsky, "In British Captivity," 8.

411   Letter from Makins to General Officer Commanding, April, 1, 1917, Canadian Archives, Trotsky file. In the rush, Captain Makins listed Chudnovsky as "Tshadnovski" and Melnichansky as "Melniczanskoi." Later reports would list these names as "Tshoodnooski" and "Melintchansky."

412   Kalpaschnikoff, 223.

413   Trotsky, "In British Captivity."

414   "Extract from German Papers re Socialists Going to Stockholm," June 18, 1917, British Archives, KV2/502. See also note to Kendall from Geo Bullock, June 6, 1917, Document 187268, British Archives KV2/502.

415   Kalpaschnikoff, 223. See also Spence, "Interrupted Journey," 5. See also Spence, "Hidden Agendas," 17; Spence, *Trust No One*, 165; and Service, *Trotsky*, 159.

416   MacLean, "Why Did We Let Trotzky Go?"

417   Steffens, *Autobiography*, 744–45.

25: NOVA SCOTIA

418   Prisoners' telegram attached to telegram from Lakatscheff to Joseph Pope, Canadian undersecretary of state, April 5, 1917, Canadian Archives, Trotsky folder.

419   Trotsky, *My Life*, 281.

420   Trotsky, "In British Captivity," and "T. Benson to Secretary, Militia Council, Ottawa, Canada," April 2, 1917, Canadian Archives, Trotsky folder.

421   Trotsky, *My Life*, 280, and "In British Captivity."

422   Telegram from Lakatscheff to Pope, April 5, 1917, Canadian Archives, Trotsky folder.

423   Letter from Pope to Lakatscheff, April 10, 1917, Canadian Archives, Trotsky folder.

424   Serge and Trotsky, 31.

425   Cameron.

426   Ibid.

427   Trotsky, *My Life*, 281.

428   Trotsky, *My Life*, 282. See also, Truro.

429   Truro; Pitzer.

430   Trotsky, "In British Captivity."

431   "Memorandum from Chief Commissioner of Police, Ottawa," May 10, 1917, in British Archives KV2/502. See also "Report on TROTZKI PARTY," British Archives KV2/502.

432   Letter from *New Yorker Volkszeitung*, as translated by British Intelligence. See "Trotsky Detained in Canada," in British Archives KV2/502.

433   *New York American*, April 12, 1917.

434   *New York World*, April 5, 1917.

435   Hillquit, 165.

436   Socialist Party resolution, April 1917, quoted in Hillquit, 166.

437   See *New York Times*, April 11, 1917; *New York Call*, April 10, 1917; and *New Yorker Volkszeitung* in British Archives KV2/502.

438   London papers, Tamiment Library.

439   Spence, "Interrupted Journey," 13.

440   Aleinikoff telegram from Canadian Archives, quoted in Sutton, 29.

441   Spence, "Interrupted Journey," 7.

442   Ibid.

443   Demand of the Menshevik executive of the Petrograd Soviet, quoted in Deustcher, 247.

444   Buchanan, 120.

445   Lenin's "The Tasks of the Proletariat in the Present Revolution," or "April Theses, was first published in *Pravda* on April 7, 1917.

446   Service, *Lenin*, 263.

447   Service, *Lenin*, 267.

448   Chkheidze quote in Service, *Lenin*, 267.

449   Buchanan, 116, 117.

450   Trotsky, *My life*, 283–84.

451   *New York Times*, April 16, 1917.

452   Ibid.

453   Ibid.

454   Trotsky, *My Life*, 282, and Truro.

455   Trotsky, *My Life*, 283.

456   Spence, "Interrupted Journey," 19.

457   Ibid.

458   On Dansey, see generally Read and Fisher.

459   See, for example, documents 170512 and 170514: memoranda to Major Dansey from Captain R. H. R., March 29, 1917, and to MI1c from C.E.D., April 5, 1917, both on the Trotsky arrest, British Archives KV2/502.

460   Document CX 015649, memorandum from C. E. Dansey, "Reference PILENAS," January 19, 1918, British Archives KV2/502.

461   Ibid.

462   Read and Fisher, 122.

463   Document CX 015649, memorandum from C. E. Dansey, "Reference PILENAS," January 19, 1918, British Archives KV2/502.

464   Spence, "Interrupted Journey," 19, and Cameron.

465   Letter from Gwatkin to Coulter, quoted in Sutton, 31.

466   Quoted in Cameron.

467   Trotsky, "In British Captivity."

468   Trotsky, *My Life*, 285.

469   Ibid.

470   Trotsky, *My Life*, 320.

471   Serge and Trotsky, 31.

26: PETROGRAD

472   Buchanan, 114.

473   Lenin's April Theses.

474   Trotsky, *My Life*, 287.

475   Serge and Trotsky, 36.

476   Volkogonov, *Trotsky*, 68.

477   Reed, 125.

478   Volkogonov, *Trotsky*, 70.

479   See Serge and Trotsky, 40.

480   See multiple references in British Archives KV2/502, including, no. 194003, "Extract Relating to Trotzky, Leo, Socialist Activities in USA," June 16, 1917, and no. 202607, "Anti-War Activities in the United States," July 28, 1917. Some quote Miliukov as the source.

481   Trotsky, *Lenin*, 69, quoted in Deutscher, 274.

482   Volkogonov, *Trotsky*, 72, and Deutscher, 276.

483   Deutscher, 277, and Serge and Trotsky, 41.

484   Trotsky, *My Life*, 299.

485   Trotsky, *My Life*, 291.

486   Serge and Trotsky, 342.

487   Clements, 120.

488   Sukarnov, *The Russian Revolution of 1917*, 276–79, quoted in Porter, 264.

489   *New York Times*, November 11, 1917.

490   *New York World*, November 11, 1917.

491   Ibid.

492   *New York Times*, November 9, 1917.

493   See *New York Times*, September 10, 1995.

494   *New York American*, November 9, 1917.

495   *New York Call*, November 13, 1917.

496   Others initial top commissars included Alexander Shliapnikoff (labor) and Anatoly V. Lunacharsky (education), with both making US speaking and fund-raising tours the prior year.

497   "Russian from U.S. Leading Lenine Radicals," by Arno Dosch-Fleurot, correspondent for *New York World* and *Saint Louis Post Dispatch*, August 25, 1917.

498   See, for instance, Howe, *World of Our Fathers*, 326.

499   *New York Times*, November 10, 1917.

500   *New York Times*, November 30, 1917.

501   "Despotism Aim of Bolsheviki," *Detroit Free Press*, January , 1918.

502   *New York Times*, December 29, 1917.

503   Quoted in *New York Times*, December 17, 1917.

504   Pratt, 137.

LOOSE ENDS

505   Marcosson, 402.

506   BBC Radio, "Christopher Hitchens on Trotsky," BBC Radio, August 8, 2006, https://www.youtube.com/watch?v=rD54qnI_Mhc, accessed May 20, 2016.

507   This famous quote is derived from a letter in which Trotsky says: "Burnham doesn't recognize dialectics but dialectics does not permit him to escape from its net." Trotsky, *In Defense of Marxism*," 273.

508   Goldman, chapter 52.

509   Hammer, 128–29.

510   Marcosson, 413.

511   See generally Trotsky, *Terrorism and Communism*.

512   Trotsky, *The Revolution Betrayed*, 200.

513   Volkogonov, *Trotsky*, 216–17.

514   From Morton, 5.

515   He summarized his opinion of Stalin this way: "It was as the supreme expression of the mediocrity of the apparatus that Stalin himself rose to his position." Trotsky, *My Life*, 501.

516   Greene, 6.

517   Letter from Bukharin to Stalin, October 12, 1937, from Radzinsky, 380.

518   Clements, 255.

519   On what has become of the family there, see "Falling Far from the Family Tree," *Forward*, July 7, 2010.

520   Shachtman notes, 6.

521   Serge and Trotsky, 219.

522   See, for instance, Wittlin, 258.

523   *Workers Vanguard*, March 31, 1989.

524   Trotsky, *Revolution Betrayed*, 204, 214–15.

525   Volkogonov, *Lenin*, 255.

526   In another example, in early 1918, needing a new Russian diplomat to represent the Bolshevik government as consul in New York, he chose John Reed, author of *Ten Days That Shook the World*, knowing that this would only irritate the Americans, since Reed had recently been indicted for violating the Espionage Act. *New York Times*, January 31, 1918.

527   On this debate, see Trotsky, *In Defense of Marxism*.

528   Interview with Esteban Volkov in the *Guardian*, February 13, 2003, and "The Fight of the Trotsky Family—Interview with Esteban Volkov, Marxism.com, August 21, 2006, http://www.marxist.com/trotsky-assassination-esteban-volkov210806.htm, accesed May 20, 2016

529   Waldman, 69.

530   Hillquit, 184.

531   Hillquit, 189.

532   *New York Times*, November 7, 1917.

533   Winners included lawyer Louis Waldman, *Forward* editor Baruch Vladeck, and Algernon Lee and Jacob Panken, who served with Trotsky on the Socialist Party Resolutions Committee.

534   *New York Evening Post*, November 7, 1917, quoted in *New York Call*, November 8, 1917.

535   *New York Times*, November 7, 1917.

536   On the Debs case, see generally Freeberg.

537   Hillquit, 291; Pratt, 141.

538   *Revolutionary Age,* March 29, 1919, 3, quoted in Draper, 154. Fraina laid out the approach more fully in a coauthored article, "The Left Wing Manifesto," a practical blueprint for harnessing unrest—from labor strikes to general strikes to conquest of power—for political purposes. See *Revolutionary Age,* July 5, 1919. The latter article became the basis for prosecutions under New York's criminal anarchy statute, resulting in the landmark Supreme Court decision in *New York v. Gitlow*, 268 U.S. 652 (1925), establishing principles of modern First Amendment law.

539   John Reed put it this way over dinner with Socialist assemblyman Louis Waldman: "Louis, stop wasting your time running for the Assembly and stupid things like that. By the time you finish your course there'll be no more lawyers. . . . The masses are revolutionary and are about to rise!" Waldman, 72.

540   *New York Call*, May 21, 1919; Draper 157–58.

541   Benjamin Gitlow, a young Socialist assemblyman from the Bronx, remembered attending the meeting and watching as another left-winger sitting near Hillquit jumped out of his seat after one of the expulsions. "You are Right Wing enemies of the revolution!" the man shouted at Hillquit, pointing his finger. "Go ahead with your dirty work! Expel us from the party! We will soon meet you in bloody battle at the barricades!" Gitlow, 30. See also *New York Communist*, June 7, 1919.

542   The raids also targeted a similar, smaller group called the Union of Russian Workers.

543   The *New York Call*, the Socialist Party's organ in New York City, briefly went out of business in 1923 and then reemerged as a biweekly called the *New Leader*. A voice of liberal anti-communism throughout the twentieth century, it featured writers as diverse as US senator Daniel Patrick Moynihan (Democrat of New York), civil rights

leader Martin Luther King Jr., journalist Irving Kristol, historian Arthur
M. Schlesinger, and novelists James Baldwin and Alexander Solzhenitsyn.

544 See Wohlforth's article on Trotskyism in Buhle et al., 829.

545 Draper, 180.

546 On Lore's role as a Justice Department agent, seen Reinhardt, 17.

547 Chambers, 392.

548 On the British connection, see Spence, "Catching Louis Fraina."

549 Corey, 109.

550 Pratt, 223.

551 Goldman, chapter 46.

552 "When Trotsky Was an Extra at Five a Day," *New York Herald Tribune*, February
14, 1932.

553 Marcosson, 404.

554 Zelman and Scharlau, 136.

555 Volkogonov, *Lenin*, 110–11, citing Ludendorff's wartime memoirs.

556 *New York World*, November 9, 1917. Notably, in November 1917 Trotsky himself
ordered files of Russian prosecutors investigating the affair to be confiscated so
that Lenin and the rest could not be accused of treason. See Volkogonov, *Lenin*,
121, and report to Trotsky from F. Zalkind and E. Polivanov, November 16, 1917,
reproduced therein.

557 Zeman and Scharlau, 246.

558 Zeman and Scharlau, 251.

559 Becker report, 3. See also *New York Times*, January 20, 1918.

560 Ibid.

561 Hearing on "Brewing and Liquor Interests and German and Bolshevik Propaganda,"
Committee on Judiciary, United States Senate, 65th Congress, 1919, quoted in
Sutton, 23.

562 On Parvus's role, see generally Spence, "Hidden Agendas."

563 Cohen, *Schiff*, 243.

564 Conspiracy theories connecting Schiff to Trotsky became so prevalent after 1920 that
even friendly accounts of Trotsky's New York visit included him. See, for instance,
Kopp.

565 See for instance RG 165, MID, files 10110-126/920 et seq. and 9140-6073 et seq. See
generally Bendersky, chapter 2.

566 "Memorandum for Colonel Masteller from M. Churchill," November 30, 1918, in
RG165, MID, 10110-920.

567 RG 165, MID, "Bolshevism and Judaism," November 30, 1918, 10110-920, 1 and
4. This remarkable document even gives shout-outs to Morris Hillquit and Mayer
London as "leaders of the Bolshevist movement in this country."[1]

568 RG 165, MID, "Bolshevism and Judaism," November 30, 1918, 10110-920, 1 and 4.

569 See, for instance, Former Russian commissar, 25.

570 Cohen, *Schiff*, 243–45.

571 *New York Journal-American*, February 3, 1949.

572 See, for instance, *New York Times,* March 18, 1917, and *New York Evening Post,*
March 19, 1917, both containing a letter from Schiff specifying his presence in West
Virginia.

573   As late as October 1915, he had offered to drop his objections and help raise $200 million for the Russian war effort on the condition that Russia grant Jewish subjects full civil rights, but Russia refused. Roberts, *Jewish Bankers*, 19.

574   See generally Roberts; Cohen, *Schiff*, chapter 7.

575   Fowler, 106.

576   Spence, "The Tsar's Other Lieutenant," 209–10.

577   See, for instance, Spence, "Hidden Agendas": "In my original article [Spence, "Interrupted Journey,"], I speculated that Wiseman's peculiar behavior towards Trotsky was driven by his desire to enlist the exile in a secret scheme to 'guide the storm' in revolutionary Russia and, above all, to keep Russia in the war. The more recent information, I believe, supports this theory."

578   Around this time many British officials worried about the flood of Russian radicals returning home. "We have reliable information that the Germans are organizing from every neutral country parties of Russian refugees, largely Jewish socialists," he would write in a confidential briefing for his superiors in London. "These parties are sent to Petrograd where they are organized by German agents posing as advanced Socialists." "Russia," May 15, 1917, Wiseman papers, Folder 255.

579   "Russia," May 15, 1917. Wiseman papers, Folder 255. Wiseman had already engaged Columbia University professor Richard Gottheil to solicit statements of support from prominent American Jews to circulate in Russia. These Jews included Supreme Court Justice Louis Brandeis, Rabbi Stephen Wise, and even Jacob Schiff. See Fowler, 109.

580   "Intelligence & Propaganda Work in Russia, July to December 1917," January 19, 1918, in Wiseman papers, File 10/261.

581   Kalpaschnikoff would be cleared of the charges and released in 1919.

582   Even after Brest-Litovsk, British officials suggested seeking Trotsky's support for British military intervention in Siberia to reopen an anti-German eastern front. Woodrow Wilson blocked the idea, convinced that Trotsky was a paid agent of Germany. The Allies, including about thirteen thousand Americans, intervened regardless. See Fowler, 176–77.

583   Trotsky, *My Life*, 283.

584   Also along these lines, in a 1919 article titled "Why Did We Let Trotsky Go?" Canadian lieutenant colonel J. B. MacLean accused his own government of losing a chance to shorten the war and blamed it for weakness and incompetence.

585   Marcosson, 404.

586   Willert, 29. An anonymous witness before the 1919 Overman Committee seemed to back up this story with a joke: "I remember it struck me as comical" that Kerensky asked the American government to provide Trotsky a passport "because he thought he could be able to help him out. And he did help him out." See "Bolshevik Propaganda: Hearings before a Subcommittee of the Committee on the Judiciary," 1919.

587   See Wise, 647.

588   Also, by early 1918 President Wilson was convinced that Trotsky was a German agent, based at least partly on the Sisson papers, a set of Russian-language documents hand-carried from Petrograd by US official Edgar Sisson, connecting German influence to top Bolshevik figures. Several of these documents were later shown to be forgeries. Fowler, 178.

589   *New York World*, November 11, 1917.

590 Trotsky speech "Revolutionary Marxist Critique of Americanism," undated, quoted in Cannon, 99–105.

591 Letter to American Bolshevik-Leninists from Constantinople, March 1929, quoted in Cannon, 99–105.

592 Trotsky, *My Life*, 270.

593 Volkogonov, *Trotsky*, 475.

594 *New York Times*, November 23, 1988.

INDEX

A

AFL *See* American Federation of Labor (AFL)

African Americans 85–86

African Blood Brotherhood 86

Aleinikoff, Nicholas 156, 162, 163, 172, 199, 262

Alexander II, Tsar of Russia 131, 132

Alphonso XIII, King of Spain 15

Amalgamated Clothing Workers of America 70, 116

American Alliance for Labor and Democracy 289

American Communist Party 59, 175, 302, 304, 308, 309, 310, 311–312, 313

American Federation of Labor (AFL) 121

American Jewish Committee 201

American Neutral Conference Committee 116

American Railway Union 69, 179

Americans for Democratic Action 314

American Trotskyists 63, 86, 233, 302, 305, 311–312, 313

Anthony, Susan B. 79

Anti-Saloon League 81

anti-Semitism 92, 107, 190, 200–203, 219, 220, 280, 318–321

Appeal to Reason 67

April Theses (Lenin) 207, 264, 265, 277

Arbeiter Zeitung 68

Armand, Inessa 210

Armed Ship Bill 149

Asch, Sholem 235

Askold (ship) 21

Astor, John Jacob 39

B

Balkan Wars 89, 193

Barc, Ernesto 23

Basch, Victor 90–93

Beautiful Bronx, The (Ultan) 75

Becker, Alfred H. 317

Beilis, Menahem Mendel 200

Bellow, Saul 328

Bennett, William F. 305

Berchtold, Leopold 115

Berger, Victor 306

Beria, Lavrenty 303

Berkman, Alexander 231, 232, 315

Berlin, Simon 172

Bernstorff, Johann Heinrich von 204

Besteiro, Julian 23

Bolshevik Revolution of 1917 17, 58, 110, 157, 284–285, 286, 291

Bolsheviks 9, 18–19, 20, 34, 35, 43, 48–49, 51, 52, 62–63, 73, 108, 111, 155, 165, 187, 201, 202, 204, 205, 207, 210, 211, 217, 235, 243, 249, 250, 263–264, 265, 274, 276, 277, 279–280, 281, 283, 284, 286–289, 291, 292, 293, 296, 298, 309, 321, 326

Boudin, Louis 58, 60, 61, 63, 177, 194, 266, 307, 312

Bourderon, Albert 140

Brandeis, Louis 319

Brasol, Boris 200–201, 321

Brice, Fannie 5

Britain 82, 91, 95, 106–107, 108, 190, 195, 197, 203–204, 221, 239–242, 244–249, 257, 263, 265, 267–272, 279, 321–323

British intelligence 104–105, 108, 195, 198, 204, 221, 239–240, 269

Brockdorff-Rantzau, Ulrich Karl von 208–209
Bronck, Jonas 76
Bronstein, David 132–134, 136
Bronstein, Lev Davidovich *See* Trotsky, Leon
Bronstein, Nina 300–301
Bronstein, Zina 300–301
Bronx Home News 287
Buchanan, George 263, 264, 273
Bukharin, Nicolai Ivanovich 34–40, 43, 44, 48, 55, 57, 58, 62–63, 66, 73, 74, 112, 119, 126, 142–143, 146, 147, 170, 185, 186, 192, 214, 217, 250, 283, 288, 296, 297–298, 329
   Economic Theory of the Leisure Class 36
   Imperialism and World Economy 36
Burns, George 6
Burton, Richard 328
Byrne, Ethel 81

C

Cahan, Abraham 45–46, 68, 152, 153–155, 161, 177, 188, 287, 319
   The Rise of David Levinsky 154
Canada 103, 240, 250, 252, 257, 258, 259, 261, 265, 267–269, 272, 323
Cannon, James P. 233, 311
Cannon, Joseph D. 179
Cantor, Eddie 5
Carnegie, Andrew 39, 120, 232
Carnegie Hall 117–119, 120–128, 149, 235, 325
Carney, Frank 13
Casals, Pablo 120
Castrovido, Roberto 23
Chambers, Whittaker 57, 313
Chernov, Viktor 279
Chezal, Ivan 84
Chudnovsky, Grigorii 43–44, 48, 55, 58, 112, 119, 170, 214, 218, 246, 258, 259, 261, 262, 272, 277, 288, 318
Churchill, Winston 202
Citizens Municipal Committee 128
Class Struggle 266, 307
Cleveland, Grover 69
Cohan, George M. 5, 214
Cohen, Stephen 37
Cold War 263, 285, 296, 320

Comintern 20, 34, 297, 312, 313
Communism 263, 285, 292, 296, 314, 327
   See also American Communist Party
Communist Labor Party 308, 309, 310, 311–312
Concors, Arthur 30, 32
Cooper Union 79–84, 86, 89
Corey, Lewis *See* Fraina, Louis C.
Coulter, R. M. 262, 268–269, 271
Crane, Charles R. 242
Cravan, Arthur 25–26
Czolgosz, Leon 70, 232

D

Daily People 59, 160
Dansey, Claude E. M. 269–272
Darrow, Clarence 178, 179, 242
Davies, Marion 231
Debs, Eugene V. 8, 45, 52, 53, 67, 68, 69, 71, 154, 178–180, 304, 306, 307, 310
Decline of American Capitalism, The (Fraina) 314
Deutch, Lev 33–34
   Sixteen Years in Siberia 33
Dewey, John 311
Die Glocke 112, 208
Die Zukunft 117
Dosch-Fleurot, Arno 286, 316
Draper, Theodore 57, 62–63
Dreyfus, Alfred 90
DuBois, W. E. B. 60
Dukhom, W. Schloima 218
Duncan, Isadora 158–159, 166
Durante, Jimmy 6
Dybenko, Paul 298
Dzerzhinsky, Felix 134

E

Eastern Review 134
Eastman, Max 136, 137
Economic Theory of the Leisure Class (Bukharin) 36
Emergency Peace Federation 162
Engels, Friedrich 90, 151
England *See* Britain
Entente Allies 7
Executive Russian Committee 194

F

Figueroa de Romanones, Alvaro de 23
Fisheleff, Liebe 246
Forward 31, 34, 44, 45–47, 68, 77, 79–80, 81, 83, 117, 148, 150–155, 166, 188, 261, 287, 305, 319, 325
Fraina, Louis C. 59–60, 63, 77, 119, 156, 157, 159–161, 162–167, 170, 171, 172, 174, 175, 177, 199, 223, 233, 266–267, 304, 306–307, 308, 313–314
    The Decline of American Capitalism 314
    The House of Morgan 313
France 15–17, 20, 21, 47, 82, 90, 91–92, 95, 108, 190, 279
Frank, Caesar 159
Frankfurter, Felix 319
Frederick VIII (ship) 204
Freeman, Elizabeth 124
Freier Arbeiter Stimme 246
Frick, Henry Clay 232
Frost, Robert 159
Furstenberg, Jakob 112–113, 207, 250, 277

G

Gapon, Gyorgy 49
Garbo, Greta 48, 299
Gardner, Augustus 120
Gaunt, Guy Reginald 197–198, 200, 239–241, 245, 270
George, Lloyd 267
Gerber, Julius 179
German Libel 316–318
Germany 7, 8, 13, 15, 16, 20, 47, 52, 82, 91, 93, 95–99, 104, 105–106, 109, 110–111, 113, 115, 116, 121, 122, 149–152, 155–156, 162, 180, 189, 190, 197, 199, 203–204, 205, 208–210, 221, 239–241, 250, 257, 267, 279, 286, 296, 316–318, 322–323
Germer, Adolph 306
Gershwin, George 5
Gilman, Charlotte Perkins 121
Gitlow, Benjamin 59, 308
Goldfarb, Max 81
Goldman, Emma 8, 231–232, 234, 292, 293, 306, 315
Gompers, Samuel 121
Gorbachev, Mikhail 297, 301, 329
Gorky, Maxim 110, 281

Gottheil, Richard J. H. 220
Grimm, Robert 140
Gruenberg, Louis 90
Guchkov, Alexander 187, 192, 206, 211
Gwatkin, Willoughby 269, 271

H

Halifax, Nova Scotia, Canada 251–258, 262, 267–272
Halifax Chronicle 256
Hall, Reginald (Blinker) 240
Hammer, Armand 78, 292, 312
Hammer, Julius 78, 119, 170, 304, 312
Hammer, Rose 78, 84, 85, 145, 226
Harlem Renaissance 86
Harlem River Casino, Harlem, New York City 231–234, 241, 317
Harris, Frank 222–223
Haywood, Bill 53, 59, 61, 71, 160, 306
Hearst, William Randolph 8, 45, 67, 95, 181, 186, 231, 287
Hebrew Sheltering and Immigration Aid Society (HIAS) 30, 43
Hellig Olav (ship) 272
Helphand, Alexander Israel *See* Parvus
HIAS *See* Hebrew Sheltering and Immigration Aid Society (HIAS)
Hill, Joe 54
Hillquit, Morris 41, 60–61, 63, 65–71, 73, 89–90, 92–93, 119, 120–128, 144, 146, 151, 154, 155–156, 160–161, 162–167, 169, 170–172, 174, 175, 177, 178, 179, 180, 188, 189, 194, 228–229, 233, 261, 273, 287, 290, 304, 305, 306, 307–308, 310, 314–315, 321, 326, 329
Hindenburg, Paul von 95
Hiss, Alger 57, 313
History of the Russian Revolution (Trotsky) 302
Hitchens, Christopher 291
Hitler, Adolf 263, 302
Holland, Francois 314
Hoopes, Darlington 310
Hoover, J. Edgar 309
Horowitz, David 255–256
Horowitz, Fanny 256
House, Edward 98, 105, 197–198
House of Morgan, The (Fraina) 313

House Un-American Activities Committee 311

Howells, William Dean 154

Hughes, Charles Evans 310

Hylan, John F. 305

I

Imo (ship) 243–244

Imperialism and World Economy (Bukharin) 36

Industrial Workers of the World (IWW) 53, 54, 59, 70–71, 121, 160, 306

Ingerman, Anna 147–148, 177, 289

Institute for the Study of the Social Consequences of the War 112

Internationalist 58, 60, 159–160, 223, 233, 266

International Socialist Review 58

Iskra 17, 18, 19, 33, 110

IWW *See* Industrial Workers of the World (IWW)

J

Jacob Jones (ship) 97

Japan 58, 59, 107, 250, 291, 319

Jewish Daily Forward 6

Joffe, Adolf 277

Johnson, Jack 25

Jolson, Al 6

Jungle, The (Sinclair) 121

K

Kahlo, Frida 302, 328

Kalpaschnikoff, Andrei 245, 247

Kamenev, Lev 249, 276, 284, 295, 296, 297, 298, 329

Katayama, Sen 57, 58–59, 60, 63, 74, 267, 307

"Morris Hillquit and the Left Wing" 61

Kautsky, Karl 52, 140, 141

Keaton, Buster 6

Keep Out of the War Committee 116–117

Kennan, George 185

Kerensky, Alexander 181, 189–190, 192, 199, 207, 211, 248, 250, 261, 262, 264, 273, 279–280, 281, 282, 283, 285, 289, 318, 321, 324, 329

Kern, Jerome 5

Kerr, Charles 53

Khrushchev, Nikita 296–297

King, Martin Luther Jr. 310

Kingsmill, C. E. 269

Knickerbocker, Cholly 320

Kolb, Fritz 149–150

Kollontai, Alexandra 28, 48–54, 57, 58, 60, 61, 71, 73, 119, 141–143, 160, 170, 207, 210–212, 249–250, 265, 283, 284, 288, 298–299

"Who Needs War" 51, 249

Kornilov, Lavr 283

Kristianiafjord (ship) 218, 219, 220, 236, 237, 239–249, 323

Kristol, Irving 328

Kronstadt Rebellion 293

Krupskaya, Nadezhka 18, 27–28, 35, 111, 139, 140, 141, 142, 204, 206, 210

L

La Follette, Robert 149

La Guardia, Fiorello 315

Lakatscheff, I. A. 254–255

Lassalle, Ferdinand 151

League of Nations 91

Lee, Algernon 80–81, 89, 90, 91, 92, 156, 162, 163, 171, 177, 179, 188

Lenin, Vladimir

April Theses 207, 264, 265, 277

Bolshevik Revolution of 1917 3, 17–21, 263–265, 284–285, 286, 293, 316, 321, 323

Bukharin, Nicolai Ivanovich 35–37

correspondence 27–28

Iskra 17, 18, 19, 109–110

Kollontai, Alexandra 28, 48, 51–54, 74, 141–144, 210–212, 249–250, 298

Krupskaya, Nadezhka (wife) 18, 27–28, 35, 111, 139, 140, 141, 142, 204, 206, 210

"Letters from Afar" 207

Parvus 111–113, 207–210, 250, 280, 316–318

Petrograd, Russia 204–207, 276–283

Russian Revolution 17, 19, 20–21, 27–28, 35, 204–210, 250, 263–265

Russian Social Democratic Party 17

Stalin, Joseph 294–295

Trotsky, Leon 17–21, 28, 54, 87, 265, 276–283, 294, 297, 302
"What Is to Be Done?" 17
Zimmerwald platform 139, 140, 165
Lenox Casino, Harlem, New York City 169–175, 177, 178, 194–195, 241, 262, 266, 304, 326
"Letters from Afar" (Lenin) 207
Liebnecht, Karl 51
Lincoln, Abraham 79
Lippmann, Walter 60
London, Jack 228
London, Meyer 68, 90, 180, 260, 262, 286
London Times 324
Lore, Lillian (Lily) 53, 56, 57, 60
Lore, Ludwig 40, 48, 51, 52, 53, 54, 56–57, 60, 62–63, 73, 74, 76, 78, 81, 83, 84, 89, 90, 118, 119, 159, 164, 166, 169, 170, 175, 194, 217, 233, 234, 236, 266, 282, 304, 307, 308, 312–313
Ludendorff, Erich von 316
Lukina, Nadezhda Mikhailovna 36
Lusitania (ship) 7, 16, 95, 116, 159
Luxemburg, Rosa 109
Lvoff, Georgy Yevgenyevich 192, 206
Lvovna, Alexandra 131–132, 133–135, 136, 137
Lynch, Frederick J. 124

M

Maclean, J. B. 247–248
Maisel, Robert 289
Makins, O. M. 241–242, 244, 245, 246, 247, 248, 269, 270, 271
Malcolm X 86, 170
Malvy, Louis 22
Marcosson, Isaac 324
Marcosson, Frederick 292
Martov, Julius 19, 43, 206, 210, 273, 278
Marx, Karl 59, 90, 131, 151
Marx Brothers 6
Marxism 3, 36, 68, 69, 90, 131, 134, 146, 324
Masses 305
Matuschka, Manfred 204
Maugham, W. Somerset 322
McCarthy, Joseph 311
McClure's 8, 242, 318

McKay, Claude 86
McKinley, William 69, 70, 232
Medzikhovsky, C. J. 106
Melnichansky, Guschon 214, 218, 246, 262
Mensheviks 9, 18, 19, 20, 33, 43, 49, 51, 62–63, 108, 143, 165, 187, 206, 207, 210, 250, 263, 264, 273
Menshoy, Alexander 287
Menson-Minkin, Alexander 288
Mercader, Ramon 303
Merrheim, Arthur 140
Mexico 150, 242, 302, 303, 328
Mezhrayontska (RSDLP) 277, 278, 283
Militant 311
Military Revolutionary Committee 284–285
Miliukov, Paul 83–84, 192–193, 199, 206, 211, 250, 262, 263, 264–266, 280, 282, 317
Mill, John Stuart 131
Mitchel, John Purroy 81, 97, 128, 158, 235–236, 305
Modern Dance 59, 60, 157, 159, 266
Mont-Blanc (ship) 243–244
Montserrat (ship) 5, 9–15, 24–26, 29, 30, 44, 326
Morris, Arthur Henry 252, 253–254, 256–257, 267–268, 271–272
"Morris Hillquit and the Left Wing" (Katayama) 61
Moscow Bolshevik Committee 250
Moskowitz, Henry 229
Most, Johann 69
Mother Earth 232
Muchin, Nikita 246
Muhammad, Elijah 170
Murphy, Charles 235
Myers, Gustavus 228

N

Nashe Slovo 15–16, 22, 31, 43, 51, 108, 111, 112
National Committee of Jewish Workmen 229
NEP *See* New Economic Policy (NEP)
New Deal 305, 313–314, 327
New Economic Policy (NEP) 293–294, 297
New International 307
New Republic 313
New Review 60

New York American 8, 95, 97, 181, 186, 192, 287

New York Call 30, 31, 44, 45, 47–48, 65, 80, 166, 177, 181, 192, 203, 254, 259, 261, 262, 287, 305, 307–308

New York Church Peace Union 124

New York City 3, 5–7, 8–9, 23, 28, 37–38, 55–56, 65–71, 96–97, 105–108, 117, 122, 127–128, 145–146, 157–159, 162, 169–175, 198–204, 225–228, 231–234, 235–237, 258–259, 266–267, 269, 286–290, 305, 324–327

New Yorker Volkszeitung 29, 31, 40, 44, 51, 56–57, 90, 117, 166, 173, 220, 261, 282, 305, 308, 312, 317

New York Evening Post 181, 190, 242, 305

New York Herald 30

New York Philharmonic 120

New York Post 312

New York Public Library 38–39, 146

New York Socialist Labor Party 59, 123, 155–156, 161, 162–167, 171, 172, 199, 228, 231–234

    Resolutions Committee 156, 159, 161, 162–167, 171, 172, 199, 262

New York Times 6, 8, 30, 70, 71, 116, 161, 178, 181, 191, 193–194, 203, 206, 261, 267, 287

New York Tribune 30, 180

New York World 8, 105, 125, 192, 286, 287, 288, 316

Nicholas II, Tsar of Russia 49, 50, 83–84, 108, 181, 187, 190, 192, 193, 210, 215, 264, 293

Norris, George W. 149

Nourteva, Santeri 156, 162, 163, 172, 194

Novaya Zhizn 281

Novy Mir 9, 23, 28, 29, 31, 32, 34, 37, 41, 42–44, 48, 53, 66, 76, 79, 81, 98, 106, 112, 117, 119, 124–126, 142, 143, 145, 146, 147, 148, 153, 154–155, 165, 170, 178, 185, 186, 187–188, 191–192, 199, 203, 213, 214, 216, 217, 218, 220, 222, 223, 227, 241, 246, 250, 258, 261, 262, 283, 287, 288, 292, 305, 306, 307, 317, 326

O

O'Connor, Dan 13

Oganesoff, Marie 312

O'Hare, Kate Richards 306

Olgin, Moissaye (Moshe) 34, 77

Original Dixieland Jazz Band 6

Oustinoff, Michael 216

Outlook 8, 185

P

Pacino, Al 75

Packard, Clara 90

Packard, Samuel 90

Paderewski, Jan 120

Palermo (ship) 13

Palmer, Alexander Mitchell 309, 310

Palmer Raids 304, 309, 310, 311, 312, 325

Panken, Jacob 156, 162, 163, 172

Parvus 103, 108–113, 130, 207–210, 250, 264, 265, 277, 280, 316, 318

Patrick, George 200

Pearl, Jeanette 159

Pearson's 222, 305

Petrograd, Russia 180–181, 185–195, 191, 192, 193, 204, 207, 210, 211, 249, 262–264, 273–285

Petrograd Workers Council 206

Pilenas, Casimir 195, 199–201, 221, 241, 245, 270–271

Plekhanov, Georgi 130

Pope, Joseph 254–255

Powell, William 231

Pravda 34, 211, 249, 250, 265, 276, 277, 278, 280, 288, 295, 297

Protocols of the Elders of Zion 200–201, 321

Pulitzer, Joseph 8, 45, 105

R

racism 85–86 *See also* anti-Semitism

Radek, Karl 20, 210

Rakovsky, Christo 112

Rand School for Social Research 80, 89, 156, 177

Rankin, Jeanette 260

Recht, Charles 65

Red Army 3, 291, 293

Red Cross 147–148, 177, 245, 289

Red Terror 293, 327

Reed, John 60, 278, 308

Reilly, Sidney 106, 199, 219, 220

"Repetition of Things Past, A" (Trotsky) 98

Resolutions Committee 156, 159, 161, 162–167, 171, 172, 199, 262

Revolutionary Age 307

Revolution Betrayed, The (Trotsky) 302

Rise of David Levinsky, The (Cahan) 154

Rockefeller, John D. 122

Rogers, Will 5

Romanchinko, Konstantin 218, 246

Roosevelt, Franklin D. 305

Roosevelt, Theodore 149, 178

Routsky, Pierre 213, 215, 216–217, 219, 245

RSDLP *See* Mezhrayontska (RSDLP)

Runyon, Damon 259

Rush, Geoffrey 328

Russell, Bertram 120

Russell, Charles Edward 121, 180, 228

Russia 58
  Bolshevik Revolution of 1917 58, 284–285, 286, 291
  Communism 263, 292, 314, 327
  coups d'etat 283, 284–285, 297
  food riots 181, 186–187
  Kronstadt Rebellion 293
  Marxism 3
  Red Army 3, 291, 293
  Red Terror 293, 327
  Russian Revolution 17, 34, 35–36, 83, 110, 115, 133, 141, 181, 185–195, 204–212, 213–219, 233, 254, 257, 263 265, 273–285, 318, 324

Russian Okhrana 200–201

Russian Revolution 17, 34, 35–36, 83, 110, 115, 133, 141, 181, 185–195, 204–212, 213–219, 233, 254, 257, 263–265, 273–285, 318, 324 *See also* Bolsheviks; Mensheviks

Russian Social Democratic Party 17

Russian Supply Committee 200

Russkaya Zemla 43

Russkii Golos 43

Russkoe Slovo 43, 194

Russo-Japanese War 59

Rutgers, Sebald J. 58, 60, 74, 267, 307

Ruth, Babe 259

S

Sagan, Carl 328

Saint Petersburg, Russia 11, 12, 33, 48–49, 110, 160 *See also* Petrograd, Russia

Saint Petersburg Workers Soviet 11, 49–50

Sanders, Bernie 314

Sanger, Margaret 8, 81, 120

Saturday Evening Post 324

Schiff, Jacob 107–108, 189–190, 201, 319, 320

Schiff-Trotsky Conspiracy 318–321

Schluter, Hermann 90, 92

Secret Intelligence Service *See* British intelligence

Sedov, Lyova 9, 14–15, 299–300

Sedova, Natalya 9, 11–12, 14, 15, 16, 23, 24, 76–77, 84, 85, 136, 145, 181, 188, 218, 223, 225–228, 248, 255–256, 275, 282 283, 301–302

Sedov, Sergei 9, 14–15, 225–228, 299–300, 329

Service, Robert 264

Shepherd, William 288–289, 323–324

Shliapnikov, Alexander 36

Shub, David 153

Shulgin, Vasili 187

Siberia 10, 11, 17, 51, 87, 134–135, 262

Sinclair, Upton 121, 228
  The Jungle 121

Sixteen Years in Siberia (Deutch) 33

Smith-Cumming, George Mansfield 104, 105

Smolny Institute 281, 284

Socialist Equality Party 312

Socialist Labor Party 68, 69, 78

Socialist Party of America 28, 45, 47, 53, 54, 57, 58, 60–63, 65–71, 93, 108, 125, 127, 143, 155, 164, 165–166, 169–175, 177, 178–180, 188, 198–199, 214, 228, 261, 262, 304–312

Socialist Propaganda League 58, 147, 159, 266

Sokolovskaya, Alexandra Lvovna 87, 275, 300, 301

Soviet Communist Party 295, 297

Soviet of Workers Deputies 187

Spain 22–23, 24

Spring-Rice, Cecil 198

Stalin, Joseph 17, 34, 249, 283, 284, 285, 291, 294–297, 302, 311, 327
  purges 296, 298
  Trotsky, Leon 294–295, 296, 303, 329

Stanton, Elizabeth Cady 79
Steffens, Lincoln 154, 239, 242, 243, 244
Stokes, J. G. Phelps 121
Stokes, Rose Pastor 121, 306
Stowe, Harriet Beecher 121
    Uncle Tom's Cabin 121
Sukarnov, Nikolai 284
Sven du Rietz (ship) 204
Svobodnoye Slovo 34

T

Taft, William Howard 68, 178
Tammany Hall 32, 46, 67, 128, 235, 304
Tchaikovsky, Pyotr Ilyich 120, 159
Third International 141, 147, 297, 311, 315
Thomas, Norman 310
Thwaites, Norman 199, 200, 219, 270
Tilden, Samuel 39
Tolstoy, Ilya 8
Trotsky, Leon 199–204
    "A Repetition of Things Past" 98
    arrests 10–11, 13, 14, 17, 23, 30, 134,
        199–204, 248, 251–255, 256–258, 261,
        262–263, 267–272, 282, 283, 322
    assassination 303, 311, 328
    Bolshevik Revolution of 1917 284–285,
        286, 289, 291
    Bronstein, David 132–134
    Bukharin, Nicolai Ivanovich 34–36,
        37–40, 55
    conspiracy theories 315–324
    emigration 9–15, 23, 24–26, 30
    exile 10, 11, 14, 17, 22, 44, 49, 50, 87,
        295, 302, 303, 311, 328
    Fraina, Louis C. 59, 159–161, 162–167,
        171, 172, 175
    France 15–17, 21–22
    Hillquit, Morris 65, 124–128, 160–161,
        162–167, 228–229, 326
    History of the Russian Revolution 302
    Jewish identity 30–31, 45, 46–47, 132,
        294
    journalism 10, 11, 15–16, 21–22, 23,
        30–31, 43–44, 80, 81, 89, 98, 111, 117–
        118, 124–126, 134, 145, 148, 193, 194,
        213, 216, 223, 278, 281–282, 303
    Kahlo, Frida 302, 328
    Kristianiafjord 239–249

Lenin, Vladimir 17–21, 54, 87, 265,
    276–283
Lvovna, Alexandra 133–135, 137
Marxism 3, 131, 134, 146, 324
Mexico 303, 311, 328
Parvus 110–111
Petrograd, Russia 273–285
The Revolution Betrayed 302
Russian Revolution 17, 188, 191–195,
    213–219, 233, 264
Sedova, Lyova (son) 9, 14–15, 299–300
Sedova, Natalya (wife) 9, 11–12, 14,
    15, 16, 23, 24, 136, 181, 188, 218, 223,
    225–228, 248, 255–256, 275, 282–283
Sedova, Sergei (son) 9, 14–15, 225–228,
    299–300
speeches 79–84, 117–119, 194–195, 199,
    229–230, 234, 241, 278, 281–282, 284
surveillance 199–204, 219–222, 232, 234,
    235, 237, 239–249
War and the International 243
Ziv, Grisha 86–87, 129–133, 136–137
Trotsky-Fraina minority report 169–175,
    178, 191, 228
Tudor, Mary 231
Tukhachevsky, Mikhail 293
Turati, Filipo 140
Twain, Mark 79

U

Ultan, Lloyd 75
    The Beautiful Bronx 75
Uncle Tom's Cabin (Stowe) 121
United Hebrew Trades 116
United States
    World War I 286–287, 304, 305, 314,
        325
Uritsky, Moises 134, 277

V

Vietnam War 310
Villa, Pancho 150, 242
Vladeck, Baruch Charney 150–153
Volgar, Nikolai 220
Volkogonov, Dmitri 328
Volkov, Esteban 301, 303
Volodarsky, V. 48, 58, 214, 277, 288

W

Wagner, Robert F. 235–236

Waldman, Louis 118, 146–147, 172, 173, 174, 303

Walling, William English 180

War and the International (Trotsky) 243

Weinstein, Alexander 106, 199, 220

Weinstein, Gregory 41, 43, 44, 45, 106, 126, 166, 170, 186, 199, 220, 258–259, 261–262, 267, 307

"What Is to Be Done?" (Lenin) 17

Whitmore, F. C. 257

"Who Needs War" (Kollontai) 51, 249

Wilde, Oscar 25

Willert, Arthur 324

Williams, John D. 58

Wilson, Woodrow 7, 8, 47, 68, 82, 91, 95–99, 105, 115, 116–117, 120–121, 127, 149, 150, 162, 177, 178, 190, 197, 214, 242, 259–260, 314, 324

Wise, Jennings C. 324

Wiseman, William George Eden 98, 103–108, 197–199, 200, 201, 202–204, 219–222, 237, 239–240, 241, 267, 270–271, 321–323

Witte, Sergius 107

Wobblies *See* Industrial Workers of the World (IWW)

Wolf, Arthur 262

Wolfe, Bertram 63

Women's Peace Party 116, 124

Woodrow Wilson Conspiracy 324

Worker Opposition Party 298

World League for Peace 91 *See also* League of Nations

World Tomorrow 310

World War I 3, 7, 8, 13, 20, 47, 51, 52, 57, 82–83, 91–93, 95–99, 103–112, 115–117, 141, 163, 179, 190–191, 198, 214, 243, 257, 259–260, 279, 286, 304, 305, 306, 314, 325

World War II 296, 299, 302, 311

Y

Yeltsin, Boris 297

Z

Zaro, Henry C. 218, 220

Zetkin, Klara 148

Ziegfeld's Follies 5

Zimmermann, Arthur 150

Zimmermann Telegram 148, 150, 151

Zimmerwald platform 17, 20–21, 51, 61, 71, 74, 139, 140, 147, 165, 277, 316

Zinoviev, Grigory 20, 37, 140, 205, 210, 284, 295, 296, 297, 298, 312–313, 329

Ziv, Grisha 80, 82–83, 86–87, 128, 129–133, 136–137